A Population Geography

A Population Geography

Huw R Jones

Harper & Row, Publishers
London

Cambridge San Francisco
Hagerstown   Mexico City
Philadelphia   Sao Paulo
New York   Sydney

First published 1981
Harper & Row Ltd
28 Tavistock Street
London WC2E 7PN

British Library Cataloguing in Publication Data

Jones, H.
    A population geography.
    1. Population geography
    I. Title
    910'.01'8   HB1951

    ISBN 0-06-318188-6
    ISBN 0-06-318189-4 pbk

Typeset by Inforum Ltd, Portsmouth
Printed and bound by The Pitman Press, Bath

Contents

PREFACE

Population geographers have not figured prominently among the stormtroopers of methodological transformation in geography in recent years, and this is why the several pioneering texts in population geography written in the 1960s have survived up to 1980 almost without competition. Inevitably they have become somewhat dated in material, approach and perspective, so that this text has been written for an undergraduate readership as an expression and review of the current state-of-the-art in population geography. It may be compared profitably with similar recent attempts, although from quite different standpoints, by Noin (1979) and Woods (1979).

Within population geography there has been a growing concentration of academic research, policy formulation and student interest in process-oriented population dynamics. In sympathy, this text accords little attention to patterns of population distribution and composition *per se*, but concentrates on evolving patterns of fertility, mortality and migration, the spatio-temporal processes that fashion them, and their interaction expressed in population growth, population problems and population policies. A major theme is the spatial expression at global national and subnational scales of cause and effect links between demographic change and the transformation of societies known widely, but interpreted increasingly critically, as development and/or modernization.

I would like to express particular thanks to: Professor J. B. Caird, for general encouragement; Mr. W. G. Berry, for computing advice and assistance; Mrs. C. Bain for supervising the preparation of figures; and Mrs. N. Ferrier and Mrs R. Murray for typing the script.

CHAPTER 1

THE NATURE OF
POPULATION GEOGRAPHY

As a response to the stresses imposed on societies and their habitats throughout the world by unprecedented increases in human numbers and appetites in this century, there has been ever-growing interest by academics, general public and governments in 'the population question' at all levels of scale from global to local. Major international organizations like the United Nations, World Bank and Population Council have concerned themselves more and more with the study of global population problems, especially with a view to incorporating appropriate population policies in overall development strategies in the disadvantaged Third World. Meanwhile the governments of many Western nations feel they can no longer shelter behind their shield of affluence and ignore the population dimension. Several such governments, such as the United States, the Netherlands and the United Kingdom, have formed special advisory commissions or panels on population, although because population tends to be viewed in crisis terms rather than as a critical element of an ever-evolving social scene, these initiatives have been poorly funded, half-heartedly supported and sometimes aborted (Nam 1979).

By the late 1970s the more hysterical outbursts of concern about population growth had abated somewhat as the more gloomy scenarios for the future interaction of population and resources had been discredited by critical examination of their assumptions. Moreover, the growth rate in world population has fallen from about 2.0 percent per annum in the 1960s to 1.7 percent in 1980, essentially due to fertility falls in all developed countries and in some Third World countries, including most notably and dramatically the population giant of China. Yet such is the in-built momentum for absolute growth in population numbers globally and such are the uncertainties about the world's ability to provide supportive resources that population questions will remain a fundamental concern of mankind for decades to come. Even if developed countries myopically consider that their modest fertility levels cushion them from a survival crisis, they will certainly be concerned with a whole host of economic, social and physical planning problems stemming from the changing age structure of their populations.

The study of human populations embraces a wide academic spectrum, and it is important to review the interests of at least some of the more central and important disciplines in the population field in order to assess how distinctive is the approach of population geography.

Demography

'Demography is the empirical, statistical and mathematical study of human populations' (Bogue 1969, p.1). It is the quantitative study of the size, distribution and composition of human population (population statics) and of the major components of change in these features (population dynamics). The dynamic components comprise fertility, mortality and migration, to which some demographers would also add marriage and social mobility. Any apparently static demographic condition or pattern represents merely a temporary equilibrium among the formative elements which are always at work within a population.

Within demography a distinction has commonly been made between formal or pure demography and population studies or social demography. The former emphasizes the demographer's prime concern with the collection, evaluation, adjustment, analysis and often projection of population data. A common core of analytical techniques comprises the standardization measures which 'control' differences in population composition in order to pinpoint more precisely the nature of the dynamic processes. Rigorous though the methods of formal demography are, it has been suggested that 'technical pyrotechnics may displace penetrating analysis and that workers with high technical standards may become reluctant to work on scientifically important problems where precision is difficult or impossible to attain' (Hauser and Duncan 1959, p.10).

Within the more general approach of population studies or social demography, the need to handle and analyse the basic demographic data objectively is not disputed, but this is regarded as the starting point in the exercise – a means to an end and certainly not an end in itself. Analysis proceeds to an attempted explanation of demographic patterns and processes from the subject matter and theories of social science disciplines like anthropology, economics, human geography and sociology. Indeed, the great majority of demographers have been trained in such disciplines before specializing in demographic research; few opportunities exist for undergraduate specialization in demography itself. The distinction then between a narrow and a broad approach to demography is a real one, although the labelling distinction is much less clear and, some would say, inappropriate. It would be difficult, for example, to make any distinction in content between the two leading English language journals in the field, *Demography* and *Population Studies*.

Population ecology

The study of human populations is regarded by some biologists as part of a single field of population study at all organic levels – microbe, animal, plant – which has been termed general demography, bio-demography or, increasingly, population ecology. Despite the diversity within plant and animal kingdoms, population ecology attempts to formulate generalizations, laws and processes for living organisms as a whole in their relations with each other and their habitats ('ecology' from the Greek *oikos* meaning home or place to live).

Particular emphasis is given to explaining fluctuations in population size over time (Solomon, 1969, and Snyder, 1976, provide concise introductions). The powers of reproduction of an organism under optimum conditions – its so-called biotic potential – are invariably considerable. For example, when grain-mites are reared under favourable laboratory conditions, an initial 100 mites would become 700 in one week and over 28,000 million in 10 weeks. Even the elephant, with its very long gestation period, was thought by Darwin to be capable of increasing from 1 couple to 19 million living descendants after 750 years. That such numbers are never accomplished in the real world is mainly due to high mortality, often operating through the pressure of competition and natural selection. There are also constraints on fertility, again reflecting environmental resistance, like the effect of food shortages on the ability to conceive, and, additionally, social conventions like territoriality which exclude parts of populations from breeding (Wynne-Edwards 1962, 1965).

This approach forms a useful context for an understanding of specifically human populations, particularly in the facilities it offers for field and laboratory experiments with animal numbers, but the point must be emphasized that man is a unique organism. Certainly man, like all organisms, functions in his environment by means of adaptation. He participates with other organisms in physical adaptation or natural selection. But man's brain size and associated mental powers have increased so much during the course of evolution that he has become uniquely able to adapt flexibly to his environment by modifying his behaviour, essentially through his cultural equipment. Culture can be regarded as learned behaviour that is socially transmitted: it includes customs, beliefs, technology and art. The culture gap between man and other animals has become so enormous that a quantitative difference along a continuum of organisms can, in effect, be regarded as a qualitative one.

Human ecology

This emerged as a subject in the 1920s through the initiative of the Chicago school of sociologists, most characteristically expressed in the work of Park (1936). Much of their initial work was in applying the fundamental theories and methods of plant and animal ecology to the study of human communities, and, in particular, to interpreting spatial ordering within communities, especially metropolitan ones, through the process of competition or 'the struggle for space'. By the 1940s classical human ecology had become discredited as crude biological determinism, and the focus of the discipline swung more to studying the spatial distribution of social phenomena by cartographic and statistical methods. Some sociologists would immediately use the term ecological to describe work which emphasizes a spatial perspective, particularly in the use of small-area data (census tracts and enumeration districts). But more discerning commentators suggest that this limited approach, often bereft of theoretical justification, can hardly form the basis of an academic discipline. As Hawley (1944, p.148) puts it clearly: 'One of the techniques employed in ecological research – mapping – has been mistaken for the discipline itself.'

In more recent years human ecology has re-established itself by focusing on studies of the ecological complex at various community scales from local to global. The representation of the ecological complex or system which has perhaps achieved greatest impact has been that of Duncan (Figure 1.1). This indicates that human ecology focuses above all on the interactions between the fundamental dimensions in the complex from a functional point of view. Emphasis is given, therefore, to the way in which a population organizes and equips itself for survival in a particular habitat. Critically important to the human ecologist is an apprecia-

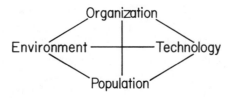

Figure 1.1
The ecological complex
Source: Duncan (1959), figure 10.   By permission of The University of Chicago Press
© 1959 by The University of Chicago.

tion of the interdependence of the various dimensions; there is no unilateral causation, only mutual interaction. The lines in the diagram are thus meant to indicate linkages of functional interdependence. It follows that if dislocating forces affect any one dimension (e.g., concentrated mortality reduction, technological innovation or rapid environmental change), a whole chain reaction of changes is set up throughout the complex as a new equilibrium is sought.

Roots of population geography

It will be argued here that the nature of contemporary population geography owes more to the radical changes in approach and methods operating throughout human geography in the 1960s and 1970s than to the particular emergence and development in the 1950s of population geography as a recognized branch of geography; yet these early roots must at least be acknowledged and traced briefly.

In authoritative reviews of the evolution and nature of geography, Hartshorne (1939) and Wooldridge and East (1951) make not a single reference to population geography, thus indicating the late entry of population geography into the recognized systematic branches of the subject. Zelinsky (1966) attributes this to the late arrival and modest impact on the academic scene of demography (compared with, for example, the role of economics in stimulating economic geography), and also to a dearth until fairly recently of population statistics, especially for subnational areas. Another factor would be the strong interests of many of the leading human geographers like Brunhes and Demangeon in settlement geography, where the distribution of population was studied through what was thought to be the more geographically acceptable medium of the cultural landscape. Population *per se* was relegated to consideration in the more sterile forms of regional geography as part of a Place-Work-People chain, with a naïve implicit assumption of unidirectional causation in that the physical environment was thought to strongly influence economic activities, which in turn controlled population patterns.

It was in the early 1950s that population geography finally emerged as a systematic branch of geography in the sense that it dealt with a recognizably distinct group of phenomena and systematically related processes, the study of which involved a particular form of training. Much of the credit must go to

Trewartha, who used the platform of his presidential address to the Assocation of American Geographers in 1953 to make a powerful case for, and an outline of, population geography (Trewartha 1953). He argued (p.97) that population was 'the pivotal element in geography, and the one around which all the others are oriented, and the one from which they all derive their meaning'. Other important formative statements were made at this time by P. George (1951) and James (1954a), and such was the growing interest in population geography that several synthesizing introductory texts appeared in the 1960s (P. George 1959, Clarke 1965, Zelinsky 1966, Beaujeu-Garnier 1966, M. G. Wilson 1968, Trewartha 1969). Illustrative of growth in the subject at this time, papers in population geography increased from 3 percent in 1962 to 13 percent in 1972 of papers presented at the annual meetings of the Association of American Geographers, and from 5 percent to 12 percent at the same time of papers in the leading American geographical journals (Hansen and Kosiński 1973, p.12).

Spatial distribution and areal differentiation of population attributes were clearly the unifying threads within population geography at this time. Thus Trewartha (1953, p.87) saw its purpose as 'an understanding of the regional differences in the earth's covering of peoples', while James (1954a, p.108) thought 'the objective of population geography is to define and to bring forth the significance of differences from place to place in the number and kind of human inhabitants'. The role of the population geographer was regarded by Zelinsky (1966, p.5) as studying 'the spatial aspects of population in the context of the aggregate nature of places', and by Beaujeu-Garnier (1966, p.3) as describing 'the demographic facts in their present environmental context'. More explicitly, Clarke (1965, p.12) stated that population geography 'is concerned with demonstrating how spatial variations in the distribution, composition, migrations and growth of populations are related to spatial variations in the nature of places'.

In these traditional approaches a focus on spatial distribution was thought sufficient to distinguish population geography from demography, which is much more concerned with the intrinsic nature and universal attributes of populations and with a temporal, rather than spatial, dimension. But a problem had always existed in specifying population attributes appropriate for direct study by the population geographer. There is agreement on a core comprising distribution, density, age-, sex- and marital-composition, fertility, mortality and migration, but opinions differ widely on the inclusion of attributes like occupation, religion, language and ethnicity. A neat rule-of-thumb way of circumscribing the field, suggested by Zelinsky (1966, p.7), is that attention should be confined to those human characteristics 'appearing in the census enumeration schedules and vital registration systems of the more statistically advanced nations', but inevitably there are data recording variations between such nations, and, more critically, there is no theoretical justification for the suggestion.

Two questions have dominated the traditional approach of the geographer to population study: Where? and Why there? The first has been responsible for considerable work in observing, identifying and, above all, depicting patterns of spatial distribution. Mapping of cross-sectional patterns thus dominated the early work in population geography, well exemplified by James (1954a) devoting more than three-quarters of his discussion of research frontiers in population geography to problems of mapping. Various commissions of the International Geographical Union have been active in this area (William-Olsson 1963, Prothero 1972, Kormoss and Kosiński 1973) and many geographers have developed considerable expertise in population mapping, prompting one human ecologist, worried about the narrow focus of his discipline at one time on the mapping of social phenomena, to exclaim: 'It is sometimes difficult to understand why this kind of work should be called anything other than geography, except possibly – out of deference to the geographers – because of the inferior cartographic skill which is often exhibited' (Hawley 1944, p.148).

Why there? takes the population geographer's approach a step further into an essentially ecological field, since 'the areal facts of population are so closely orchestrated with the totality of geographic reality' (Zelinsky 1966, p.127). Consequently, the analysis and explanation of 'complex inter-relationships between physical and human environments on the one hand, and population on the other . . . is the real substance of population geography' (Clarke 1965, p.2). But for some time there has been a nagging unease among population geographers about what some regard (retrospectively, of course!) as inadequate theoretical and analytical rigour in much of their traditional work. The problem has been addressed explicitly by Woods (1979) in his attempt to introduce population geographers to a wide range of analytical methods from formal demography.

Modern population geography: its changing emphasis

The spatial and ecological approach to population phenomena remains the dominant and distinctive dimension of population geography, but the practice of the subject has changed appreciably in response to the winds of conceptual and quantitative change which have swept through human geography in the last two decades (M. Chisholm 1975, Johnston 1979). Nearly all of these changes were introduced and developed in branches of the subject outside population geography, most notably in economic and urban geography where the new outlooks and procedures were derived from other social science disciplines, but their take-up by population geographers has been rapid and substantial – so much so that the methods they adopt have become less unique to demography and population geography, and more representative of the methods widely practised throughout human geography. Some might regret this as eroding the *raison d'être* of population geography, but an alternative view is that such integration of methods and communality of ideas augurs well for the health of the greater body, the parent discipline of geography. Indeed, this brings us back to an early statement by James (1954a, p.108): 'To recognize population geography as a distinct topical speciality is not to think of it as separable from the whole field of geography.'

Several strands of methodological transformation can be identified, although they are obviously more interactive and less compartmentalized than the following list suggests.

(i) *Quantification*

The traditional geographical means of presenting and analysing population patterns has been essentially cartographic. Thus 'the map is the fundamental instrument of geographic research' (James 1954b, p.9), with particular reliance on dot maps for population distribution and on choropleth maps for the distribution by area of population characteristics. The nature of such maps as essentially graphic devices greatly limits their use as analytical tools, and for explanation of patterns population geographers have often resorted to subjective and unreliable visual comparison of distributions in an attempt to assess correspondence and possible causal connection.

But with the growing awareness of quantitative methods within geography, an alternative means of describing numerical distribution within space has been adopted increasingly – the matrix – since this offers superior opportunities for subsequent analysis. A matrix is an ordered array of numbers, and the general form of a geographical data matrix is shown in Figure 1.2. The vertical axis indicates units of observation, like administrative areas, and the horizontal axis represents variables or attributes of place like sex ratio and number of immigrants. The particular importance to the population geographer of the matrix approach to data handling is that the great bulk of population data, by the very nature of its collection and publication, is arranged by areal units at all levels of scale from whole countries to the smallest census recording units.

Each row of the matrix presents an inventory of a place or area, each column indicates how the incidence of a particular characteristic varies spatially, and each cell defines a geographic fact; thus cell ij in Figure 1.2 shows the value assumed by characteristic i at place j, and this may be expressed by the symbol x_{ij}. Comparison of rows facilitates areal differentiation and therefore regional geography, while comparison of columns promotes the study of spatial association or covariation of phenomena, which is perhaps the most widespread general method currently adopted in population geography. The traditional visual comparison of map patterns has invariably been supplemented and often replaced by the use of correlation and regression methods on geographical data matrices (for a concise review of such methods and their applications, see D. M. Smith, 1975, chapter 8). Such methods allow spatial associations to be described with precision, and if analysis is extended into a consideration of residuals, hypotheses can often be generated about the identification and role of additional related variables. Nevertheless, one must be alert to a range of difficulties in applying standard statistical procedures like correlation and regression to spatially distributed data. There is the technical problem posed by the contiguity and spatial dependence of observations (Cliff and Ord 1973), and it has been shown that varying the size of the areal units can alter the value of the correlation coefficient (A. H. Robinson 1956, E. Thomas and Anderson 1965). More broadly, the distinction must always

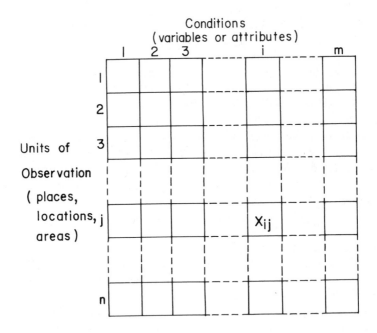

Figure 1.2
A geographical data matrix
Source: D.M. Smith (1975), figure 1.2

be made between the establishment of a measure of association and its use to infer a causal relationship; such a relationship must always be set within a plausible theoretical framework. In addition, there is the problem common to all forms of ecological correlation, that of making inferences about individual behaviour from essentially group or areal observations, as illustrated by the work of W. S. Robinson (1950) and Goodman (1959) on colour and illiteracy data in the United States.

The statistical analysis of areally based data sets is taken a step further into the realm of multiple correlation and multiple regression (Johnston 1978) by those population geographers who seek relationships between one dependent variable, whose spatial pattern they are seeking to explain, and several hypothesized independent variables. Additional examples of the advanced statistical methods increasingly adopted in population geography would be tedious at this stage when no reference is being made to specific findings.

(ii) *Computergraphics*

Increasing access to and familiarity with computers has stimulated the adoption, not simply of advanced statistical methods, but also of automated cartography. Population geographers have benefited from the use of computer mapping systems like SYMAP, which produces choropleth and isopleth maps by printing or over-printing characters or symbols to produce required densities.

The advantages over conventional hand-drawn maps are essentially in accuracy and speed of production when maps of several variables are required for a common areal base, thus allowing the initial programming and data preparation time to be effectively spread. Such mapping is particularly suitable, therefore, for the production of atlases portraying census variables; examples are provided by Rosing and Wood (1971) and Compton (1978a) in portrayals of census ward and enumeration district data for the West Midlands conurbation and Northern Ireland respectively. Automated cartography comes fully into its own where data are available for grid-squares. Such was the case in the 1971 UK Census when grid referencing of households was undertaken for the first time, thereby permitting the production of a population atlas based on square-kilometre data for Great Britain (Office of Population Censuses and Surveys 1981).

(iii) *Models*

Much of the traditional work in geography adopted a descriptive, historical approach to what were considered to be unique situations, but growing familiarity with the methods of physical and social sciences has encouraged geographers to seek assiduously for patterns, regularities and order in space. This approach is expressed in the formulation and testing of generalizing concepts, law-statements and, above all, models. A model may be regarded as a representation of reality whose purpose is to give 'a conceptual prop to our understanding, and, as such, provide a simplified apparently rational picture for teaching and a source of working hypotheses for research' (Haggett 1972, p.15).

The response of population geographers to this search for regularity was, initially, a qualified and hesitant one. Thus James (1954a, p.112) described the important pioneering of Stewart (1947) on a formula to describe population grouping around urban centres in these terms: 'As a device for uncovering some kind of theoretical order in the processes leading to the distribution of people this paper may be of great importance, although the geographer is more especially concerned with the modifications of the process in particular places.' Likewise, Zelinsky (1966, p.24) warned that the complexity of population patterns 'denotes relatively strong individuality for specific areas and wide, if potentially explainable, departures from predicted patterns. There may, then, be no simple formulas to explain the geography of the world's population; at best, only useful fragments of such laws may be available.' But more recent work in population geography, particularly in the study of migration as a form of spatial interaction, has conformed to the regularity-seeking trend in geography as a whole, as Zelinsky's own work (1971) on the mobility transition demonstrates.

(iv) *Process study*

There has been a growing awareness in human geography that too much attention in teaching and research has been given to the observation and identification of spatial patterns and too little attention to the processes which create and subsequently modify such patterns. More and more it is being appreciated that form and structure – the statics – are dependent on process and spatial interaction – the dynamics. Indeed, 'in proper perspective, the distinctions we make between spatial process and spatial structure disappear because they are based upon a limited time perspective. . . . Process and structure are, in essence, the same thing. . . . When we distinguish spatial process from spatial structure we are merely recognizing a difference in relative rapidity of change. . . . Properly considered, the spatial structure of a distribution is viewed as an index of the present state of an ongoing process' (Abler, Adams and Gould 1971, p.61).

Accordingly, geographers have become reluctant to infer process from structure, but ever more anxious to research the nature of the formative processes, not simply to explain past and present patterns but also to provide the basis of sound forecasting. Moreover, an important logistical advantage noted by Brookfield (1973, p.15) is that 'our fundamental shift away from the study of differentiation toward that of process carries with it liberation from any blanket-like constraint of scale in defining a geographical problem. The appropriate level of resolution becomes that at which the relevant process may best be recognized and analysed.'

Writing in 1967, Heenan (1967, p.714) argued convincingly that 'population geographers have hitherto tended to concentrate their interest very heavily upon the end product or summation of change in preference to the study of those dynamic processes whereby change is wrought.' But more recently population geography has been among the most responsive branches of human geography to the new emphasis on process-oriented study. A collection of papers on population geography by Demko, Rose and Schnell (1970) is clearly designed to place reader attention on the process dimension, as are reviews by Clarke (1973, 1977, 1978, 1979). The structure of this book has been designed specifically to recognize the prime explanatory importance in contemporary population geography of the dynamic components – fertility, mortality and migration – and the processes that fashion them; it is their spatial and temporal interaction which produces changes in population numbers, distribution and composition. Interaction is all important, and none of the dynamic components and their associated processes can be studied effectively in isolation. Consider, for example, how appreciable emigration (selective in terms of young male adults) from congested, famine-ridden Ireland in the nineteenth century promoted changes in the age-, sex- and marital-structure of Ireland, which in turn had repercussions on the level of birth, death and marriage rates and on a wide range of social and economic structures.

It has been the spur of process study that has stimulated the theoretical, model-based and simulation-oriented work on the spatial diffusion of ideas, behaviour and technology which arguably has been one of the very few significant strands of indigenous theory developed within geography, as opposed to theory derived from other sciences. Diffusion studies of the type pioneered by Hagerstrand (1968) have a clear relevance to an understanding of many of the key demographic processes. It is possible, for example, to consider, although not necessarily to accept, that spatial patterns of both fertility and mortality reduction reflect the spatial diffusion of innovations like contraception knowledge and public health technology, with diffusion from metropolitan innovation centres being controlled by spatial and urban hierarchical proximity.

(v) *Behavioural geography*

As a response to what some geographers regard as the excesses of macro-level deductive theorizing, of mechanistic quantification and of spatial fetishism, links are being forged increasingly with the behavioural sciences in order to appreciate better how the decisions which collectively form the basis of geographical processes and patterns are made. This approach has been used extensively and fruitfully by population geographers in studies of the socio-psychological determinants of migration – one of the most overt expressions of spatial behaviour. Wolpert (1965, 1967) provided the seminal geographical work in this field in his attempts to model the behavioural processes underlying the migration patterns which traditionally had been analysed by spatial scientists using little more than aggregate census data.

(vi) *Applications and relevance*

Despite a widespread satisfaction in geography with the intellectual rigour imparted to the subject by recent conceptual and technical developments, there exists an equally widespread concern that the subject has not been contributing powerfully to solving the pressing problems facing mankind. House (1973, p.273) maintains that 'particularly disadvantageous to geography is the widespread inability or disinclination by administrators to view problems, decisions or policies in a spatial framework, or even as having an important spatial implication.' Yet others, like D. M. Smith (1977, p.368), feel that 'the spatial or areal perspective imbued by geographical training may itself impose blinkers that obscure the operation of "non-geographical" variables.'

Population geographers in the Soviet Union have been centrally involved in settlement and economic planning (Clarke 1973), but in the West their applied role has been more tentative (Udo 1976). Yet a modest growth in applied and socially relevant work can be illustrated by reference to three areas. First, effective development planning in the Third World is enhanced by a full appreciation of the spatial population patterns traditionally prepared by population geographers from census and other data; examples from Africa include the work of Hilton (1960), Clarke (1966), I. D. Thomas (1968, 1972) and Gould (1973). Second, the geographer's interest in optimization or 'best location' has important applications in the population field. Work by Robertson (1972, 1974) is an example of the application of statistical and cartographic methods to a matrix of population data on a regular grid to give precise yet flexible answers to problems of facility location when maximum accessibility of population to facilities is desired. Third, significant contributions are being made by some population geographers to the construction of spatially disaggregated population-forecasting models (Rees and Wilson 1977).

(vii) *Ideology*

Often associated with calls for a more socially relevant, humane and welfare-oriented approach in geography have been strictures about the value judgements implicitly adopted in academic studies. Harvey (1974) has demonstrated powerfully, with particular relevance to the then active debate on the global population-resource balance, that in geography as elsewhere there is no such thing as an ethically neutral scientific methodology, and Hurst (1973) has accused human geography of largely supporting the status quo and predisposing people to an acceptance of the social ills accompanying capitalism.

Perhaps the area of population geography most influenced by a modern radical perspective has been that of development-related population processes in the Third World. Brookfield (1973, 1975) has shown that geographers, because of their deep commitment to Eurocentric values, have uncritically viewed development as a desirable process of diffusion of Western culture and technology to less favoured areas. It is now being recognized that alternative explanatory models are available, notably the inequality-perpetuating 'core-periphery' or 'dominance-dependency' relationship, and that goals like the achievement of self-respect and self-reliance might be considered no less desirable in a meaningful development process than material gain. One radical geographer has also argued with reference to the Third World that 'the poverty which is regarded as symptomatic of reckless population growth is rather a *structural poverty* caused by the irresponsible squandering of world resources by a small handful of nations' (Buchanan 1973, p.9) and that the current Western promotion of birth control programmes arises less from genuine humanitarianism than from the attempt of white northern imperialism to preserve the global status quo and its own privileged access to the resources of the dependent international periphery. Whether or not a Marxist mode of analysis gives more perceptive insights to population study than those grounded in capitalism is perhaps a less important matter to population analysts than the need to at least recognize and acknowledge the guiding framework of one's ideology and values.

CHAPTER 2

MORTALITY: INTERNATIONAL VARIATIONS

Both fertility and mortality rates are high in traditional, less developed societies, and both are low in modernized, economically advanced societies. Population growth through natural increase is consequently low at both ends of the conventional development/modernization spectrum, but in between it is considerable as mortality invariably falls in advance of fertility through its earlier response to modern economic and social influences. This is the essence of the demographic transition, which has been aptly described by Demeny (1972, p.153) as 'the central preoccupation of modern demography', not simply for its intrinsic intellectual interest, but also because it has brought about the global population explosion which threatens the preservation of social systems. Thus, although in individual life-cycles birth obviously occurs before death, it is mortality that merits initial consideration in any systematic treatment of demographic components and processes.

Measures of mortality

To study spatial and temporal variations in mortality it is necessary to use comparative measures or indices of mortality for the periods and areas under consideration. The basic measures are essentially rates of incidence, relating the number of deaths to a unit of population in a particular interval of time. The unit of population is commonly 1000, although its adoption in place of 100, 1 million or indeed any number is little more than demographic convention. The time interval is invariably one year, to avoid the complicating effect of seasonal mortality variations on comparability of rates.

Crude death rate
This is the simplest measure, indicating the number of deaths in a particular year per 1000 of the population:

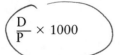

$$\frac{D}{P} \times 1000$$

The mid-year population is used, ideally, as the best available approximation to the average number of people exposed to death, or 'at risk', during the year. The term 'crude' is used advisedly, since no allowance is made for often considerable differences between communities in those aspects of population composition, particularly age and sex, which strongly influence mortality probabilities. It will be shown that mortality rates increase with age from late childhood, and that at nearly all ages mortality is higher for males than females. Consequently, age and sex structure plays an important role in influencing crude death rates, regardless of factors like living standards and health programmes. This is why care has to be taken in interpreting international differences in crude death rates. There are some less developed countries (e.g., Costa Rica, Guyana, Jamaica, Sri Lanka) which have lower crude death rates (about 5–7 per 1000 in the late 1970s) than the economically and medically advanced countries of North America and northwestern Europe (about 9–12 per 1000). Clearly this is due to much younger age structures in less developed countries, resulting from their high fertility in the immediate past.

Age- and sex-specific death rates

A more critical appreciation of mortality level can be derived from a table of mortality rates disaggregated by age and sex. An age- and sex-specific death rate is the number of deaths during a year of persons of a given age and sex per 1000 people of that age and sex:

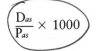

$$\frac{D_{as}}{P_{as}} \times 1000$$

It is, in essence, a crude death rate for a particular age and sex group. It is conventional to use five-year or ten-year age groups, as a compromise between unnecessarily detailed and tediously compiled one-year groups and excessively generalized and often internally heterogeneous larger age groups. However, because of the importance of infant deaths, separate rates are usually calculated for the under one and one–four age groups.

Examples of age- and sex-specific death rates are given in Table 2.1 for a developed and a less developed country. Although levels of mortality differ between the United States and Costa Rica, the overall pattern of mortality by age and sex is similar. Mortality rates fall from relatively high levels in the first year of life to a minimum in the five–fourteen age group and then rise in successive age groups, although the mortality level in the first year is not exceeded until old age. The lower

Table 2.1 Age- and sex-specific death rates (per 1000), United States (1975) and Costa Rica (1974)

	United States		Costa Rica	
	male	female	male	female
Under 1	18·3	14·4	49·5	35·3
1– 4	0·8	0·6	2·0	2·0
5–14	0·4	0·3	0·6	0·5
15–24	0·8	0·6	1·6	0·8
25–34	2·0	0·9	2·5	1·0
35–44	3·5	1·9	3·5	2·3
45–54	8·6	4·6	7·0	4·5
55–64	20·3	10·1	14·5	10·5
65–74	44·1	22·5	36·0	30·1
75–84	95·2	60·3	81·9	72·5
85+	175·7	140·3	160·7	165·4

Source of data: UN Demographic Yearbook 1976

mortality of females is found in all the United States age groups and almost all in Costa Rica. Traditional explanations include the greater exposure of men, in general, to warfare, occupational and recreational hazards and occupational tension, but the excess male mortality at infant and even foetal stages suggests that a biological difference is the decisive factor – the gentler sex being the stronger sex, at least for survival (Madigan 1957, Enterline 1961, Koller 1963).

Sets of age- and sex-specific death rates represent refined measures of mortality, but they are cumbersome and difficult to assimilate. It is desirable, therefore, to have a summary measure which epitomizes a whole set of rates but which avoids the crudity of the crude death rate. Demographers have used their technical ingenuity to produce several such measures, and two of the most widely used will now be discussed to illustrate the process known as standardization. By this procedure death rates are adjusted or standardized for, commonly, the age and sex composition of the population. Standardization can be regarded as a means of holding age and sex constant, in a not dissimilar way to the holding of altitude constant in the calculation of temperature or pressure 'reduced to sea level'.

Standardized death rate

This is a hypothetical figure which indicates what the crude death rate would be if the population being studied had the same age and sex composition as a population (any population, real or assumed) which is used as the standard. It is calculated (in the so-called direct method of standardization) by applying the age- and sex-specific death rates for each population under consideration to the age and sex composition of the standard population:

$$\frac{\sum (P_{as} \, D_{as})}{P} \times 1000$$

P = standard population
P_{as} = number in standard population of age and sex category *as*
d_{as} = specific annual death rate of age and sex category *as* in the population under study.

It is a weighted average of the age- and sex-specific death rates in a population, using as weights the age and sex distribution of the standard population. Worked examples for the United States and Costa Rica are shown in Table 2.2, using the population of another country, Japan (an arbitrary choice), as the standard. The standardized death rates, calculated on this basis, confirm a theoretically reasonable expectation that mortality is somewhat lower in the United States than in Costa Rica, despite crude death rates for the years in question of 8.9 per 1000 in the United States and a mere 5.0 in Costa Rica. It should be emphasized that standardized death rates have little intrinsic meaning; they are meaningful only in relation to each other and to the selected standard population.

Table 2.2 Calculation of standardized death rate, United States and Costa Rica

| | Standard population Japan 1975, '000 | | United States | | | | Costa Rica | | | |
| | | | Age-specific death rates 1975 (per 1000) | | Expected deaths in standard population | | Age-specific death rates 1974 (per 1000) | | Expected deaths in standard population | |
	M	F	M	F	M	F	M	F	M	F
Under 1	973	933	18·3	14·4	17,806	13,435	49·5	35·3	48,164	32,935
1– 4	4,121	3,937	0·8	0·6	3,297	2,362	2·0	2·0	8,242	7,874
5–14	8,813	8,410	0·4	0·3	3,525	2,523	0·6	0·5	5,288	4,205
15–24	8,606	8,386	0·8	0·6	6,885	5,032	1·6	0·8	13,770	6,709
25–34	10,120	10,012	2·0	0·9	20,240	9,011	2·5	1·0	25,300	10,012
35–44	8,337	8,295	3·5	1·9	29,180	15,760	3·5	2·3	29,180	19,079
45–54	6,293	6,868	8·6	4·6	54,120	31,592	7·0	4·5	44,051	30,906
55–64	3,983	4,941	20·3	10·1	80,853	49,904	14·5	10·5	57,754	51,881
65–74	2,715	3,305	44·1	22·5	119,732	74,362	36·0	30·1	97,740	99,481
75–84	998	1,441	95·2	60·3	95,009	86,892	81·9	72·5	81,736	104,472
85+	124	275	175·7	140·3	21,787	38,582	160·7	165·4	19,927	45,485
	111,886				452,434	329,455			431,152	413,039

Standardized death rate:

$$\text{United States}$$
$$\frac{(452{,}434 + 329{,}455)}{111{,}886{,}000} \times 1000$$
$$= 6.99 \text{ per } 1000$$

$$\text{Costa Rica}$$
$$\frac{(431{,}152 + 413{,}039)}{111{,}886{,}000} \times 1000$$
$$= 7.55 \text{ per } 1000$$

Source: data from UN Demographic Yearbook 1976

Expectation of life at birth

This is the average number of years that would be lived by a group of persons born in the same year, assuming (unrealistically from the point of view of forecasting) that the age-specific death rates of that year would be maintained throughout the life history of the cohort. It is a measure of mortality in a particular year, and that year only, and is normally derived from a national life-table. An extract from a United States life-table is shown in Table 2.3. It adopts the standard practice of setting up a hypothetical birth cohort of 100,000 persons and then plotting its diminution over time on the basis of age-specific mortality rates applying in the year of calculation, an average of 1959–1961 in this particular example. In essence, it provides a cross-section or snapshot of mortality at one particular time.

Table 2.3   *Extract from life-table of United States, 1959–1961*

Age interval x	No. living at beginning of interval l_x	No. dying during interval d_x	Average remaining lifetime in years at beginning of interval e_x
0–1	100,000	2,593	69·89
1–2	97,407	165	70·75
2–3	97,242	101	69·87
3–4	97,141	78	68·94
.			
.			
.			
.			
.			
109–110	1	1	1·29

Source: Shryock and Siegel (1976), p.252

The first figure in the final column (e_x) gives the expectation of life at birth, calculated in the following manner. Consider from column d_x that 2593 persons die in the first year of life. They can be regarded as having lived, on average, about half a year, so that they contribute $2593 \times \frac{1}{2}$ years to the total years lived by the original 100,000 birth cohort. The 165 dying in the second year live, on average, $165 \times 1\frac{1}{2}$ years. Thus the average length of life for the birth cohort can be regarded as:

$$\frac{(2593 \times \frac{1}{2}) + (165 \times 1\frac{1}{2}) + \ldots + (1 \times 109\frac{1}{2})}{100,000} = 69.89$$

The formula, using the notations of Table 2.3, is:

$$e_0 = \frac{\sum_{x=0}^{x=109} d_x (x + \frac{1}{2})}{100,000}$$

As refined measures of mortality, expectation of life at birth and the standardized death rate should be expected to give broadly consistent results in comparative analyses. In the case of the United States and Costa Rica in 1974–1975, standardized death rate calculations (Table 2.2) have given figures of 6.99 and 7.55 per 1000 respectively, which are consistent with the life expectancy at birth figures for those countries at that time of seventy-two and sixty-eight years respectively.

Infant mortality rate

This is a widely used indicator of health conditions and general living standards which recognizes the concentration of deaths in the first year of life (Tables 2.1 – 2.3). The rate is conventionally defined as the number of deaths of children under one year of age in a particular year per 1000 live births in that year:

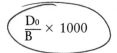

$$\frac{D_0}{B} \times 1000$$

It is almost, but not quite, the same as the specific death rate in the under one-year-old age group.

Data quality

A word of warning is necessary at this stage, since there is a danger that preoccupation with sophisticated statistical methods might blind one's eyes to the often unreliable primary data on deaths and ages. Clearly, any statistical analysis is only as sound as the quality of the data it uses.

The basic data on deaths are normally obtained from a country's vital statistics registration system. The legal requirement for registration of births, deaths and marriages is far from universal, and when it is absent registration will inevitably be incomplete. Many less developed countries collect death statistics by registration in only a part of the national territory, because of problems like nomadism, civil disorder and inadequate administrative systems. Another source of under-registration, common practice in many less developed countries, is that babies dying before the end of the legal registration period for births are not registered as births or deaths. Such is the extent of under-registration that a United Nations analysis in 1951–1955 suggested that only about 33 percent of the world's deaths were then being registered, the proportion varying regionally from some 7 percent in East Asia to almost 100 percent in Europe and North America (Shryock and Siegel 1976). Even in some developed countries, the establishment of comprehensive death recording has been achieved only fairly recently. Thus in the United States the registration area at the beginning of this century embraced only 40 percent of the country's population. Complete territorial coverage was not achieved until 1933, and even then a completeness of registration of only 90 percent of deaths was the condition for joining the national death registration area. A useful, but by no means infallible, indication of the completeness of current national mortality data is given in the UN *Demographic Yearbooks*.

The accuracy of annual mortality rates is also affected by the practice in a substantial minority of countries (e.g., Egypt, Mexico, Singapore, Scotland) of recording deaths on a year-of-registration and not year-of-occurrence basis. Most mortality rates also require for their computation the appropriate age and sex distribution of the population from a census or sample survey. Errors in the recording of age are thought to be widespread and may be due to a host of causes: ignorance of correct age; the reckoning of age in parts of Asia by the so-called Chinese system and not by completed solar years since birth; deliberate misrepresentation for personal and sometimes practical reasons; and a tendency to give age in figures ending in certain digits, particularly 0, 5 and even numbers.

Demographers have evolved methods of adjustment and smoothing to minimize such data deficiencies (Brass et al. 1968, Preston 1980) but it is well to be aware that for much of the world the data on mortality still rest essentially on estimates of varying authority.

Mortality and development

It is well known that the modern period of world mortality decline and consequent population growth, dating essentially from the eighteenth century, was initiated and consolidated in the economically advanced parts of Europe and North America before spreading to less developed parts of the world, reaching the bulk of the world's population in Asia, Africa and Latin America only in the last half century. As a prelude to a discussion of the manner and mechanism of mortality decline, it is useful to consider the current relationship between national levels of mortality and economic development.

Table 2.4 presents a correlation matrix, based on data from 150 countries in the late 1970s, of the relationships between three measures of mortality and the best-known, most widely used, yet increasingly controversial, measure of development – Gross National Product (GNP) per head. The processes of development and underdevelopment have come under close and critical scrutiny in the social sciences in recent years (well-summarized for geographers in D. M. Smith, 1977, chapter 8). It is now widely appreciated that development is not simply concerned with the production of goods and services measurable in monetary terms. Rather, it is a multifaceted phenomenon embracing social as well as economic change, and distributional as well as aggregate performance; and it is subject always to values, goals and standards which are not universal.

Several attempts have been made to construct a composite index of development based on the empirical association between many individual indicators (Adelman and Morris 1967, Drewnowski and Scott 1968, McGranahan et al. 1972). However, the incorporation of health and mortality variables in these indices makes it technically undesirable, because of circularity problems, to use such indices in a consideration of possible functional relationships with international levels of mortality – hence the use in Table 2.4 of the traditional GNP index of development.

Table 2.4   Coefficients of linear correlation between gross national product per capita and mortality, 150 countries,* 1976–1978

	CDR	ELB	IMR
GNP per capita	−0·39	0·68	−0·65
log GNP per capita	−0·67	0·88	−0·82
CDR		−0·88	0·86
ELB			−0·95

CDR = Crude death rate,   ELB = Expectation of life at birth,
IMR = Infant mortality rate

* For a substantial number of less developed countries, data are estimated. Oil-rich (OPEC) countries are excluded because of disparities there between GNP per capita and other development indicators.

Source: data from Population Reference Bureau, World Population Data Sheet, 1980

The first row of Table 2.4 shows a clear relationship between national levels of GNP per capita and of mortality. Predictably the relationship is stronger for the age-standardized measures of mortality than for the crude death rate, bearing in mind the young age structure of less developed countries. Alternative indicators of development can be used to confirm the general relationship with mortality. Thus in a correlation matrix established by McGranahan et al. (1972, p.53) on the basis of 1960 data for 115 countries, there are correlation coefficients for expectation of life at birth of 0.85 with literacy percentage in the over-fifteen age group and −0.90 with proportion of male labour force in agriculture.

But a scattergraph (Figure 2.1) of GNP and expectation of life at birth indicates that the relationship is very far from a linear one. Life expectancy increases rapidly at first as GNP rises, but tends to level off in the richer group of countries at just above the biblical allotment of three score years and ten. Thus at high levels of economic development substantial increases in GNP per capita bring little or no reduction in mortality level. It is now widely recognized that such a pattern of strongly diminishing returns is common in the development process, in that increasing wealth and investment add progressively less economic and social benefit.

In order to transform the curvilinear graphical pattern into a linear one, log GNP values have been used in the second row of Table 2.4 and in a second scattergraph (Figure 2.2). The linear correlation coefficient values increase accordingly, although the hint of curvilinearity still found in Figure 2.2 at higher GNP levels indicates that the relationship between GNP and mortality is a very tenuous one at high levels of economic advancement. It is almost certainly influenced by the variable distribution of income and other benefits within national societies. In the United States, for example, mortality reduction to the very lowest levels predicted on the basis of GNP may well be prevented by the heterogeneity of its population, a

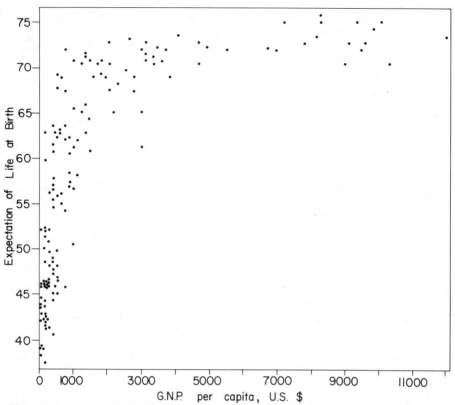

Figure 2.1
Expectation of life at birth (in years) by gross national product per capita (US$), 150 countries,* 1976-1978
Source: data from Population Reference Bureau, *World Population Data Sheet, 1980*
*see Table 2.4

sizeable segment belonging to groups which are still severely disadvantaged. An obvious contrast is provided by Scandinavian countries.

Figure 2.3 depicts the international pattern of survival based on actual or estimated 1976 age-specific death rates. A zonal pattern, dependent on development differences, is the dominant feature, with the two ends of the survival spectrum being the temperate-latitude developed countries, on the one hand, and the hard-core disadvantaged countries of intertropical Africa, the Indian subcontinent and parts of Southeast Asia on the other.

The evolving pattern of mortality decline

The temporal and spatial processes which have created the current world pattern of mortality can now be explored through a consideration of three groups of countries picked out by their differing onset, pace and pattern of mortality decline.

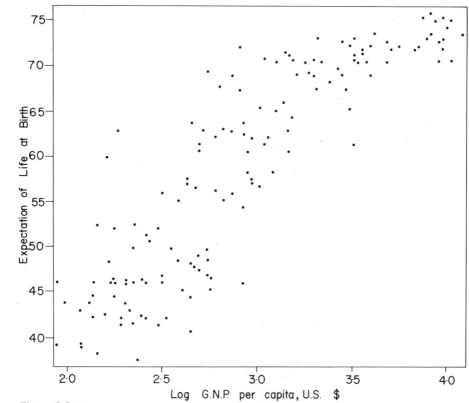

Figure 2.2
Expectation of life at birth (in years) by log GNP per capita (US$), 150 countries,*
1976-1978
Source: data from Population Reference Bureau, *World Population Data Sheet, 1980*
*see Table 2.4

Northwestern Europe and North America

The nature of population growth from about the mid-seventeenth to the mid-
nineteenth century in the northwestern European core area of world population
expansion is still a matter of controversy, although the scale and extent of growth is
not disputed. The essence of the debate is captured by a popular examination
question: 'Did the Industrial Revolution create its own labour force?' There are
those who argue that associated revolutions in agriculture, industry and transport
directly stimulated population growth, although the traditional view that this was
achieved through lowered mortality rather than by increased fertility is not universally accepted (Krause 1958, Langer 1963, Habbakuk 1971). Others argue for the
primacy of population growth as an independent variable, promoting in its wake a
series of economic changes. Consider, for example, the population growth in
Ireland from 3 million at the beginning of the eighteenth century to just over 8
million at the 1841 census immediately preceding the Great Famine. This growth is

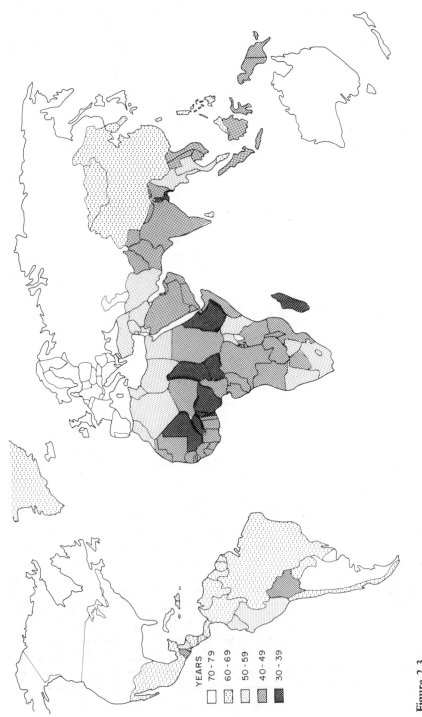

Figure 2.3
Expectation of life at birth for females, 1976
Source: OPCS, *Population Trends* 16, p.31, based on UN publications data. Crown Copyright

often attributed, in an entirely derivative fashion, to the widespread adoption of the potato, to subdivision of large farms and to reclamation of bogland, all of which could be expected to lower mortality and promote earlier marriage and hence higher fertility (Connell 1950). But it can also be argued that it was population pressure, however caused, that was the primary stimulus during this period to Irish agricultural change (Grigg 1976).

Deficiency of data is clearly the factor preventing a definitive interpretation of demographic trends before the nineteenth century. Civil registers, maintained by state officials, of births, deaths and marriages only became common in the nineteenth century (instituted, for example, in 1806 in France, 1837 in England and Wales and 1855 in Scotland), and only a minority of European countries began national censuses of population before well into the nineteenth century (Iceland 1703, Sweden 1749, Denmark-Norway 1769, France 1801, England and Wales 1801). A variety of sources has therefore been used to reconstruct past demographic patterns. Amongst the most bizarre is a scrutiny of Roman tombstone inscriptions, which led Durand (1960) to estimate the expectation of life at birth in the Roman Empire during the first and second centuries as twenty-five–thirty years. Such methods illustrate the risk of superficial generalization from unrepresentative data, since there can be little doubt that the provision of burial memorials varies by age, sex, class and other factors. For example, Henry (1957) found less than 10 percent of funerary inscriptions at a Lyon cemetry in the early nineteenth century were for ages below fifteen, whereas over 40 percent of all deaths in France were in this age group.

The most widely used demographic sources for the pre-civil registration era are the ecclesiastical registers of births, deaths and marriages. The extraction, analysis and interpretation of their data form the core of the widely practised, interdisciplinary field of historical demography, whose methods are described in Fleury and Henry (1956), Henry (1967) and Wrigley (1966a). At various times from the fifteenth to the eighteenth centuries it became common for European clergy to keep local registers of vital events, often stimulated initially by diocesan initiative but later by royal requirement. In England, for example, the keeping of parish registers dates from Thomas Cromwell's Ordinance of 1538. Invaluable as the registers are as raw demographic data banks, and ingenious as are some of the extractive methods adopted, they are subject nevertheless to major problems of error, bias and uncertainty, which can readily contaminate historical demographic data; it is also rare for complete sets of registers to survive.

The most critical deficiency of the registers is underenumeration of vital events (Krause 1965). There was rarely any check on an individual's diligence in register keeping, and Hollingsworth (1972, p.79) notes that, for the clergyman, 'keeping a parish register may have been like keeping his diary. He remembered to write the event down at once perhaps 80 percent of the time; sometimes he forgot and never wrote it up afterwards.' Growth of anticlericalism and nonconformity clearly promoted underenumeration, since the events recorded in the registers by the established church were essentially religious events – baptisms and burials rather than births and deaths. In Britain, it is widely recognized that growth of dissenting congregations diminishes greatly the demographic value of parish registers from the late eighteenth century, although another factor was the inability of the ecclesiastical recording system to cope with rapidly increasing urban populations. Yet another defect relates specifically to infant deaths in the period between birth and baptism, which averaged almost one month in late eighteenth-century England (Berry and Schofield 1971). Invariably both birth and death were unrecorded in such cases. It has been estimated that between one-third and one-half of infant deaths were unrecorded in English parish registers, leading to total deaths being undercounted by some 10 percent (R. E. Jones 1976).

The data base of historical demography has been created so recently, essentially dating from Henry's seminal work on French parish registers in the 1950s, that it represents 'a harvest so summarily gathered that more grain remains to be garnered than has yet been stored' (Henry 1972, p.43). Yet as more and more individual studies are completed and collated, so is our appreciation of the general pattern of demographic trends in pre-industrial Europe enhanced. Illustrative of this general pattern are the crude birth rates and crude death rates of Norway between 1735 and 1865 (Figure 2.4), derived by Drake from the ecclesiastical registers and population censuses of the time. He observes that 'the evidence of the vital statistics and census returns support each other, suggesting a high degree of diligence and skill on the part of the clergy of the Norwegian state church who were responsible for their collection. The clergy were aided by co-operation and homogeneity of the public – nonconformity was not a problem – and by the efficiency and continued interest of the central administration. Fortunately too, they were spared the rapid growth of urban areas which bedevilled English vital registration in the late eighteenth and early nineteenth centuries' (Drake 1969, p.150).

The pattern of Norwegian population growth revealed by Figure 2.4 is consistent with that found elsewhere in northwestern Europe. For the eighteenth and presumably previous centuries growth is restricted not simply by a high level of average mortality, but even more by the intermittent peaks in mortality commonly referred to as demographic crises or catastrophes. In the very nature of things, the theoretical range of fluctuation for the death rate – from no one to everyone dying in a particular year – is much greater than for the birth rate, and it is clear that the demographic crises were an immediate response to the onset of famine and epidemics. Thus, of the three major peaks in Norwegian mortality revealed by Figure 2.4, that of the early 1740s is related to climatically induced harvest failures and to pandemics of influenza and typhus which raged throughout Europe in those years (Helleiner 1957), that of the early 1770s to the harvest failures and acute distress then present throughout Scandinavia (Gille 1949–1950), and that of the very early nineteenth century to the collapse of the herring and cod fisheries along the west coast of Norway, to failures in the grain harvest and to the disruption of shipping and timber trades during the Napoleonic Wars (Drake 1969). An interesting demographic feature revealed by Figure 2.4 and confirmed by parish register data in Scotland (Flinn 1977) is that in the years immediately following a demographic

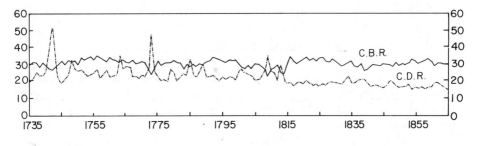

Figure 2.4
Crude birth rates and crude death rates per 1000, Norway, 1735-1865
Source: Drake (1969), figure 2. By permission of Cambridge University Press.

crisis, mortality rates generally fell to very low levels, which suggests that disease and famine tended to weed out the physiologically weak, leaving a relatively tough and resistant population. But of much greater import is the elimination in Norway of demographic crises in the nineteenth century, so that population growth was not terminated, as in previous epochs, by catastrophe.

The secular downward trend of mortality throughout northwestern Europe, typified by the Norwegian experience, can be explained by the interaction of several processes, most but not all of which are associated, directly or indirectly, with economic development.

(i) Improved nutrition

To Malthus and many other students of population the fundamental resource constraint on population growth is food supply, but there is overwhelming evidence for a considerable increase in agricultural output throughout northwestern Europe from the early eighteenth century. Langer (1975) attributes this largely to the widespread adoption of the new wonder crop from America, the potato, with its enormous calorific yield per acre. Drake (1969) attaches great demographic importance to the introduction of the potato to Norway in the 1750s, since it rapidly proved to be a more reliable provider of subsistence in agriculturally marginal climates than traditional grain crops. More generally, however, the increased European food supply can be attributed to a series of agricultural advances which, in the case of Britain, collectively have been termed the Agricultural Revolution. Major advances in Britain included: the enclosure of open fields and the reclamation of fenland and moorland; the introduction of new crops, notably turnips and clover, providing winter fodder for animals that formerly would have been killed in autumn; the development of balanced crop rotations in place of the traditional grain-fallow rotation; the conservation of soil fertility by marling, liming and mixed farming. In addition, regional famines were eliminated by the growing economic integration of national territory promoted by road and canal developments in the eighteenth century and railways in the nineteenth. By such means Britain was able to feed, almost entirely from its own resources, a population which trebled between 1700 and 1850, although Razell (1974) suggests provocatively that per capita food consumption may not have increased during this period. Later in the nineteenth century substantial imports of food were required, above all from the newly opened up wheatlands of the North American interior.

The more substantial and varied food supply lowered mortality rates by reducing the ravages of infanticide, starvation and infectious diseases. There is no direct statistical evidence on infant mortality through wilful neglect or violence, but there is appreciable documentary evidence for its wide practice until this century in Europe and for its basic cause being the inability of parents to feed their growing families (Langer 1974, Sauer 1978). Contemporary observers noted that parents were frequently indifferent to the loss of a child and that smallpox was commonly referred to in Britain as 'the poor man's friend'. Illustrative of parental inability to cope with large families were the foundling hospitals or orphanages present in all large cities of nineteenth-century Europe. Langer (1963) suggests that in the 1817–1820 period about one-third of the children born in Paris were abandoned to these institutions, and he shows that many contemporary writers denounced the practice as legalized infanticide, one even suggesting that foundling hospitals should erect a sign reading 'Children killed at government expense'.

Reliable figures on deaths wholly attributable to starvation are just as difficult to obtain, but the weight of opinion among medical historians is that starvation deaths *per se* have often been exaggerated in historical accounts of demographic catastrophes in pre-industrial Europe. Current opinion places much more emphasis on the way in which malnutrition induced death through the medium of infectious diseases like typhus, tuberculosis, measles and plague. Among the most authoritative statements is that by McKeown (1976, pp.128–129):'Extensive experience in developing countries leaves no doubt about the profound effect of nutritional state on response to micro-organisms; malnourished populations have higher infection rates and are more likely to die when infected. The predominance of infectious disease in pre- and early industrial societies was due largely to malnutrition, and an improvement in nutrition was a necessary condition for a substantial and prolonged reduction of mortality and growth of population.' There is clear historical evidence for the coincidence of epidemics with bad harvests (Gille 1949, Flinn 1977), and a supplementary factor is that at such times the rodents which transmit some major diseases move closer to man (Sigerist 1943).

(ii) Increased manufacturing output

The change from domestic handcraft to factory mass-production systems, which comprises the Industrial Revolution, greatly increased the amount and variety of goods, many of which like soap, iron bedsteads, washable cotton underclothes and heavy winter clothing had a direct role in warding off illness and death (for example, in ridding bodies of lice, the vectors of typhus). More indirectly, many of the technologically based advances in agriculture and public health in the second half of the nineteenth century were dependent on an abundant production of commodities like agricultural machinery, chemical fertilizer, iron pipes and pumping systems.

(iii) Medical advances

The views of Griffith (1926), attributing much of the eighteenth-century fall in mortality to medical developments, were widely accepted until the 1950s. He had been impressed by the expansion of hospital, dispensary and midwifery services (the number of hospitals in England increasing from 2 in 1700 to over 50 in 1800), by advances in the understanding of anatomy and physiology, and by the introduction of a specific protective measure, inoculation against smallpox. At least one modern historian (Razzell 1965, 1977) supports the important demographic effect of inoculation, a crude method of immunization introduced from the Middle East into Europe at a time when vaccination was unknown. The method consisted of inoculating, i.e., infecting, a healthy person with pus from a mild case of the disease, thus conferring protection against a more serious attack.

These conclusions on eighteenth-century mortality decline have been severely questioned by McKeown and Brown (1955) and others. They emphasize that effective medicines were nonexistent, that hospitals furthered rather than controlled infectious disease (hence the well-known statement by Florence Nightingale that the first requirement of a hospital is that it should do the sick no harm), and that the crude and dangerous measure of inoculation is thought likely by present-day smallpox virologists to have spread rather than limited the disease; but for a less pessimistic view of the role of early hospitals, readers may refer to Cherry (1980).

Even for most of the nineteenth century, medical developments are likely to have had little or no influence on falling mortality rates, essentially because there was no appreciation until the work of Pasteur and Koch in the 1870s and 1880s of the existence of germs, their manner of reproduction and transmission, and their specificity in causing disease. Similarly, society had to await Lister's work in the 1880s before a start could be made on aseptic and antiseptic surgery through the sterilization of instruments, the use of masks, and the scrubbing of operating theatres with carbolic acid. Even as late as 1870–1871, 10,000 out of 13,000 amputations performed by French army surgeons in the Franco-Prussian War proved fatal (Newsholme 1929, p.30). Effective medical therapy, acting directly on the infective micro-organism, was delayed until the introduction of chemotherapeutic agents, particularly sulphonamides and antibiotics, from the 1930s.

Probably the only medical measure to contribute significantly to mortality reduction before this century was vaccination against smallpox by the cowpox vaccine developed by Jenner in 1798, but opinions differ on its contribution to overall mortality decline. In Britain, where vaccination was made compulsory for infants in 1854 although not legally enforced until 1871, data from McKeown (1976) suggest that mortality decline from smallpox accounted for about 5 percent of total mortality decline in the second half of the nineteenth century. But for Norway, Drake (1969) attributes to vaccination a role second only to the potato in overall mortality reduction. He shows that vaccination was made compulsory in 1810 and was enforced by the refusal of the church to confirm or marry unvaccinated persons, so that by the 1850s the annual number of vaccinations amounted to 82 percent of live births.

A strong statement of the very limited role of medicine in bringing about mortality decline, even in the twentieth century, is provided by the view of Mc-Keown (1976, p.162) that 'the health of man is determined essentially by his behaviour, his food and the nature of the world around him, and is only marginally influenced by personal medical care.' One should note, however, that exposure to infection has been considerably reduced in this century by medically stimulated measures like pasteurization and bottling of milk, which M. W. Beaver (1973) regards as a major factor in reducing infant mortality in Britain. There is also the important role of health education, whereby people become aware of the need for cleanliness in body, in food preparation and in domestic waste disposal. Razzell (1974) has argued that there were significant improvements in this field in Britain in the first half of the nineteenth century, before, in fact, the germ theory of disease was appreciated. He quotes C. Wilson (1954, p.6) as summarizing the transformation of personal hygiene: 'By the 1860s a daily bath was usual among those who could afford the coal for heating the water and the labour to carry the great jugs from which the hot water was poured into the movable tub. A little lower in the social scale, the bath was a weekly ritual but washing took place daily, and everywhere the wash-hand stand, with its basin, jug and soap dish, was making an appearance in the Victorian bedrooms.' One suspects, however, that such an account inadequately embraces working-class conditions.

(iv) Public health developments

Drinking water, contaminated with human faeces or urine, was clearly the major medium for transmission of intestinal diseases (typhoid, cholera, dysentry) in crowded and unsanitary urban environments before the gradual provision of public utility systems during the nineteenth century. London provides an illustration of this provision, although as capital of the most materially advanced country in the world at that time its dates of provision were atypically early. In 1829 a start was made on water purification by the use of sand filters for Thames river water (although chlorination had to await the turn of the century); in 1848 public agencies for refuse removal began operation; and in 1865 a network of sewers was completed, to take the place of open ditches and cesspools.

A striking example of how public utility provision contributed to mortality decline in nineteenth-century Europe has been provided by Preston and Van de Walle (1978). They present graphs (Figure 2.5) of life expectancy at birth for the three departments which contain the largest cities in France: Seine (Paris), Rhône (Lyon) and Bouches-du-Rhône (Marseille). The fact that life expectancy is much lower in all three urban departments than in France as a whole reflects an important urban-rural differential in mortality which will be discussed in the next chapter. What demands immediate attention from Figure 2.5 is the striking divergence in mortality experience between the three departments from the middle of the nineteenth century. This is attributed to their differing progress in the provision of public health utilities. In Lyon, the provision of filtered, piped water and a sewerage system occurred in the 1850s. In Paris, water and sewerage

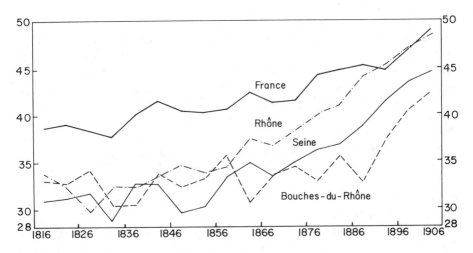

Figure 2.5
Nineteenth-century trends in life expectancy at birth (in years) in France and the departments of Seine, Rhône and Bouches-du-Rhône
Source: Preston and Van de Walle (1978), figure 2

improvements were less decisive and were spread more gradually throughout the 1850–1900 period. Cause-of-death data (Table 2.5) show that by far the greater part of overall mortality decline in Paris at this time was due to the reduced impact of water- and food-borne diseases, particularly cholera. The most retarded development was in Bouches-du-Rhône, where Marseille, almost up to the end of the century, had sewers only in a few privileged neighbourhoods and derived its water from the Durance by an uncovered 83km canal which passed through several contaminating settlements. It took a severe cholera epidemic in 1884–1885 to sting city authorities into providing appropriate utilities in the 1890s.

Table 2.5   Crude death rate (per 1000) by cause in nineteenth-century Paris

	1854–1856	1887–1889	
Airborne diseases	7·2	6·9	
Water- and food-borne diseases	8·6	2·2	
Typhoid		2·0	0·5
Diarrhoea, gastritis, enteritis		3·7	1·7
Cholera		2·9	0·0
Other causes	14·9	13·4	
All causes	30·7	22·5	

Source: Preston and Van de Walle (1978), table 3

(v) Changing internal character of infectious diseases

A contribution to mortality decline, entirely independent of economic development, might have been made by the ever-evolving relationship between micro-organisms and man. Thus a reduction in the virulence of an infective organism would bring about a spontaneous or autonomous mortality decline, and at least one historian (Chambers 1972) assigns a critical demographic role to this random biological influence. Firm evidence is hard to come by, although there seems little doubt that scarlet fever behaved in this fashion in nineteenth-century Europe (McKeown et al. 1972). It has often been hinted that the disappearance from western Europe in the eighteenth century of perhaps the most dreaded epidemic killer, bubonic plague, was also of this form, although retrospective evidence is particularly difficult to evaluate because of the critical role of fleas and rats in the transmission process. Shrewsbury (1970) argues, for example, that plague disappeared from Europe essentially because the development of a direct oceanic trade route between Asia and western Europe destroyed the traditional caravan route to the Levant which had acted as a 'rodent pipeline' for the spread of plague from its Asiatic homeland.

Table 2.6   Standardized* death rates (per 1000) by cause, England and Wales

	1848–1854		1901		1971	
Conditions attributable to micro-organisms:						
1. Airborne diseases	7·3		5·1		0·6	
Respiratory tuberculosis		2·9		1·3		0·1
Bronchitis, pneumonia, influenza		2·2		2·7		0·6
Scarlet fever, diptheria		1·0		0·4		0·0
Smallpox		0·3		0·0		0·0
2. Water- and food-borne diseases	3·6		1·9		0·0	
Cholera, diarrhoea, dysentry		1·8		1·2		0·0
3. Other conditions	2·1		1·4		0·1	
	12·9		8·5		0·7	
Conditions not attributable to micro-organisms	8·9		8·5		4·7	
All diseases	21·9		17·0		5·4	

* Standardized to 1901 age and sex distribution
Source: McKeown (1976), tables 3.1 and 3.2

There is general agreement that the continued mortality decline from the eighteenth century in northwestern Europe is due to a combination of the five processes discussed above, although the particular combination in terms of weighting varies temporally and spatially. There is little doubt that overall mortality decline has been achieved essentially by a reduction in the death toll of infectious diseases. This can be illustrated (Table 2.6) by cause-of-death data for England and Wales, although there are obvious problems of reliability and comparability of data arising from vagueness and inaccuracy of diagnosis, from changes in nomenclature and classification, and from exclusion of infanticide. Table 2.6 indicates that mortality from infectious diseases ('conditions attributable to micro-organisms') accounts for almost all of overall mortality decline in the second half of the nineteenth century and for the greater part of that during this century. The Scottish experience has been almost identical (Flinn 1977), but in other developed countries the proportion of overall mortality decline attributable to the infectious diseases group has been less, although still substantial (Preston and Nelson 1974).

The temporal pattern of mortality reduction by age groups is shown in Table 2.7 for England and Wales. The dramatic reduction in infant and child mortality, contrasting with very modest reductions in the old age groups, clearly reflects the conquest over death from infectious diseases, to which young children, not having developed a natural immunity, have always been particularly subject. Indeed, the extent of mortality reduction in the under-five age group is underestimated by Table 2.7 since it is likely that some infant deaths, especially from infanticide, were still not being recorded in the early years of civil registration. Further striking illustrations of the changing age pattern of mortality are given in Table 2.8 and Figure 2.6. So dramatic have been reductions in mortality in young age groups that

Table 2.7 Age-specific death rates (per 1000), England and Wales

	1841–1850	1901–1910	1961–1970
0– 4	66·0	46·0	4·73
5– 9	9·0	3·6	0·37
10–14	5·3	2·1	0·33
15–19	7·5	3·0	0·68
20–24	9·3	3·8	0·74
25–34	10·3	5·1	0·88
35–44	13	8·3	2·1
45–54	17	14	5·8
55–64	30	28	16
65–74	64	59	39
75–84	142	127	93
85+	301	261	218

Source: Office of Population Censuses and Surveys (1978a), table 1.1, Crown Copyright

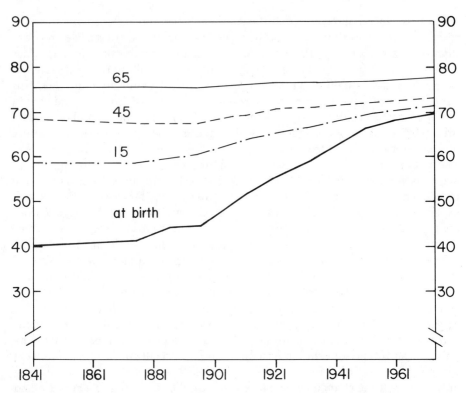

Figure 2.6
Life expectancy (in years) for males at different ages, England and Wales, 1841-1975
Source: data from Office of Population Censuses and Surveys, *Mortality Statistics 1975*, table 21

survivorship curves for man are now strikingly different from those for animals and plants (Figure 2.7).

The pattern of mortality decline in relation to development which has been described for northwestern Europe is likely to have been replicated, broadly, by North American experience, although nutritional improvements are not likely to have played such a decisive role, bearing in mind the always more favourable ratio between population numbers and resources in the New World.

Table 2.8   Percentage distribution of deaths by age group, England and Wales

	1838–1844	1975
0–14	47	2
15–64	34	23
65+	19	75

Source: Office of Population Censuses and Surveys (1978a), table 1.2, Crown Copyright

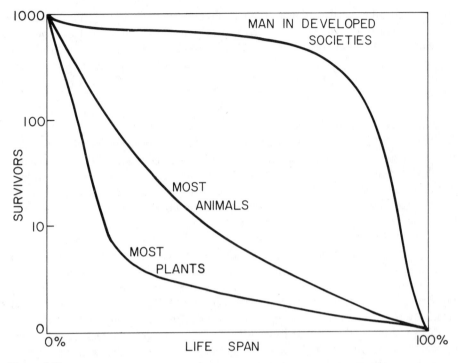

Figure 2.7
Number of survivors by age from a birth cohort of 1000. Age is measured in relative units of
mean life-span, which is the maximum length of life reasonably to be expected for a normally
endowed organism under optimal environmental conditions.
Sources: Deevey (1950), p. 59, Thomlinson (1965), figure 2.   By permission of Random
House Inc.

There is a dearth of reliable mortality data for much of North America before the
twentieth century. Between 1900 and 1905 a minority of the population of the
United States resided in states where registration systems were adjudged sufficiently accurate for them to belong to the national death registration area; and it
was not until 1933 that a 100 percent coverage was achieved by the admittance of
Texas. Nevertheless, the somewhat sporadic data do bear out northwestern European experience (Omran 1977).

Life expectancies at birth for Massachusetts in the 1850s of thirty-eight (M) and
forty-one (F) and for the United States death registration area in 1900 of forty-six
(M) and forty-eight (F) (US Bureau of the Census 1960) are very similar to those
recorded for the same years in England and Wales (Figure 2.6) and other northwestern European countries. Another close comparison with European experience
comes from the finding of Condran and Crimmins-Gardner (1978) that almost 80
percent of overall mortality decline in 28 cities of the United States between 1890
and 1900 is accounted for by deaths in four infectious disease categories: typhoid,
tuberculosis, diptheria and diarrhoeal diseases. One must beware, however, of

inferring continental trends from the reasonably favourable mortality experience in the northeastern sector of the United States. In the Canadian province of Quebec, for example, the crude death rate for the Catholic population averaged about 24 per 1000 in the 1870s and 22 per 1000 in the 1890s (Henripin and Peron 1972), compared with equivalent figures for Massachusetts of 19 per 1000 at both periods.

i̧ Southern and eastern Europe, the Soviet Union, Japan

In the onset and pace of general mortality decline, this group has an intermediate position between the economically advanced countries of the West and the less developed countries of Africa, Asia and Latin America. Progress towards modern economic development and diversification in this group had been delayed until the late nineteenth century, so that conditions of high mortality were maintained until that time. In Spain, for example, life expectancy at birth has been estimated at a mere twenty-nine years in 1877–1887 and thirty-five in 1900 (Livi-Bacci 1972).

However, the rapid pace of mortality decline in these countries in the twentieth century is demonstrated in Table 2.9. Crude death rates were substantially above those in northwestern Europe and the United States at the beginning of the century but had been reduced to equivalent levels by the 1950s. The distorting effect of relatively young age structures in producing the particularly low crude death rates of the 1970s should be borne in mind, since current age-standardized measures indicate a broad uniformity between the groups distinguished in Table 2.9. In fact, the higher mortality levels, although only marginally so, are still found in some of the countries of southern and eastern Europe, notably in Albania, Rumania, Yugoslavia and Portugal, where life expectancies at birth had still not reached seventy years by 1975.

Table 2.9   *International trends in crude death rate (per 1000)*

	1906–1910	1935–1938	1955–1958	1972–1975
Denmark, England & Wales, Netherlands, Norway, Sweden	14·1	10·7	9·3	10·5
Remainder of western Europe	17·7	13·3	11·3	11·3
USA	14·9	11·0	9·4	9·4
Southern Europe (Portugal, Spain, Italy, Greece)	21·7	15·6	9·4	9·2
Eastern Europe	24·5	15·7	10·0	9·8
USSR	28·9	19·5	7·7	6·6
Japan	25·0	17·2	7·8	6·6

Sources: data from Bogue (1969), table 16.4, and Population Reference Bureau, *World Population Data Sheets*

In this intermediate group of countries it is generally agreed that specific advances in the sciences and technologies of public health and medicine, derived externally, have played as important a role in mortality reduction as the general forces of socio-economic development. In Italy, Cipolla (1965, p.582) maintains that 'gains in infant mortality seem to be imputable more to improved medical and hygienic practices than to changes in economic conditions' and Taeuber (1958, p.284) regards Japan as giving 'the first major demonstration that reduced and even low mortality could be achieved in somewhat unfavourable environmental conditions'. The remarkable mortality reduction in Japan in the decade following the Second World War (Table 2.9) is widely attributed to the introduction at that time, under the initial stimulus of the American occupation, of antibiotic wonder drugs, mass programmes of inoculation and vaccination and the establishment of a dense network of community health centres.

Less developed countries

It has become conventional to refer to countries outside Europe, North America, Australasia, the Soviet Union and Japan as the less developed, the underdeveloped, the developing or the emerging countries. The terms are invariably regarded as interchangeable, although some regard 'less developed' as the most appropriate term, since it carries no implication that development is necessarily a universal or desirable process. More recently, the term Third World has been widely used to distinguish such countries from the materially privileged First (Western capitalist) and Second (centrally planned communist) Worlds. For our immediate purpose, which is the recognition of countries with a relatively common pattern of mortality decline, the designatory terms are not of critical importance.

The most outstanding characteristic of mortality decline in less developed countries has been its rapidity. A spectacular, although not typical, example of such concentrated mortality decline (and the associated problems of population growth and congestion) can be seen in the Indian Ocean island of Mauritius. Figure 2.8 shows that for much of this century there was little natural increase. There were appreciable fluctuations in the death rate, with peaks being associated with adverse health and economic conditions like the influenza epidemic of 1919, the depression and low wages in the sugar industry in the early 1930s, and a devastating hurricane in 1945 which halved the sugar crop and wreaked immense destruction (Brookfield 1957–1958). But between the mid-1940s and the late 1950s the death rate fell from about 30 per 1000 to 12 per 1000, achieving in less than 15 years what had taken over 150 years in northwestern Europe.

It has already been emphasized that the use of crude death rates exaggerates mortality decline in a country like Mauritius where high fertility induces a young age structure. There might also be exceptional forces at work in a small country. It is instructive, therefore, to consider age-standardized measures of mortality for a representative group of less developed countries. Figure 2.9 shows trends in life expectancy at birth for a group of eight Latin American countries in comparison with a group of developed European and North American countries.

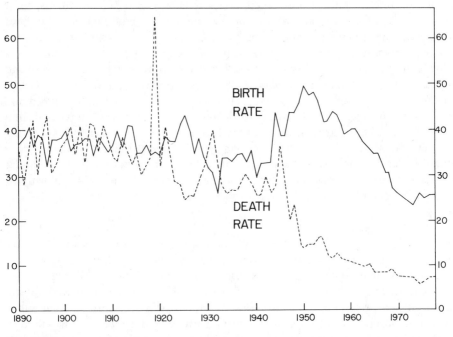

Figure 2.8
Crude birth rates and crude death rates (per 1000), Mauritius, 1890-1977
Sources: data from Titmuss and Abel-Smith (1961), figure 2, and UN *Demographic Yearbooks*

Compared with the uniform rate of improvement in the developed countries, the Latin American pattern is one of an ever-increasing rate of advance, at least until 1960. Life expectancy in the Latin American countries had been extremely low until well into this century, only reaching thirty years in 1920 and thus barely reaching levels achieved in eighteenth-century northwestern Europe; yet by 1970 the Latin American figure had doubled to sixty years.

Within the global set of less developed countries, there is certainly a relationship between development and mortality (Figures 2.1–2.3). But the rapidity of mortality decline – in some cases in countries like Mauritius showing only modest economic development – suggests that factors other than general development have contributed extensively to the recent concentrated mortality reduction. These factors are essentially medical and public health programmes imposed on often passive populations by colonial rules and more recently by newly independent governments supported by the UN World Health Organization and external aid agreements. The Second World War initiated several such programmes, since many important control measures for tropical diseases were first demonstrated by Allied troops. So successful have been health programmes based on insecticide spraying, antibiotic drugs and health centre networks, that mortality levels have often fallen spectacularly despite the continuance of largely unfavourable economic and

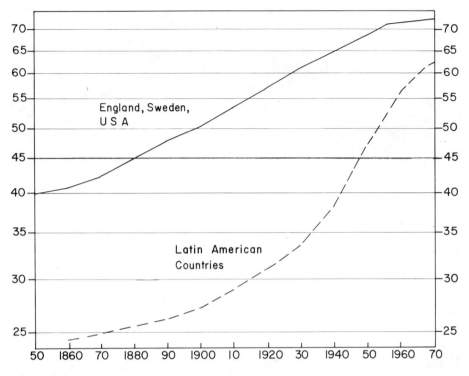

Figure 2.9
Trends in life expectancy at birth (in years) for: (i) England and Wales, Sweden and USA;
(ii) Brazil, Chile, Columbia, Costa Rica, Dominican Republic, Guatemala, Nicaragua and
Panama
Sources: data from Arriaga and Davis (1969), table A-4, and UN
Demographic Yearbooks

environmental conditions – an experience quite contrary to that of Western
developed countries. It is estimated, for example, that only 22 percent of the rural
population of less developed countries had access to safe drinking water in 1975,
and a mere 15 percent had adequate disposal of sewage (*WHO Chronicle* 1978).

Figures 2.10 and 2.11 demonstrate the potential of externally derived programmes. Until recently smallpox, one of the great scourges of mankind, had been
endemic in much of the intertropical world. But an intensified programme of
smallpox eradication initiated by the World Health Organization in 1966 has
practically eliminated the disease, so that the number of countries where the disease
is endemic fell from 30 in 1967 to 4 in 1973. The striking progress of smallpox
eradication can be attributed to the 'detection and isolation of cases, to the
widespread use of potent freeze-dried vaccine and to the excellent international
collaboration of systematic vaccination programmes' (Bruce-Chwatt 1974a, p.249).
The greatest risk of smallpox infection today comes from stocks of virus kept by
research laboratories, as shown by a smallpox fatality in Birmingham, UK, in 1978.

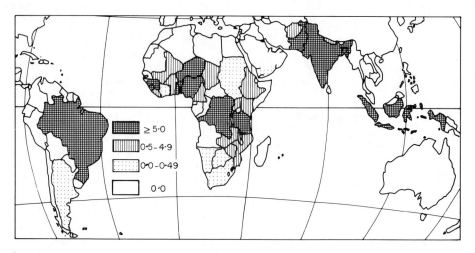

Figure 2.10
Notified smallpox cases per 100,000 population, 1967
Source: Bruce-Chwatt (1974a), figure 3

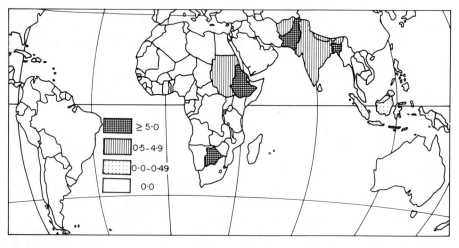

Figure 2.11
Notified smallpox cases per 100,000 population, 1972
Source: Bruce-Chwatt (1974a), figure 4

The most extensively discussed case of externally imposed disease control has been the malaria eradication programme immediately following the Second World War in Ceylon (now Sri Lanka), Mauritius and British Guiana (now Guyana). All three countries depart significantly from the general relationship between mortality and GNP depicted in Figures 2.1 and 2.2, in that their life expectancies are considerably higher than their development level warrants. But the difficulties of disentangling and evaluating the contributory factors to mortality decline have proved formidable, as the case of Ceylon will illustrate.

An all-out war on mosquitoes, the vector of malaria parasites, began in Ceylon in 1945 when commercial supplies of the newly discovered wonder insecticide DDT became available. Mass spraying of breeding grounds and dwelling walls dramatically reduced parasite rates in the population to about 5 percent of prewar levels by 1949, and the number of deaths reported as due to malaria fell from some 8000 per annum in 1944–1946 to 2400 in 1949 and less than 200 in 1956. At the same time the crude death rate plunged from 20 per 1000 in 1946 to 13 per 1000 in 1949 and 10 per 1000 in 1956. Although the reduction in recorded malaria deaths accounts statistically for only about 20 percent of overall mortality decline, some authorities argue that malarial deaths were often misdiagnosed and that endemic malaria is a debilitating disease which severely undermines resistance to other, often fatal diseases. Thus Newman (1965, 1970) attributes to malaria control 42 percent of the decline in mean crude death rate between 1930–1945 and 1946–1960.

However, other researchers look elsewhere for the dominant influences. Frederickson (1960, 1961) points to the role of postwar economic buoyancy in Ceylon associated with the rise in world prices for plantation products, and to the nutritional improvements prompted by the postwar resumption of food imports and confirmed by data showing increased height and weight among schoolchildren. Meegama (1967), on the other hand, emphasizes the concentrated improvement in general health facilities in the late 1940s. He shows that between 1945 and 1950 the number of hospitals increased from 153 to 263, maternity homes from 34 to 99, health centres from 503 to 701 and midwives from 542 to 1053. He also demonstrates that an antimalaria campaign under international auspices in Guatemala in the late 1950s of comparable scale and effectiveness to that in Ceylon was associated with a much smaller reduction in crude death rate (from about 20 per 1000 in the mid-1950s to 17 per 1000 in the mid-1960s), because improvements in health services were negligible.

The most recent comprehensive attempt to review the problem has been by Gray (1974). His general conclusion (p.226) is that 'malaria control was responsible for approximately 23 percent of the total national postwar decline of mortality in Ceylon, largely through the reduction of the excess mortality in the more malarious areas. Improvements in medical services, therapy, nutrition and possibly economic factors contributed individually indeterminate amounts to the residual decline.' He considers it possible that the main contribution of economic development to mortality decline was mediated via the increased health expenditure which the improved postwar financial situation permitted. Of particular interest to population geographers is the considerable use in this continuing debate of district data for cartographic and statistical analysis. This will be examined in the following chapter on mortality variations within countries.

Studies of mortality decline in Guyana provide broadly similar analytical problems and results to those in Ceylon. Here the crude death rate fell from about 25 per 1000 in the 1920s to 20 per 1000 in the late 1930s and 10 per 1000 in the mid-1950s. Newman (1965) and Mandle (1970) estimate that between 40 and 50 percent of mortality decline between prewar and postwar periods was due to malaria eradication. Mandle suggests that there was little economic improvement at this time; he shows, for example, that calorie and protein intake per capita declined in the 1938–1952 period. It is to general public health improvements, notably the provision of waste removal and of water supplies from artesian wells in place of drainage and irrigation ditches, that he attributes most of the prewar and some of the postwar mortality decline.

Useful contributions to the overall debate can be made at very different scales of analysis. Through regression analysis of national scale data from a set of less developed countries, Preston (1980) estimates that less than half of life expectancy gain between 1940 and 1970 may be attributed to development variables. At a more intimate scale, Orubuloye and Caldwell (1975) approach the problem by selecting two villages in Nigeria closely matched in culture, socio-economic conditions, water supply and waste disposal, but contrasting in medical services provision. One village had a rural hospital and trained doctor for more than ten years, while the other did not even possess a dispensary or chemist's shop within ten kilometres. Partly on the basis of mortality rates being twice as high in the latter village, the authors argue that mortality decline in rural Nigeria during the last half century may be almost wholly explained by the introduction of modern health services. Support for this general view is provided by a study (Faulkingham and Thorbahn 1975) of a village in southern Niger at the heart of the Sahel zone just south of the Sahara. Drought and food shortages have exacted heavy tolls throughout this area since 1968. Yet in this particular village mortality rates continued to fall in the drought period, the authors attributing this to the population's ready access to a nearby hospital and dispensary.

The likely future trend of mortality in less developed countries can now be considered briefly. In the long run it might seem reasonable to expect a convergence towards the mortality levels achieved by today's developed countries, although this would seem to depend on the present population – resources ratio being at least maintained by global fertility reduction. The more developed of Third World countries like Taiwan and Singapore have almost reached this stage, even though their crude death rates (as opposed to standardized measures) will rise in the next few years as continued fertility reduction there has its effect on age structures. In the poorer Third World countries the potential for rapid mortality improvement is clearly suggested by the apparent responsiveness of mortality to economic development in low-income countries (Figure 2.1) and by the proven impact in several countries of imported medical and public health knowledge, technology and personnel.

But progress in economic development should not necessarily be assumed for some of the poorer countries, and some leading childhood diseases (dysentry, diarrhoea, pneumonia) are proving difficult to control in some Third World environments since they respond to nutritional and living conditions rather than modern medicines. A contributory factor which has received considerable recent attention (L. Williams 1979) and the 1979 War on Want report, *The Baby Killer*) has been the disturbing promotion by Western food companies of powdered baby milk in the Third World. The benefits of breastfeeding in terms of a balanced infant diet and child survival, as well as the subsidiary contraceptive effect, are well known, and there is no doubt that bottlefed infants have a higher mortality wherever there is lack of clean water, of facilities for sterilizing bottles and of refrigeration for the formula. It is ironic that bottlefeeding is often seen as a modern advance in Third World countries at a time when breastfeeding is thought to be on the increase in the West, at least among better educated women.

There are also recent indications of the sometimes fragile nature of externally imposed disease control when environmental conditions remain poor. A spectacular example is the resurgence of malaria since the mid-1960s in many countries, including Sri Lanka, from which it had almost been eliminated (Table 2.10). In India the number of known active cases rose from about 100,000 in 1965 to some five million in 1975 (Akhtar and Learmonth 1977). The reasons seem to lie in the complacency with which programmes were conducted when elimination seemed just around the corner, but also, more disturbingly, in the way in which certain strains of mosquito have developed resistance to residual (long-lasting) insecticides like DDT and Malathion. There is an intensive medical search for more effective antimalarial drugs than chloroquine, to which some strains of malaria parasite have developed a resistance, but there is no immediate prospect of a safe vaccine becoming available. The resurgence of malaria thus provides a salutary antidote to a blind belief in the effectiveness of the 'technical fix' approach to human inprovement.

Table 2.10   Number (in thousands) of autochtonous malaria cases reported 1972–1976 by WHO region*

	1972	1973	1974	1975	1976
Americas	284	280	269	356	379
S. E. Asia	1920	2694	4210	5992	6539
Europe	21	13	8	12	39
E. Mediterranean	855	883	524	447	350
W. Pacific	171	203	170	197	210
	3251	4073	5181	7004	7517

* The figures refer only to cases confirmed by laboratory analysis and reported by the malaria services. Africa is excluded since malaria has never been reported on a systematic basis south of the Sahara.

Source: WHO *Chronicle* 32 (1978), p.227

Structure of mortality

It is appropriate to review at this stage some of the major differences between developed and less developed countries in the structure of their present patterns of mortality. There is, of course, a continuum from lesser to more developed countries, so that differences between the upper and lower ends should be interpreted in this light. Attention will be focused on three major differences.

Cause

There are obvious problems in obtaining adequate data for international comparisons of cause of death, because of international differences in the extent, accuracy and classification of death diagnosis. Particular problems in many less developed countries are the lack of adequate medical education of certifying officers and the lack of ante- and post-mortem diagnostic facilities. To lessen the problems in international comparability, it is desirable to concentrate individual causes of death into broad and well-recognized groups. This permits the establishment of a model (Figure 2.12) showing how the cause-of-death pattern varies over time and space in relation to life expectancy (and, through this, to development). The less developed countries of intertropical Africa may thus be regarded as conforming to the initial stage of the model, while the economically advanced countries of Europe and North America are represented by its final stages.

Infectious, parasitic and respiratory diseases (Group 1) account for nearly half of deaths in countries with life expectancies as low as forty years. The role of inferior socio-economic conditions in promoting these diseases is well known, but it should be noted that the great majority of less developed countries with very low life expectancies are currently in low latitudes, where a warm humid climate is ideal for the propagation of infective micro-organisms or germs and their transmission by animal vectors like flies, mosquitoes and snails. Tropical and subtropical areas are thus affected by infectious diseases like yellow fever, malaria and bilharzia which did not occur or were much less serious in the early development stages of Western nations. Group 1 diseases are now of trivial significance in developed countries, except for pneumonia and influenza in old age groups.

Group 2 and 3 diseases, largely cancer, heart disease and stroke, are essentially deteriorative diseases associated with older adulthood. They have thus become the dominant causes of death in developed countries, largely as a function of their relatively old age structures. But even when age structure is held constant (as in Figure 2.12), these diseases still dominate the cause-of-death pattern. It is not so much that the age-specific rates of these diseases have increased with development or modernization. They may well have, but the overall evidence from several developed countries is that these rates have remained fairly stable in recent decades. In England and Wales, for example, increases in age-specific death rates in these disease categories between 1951 and 1973 are confined to males – in the over-fifty-five age groups for cancer (big increases in lung cancer outweighing decreases in other sites) and in the under-sixty-five age groups for circulatory diseases (Office

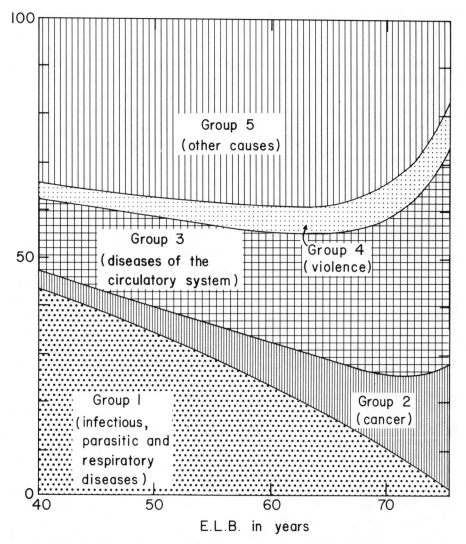

Figure 2.12
Likely percentage distribution in a standard population of causes of death for levels of
expectation of life at birth ranging from 40 to 76 years
Source: United Nations, *Population Bulletin* 1962, no. 6.

of Population Censuses and Surveys 1978a). The essential point is that the incidence of these diseases has not declined with development, setting them apart from
other causes of death. It follows that there have been only very slight increases in
life expectancy in developed countries in recent years.

   Deaths due to violence (Group 4) make a fairly constant proportional contribution to the mortality pattern at different development levels. Decline is prevented

by the importance of motor vehicle accidents. It is difficult to comment meaningfully on the residual 'other causes of death' (Group 5) because of it diversity. But diarrhoeal diseases are prominent and these 'can neither be prevented nor cured by injections or other direct remedies readily dispensed through public health programmes. Even purification of water supplies has had limited benefits. Diarrhoeal disease is prompted by poverty and ignorance' (Preston and Nelson 1974, p.43). This partly explains the retarded reduction of Group 5 mortality in Figure 2.12. It also helps to explain why infant mortality rates of some 100–200 per 1000 characterize the poorer Third World countries, compared with rates of 10–15 per 1000 in northwestern Europe and North America.

Sex

Almost universally, mortality rates are lower for females at nearly every age group, thereby establishing the well-known demographic feature that life expectancies at birth are substantially higher for females than males. Sex ratios are directly affected and, in turn, marriage possibilities, expected length of widowhood and a host of other demographic and social variables. But the extent of female superiority in survival varies by development level (Preston 1976), being comparatively modest under conditions of high mortality in less developed countries and appreciable in economically advanced societies. The 1976 *Demographic Yearbook* indicates that the great majority of less developed countries record a female superiority in life expectancy at birth of one–three years, with a very small minority (India, Pakistan, Jordan, Upper Volta, Nigeria, Liberia, Sabah and Papua New Guinea) showing a very slight male superiority; but in the developed countries of Europe and North America the female superiority amounts to six–eight years.

Given the appreciable evidence, noted earlier in this chapter, for the innate biological basis of the sex differential in mortality, it remains to consider what factors reduce its impact in less developed societies and enhance it in the developed world. Significant factors in less developed societies appear to be the subordinate position of women, the relative aversion to female children, and the maternal mortality rate under poor conditions of medical care. The role of such factors has been discussed for the Indian subcontinent by El Badry (1969), while a local study example of the differential treatment, particularly in nutrition, of male and female children is provided for rural Guatemala by Cowgill and Hutchinson (1963).

A useful indication of how the sex differential has widened over time in developed societies is provided by Figure 2.13. This shows that there are now two distinct 'humps' of excess male mortality. In the ten–thirty age group the excess is due largely to deaths from accidents and violence (especially road accidents). In the post-fifty age groups, the critical factor has been the greater vulnerability of males to cancer (above all, lung cancer) and heart diseases. It has been argued (Moriyama et al. 1958) that the attainment of a high level of modernization in a society may have placed women in their optimal exercise range but men well below theirs. There are also obvious relationships between modernization and cigarette and alcohol consumption, in which the sexes participate differently. But there are signs

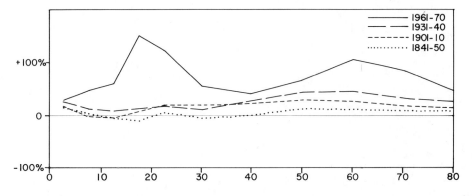

Figure 2.13
Percentage excess of male over female death rate by age, England and Wales, 1841-1970
Source: Office of Population Censuses and Surveys (1978a), figure 1.4.
Crown Copyright.

that the sex mortality differential may have reached its maximum in the most modernized societies, as the life-styles of the sexes increasingly merge.

Season

In most, but certainly not all, of the less developed countries there tends to be a mortality peak in summer, when the hot wet season of many tropical and subtropical countries stimulates micro-organic activity, accounts for much of the year's agricultural work and provides, before the main harvests, little readily available food. This disease-inducing seasonal concentration of high micro-organic activity, heavy energy expenditure and low energy intake is particularly noticeable where there are distinctive wet and dry seasons, notably in the savanna lands across West Africa (Hunter 1967).

In highly developed countries, generally occupying high latitudes with relatively severe winters, the seasonal peak tends to be in mid-winter. Thus in 1972 the proportion of deaths in the December–February quarter was 30.3 percent in the United Kingdom, 28.0 percent in France and 27.4 percent in the United States.

This chapter has demonstrated how the onset, pace and, to some extent, structure of mortality decline have varied in relation to national development experience. But to appreciate more fully the processes involved in mortality reduction, it is desirable to disaggregate national populations into their differing and sometimes conflicting components. This will be undertaken in the following chapter.

CHAPTER 3

MORTALITY: VARIATIONS WITHIN COUNTRIES

In the recognition, description and interpretation of cross-sectional mortality variations within countries, there tends to be two, often distinct, academic approaches. First, there is the traditional interest of demographers and medical sociologists in the field known as differential mortality – the way in which mortality varies in relation to social categories of class, marital status, ethnicity, community of residence, etc. Second, there is a central concern of medical ecologists, epidemiologists and medical geographers with spatial patterns of disease and associative environmental factors. It is unfortunate that many demographers seem unaware of the spatial implications of differential mortality, notably the way in which social categories are often spatially concentrated. Likewise, some medical geographers fail to appreciate that disease distributions can be understood perhaps as much through the spatial distribution of social categories as through basic environmental influences like water supply and atmospheric pollution. Consequently, a major theme of this chapter will be an attempted integration of the two approaches.

Differential mortality

An extensive systematic review of this field will not be undertaken here, since useful summaries have been provided by Benjamin (1965) and Antonovsky (1967). Attention will be focused on what arguably are the two most important independent variables in differential mortality: social class and community of residence. Many other variables conventionally recognized as influencing mortality are often themselves controlled by these two primary variables.

Social class
Social class is a multidimensional concept of social stratification based on the broad relationships which exist between specific components of socio-economic status like education, occupation and income.

England and Wales
The best-known and most authoritative evidence for the association between social class and mortality is derived from mortality data by occupation assembled at ten-year intervals from as early as 1861 by the Registrar General's office in England and Wales. Occupational mortality rates are derived by the Registrar General from two data sources. The death registration system provides the last full-time occupation of the deceased, and the decennial census of population records occupation, often on a 10 percent sample basis. Accordingly, for any particular occupational group one can relate national deaths in a period of years straddling census year (enumerator) to the census population (denominator) to provide an occupational mortality rate. It is difficult to define occupation meaningfully and consistently for retired older persons, so that occupational mortality rates are typically limited to the fifteen–sixty-four age group. A three- or five-year period is used to provide sufficiently large numbers of deaths to ensure statistically reliable results in all but

the smaller occupational groups and minor causes of death. The most recent Decennial Supplement relates 1970–1972 deaths to 1971 census occupation data.

Since 1921 occupations have been grouped into five social classes, with the implication that occupation is a meaningful indicator of life-style, embracing income, education, housing, leisure, diet, etc. (Leete and Fox 1977).

　I Professional occupations (e.g., doctors and lawyers)
　II Managerial and lower professional occupations (e.g., managers and teachers)
　IIIN Nonmanual skilled occupations (e.g., clerks and shop assistants)
　IIIM Manual skilled occupations (e.g., bricklayers and coalminers)
　IV Semiskilled occupations (e.g., postmen and bus conductors)
　V Unskilled occupations (e.g., porters and labourers)

The appreciable differences in mortality by social class revealed by the England and Wales data for the last half century are shown in Table 3.1. The index

Table 3.1   Standardized mortality ratios by social class, males 15 (or 20) – 64 years, England and Wales

| | Social Class | | | | | | |
	I	II	IIIN	IIIM	IV	V	All
1930–1932	90	94	97		102	111	100
1949–1953	86	92	101		104	118	100
1959–1963	76	81	100		103	143	100
1970–1972	77	81	99	106	114	137	100

Source: Registrar General (England and Wales), Decennial Supplements

Table 3.2   Selected mortality data, males 15–64 years, England and Wales, 1970–1972

| | All Social Classes | | | Social Class I | |
	Population 1971	Deaths 1970–1972	3-year death rate (per person)	Population 1971	Deaths 1970–1972
15–24	3,584,320	9,935	0·0028	95,190	193
25–34	3,065,100	9,238	0·0030	214,680	431
35–44	2,876,170	19,911	0·0069	171,060	854
45–54	2,965,880	64,045	0·0216	137,080	2,079
55–64	2,756,510	170,000	0·0617	100,000	5,029
Total	15,247,980	273,129	0·0179	718,010	8,586

Source: Office of Population Censuses and Surveys (1978b), table 2.3. Crown Copyright

commonly used to standardize for differences between classes in age composition is the Standardized Mortality Ratio (SMR).

A SMR is the ratio of observed to expected deaths for each category of the total population being considered:

$$\text{SMR} = \frac{\text{observed deaths}}{\text{expected deaths}} \times 100$$

The expected deaths are those that would occur if the age-specific death rates for the total population were to apply in the specific category being studied. To provide a worked example, the mortality data from Table 3.2 can be used to calculate the 1970–1972 SMR for Social Class I (males, fifteen–sixty four) as follows:

```
Obseved deaths in Social Class I    = 8,586
Expected deaths in Social Class I   = 95,190 × 0.0028
                                    + 214,680 × 0.0030
                                    + 171,060 × 0.0069
                                    + 137,080 × 0.0216
                                    + 100,000 × 0.0617
                                    = 11,223
```

$$\text{SMR} = \frac{8,586}{11,223} \times 100 = 77$$

A SMR of 100 indicates that the age-standardized mortality level in the category being studied is the same as in the overall or standard population (observed deaths = expected deaths), so that a SMR of 77 in Social Class I indicates a mortality level well below that of the overall population.

Attention can now be turned to the differences in mortality level by social class revealed by Table 3.1, but there are some important problems of data quality and interpretation that need to be borne in mind. First, one should note that a social class is not assigned for the disabled, the armed forces, full-time students and inadequately described occupations; these categories account for 11 percent of the fifteen–sixty-four male census population in 1971 and 4 percent of male deaths in that age group in 1970–1972. Second, the self-recording of occupation at the census can sometimes be inconsistent with a relative's description of the deceased's occupation at death registration. Third, there have been definitional changes in social classes from one decade to another posing severe difficulties for longitudinal comparison. Fourth, occupational mortality differentials may be subject to some exaggeration as a result of men, because of poor health, working at jobs prior to death that are below the status of their normal occupations.

These technical and interpretative problems cannot, however, throw doubt on the striking pattern of class mortality revealed by Table 3.1. Meaningful comparisons can only be made within each row, where there is a progressive increase in mortality level from Class I to Class V at every cross-section in time. Far from there being a theoretically plausible narrowing in class mortality differentials associated with growth of egalitarianism and the modern welfare state, there may have been a widening of the class gulf in survival. In particular, Social Class V stands out as a markedly underprivileged 'underclass', comprising about 7 percent of the active male population in 1971.

Some of the mortality differences between classes could be associated with the pursuit of occupations on which they are based. Manual workers, in general, will be more subject to industrial hazards and accidents than nonmanual workers (note, for example, SMRs for 1970–1972 of 171 for fishermen, 141 for coalminers and 164 for steel erectors and riggers). Higher proportions of the less skilled classes than of the professional classes work out of doors or in noisy factories, and have poorer access to high wages, sick pay, pensions, holidays, job security and job satisfaction – all of which can be expected to affect health. But perhaps of greater importance are the broad differences between social classes in home environment and way of life, embracing household amenities, overcrowding, use of health services and habits of personal hygiene, smoking, alcohol consumption and diet. Such class differences were highlighted in a 1980 research report, *Inequalities in Health,* commissioned by the Department of Health and Social Security, but given a restricted distribution because of what was thought to be an embarrassing indictment of government policies. Tables 3.3. and 3.4 provide telling examples of social class differences in just two of these critical health areas, while some geographers have demonstrated that health care delivery systems compound the socio-economic disadvantages of poor people living in poor neighbourhoods. This occurs particularly under a largely free-enterprise health care system as in the United States (Shannon and Dever 1974, Pyle 1979), but even within supposedly egalitarian welfare state systems inequalities of access exist, as shown by the marked underdoctoring of peripheral public housing estates in British cities (Knox 1978).

Table 3.3   Use of health services by children up to age of 7 by social class of father, Great Britain

| | Percentage of children who had never: | | | |
| | Visited a | been immunized against | | |
	dentist	smallpox	polio	diptheria
I	16	6	1	1
II	20	14	3	3
IIIN	19	16	3	3
IIIM	24	25	4	6
IV	27	29	6	8
V	31	33	10	11

Source: *Social Trends* 6, 1975, p.27

Table 3.4   Male cigarette smoking by socio-economic groups, Great Britain, 1976

	Current smokers (%)	Never or only occasionally smoked (%)	Ex-regular smokers (%)
Professional	25	46	29
Employers and managers	38	28	34
Intermediate and junior nonmanual	40	32	29
Skilled manual and own account nonprofessional	51	23	26
Semiskilled manual and personal service	53	21	25
Unskilled manual	58	18	23
All males 16+	46	27	27

Source: General Household Survey 1976, table 8.33, by permission of H.M.S.O.

A significant class gradient in mortality is also found among infants, children and married women classified by social class of father or husband (Table 3.5 and Figure 3.1). The particularly high infant and child mortality in Class V shows clearly to policy-makers the considerable scope that still exists for health improvement in that group. New-born males subject to the age-specific death rates of Social Class V

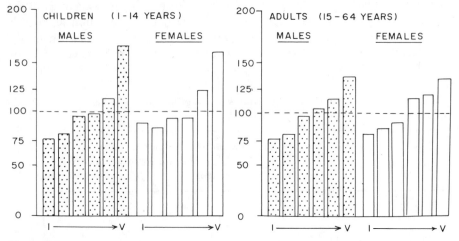

Figure 3.1
Standardized mortality ratios for social classes I-V, England and Wales, 1970-1972. For children and married women, social class is defined by occupation of father and husband respectively.
Source: Office of Population Censuses and Surveys (1978b), figure 9.1 and appendix 2. Crown Copyright.

Table 3.5   Infant mortality rate (per 1000) by social class of father

	England and Wales 1970–1972*	Scotland 1977
I	12·0	9·2
II	13·6	12·6
IIIN	14·7	
IIIM	17·1	14·2
IV	19·7	15·3
V	31·2	21·5
All	17·7	16·1

* In 1977 the overall rate in England and Wales had been reduced to 13·8 per 1000

Sources: Office of Population Censuses and Surveys (1978b), p.158, and Registrar General
(Scotland), *Annual Report* 1977 Pt.1, table F2.3, Crown Copyright

in 1970–1972 could expect to live seven years less than those subject to Social Class
I rates (J. Fox 1977, p. 13).

Figure 3.2 indicates that there are interesting variations in mortality class gradient among the three major causes of death, which accounted for over 80 percent
of all deaths to people of fifteen–sixty-four years in 1970–1972. A particularly
steep gradient for both males and females is shown by respiratory diseases, for
which environmental as opposed to genetic and behavioural causes are likely to be
dominant. Consider, for example, the extreme SMRs among miners and quarry-
men, heavily exposed occupationally to dust, of 245 for bronchitis, 331 for
respiratory tuberculosis and 2097 for pneumoconiosis. The cancer gradient for
males is fairly appreciable, reflecting the steep male gradient for lung cuncer (44
percent of all fifteen–sixty-four male cancer deaths) from a SMR of 53 in Social

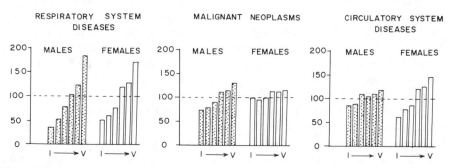

Figure 3.2
Mortality by social class (I-V) and selected cause of death, England and Wales, 1970-1972:
standardized mortality ratios for men and married women (by husband's occupation) aged
15-64
Source: Office of Population Censuses and Surveys (1978b), figure 4.4.
Crown Copyright.

Class I to 143 in Social Class V. Women engage in smoking to a lesser extent than men (39 percent compared with 60 percent of the over-sixteen age group for any form of smoking: *1976 General Household Survey*), so that their mortality from lung cancer is much less and their class gradient in overall cancer mortality very modest. Despite a common view that associates heart disease and stressful executive-type occupations (Social Classes I and II), the normal gradient in class mortality is found for diseases of the circulatory system, although it is, for males, a fairly gentle gradient. For all the important specific diseases in this group, notably ischaemic heart disease and cerebrovascular disease, the normal gradient is present.

United States

Analyses of death registration and census data, using similar methods and providing broadly similar results to the England and Wales analyses, have been conducted in the United States (Moriyama and Guralnick 1956, Guralnick 1963). There is also an invaluable study of differential mortality by social class components, accomplished by a matched records study of 1960 data (Kitagawa and Hauser 1973). Some 340,000 deaths that occurred in May–August 1960 were matched individually with census records to obtain socio-economic characteristics of the deceased as reported at the April 1960 national census of population. Although the study does allow separate evaluation of the relationship between mortality and each of several components of socio-economic status, there are interpretative problems as in the British data arising from the essentially cross-sectional nature of the analysis. Ideally, one would like to have a longitudinal profile for each person which would allow some evaluation of status mobility.

Tables 3.6, 3.7 and 3.8 demonstrate the strength of the mortality gradients by occupation, income and education revealed by the matched records study. The most meaningful gradient is that for education, since education level as an index of class has the advantage of being relatively stable by the age of twenty-five. Income and occupation, on the other hand, can vary over time and, in particular, may be adversely affected by the onset of poor health which also brings about death, thereby causing a 'chicken-and-egg' interpretative problem of causative sequence. The three components of status are obviously intercorrelated, but the kind of data available from the matched records study makes it possible to hold constant, or standardize for, any of the components. When this is done, all three components emerge as having important *independent* associations with mortality.

The strength of class differentials in mortality in Britain and the United States indicates the considerable scope that still exists for mortality improvement in economically advanced societies. In societies which pay lip service to the goal of equal opportunities, there are stark *inequalities* in the ability to survive, which derive partly from differential access to health care but more particularly from the harmful life-styles of lower status groups. Policy-makers should be aware that future improvements in health and survival are likely to be achieved more through improved socio-economic conditions than by advances in biomedical knowledge and programmes.

Table 3.6 Standardized mortality ratios by occupation* for white males aged 25–64, United States, 1960

White-collar workers	92
Craftsmen and operatives	101
Service workers and labourers	128
All workers	100

* The three specified groups incorporate 89 percent of all white occupied males in 1960. Persons not employed at 1960 census are classified by last occupation.

Source: Kitagawa and Hauser (1973), table 3.2

Table 3.7 Standardized mortality ratios by family income for white family members aged 25–64, United States, 1960

Family income 1959	Males	Females
Under $4000	132	115
4000–6000	99	100
6000–8000	88	97
over $8000	88	88
All	100	100

Source: Kitagawa and Hauser (1973), table 2.7

Community of residence

A spectacular differential in mortality associated with economic development and urbanization in nineteenth-century Europe and North America is the rural-urban gradient. The insanitary, congested living conditions which spawned epidemics of often calamitous proportions in the major cities of that era have been vividly described by social historians and novelists. The particularly high mortality rates of

Table 3.8 Standardized mortality ratios by school years completed for population aged 25–64, United States, 1960

	White males	White females	Nonwhite males	Nonwhite females
0–4 years	115	160	114	126
5–8 years	109	111	97	106
High school or college	91	87	87	74
All	100	100	100	100

Source: Kitagawa and Hauser (1973), tables 2.1 and 2.2

Paris, Lyon and Marseille at that time have already been noted (Figure 2.5), while in Britain male life expectancy at birth in 1841 was a mere twenty-four years in Manchester, twenty-five in Liverpool and thirty-five in London, compared with forty for England and Wales as a whole and forty-four for the then rural county of Surrey (Glass 1963–1964, p. 265).

Although urban-rural differentials have narrowed considerably in this century, they are still recognizable in most, although not all, developed countries (Federici et al. 1976). In the United States in 1959–1961 the age-standardized mortality of both males and females was 5 percent higher in metropolitan areas than in nonmetropolitan counties (Kitagawa and Hauser 1973, p. 120), while for England and Wales in 1969–1973 an overall mortality gradient by degree of urbanization is clearly demonstrated by Table 3.9. A major interpretative problem is to identify those dimensions of urban life which promote higher mortality. These might be grouped into either class-related factors such as occupation, income, diet and smoking, or into factors associated more specifically with the physical nature of urbanism, notably housing, residential and working densities, leisure opportunities and atmospheric pollution.

Rural populations as an aggregate group pose a particular problem of interpretation since they span the spectrum from affluent big city commuters to the physically isolated rural poor. Thus in the United States some of the lowest age-standardized mortality rates are found in the wealthy 'rururban' fringes of the northeastern cities, while very high rates are found among the black rural poor of the South. There is a particular problem with the urban-rural classification for England and Wales used in Table 3.9, since the classification (before the reorganization of local government in 1974) depended on the historically derived administrative status of local authorities as urban or rural areas. Some nominally rural areas of recent settlement expansion were clearly urban in all but official designation. To obviate this problem, a particularly useful urban-rural classification of vital statistics data

Table 3.9   Standardized mortality ratios for males for selected causes of death by degree of urbanization, England and Wales, 1969–1973

	All causes	Circulatory diseases	Cancers	Respiratory diseases	Accidents
Conurbations	105	100	111	113	99
Urban populations					
> 100,000	104	102	106	108	101
50,000–100,000	99	100	98	98	96
< 50,000	100	104	95	96	97
Rural populations	91	95	87	83	106
All	100	100	100	100	100

Source: Chilvers (1978), table 1, Crown Copyright

has been made since 1975 by the Registrar General for Scotland. Addresses of usual residence are assigned by their postcode to a fivefold urban-rural classification based on the population size of the continuously built-up area containing the postcode. Table 3.10 shows Scottish infant mortality rates in 1977 for this classification, and it reveals that the truly rural areas (with less than 1000 population), while having slightly lower mortality than Scotland as a whole, have higher mortality than urban units of less than 100,000.

Table 3.10 Infant mortality rate (per 1000) by population units, Scotland, 1977

Over 1 million	18·4
100,000–1 million	16·7
10,000–100,000	14·1
1,000–10,000	14·9
under 1,000	15·8
Scotland	16·1

Source: Registrar General (Scotland), *Annual Report* 1977 Pt. 1, table F2.8, Crown Copyright

These sensitive recent data from Scotland seem to suggest that rural areas may no longer be retaining their privileged mortality position in developed countries. Indeed, there has been growing concern about the acute disadvantage suffered by major segments of the rural population in terms of access to health care personnel and facilities (Moseley 1979, J. M. Shaw 1979). The spatial perspectives and techniques of geographical analysis have been profitably employed by Shannon and Dever (1974) to demonstrate this unequivocally in the United States. They show that during the course of this century physicians, particularly younger ones, have been leaving and avoiding rural areas due to the pull of urban client wealth, the urban home background of an increasing majority of medical students, the attraction of urban cultural facilities, and, perhaps most important of all, the growing dependence of physicians on the equipment and auxiliary personnel of city hospitals. They also demonstrate that there is a clear distance-decay function in the use of medical facilities and that people living at greater distances from such facilities tend to make their visits for curative rather than preventive purposes. All these findings are confirmed by a recent study of rural health care in the American South (Davis and Marshall 1979). Nevertheless, it is possible to exaggerate the contribution of medical care to health provision in developed countries, since rural populations in general are still not experiencing poorer mortality records than urban populations.

In less developed countries the pattern is very different. Although it is difficult to obtain reliable comparative data, it is widely recognized that urban mortality rates are significantly lower than those in rural areas, with the lowest rates being in capital cities (G. Johnson 1963–1964, Caldwell and Okonjo 1968, Federici 1976).

A major reason is the metropolitan concentration of modern medical facilities and public health services. Such systems have been modelled on European and North American systems originally designed for highly industrialized, commercialized and urbanized societies, so that the spatial concentration they have developed in the Third World is inevitable, regardless of further bias given by governing urban élites in the spatial allocation of resources. This bias has been exposed recently in stark terms by Lipton (1977, p. 13): 'The most important class conflict in the poor countries of the world today is not between labour and capital. Nor is it between foreign and national interests. It is between the rural classes and the urban classes. The rural sector contains most of the povery, and most of the low-cost sources of potential advance; but the urban sector contains most of the articulateness, organisation and power. . . . Scarce investment, instead of going into water pumps to grow rice, is wasted on urban motorways. Scarce human skills design and administer, not clean village wells and agricultural extension services, but world boxing championships in showpiece stadia.' In some less developed countries the highest mortality is found in small and medium-sized towns, since these have the health problems associated with urban crowding but lack the piped water supplies, sanitation and medical facilities of the large cities.

The World Health Organization (WHO) has become increasingly concerned about health care deprivation in rural populations of the Third World: 'The few trained workers who do work in rural areas – against their will – discover that they are completely unprepared to deal with the specific problems of the communities they serve; their training syllabuses were copied from European models and they received their training in establishments situated in urban areas. They work under bad conditions and are often poorly managed and supervised' (WHO 1976, p. 14). WHO has accordingly evolved a policy of primary health care, essentially to provide the rural populations of less developed countries with at least the bare minimum of health services. Its population catchment recommendations for the establishment of a hierarchical network of health centres are:

Dispensary	5,000–10,000
Rural Health Centre	40,000–100,000
Rural or District Hospital	100,000–200,000
Provincial or National Hospital	1,000,000

The relevance of central place theory and geographical methods of analysis in the planning of such networks is obvious, as has been demonstrated by the classic study of Godlund (1961) of medical services in Sweden.

But modern health planning in disadvantaged rural sectors of the Third World is not simply about provision and location of modern facilities. Increasing attention is being paid to the possibilities of harnessing the appreciable manpower of traditional medicine as practised by folk doctors, native midwives, herbalists and the like (WHO 1978). Modern health planners no longer deride and reject traditional medicine as being unscientific and ineffective. There has clearly been some success, modest in India but substantial in China, in the integration of modern and traditional medicine to form comprehensive systems of primary health care, but there are formidable logistical problems, as Nicholas et al. (1976) demonstrate for rural Ghana.

Then again, sheer poverty is a major cause of low health standards in the rural areas of the Third World, so that there is a clear need for health administrators to participate actively in rural development in its widest sense (Abel-Smith 1978). The whole emphasis of Third World development strategy has been changing in the 1970s: 'Some of the most fundamental development dogmas of the whole period since World War II are being challenged. These include the prior place of industrial growth, the desirability of shifting people out of agriculture into the "modern sector", and the very concept of a "modern sector" closely linked by technology and finance to the internationalist capitalist system as the principal engine of progress. An emergent doctrine of "self-reliant development" is increasingly being advocated. . . . Given that the poor remain poor, and that most of them are rural, there is new priority given to rural development' (Brookfield 1978, pp. 124–125).

In Tanzania, as part of a drive towards self-reliance through communal and co-operative activity, there has been appreciable decentralization of health services, and the guiding socialist principle of mobilizing the masses has stimulated participation by local communities in the development of health services at the critical village level. Dispensaries are built by villagers, with the state providing equipment and materials not locally available; they also help to construct water supply networks and are encouraged to build their own latrines. Extension agents are assigned to villages to promote rural development, and their training includes a grounding in hygeine and preventive medicine. This is one of the clearest cases of health planning being conceived and implemented as an integral part of overall community development.

Other differentials

Demographers have recognized mortality variations within societies by social categories based on several other variables, including marital status, parity (completed fertility) and ethnicity. But it is often difficult to specify the independent role of such variables, since they are often correlated with one another and with the two primary variables discussed above. Consider the long-standing, although narrowing, racial mortality differential in the United States. In 1976 life expectancy at birth was 73.5 years for whites and 68.3 years for nonwhites, and their respective infant mortality rates were 13.3 and 23.5 per 1000. Biological differences in survival potential are unlikely to have made a significant direct contribution. Rather the answer lies in the disadvantaged position of nonwhites in housing, income, education, diet and health care. In other words, 'the race differentials, in general, are consistent with the inverse relationship between mortality and socioeconomic status' (Kitagawa and Hauser 1973, p. 102).

Spatial patterns

The spatial distribution of disease mortality and morbidity within countries is the central concern of medical geography. Whether this branch of geography should be regarded more appropriately as a component of population geography, for which a strong theoretical case can be made, or as an independent subdiscipline, which tends to be its current status, is essentially a matter of academic organization which need not concern us unduly. It is more important to appreciate the three overlapping dimensions which characterize the geographer's approach to studies of disease.

Ecological

Ecology is the study of relationships between living organisms and their surroundings. Since geography has developed primarily as an ecological discipline, it can be argued that 'the geographer's contribution to medical knowledge can properly be expected to lie chiefly in the field of environmental studies and the relation of disease distribution to other geographic variables' (McGlashan 1967, p. 333).

The roots of medical geography are often traced to the environmental awareness of Hippocrates, notably his appreciation of the links between climate and disease in *De aëre, aquis et locis* (*On Airs, Waters and Places*). But for practical purposes the foundations of medical geography were laid in the 1950s. In the Soviet Union there was a concentration by Pavlovsky and others on 'landscape epidemiology' which 'delimited the foci of infectious, zoonotic diseases by analysing the associations of vegetation, animal and insect life, soil type and acidity, precipitation regime, and other elements of the natural landscape. General landscape patterns could be used to assess the likely presence of the infectious agents of diseases' (Meade 1977. p.380).

In the West, the critical influence was that of May. In his prolific writing (e.g., May 1950, 1958, 1961) he guided medical geography towards understanding the processes of medical ecology. Since his interest was largely in tropical diseases, he paid particular attention, as in the Soviet studies, to natural environmental risk factors, in which he distinguished between inorganic influences (climate, hydrology, geology, etc.) and organic influences (especially the cycles of interdependence between infective micro-organisms, plants, animals and man). But man has always been a critical element in the ecosystem, as May and his followers came to recognize in their appreciation of socio-cultural influences. As societies become modernized and more complex it is increasingly difficult to attribute disease to the natural environment, as studies of differential mortality based on socio-economic variables have demonstrated.

Even in less developed societies man himself often creates the necessary habitat conditions for foci of disease. Consider, for example, how the construction of dams and the associated provision of perennial irrigation in parts of the tropics has led to a world increase, especially in Africa, in the incidence of schistosomiasis (often termed bilharzia), a debilitating disease which the WHO estimates as affecting 200 million people in the late 1970s. The disease is caused by parasitic blood flukes of the genus *Schistosoma* which are carried among the human population (the main host) by snails (the intermediate host). Fork-tailed larvae (cercariae) of *Schistosoma* emerge from snails and can be transmitted to man by skin penetration or by drinking water. They then proceed to develop their life-cycle in the human host, with eggs being expelled in faeces or urine, and thereby often entering fresh water. Here they hatch and release larvae, some of which develop further in snail hosts, so that the transmission cycle continues (Rée 1977). Irrigation schemes have extended both the habitat of the snails and the contact of man with the parasite-infected water (Kloos and Thompson 1979). This is notoriously the case in Egypt, where seasonal irrigation associated with the annual Nile flood has been replaced since the mid-nineteenth century by perennial irrigation networks fed from storage reservoirs, the latest and largest of which is the Aswan High Dam.

The ecological approach in medical geography has increasingly moved, therefore, towards an appreciation of the holistic system of interaction between population and health environments, wherein disease may be regarded as a maladaptive interaction between population, environment and culture (Meade 1977).

Cartographic

The spatial occurrence of disease has been neglected until recently in most health fields outside epidemiology. This has stimulated geographers to make what they feel is a positive contribution to the understanding of disease aetiology through the mapping of disease incidence and possible associative factors. An early and influential expression of this view was by Stamp (1964, pp. 66–67), who was 'convinced that no more important work is waiting to be done than the very detailed mapping of the incidence of different forms of cancer and the search for possible correlation with causative factors. With all the many millions being spent on cancer research, this approach is being seriously neglected.' An example of a geographical approach in this field has been the recognition by McGlashan (1972) of a cartographic association in central Africa between cancer of the gullet and a particular indigenous distilled spirit. Strong areal correlation does not in itself establish a direct causal link, although it is highly suggestive when backed by evidence like the particularly high incidence in France of gullet cancer in Normandy and Brittany, where home-manufactured apple spirit is suspect (Tuyns 1970).

One should not pretend that geographers have a monopoly of cartographic expertise, and Learmonth (1972) has shown that the majority of the great atlases of disease have been produced by medical men with professional cartographic assistance. Yet geographers have skills in the conceptual and technical aspects of cartographic presentation and analysis that should not be undervalued, particularly when maps are being used as serious tools of analysis and not simply as illustrations. The innovative use of cartograms or demographic base maps for disease mapping has been demonstrated by Forster (1966) and Howe (1970b), and the use of computer mapping in medical geography has been reviewed by Armstrong (1972) and exemplified by the *Atlas of Cancer Mortality for U.S. Counties* (Mason et al. 1975).

Statistical

The statistical awareness and skills which geographers have increasingly acquired have been applied profitably to medical geography in three key areas, particularly with a view to countering the not uncommon charge that medical geography is merely descriptive. First, statistical tests are now applied routinely to distributions to assess whether or not patterns are likely to have occurred by chance. A simple example is McGlashan's use of the chi-squared test (Table 3.11). The null hypothesis, which postulates no relation in this example between the distribution of oesophageal (gullet) cancer and the drinking of a particular alcoholic spirit, is decisively rejected; statistically the null hypothesis would be justified less than once in a thousand. Another example is the way in which Howe (1970a) has calculated standard errors for local authority SMRs as a means of assessing whether or not the difference in SMR level between a local authority and the country as a whole (100) is statistically significant (i.e., is unlikely to be the result of chance factors).

Table 3.11   *Number of hospitals reporting oesophageal cancer in central Africa*

		Annual number of cases			
		0	1	2–51	All
Observed no. of hospitals					
Kachasu	Yes	8	10	19	37
drunk locally?	No	38	21	4	63
Expected no. of hospitals					
Kachasu	Yes	17·0	11·5	8·5	37
drunk locally?	No	29·0	19·5	14·5	63
All hospitals		46	31	23	100

$n = 2$ $\chi^2 = 28$ $p < 0.001$

Source: McGlashan (1972), table 18.1, By permission of Methuen & Co. Ltd.

Second, correlation and regression techniques are being used to measure the degree and form of correspondence between the spatial incidence of disease and of postulated associative factors. Classic cartographic correlation by visual inspection of patterns is still important, but its value is limited by subjectivity, particularly in assessing the multivariate relationships of most diseases which occur only when several factors coincide in time and space. Spatial data can normally be arranged in a matrix — by variable and by unit of observation — and are thus suitable for correlation and regression analysis at bivariate and multivariate levels. The basic functional multivariate model of disease can be expressed as:

$$Y = f(X_1, X_2 \ldots X_n)$$

where : Y = disease incidence by area
    $X_1 - X_n$ = physical, economic and social characteristics by area.

A more precise expression of a linear relationship is:

$$Y = a + b_1X_1 + \ldots + b_nX_n + u$$

where : a = regression constant

$b_i - b_n$ = regression coefficients

u = the error or disturbance term representing all unmeasured influences on Y.

Readers unfamiliar with multiple regression may be referred to a teaching case study by P.J. Taylor (1980).

Third, statistical and cartographic methods have been combined profitably in geographical studies of disease diffusion through time and space. In the case of epidemic waves, an outward spread from an innovative centre can be modelled mathematically in relation to postulated barrier and enhancement effects (Brownlea 1972, Kwofie 1976, Haggett 1976).

Consideration can now be given to an interpretation of selected spatial patterns of disease mortality and morbidity.

Great Britain

The regional pattern of life expectancy at birth for males in 1974–1975 is depicted in Figure 3.3. There is a well-marked gradient (also found for females) from the older industrial areas of the North and West to the more affluent and economically dynamic regions of the South and East – a regional mortality gradient shown by the Registrar General's Decennial Supplements to have been remarkably stable throughout this century. It is important to put into perspective the absolute regional range in life expectancy: 3.7 years for males and 2.9 years for females in 1974–1975. It has taken twenty-seven years (from 1948 to 1975) for the average male life expectancy to have increased by as much as the mid-1970's regional range. Put another way, the elimination of cancer as a cause of death would increase life expectancy at birth by about 2.9 years for men – by less than the current regional range which is often accepted as a matter of course rather than a cause for concern (Gardner and Donnan 1977).

In interpreting this regional pattern, it is useful to bear in mind the appreciable variations in mortality by social class which have already been identified. Since the regional distribution of social classes is not uniform, it seems plausible for social class distribution to control the regional mortality pattern. In other words, the poorer survival prospects in Wales and northern England might simply reflect a relatively high proportion in their populations of the disadvantaged classes IV and V. In order to test this hypothesis, regional mortality data can be standardized for class as well as age. The results (Table 3.12) are a surprisingly decisive rejection of the hypothesis, since standardization for class effects only a modest narrowing of the regional differential in infant mortality and none at all in adult male mortality. Table 3.13 shows clearly that for any particular social class there is an appreciable and fairly regular regional gradient. Nor can regional differences in mortality be

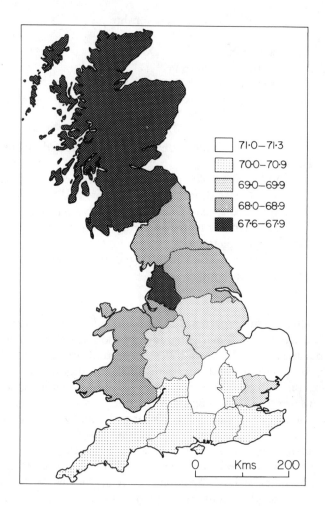

Figure 3.3
Male life expectancy at birth (in years), regional health authorities of Great Britain, 1974-1975
Source: data from Gardner and Donnan (1977), table 1

Table 3.12   *Mortality by region standardized for age and social class, England and Wales, 1970–1972*

| | Males 15–64 | | Infants less than 1 year | |
| | SMR standardized for: | | Regional IMR as % of national IMR | |
	age	age and social class	Crude	Standardized for social class of father
North	113	113	107	103
Yorkshire and Humberside	106	105	112	111
Northwest	116	116	113	109
East Midlands	96	94	101	102
West Midlands	105	105	104	103
East Anglia	84	83	88	88
Southeast	90	90	90	92
Southwest	93	93	94	96
Wales	113	116	100	97
England and Wales	100	100		

Source: Fox (1977), table 2, Crown Copyright

Table 3.13   *Standardized mortality ratios by social class and region for males aged 15–64, England and Wales, 1970–1972*

| | Social Class | | | | | | |
	I	II	IIIN	IIIM	IV	V	All
North	99	110	109	115	109	120	113
Yorkshire & Humberside	115	108	107	103	110	99	105
Northwest	113	118	114	116	116	114	116
East Midlands	98	95	99	92	98	88	94
West Midlands	97	103	104	104	102	108	104
East Anglia	87	92	95	82	76	81	83
Southeast	96	91	93	89	90	88	90
Southwest	93	96	98	90	95	90	93
Wales	117	116	109	120	112	110	116
England and Wales	100	100	100	100	100	100	100

Source: Office of Population Censuses and Surveys (1978b), table 8.4, Crown Copyright

explained readily by differing regional distributions of urban and rural population. Consider, for example, how the rural populations of the North, Northwest, Wales and Scotland regions have 1969–1973 SMRs of over 100, while the Greater London conurbation has a SMR of 97 (Chilvers 1978, p. 19).

In the case of England and Wales, therefore, regional variations in mortality seem to owe remarkably little to regional variations in the two most important variables commonly recognized in differential mortality. This does not necessarily mean that these variables are unimportant influences on spatial mortality patterns; it is simply that their influence is not evident at a regional scale of analysis. Indeed, at the intra-urban scale Griffiths (1971) has shown that social class and housing variations contribute strongly to spatial mortality variation within Exeter.

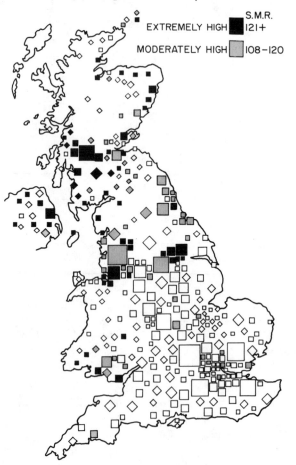

Figure 3.4
Ischaemic heart disease among males in the United Kingdom, 1959-1963: distribution of high standardized mortality ratios
Source: Howe (1972), figure 81

What then are the major factors behind the regional mortality pattern? Useful clues are provided by the detailed mortality mapping of the country by local authority areas accomplished by Murray (1967) and particularly Howe (1970a, 1979). Simplified extracts from Howe's maps of specific diseases are provided by Figures 3.4, 3.5 and 3.6. The so-called demographic base maps have symbols (squares for urban populations and diamonds for rural) proportional to the populations they represent. Relative geographical positions are maintained as far as possible, and a stylistic coastline added. The purpose of this is to avoid the way in which choropleth maps using a conventional geographical base exaggerate the importance of large, sparsely peopled areas at the expense of compact urban populations. Although the patterns of the three maps are broadly similar, there are

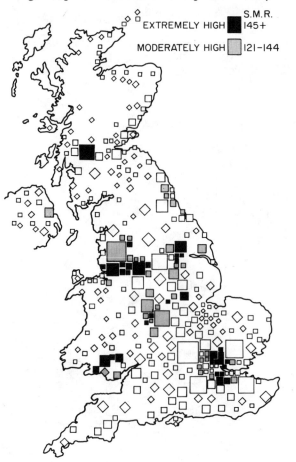

Figure 3.5
Chronic bronchitis among males in the United Kingdom, 1959-1963: distribution of high standardized mortality ratios
Source: Howe (1972), figure 83

important differences which suggest the complexity of interaction between the various physical, cultural and biological determinants of disease.

Britain exhibits considerable variety in physical environmental conditions. The relationship of weather and climate to disease has been reviewed by Tromp (1973), but more important are thought to be the geological influences operating on health through background radiation, trace elements in the soil and water quality. The sedimentary rocks of lowland Britain (the Southeast) have a lower content of radio-active elements and thus less gamma-ray background than the igneous rocks of highland Britain (the North and West), although in terms of human exposure it is type of building material, which may not be derived locally, that seems to be the decisive factor.

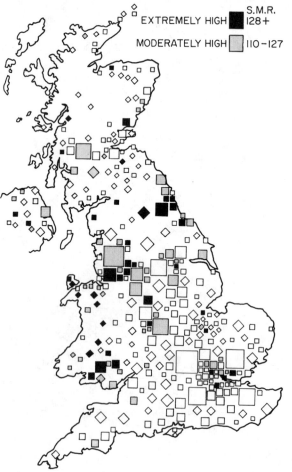

Figure 3.6
Stomach cancer among males in the United Kingdom, 1959-1963: distribution of high standardized mortality ratios
Source: Howe (1972), figure 85

Trace elements are present in the atmosphere and especially in the soil, where they act as important micronutrients. Soils derive their trace elements from the underlying geology and transmit them to the vegetation and thereby to human diets. Both deficiencies and excesses of certain trace elements are known to be harmful to health (Cannon and Hopps 1972, Warren 1973). Excesses of nickel, cadmium, mercury and lead are notorious hazards, and British readers may recall the formal warning given in 1979 by the Department of the Environment to villagers at Shipham, Somerset, not to grow vegetables in their gardens because of dangerously high levels of cadmium derived from the spoil heaps of a long-defunct zinc mine. This illustrates how man's activities can significantly and sometimes harmfully alter trace element concentrations by mining, by fertilizer and pesticide application and by industrial and automobile emissions.

Quality of water supply, particularly its degree of hardness, almost certainly contributes to the British pattern of regional mortality. 'Hardness' is an imprecise term referring to the presence of particular ions in water, the most important being calcium and magnesium. Figure 3.7 indicates a marked regional division in Britain, with the hard water of the South and East, usually obtained from subterranean water-bearing formations like chalk, sandstone and pebble beds, contrasting with the soft water in the North and West obtained from surface supplies off peat-covered uplands. There appears to be a fairly consistent relationship, based on world-wide evidence, between soft water and high levels of heart disease (Schroeder 1960, Reid 1973), but how the relationship is effected is open to doubt. There are two favoured hypotheses: first, that calcium and particularly magnesium have positive preventive effects; and second, that soft acidic water acts as a solvent for harmful metals like lead, zinc and copper from mining spoil heaps in upland Britain or, more universally, from water piping and cooking vessels. Crawford et al. (1961, 1968) have shown clear statistical relationships between water hardness and cardiovascular mortality in a set of 83 British cities. They also show (Crawford et al. 1971) that in the 11 cities where water hardness had been changed substantially in a preceding period of thirty years (and where other factors could be controlled) a hardening of the supply had a favourable effect on the cardiovascular mortality rate, while softening had an unfavourable effect. This confirms evidence from New York where a major change in water supply from well water to softer river water in 1940 was followed by an increase in the heart disease mortality rate (Muss 1962). The general practice, therefore, of indescriminately softening water for practical and aesthetic reasons needs to be reconsidered, and perhaps confined to industrial water and to hot water supplies for domestic appliances.

The cultural environment provides several, spatially concentrated, health hazards which contribute to regional mortality variations (Chilvers and Adelstein 1978). Three examples are air pollution, diet and smoking habits. Pollution of the atmosphere in cities and industrial areas by dust, smoke and noxious gases is clearly associated with a high incidence of respiratory diseases (Table 3.9 and Figure 3.5). A classic British example was the great London smog of December 1952, when a temperature inversion prevented for four days the escape of

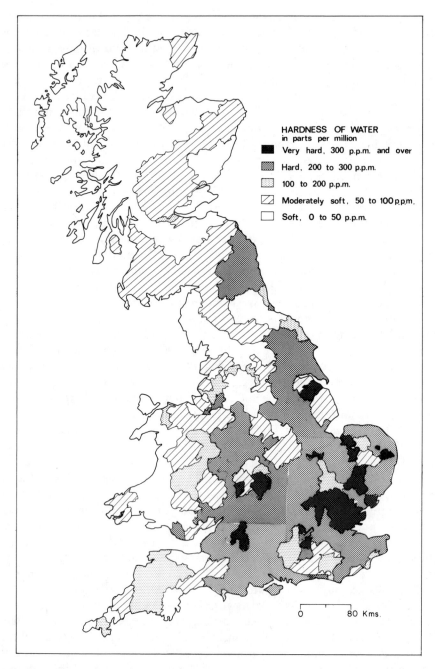

Figure 3.7
Degree of hardness of water for direct supply water undertakings in Great Britain
Source: Howe (1972), figure 20, based on data from *Water Engineer's Handbook 1968*

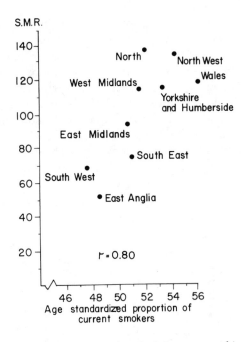

Figure 3.8
Regional levels of mortality from bronchitis and of cigarette smoking, males aged 15-64, England and Wales, 1969-1973
Source: Chilvers (1978), figure 5. Crown Copyright.

impurities into the upper air. It is thought that this was directly responsible for almost 4000 deaths from chronic bronchitis (Howe 1972, p. 78). The enforcement of Clean Air Acts has led to appreciable improvements in atmospheric quality in British cities since 1960, but anyone who has sampled the atmosphere associated with chemical complexes like Teesside will appreciate that atmospheric problems persist, and may well show an association with mortality such as E.J. MacDonald (1976) was able to demonstrate for cancer within the Texas city of Houston.

Diet is clearly an important variable factor in health. In the case of stomach cancer, for example, almost every dietary constituent that can be thought of has been brought under suspicion by one researcher or another (Logan 1976). There are significant regional variations in diet composition in Britain (Howe 1976, figure 24), but relating these to mortality patterns is a contentious matter (Stocks 1947). Is there any link, for example, between the extremely high regional rates of stomach cancer (Figure 3.6) and of butter consumption in Wales?

Smoking habits vary not only by class (Table 3.4) but also by region, and Figure 3.8 demonstrates a clear relationship between regional indices of cigarette smoking and of mortality from bronchitis.

An aspect of the biological environment which is thought to influence spatial mortality patterns is the distribution of genetic traits in the population which may well give some people a predisposition and others a resistance to certain diseases.

There is strong evidence of relationships between blood groups and diseases (Mourant et al. 1978). Human beings belong to one of four blood groups (A, B, AB and O) which are stable from birth to death and which are determined by heredity. The distributions of the two most important blood groups in Britain are shown in Figures 3.9 and 3.10, and the broad relationship with regional mortality is an obvious one. It is possible, therefore, that the distribution of ancestral populations, based essentially on the different origins and modes of colonization of the highland and lowland zones (C. Fox 1947), is still influencing spatial mortality patterns today, despite the blurring of spatial biological traits by centuries of migration and intermarriage. It has also been suggested that selective migration of healthy indi-

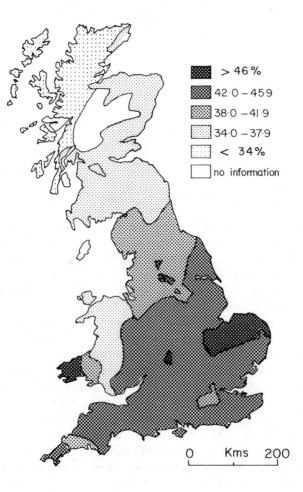

> 46 %
42·0 – 45·9
38·0 – 41·9
34·0 – 37·9
< 34 %
no information

0   Kms   200

Figure 3.9
Percentage frequencies of the blood group A gene in Great Britain, based on blood donor evidence
Source: simplified from Howe (1972), figure 4

viduals from north to south in twentieth-century Britain may have contributed to regional mortality differences (Chilvers 1978).

United States

It was a population geographer (Murray 1967) who was the first to attempt a portrayal of areal variations of mortality in the United States on any kind of detailed basis. His depiction of age-standardized death rates by county for the 1950–1959 period indicated a strong spatial association between high mortality and areas of traditionally poor socio-economic circumstances – the South, north-ern inner cities, Indian reservations and Spanish-American districts. In contrast,

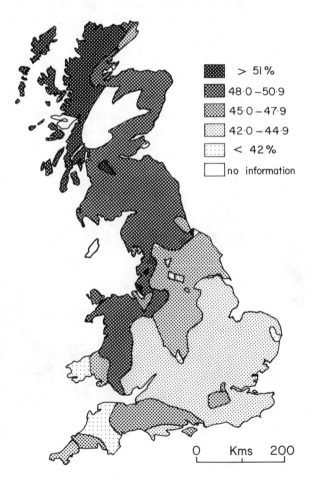

> 51%
48·0 – 50·9
45·0 – 47·9
42·0 – 44·9
< 42%
no information

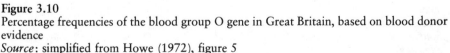

O   Kms   200

Figure 3.10
Percentage frequencies of the blood group O gene in Great Britain, based on blood donor evidence
Source: simplified from Howe (1972), figure 5

low mortality characterized much of the agricultural interior, California and the Pacific Northwest. This pattern is confirmed broadly by more recent, but areally coarser, mortality data, again standardized for age (Figure 3.11).

Attempts have been made to explain the spatial mortality pattern of the United States by bivariate and multivariate analysis. For example, Kitagawa and Hauser (1973, p. 143) show that variations between states in the Negro proportion of the population and in median family income, considered together, account for 48 percent of the variation in 1959–1961 age-adjusted state death rates for males and 61 percent for females (multiple correlation coefficients of 0.69 and 0.78 respectively, giving r^2 values of 0.48 and 0.61). They also show (p. 149) that 58 percent of the variation in male, age-adjusted 1959–1961 death rates in 212 Standard Metropolitan Statistical Areas could be accounted for by the incorporation of several socio-economic variables in a multiple regression analysis; for females the proportion was 72 percent.

Sri Lanka

The important role in mortality reduction of the post-World War II programme of malaria eradication has been discussed in Chapter 2, but the spatial pattern of malaria incidence at that time remains to be considered. It provides an excellent

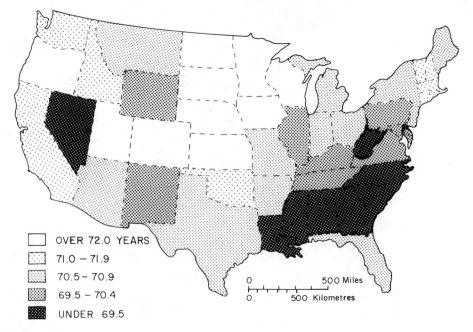

OVER 72.0 YEARS

71.0 – 71.9

70.5 – 70.9

69.5 – 70.4

UNDER 69.5

0   500 Miles

0   500 Kilometres

Figure 3.11
Life expectancy at birth, United States, 1969-1971
Source: data from US National Center for Health Statistics, *Decennial Life Tables 1969-71*, Washington, D.C.

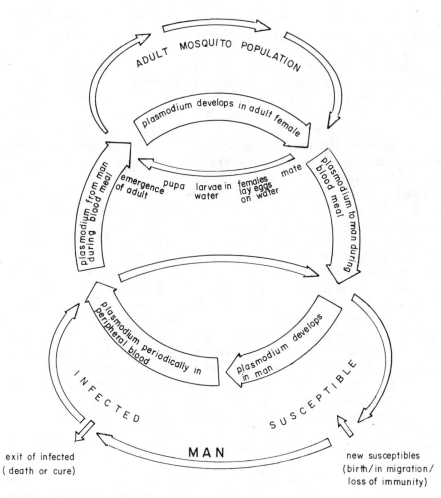

Figure 3.12
The malaria cycle viewed as the interlocking relations of parasite, vector and man
Source: Learmonth (1977), figure 16, and *The Population Explosion, an Interdisciplinary Approach,* Understanding Society Course, The Open University Press, 1971, figure 33.6

example of how ecological forces can fashion spatial patterns of disease in less developed societies.

Malaria is a three-factor disease embracing: the causative organism, malaria parasites of the genus *Plasmodium*; the host, man; and the vector (strictly speaking an alternative host), female mosquitoes of the genus *Anopheles*. There are thus three separate ecologies in that each individual factor interacts with its total environment, which includes the other two factors. Several of these interactions are summarized (Figure 3.12) in a particularly useful representation of the malaria cycle provided by Learmonth (1977).

Figure 3.13 depicts the typical distribution of malaria in Sri Lanka in the pre-control era. The index of malaria prevalence is the spleen rate, the percentage of a sampled population with the splenic enlargement associated with malaria. The distribution pattern is closely related to the island's physical and human geography, particularly to the fundamental and universally recognized regional division between Wet and Dry Zones (Figure 3.14 and 3.15).

The Wet Zone receives the bulk of its appreciable rainfall from onshore winds during the southwest monsoon from May to July, but its southerly latitude ensures the adjacency of the Inter-tropical Convergence Zone throughout the year, so that there is normally no rainless season. The Dry Zone, on the other hand, in the north and east of the island has its more limited and essentially seasonal rainfall during the relatively weak and unreliable northeast monsoon from October to February, since the uplands in the south-centre of the island impose a rain-shadow effect on the Dry Zone in the southwest monsoon period.

The epidemiological significance of these contrasting climatic conditions lies in the breeding habits of the vector mosquito *Anopheles culicifacies*, which requires fresh and still water sites like river pools, irrigation ditches and rain puddles for egg laying and the development of larvae. Water flow in the Wet Zone is normally continuous and fast enough to keep the stream beds flushed and clear of larvae, and the limited amount of irrigation practised is not of the tank-storage type. However, when the southwest monsoon occasionally fails, stagnant water does collect in riverbed pools, leading to the rapid multiplication of mosquitoes and epidemic outbreaks of malaria. Such conditions often result in high mortality, as in the devastating outbreak of 1935, since the Wet Zone population, not being continually exposed to malaria, has little natural resistance to the disease.

In the Dry Zone, optimum breeding grounds for larvae are provided by the reduced river flow of the dry season and by irrigation tanks, canals and ditches, particularly when silted up and abandoned. Figure 3.16 shows the abundance of tanks and canals in a typical part of the Dry Zone. A few large tanks are formed by barrages on fair-sized rivers, while others derive their water by diversion weirs from rivers; but the great majority of tanks are small reservoirs tapping localized catchments. There is only one exception to the Dry Zone pattern of endemic malaria, as Figure 3.13 indicates: the Jafna district in the extreme north. Here limestone prevents surface rivers, and well irrigation is the mainstay of agriculture. There are no tanks, and the industrious Tamils have refurbished the ancient irrigation channels, allowing constant water flow and consequent avoidance of malarial hazards.

Gray (1974) has provided some interesting results by correlating for a set of 21 districts the spleen rate for 1938–1941 with: (i) the average crude death rate for 1936–1945 (r = 0.91), (ii) the average crude death rate for 1949–1952 (r = 0.17), and (iii) the percentage decrease in average crude death rate between 1936–1945 and 1946–1960 (r = 0.91). Clearly the spatial correlation between malaria incidence and overall mortality breaks down after the malaria control programme of 1946–1948, when mortality becomes spatially homogeneous on the island. The

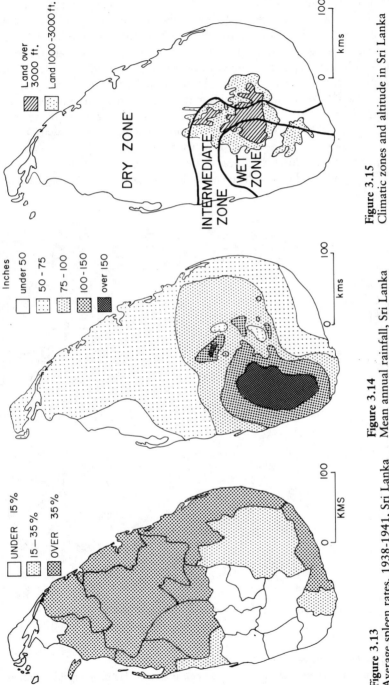

Figure 3.13
Average spleen rates, 1938-1941, Sri Lanka
Source: data from Gray (1974), table 1

Figure 3.14
Mean annual rainfall, Sri Lanka
Source: simplified from B.L. Johnson
(1969), figure 5.1.2.   By permission
of Heinemann Educational Books Ltd.

Figure 3.15
Climatic zones and altitude in Sri Lanka

average of district crude death rates for 1936–1945 is 24.5 per 1000, with a standard deviation of 6.3; for 1946–1960 the respective figures are 11.7 and 1.3.

The world-wide resurgence of malaria in the 1970s has been commented on in Chapter 2. Sri Lanka has shared in this, with about 1.5 million cases being reported in the 1968–1970 period. One of the world's leading authorities on malaria has declared with reference to Sri Lanka that 'should some combined climatic, ecological or other causes create conditions for a widespread transmission of falciparum malaria from the remaining few foci, few people will be surprised if the tragic history of 1934–1935 with its 80,000 dead repeats itself' (Bruce-Chwatt 1974b, p.65). Unfortunately there does not seem to be any detailed spatial study of resurgence in Sri Lanka along the lines of the Indian study of Akhtar and Learmonth (1977), in which they produce choropleth maps of malaria incidence for

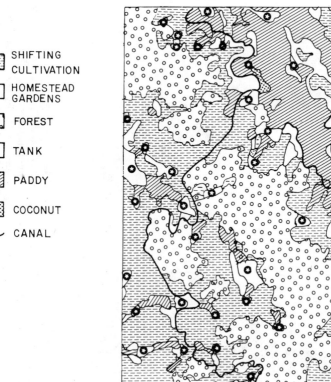

Figure 3.16
Land-use in the Dry Zone of Sri Lanka: a representative area
Source: B.L. Johnson (1969), figure 5.2.5.   By permission of Heinemann Educational Books Ltd.

various years between 1965 and 1976. They are able to identify four foci in the diffusion of malaria – the Kutch salt marsh area and the hill forest tracts of Madhya, Orissa and Assam. Preliminary examination of rainfall anomaly maps suggests to these researchers that the role of wet years in areas normally arid, semi-arid or moderately humid might be crucial in the diffusion process.

Microscale and metropolitan studies
The application of geographical methods to medical problems, not necessarily by geographers, has also proved fruitful at subnational scales of analysis. Three examples will be used to demonstrate this at a local community scale.

The mapping of residences of nineteenth-century cholera victims in the British cities of Leeds, Exeter and Oxford by Baker, Shapter and Acland respectively (Stamp 1964, p. 27) gave useful clues to the nature and transmission of the disease, but the critical mapping work was that of a London general practitioner, Dr. John Snow. During an acute outbreak of cholera in the Soho district of London in August–September 1848, Snow marked on a large-scale map the residences of the 500 victims (Figure 3.17). He was obviously testing a hypothesis, since he also marked the standpumps which supplied drinking water to the population. As Figure 3.17 indicates, there was a heavy clustering of deaths around the Broad Street pump, and when the pump handle was removed at Snow's insistence the cholera outbreak subsided. Sceptics argue that the outbreak was self-limiting and that the dismantling of the pump was essentially symbolic, yet it was Snow's map that clearly established the critical role in cholera transmission of contaminated drinking water. It was not until 1883 that the infective micro-organism, *Vibrio cholerae*, was identified by the German bacteriologist Robert Koch.

Links between cancer mortality and water supply have been suggested strongly by the mapping of over 5000 deaths, classified as either cancer deaths or deaths from other causes, in West Devon (UK) over a twenty-year period (Allen-Price 1960). An extract from the maps is shown in Figure 3.18 for the village and environs of Horrabridge. This indicates that to the north of the River Walkham there are 25 cancer deaths and 73 other deaths, compared with only 18 cancer deaths and as many as 130 other deaths to the south of the river. Chi-squared analysis indicates that there is a probability of between 95 and 99 percent that the observed differences are not the result of a chance occurrence within the standard null hypothesis. Allen-Price comments (p. 1238) on the Horrabridge pattern: 'Here there is a homogeneous group, following the same occupations, eating the same food, and in an identical environment, and merely separated one from another by the natural boundaries of the river Walkham, which is crossed by a bridge. Here, for generations, the people have intermarried freely, and their social activities have been confined, yet each artifical section of the community has a widely different cancer mortality. As far as can be assessed, the only difference that could account for this is their water supply.' He was able to show that for West Devon as a whole the highest incidence of cancer was in populations deriving their water from highly mineralized rocks.

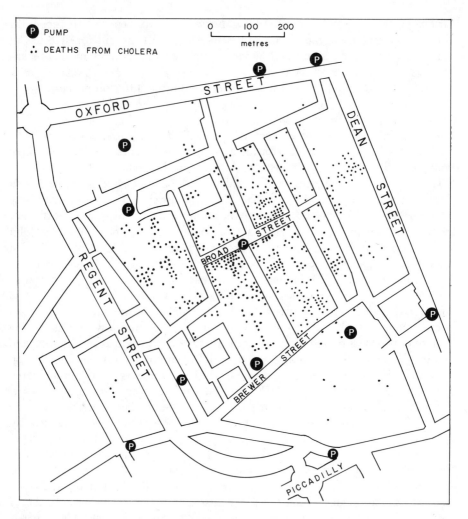

Figure 3.17
Snow's map of cholera deaths in the Soho district of London, August-September 1848
Source: Stamp (1964), figure 9

A third example is the mapping by Young (1972) of cases of illness diagnosed as food poisoning in the English town of Consett. He was able to demonstrate a pattern dominated by locations downwind from an iron and steel plant. A strong supposition arose that the majority of food poisoning notifications were, in fact, derived from iron oxide dust pollution.

At a metropolitan scale of analysis it is significant that some of the most active work on spatial mortality patterns has been accomplished in Chicago, the academic home of human ecology. Kitagawa and Hauser (1973) demonstrate that socio-economic differentials within Chicago have a spatial expression which contributes to the spatial metropolitan pattern of mortality. For 1950 and 1960 they group census tracts on the basis of median family income into five divisions for whites and three for nonwhites. They then calculate age-adjusted death rates by colour for these divisions and thereby demonstrate clear gradients in mortality for both whites and nonwhites from high-income to low-income divisions. The particularly high level of mortality in the lowest income division is yet another expression of the acute social and spatial disadvantage present within the metropoli of ostensibly advanced societies.

More detailed analyses of the spatial mortality pattern within Chicago have been provided by Pyle (1971) and Pyle and Rees (1971). The former study is particularly noteworthy for its innovative use of trend surface analysis (Chorley and Haggett 1965) in urban disease mapping. For 271 subareas of Chicago an overall relationship is calculated between the crude death rate in a disease group (dependent

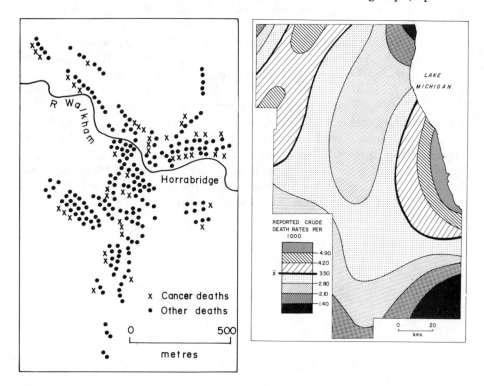

Figure 3.18
Distribution of deaths from cancer and from all other causes in Horrabridge, UK, 1939–1958
Source: simplified from Allen-Price (1960), figure 2

Figure 3.19
Total heart disease mortality, Chicago, 1967
Source: Pyle (1971), figure 14

variable) and the subarea spatial co-ordinates (independent variable). When mapped, these relationships provide generalized or smoothed patterns of disease mortality which over-ride nonsystematic, local and chance variations (Figure 3.19), although it is unfortunate that age-standardized mortality rates could not be used. The aim of the study is not simply to describe and interpret spatial mortality patterns within Chicago, but rather to use these patterns as data input in the development of a locational efficiency model for health care facilities in 1980.

Some of the growing volume of work by geographers on inequalities of access to health care has also been accomplished in Chicago (DeVise 1969, Earickson 1970, Morill et al. 1970), and there is a growing appreciation of the essentially subtle relationships between spatial and behavioural influence in this field. Geographers no longer rely on simple physical or time-distance modelling to demonstrate what Hart (1971, p. 412) has called the Inverse Care Law, whereby 'the availability of good medical care tends to vary inversely with the need of the population served'.

It is at the metropolitan scale that medical geographers are likely to make their most useful contributions in the near future. Pyle (1979, p. 245) has argued: 'One of the best combinations of skills the geographer has to offer consists of methodologies for the collection, organisation, and analysis of information made available on the basis of small subareas within the larger Health Systems Areas.' The 1970s has seen the emergence in many cities of the developed world of computerized geographic base files where recording is by street segment, city block, postcode or National Grid reference. The areal matching of health files with housing, planning, social work, crime, census and other geocoded files is thus permitted, as well as the ready aggregation of data to prescribed areas and, given the availability of explicit spatial co-ordinates, the drawing of computer maps (Levy 1972, Pyle 1979, chapter 8, and work in progress in 1980 at the Census Research Unit, University of Durham).

CHAPTER 4

FERTILITY PATTERNS: DEVELOPED COUNTRIES

The volatile and often unpredicted movements of fertility in recent decades in developed countries have emphasized to policy-makers and general public alike the critical contribution made by fertility levels to population growth and composition and, consequently, to a whole host of social and economic structures and processes. The geographer's prime interest in fertility studies is that of recognizing, depicting, analysing and interpreting spatial variations at all levels of scale from neighbourhood to nation. A particularly useful approach to an understanding of such variations, at least at larger scales of analysis, is through demographic transition theory. This should be viewed as a paradigm which links socio-economic and demographic change through sociological, economic and psychological arguments and through the empirical observation of demographic evolution in developed countries, but which is sufficiently open-ended to leave several problems for individual researchers to resolve.

The demographic transition

This is probably the most actively discussed and debated field of demography in terms of theory formulation, empirical testing and policy implications, despite the apparent simplicy of its core theory that fertility declines appreciably and probably irreversibly as traditional, nonindustrial, usually agrarian societies are transformed by modernization or development into bureaucratic urban societies. The effect of such transformation on a population's fertility level is mediated through changes in the norms and values relating to child-bearing and parenthood. Such changes have been discussed extensively in sociological literature (consisely reviewed by S.E. Beaver 1975), and may be summarized as follows:

(a) The breakdown of extended kinship systems lessens the status value of large families and places the physical and emotional costs of child-raising much more centrally on parents.

(b) The labour value of children diminishes when the family is no longer the basic productive unit. In peasant societies children contribute to the farm labour force from very early ages, so that they are commonly regarded as economic assets. But in urban environments, particularly following the introduction of compulsory education and restrictions on child labour, the very real costs of child-rearing are more keenly felt by parents.

(c) There are greater opportunities in a modernized society for women to achieve economic support and personal satisfaction outside the roles of wife and mother. Female employment, in particular, may be regarded as incompatible with continuous child-bearing.

(d) In so far as most religions actively or passively uphold the ideal of large families ('Be fruitful and multiply'), the decline of religious practice and growth of secular education which often accompany modernization can be expected to undermine large-family norms.

(e) In inert pre-industrial societies there is little scope for personal advancement, so that an individual's status is invariably that to which he is born. There tends to be a fatalistic acceptance of one's lot, including family size. But with economic diversification new opportunities arise, and it becomes widely appreciated that one's destiny can be affected by one's deeds. The opening of class structures permits greater social mobility, leading Dumont to observe in his renowned theory of *Capillarité Sociale* formulated in the late nineteenth century that, just as a column of liquid has to be thin in order to rise under the force of capillarity, so a family must be small in order to ascend the social scale. Children thus become regarded as competing for limited family resources of income, time and effort with the goods and activities which determine social rank.

(f) Mortality reduction, particularly of young children, is a standard component of the development process. Although initially this may promote higher fertility, for reasons to be discussed later, the long-term impact is to reduce fertility, since several births per family are no longer required to ensure an ultimate family size capable of meeting parental needs for labour, security and inheritance.

These changing attitudes towards family size are so powerful that level of modernization has clearly been the critical factor controlling spatial variations in fertility at national and regional levels. Some demographers have emphasized the intermediate importance of innovation and diffusion processes, whereby the small-family norm and particularly the means of achieving it through contraceptive knowledge are initiated in metropolitan upper and middle classes before trickling down the social and settlement scales into smaller urban centres and, eventually, the countryside; it is transmission of information which is seen as controlling this diffusion pattern. This is how Hofstee (1968) explains regional differences of fertility in the Netherlands. He regards birth control as emanating from a highly urbanized core in the West-Centre of the country, so that the most distant regions from this core – North Brabant and Limbourg in the South and Drenthe, Groningen and Friesland in the Northeast – have maintained the highest fertility. This type of explanation is intuitively attractive to geographers well versed in diffusion theory, but is critically regarded by most contemporary demographers. They emphasize the presence in pre-industrial societies of folk methods of birth control like *coitus interruptus* (withdrawal) which, although unreliable at an individual level, are capable of reducing aggregate fertility levels considerably. Accordingly, in framing a strategy of fertility change, such demographers attach little weight to information but considerable importance to motivation as it adjusts to social change.

The whole problem has been discussed penetratively by Carlsson (1966), using spatial and temporal fertility data from Sweden. He concludes (p. 172) that the 'growth of the proportion of [fertility] controlling parents should be regarded not as the spread of a new social invention but rather as a shift in a stimulus balance between old-style and new-style ideals. . . . Geographical diffusion models do not seem very helpful for the understanding of this shift.'

Geography and the study of fertility

In multidisciplinary·fields of study it is customary for writers to emphasize the importance of their own discipline's contribution. But in the case of population geography there can be no avoiding the slightness of its contribution to fertility studies. There is no equivalent to the work on mortality, morbidity and access to health care by medical geographers, presumably because the set of environmental and behavioural influences to which fertility responds may be regarded, rightly or wrongly, as less intrinsically geographical than those which influence health.

The neglect of fertility studies in geography is, indeed, spectacular. They barely rate a mention in a review of major research themes in population geography (International Geographical Union 1973), while in a review by Clarke (1973) of work in population geography by mainly, but not exclusively, British authors, not more than two of the 140 works cited can be regarded as dealing in any central way with spatial fertility variations. In the 35 articles chosen by Demko et al. (1970) to constitute a reader in population geography, there is only a single article by a geographer on fertility. It also needs to be said that most of the scattered work on fertility by population geographers, whether based on cartographic or statistical methods, is essentially descriptive, contributing little to theory in a field dominated by sociologists, economists and social historians.

Despite the dearth of professional geographical involvement in fertility analysis, there is no question that appreciable spatial variations in fertility exist at all scales of aggregation and at most periods of time. Such cross-sectional variations have often been studied by nongeographers as a means of identifying and monitoring the evolving relationship between development and fertility decline, although some rightly emphasize like Rindfuss and Sweet (1977, p. 79) that 'region is an imperfect indicator of a variety of diverse variables ranging from ethnic group membership to lifestyle to cost of housing.' Population geographers could, and indeed should, offer particular expertise in such cross-sectional studies, not simply in the presentation of areal data in map or matrix form, but more importantly in an appreciation of the analytical problems posed by scale (Clarke 1976) and spatial auto-correlation (Cliff and Ord 1973).

It has often been predicted that spatial and other differentials of fertility will narrow and eventually collapse as high levels of modernization are universally achieved. Yet spatial variations in fertility are remarkably persistent even in highly modernized societies; for example, H. R. Jones (1975) demonstrates that in 1971–1972 the coefficient of variation for age-standardized birth rates in 31 divisions of Scotland was higher than that for age-standardized death rates.

Measures of fertility

Before proceeding to analyse fertility patterns, it is obviously necessary to appreciate the ways in which fertility is commonly measured. The principles and procedures are very similar to those of mortality measurement presented in Chapter 2.

Crude birth rate

This is the simplest and commonest measure, being defined as the number of births in a year per 1000 of the mid-year population:

$$\frac{B}{P} \times 1000$$

It has the advantage of showing the exact rate at which additions are made to a population through births, but for temporal or spatial comparisons it has the disadvantage of including in its denominator a large mass of males and of female children and older adults not 'exposed' to child-bearing. H.R. Jones (1975) has demonstrated that 71 percent of the variation in crude birth rates among 31 areas of Scotland in 1971–1972 was due solely to areal variations in female age structure ($r = 0.84$, $r^2 = 0.71$).

Accordingly, the more refined and analytically useful measures of fertility attempt to standardize for the variable age and sex composition of the population, so that births are related specifically to the female population 'at risk'.

General fertility rate

This measures the number of births in a year per 1000 women of normal reproductive age:

$$\frac{B}{P_{f15-44}} \times 1000$$

Sometimes the somewhat larger fifteen–forty-nine age group is used, but since women of forty-five–forty-nine contribute relatively few births it is preferable to avoid dilution of the denominator by this low-risk group. Even so, there is still only a partial standardization for age, since populations differ in age composition *within* the fifteen–forty-four age group. This is important for fertility measurement since the rate of child-bearing is appreciably higher in the twenty–twenty-nine group than in the fifteen–nineteen and thirty–forty-four groups.

Child-woman ratio

This is the ratio of children under five years of age to women of child-bearing age:

$$\frac{P_{0-4}}{P_{f15-49}} \times 1000$$

In this case the fifteen–forty-nine rather than the fifteen–forty-four group is conventionally used, since children under five may have been born up to five years prior to the census, when the mothers were up to five years younger. Its great operational advantage is that the basic data are available from census age-tables. This is important in less developed societies with poor systems of birth registration, while even in countries with good registration data the child-woman ratio is often the only means of measuring fertility in small areas for which births data are not tabulated. The child-woman ratio is thus used extensively by population geographers for microscale spatial studies of fertility.

Nevertheless, the ratio has several deficiencies. It is only partially standardized for age, not taking account of age distribution within the fifteen–forty-nine range; the number and age of young children may be misreported to census enumerators; the ratio is essentially a measure of survivors of births, so that it is affected by differences between populations in child mortality; and there are further complications caused by migration, as in the case of women in some less developed countries moving to urban areas but having their children brought up by grandparents in the countryside.

Age-specific birth rate
Such a rate measures the number of births in a year to women of a given age group (B_{fa}) per 1000 women in that age group (P_{fa}):

$$\frac{B_{fa}}{P_{fa}} \times 1000$$

Sets of age-specific birth rates allow detailed but cumbersome comparisons between populations. For more effective comparisons, demographers have evolved single-figure indices from sets of age-specific birth rates.

Standardized birth rate
This can be calculated from a set of age-specific birth rates in the manner demonstrated in Table 4.1. It indicates what the crude birth rate would have been in a population if the age and sex composition of that population was the same as in a population selected as the standard. In the so-called direct method of calculation used in Table 4.1 the age-specific birth rates of the population being studied (England and Wales, 1977) are applied to the age structure of the standard population (Great Britain, 1961).

Total fertility rate
Demographers tend to regard this as the most sensitive and meaningful cross-sectional measure of fertility. It indicates the number of children that would be born to 1000 women passing through the child-bearing ages assuming, firstly, that none of the women die during this period and, secondly, that age-specific birth rates remain the same as for the year of calculation. The number is obtained by summing the age-specific birth rates for the relevant age intervals and multiplying by the number of years in the age interval. In the case of quinquennial groups:

$$5. \sum_{15-19}^{45-49} \left(\frac{B}{P_f} \times 1000 \right)$$

Table 4.1 demonstrates how a total fertility rate of 1675 per 1000 is calculated for England and Wales in 1977.

It is important to appreciate that the total fertility rate is an entirely hypothetical figure based on age-specific birth rates in one year only. It has sometimes been used to assess whether the population is replacing itself, particularly when it is modified to form the *gross reproduction rate* (taking account of female births only) and the *net reproduction rate* (taking account of female births only and also of female mortality between birth and normal completion of child-bearing). But calendar year reproduction rates in any shape or form are now recognized as being very imperfect measures of replacement. Only a persistent trend of annual rates substantially above or below unity might be an indication of a growing or declining population.

Rates adjusted for marital status and duration

It can be argued convincingly that the age-standardized fertility indices discussed above do not entirely restrict their denominators to persons truly exposed to the 'risk' of child-bearing, since they include unmarried as well as married females. The importance of this can be gauged by the 85 percent of all live births in England and Wales in 1976 which were conceived within marriage (Office of Population Cen-

Table 4.1   Age-specific birth rates, standardized birth rate and total fertility rate, England and Wales, 1977

Age	Age-specific birth rate per 1000 women	No. of females in standard population* (thousands)	Expected births in standard population
15–19**	29·7	1765·4	52,432
20–24	104·7	1617·5	169,352
25–29	118·9	1566·1	186,209
30–34	59·0	1652·4	97,492
35–39	18·3	1802·5	32,986
40–44	4·1	1710·0	7,011
45–49	0·3	1823·7	547
Total	335·0		546,029

Standardized birth rate (per 1000 population):

$$\frac{546,029}{51,283,892} \times 1000 = 10 \cdot 65$$

Total fertility rate (per 1000 women):

$$335 \cdot 0 \times 5 = 1675$$

* Great Britain, 1961; total population (male and female) of 51,283,892

** The small number of births to mothers of under 15 and over 49 years are attributed to the 15–19 and 45–49 age groups respectively

suses and Surveys 1978c, p. 23). Accordingly, demographers have often found it useful to compute measures like the general fertility rate, child-woman ratio and total fertility rate on the basis of the currently married or the ever-married female population. One can refine further by standardizing for duration of marriage.

Cohort measures

All the fertility indices so far presented are based on births occurring in a particular year; they are thus described as annual or period measures. But births in any one year occur to only a cross-section of women, and changes in period measures of fertility may reflect changes in the tempo of family formation as well as in completed family size. Thus a fall in total fertility rate might simply reflect a lengthening – temporary or permanent – of intervals between births.

In order to avoid the interpretative problems associated with measures of one-point-in-time reproductive performance, demographers have increasingly adopted measures of cohort fertility – a cohort being regarded in these cases as a group of women born or married in a particular period. An extensively used measure is that of completed or lifetime fertility, which may be regarded to all intents and purposes as the average number of live births achieved in their lifetime by women of fifty years of age. The measure can be calculated for all such women, or restricted to the ever-married, the still-married or to women married at particular ages.

A particularly refined measure of cohort fertility has been adopted by a population geographer in a spatial study of fertility in Scotland. M.G. Wilson (1978a) derived for 31 areal units a cumulative marital fertility ratio standardized for age at, and duration of, marriage. The ratio is that between, on the one hand, the number of children ever born to once- and still-married women of under forty-five years in an area and, on the other, the number expected there on the basis of Scottish national rates of fertility being applied to each area's particular structure of age at, and duration of, marriage.

Inter-relationships between measures

At a national level the relationships between fertility measures are usually very close when assessed statistically. For example, Bogue and Palmore (1964) calculate a correlation coefficient of 0.996 between the general fertility rate and the total fertility rate for 50 countries in the late 1950s. But at a local scale, where demographic structure is much less regular, there may well be significant discordancies between the patterns of individual measures. M.G. Wilson (1971a) shows that for local government areas in Victoria in 1966 there are only modest levels of correlation between the child-woman ratio and each of the general fertility rate ($r = 0.64$), the marital fertility rate ($r = 0.51$) and the total fertility rate ($r = 0.60$). Contributory factors to discordancy in these cases are: (i) local variations in survival of children to five years of age, (ii) local variations in child migrant flows, (iii) differences in 1966 birth totals relative to those of previous years. It is important, therefore, for analysts of spatial fertility to be aware that a study using a particular fertility index may not always provide results entirely compatible with those using alternative indices.

Fertility decline and modernization: the international pattern

There is general agreement that economic development and the associated transformation of social institutions brought in their wake a secular trend of declining
fertility in today's developed countries. To that extent the theory of the demographic transition is upheld, but several demographers feel, like Coale (1969, p. 19),
that 'the process was more complex, subtle and diverse than anticipated; only an
optimist would still expect a simple account of why fertility fell.' The identification
of a threshold level for the commencement of fertility decline has proved elusive,
and it may be argued that in northwestern Europe there have been *two* demographic transitions.

The pre-modern transition

Through the assiduous work of historical demographers in recording and collating
demographic material from ecclesiastical registers of baptisms, burials and marriages in centuries preceding the regular collection by the state of vital statistics, it is
now well known that fertility fell between the sixteenth and eighteenth centuries in
wide areas of northwestern Europe to levels below those presumed to occur
elsewhere in the world at that time and known to occur in less developed countries
in the twentieth century. Crude birth rates of about 35–40 per 1000 were typical,
although in Scandinavia rates barely exceeding 30 per 1000 were common in the
eighteenth century (Figures 2.4 and 4.1). This widespread, although by no means
dramatic, fertility fall in agrarian, pre-industrial societies is attributed largely to a
pattern of late marriage and widespread celibacy which Hajnal (1965) recognized
as emerging from the sixteenth century in Europe to the west of a line drawn from
Leningrad to Trieste. He demonstrated that married women comprised only about
40–50 percent of all women aged fifteen–forty-five in this area, compared with
proportions of 60–70 percent in eastern Europe, Africa and Asia. The average age
at first marriage estimated by Andorka (1978) from many microlevel reconstitution studies was between twenty-seven and thirty-two years for men and between
twenty-four and thirty-one years for women. The effect of this marital pattern on
overall fertility was clearly substantial, bearing in mind that illegitimate births are
estimated to have comprised well under 5 percent of all births in western Europe at
that time (Shorter, Knodel and Van de Walle 1971).

But what caused the emergence of this distinctive pattern of marriage, which
must surely be regarded as oppressive and contrary to human inclination? A
popular explanation in historical demography embraces marriage-inheritance
theory. It is assumed that having the means to an adequate livelihood was a
prerequisite to marriage, and that in those peasant societies where the supply of
land was not expanding such means were obtained through land inheritance.
Hence marriages often had to be delayed until the incapacity or death of the father,
particularly under impartible inheritance systems, in which peasants do not divide
their land (Berkner and Mendels 1978).

In a visit to Switzerland in the early nineteenth century Malthus encountered this
argument from a peasant who 'appeared to understand the principle of population

almost as well as any man I ever met. . . . [The] habit of early marriages might really, he said, be called *le vice du pays*; and he was so strongly impressed with the necessary and unavoidable wretchedness that must result from it that he thought a law ought to be made restricting men from entering into the marriage state before they were forty years of age, and then allowing it only with *des vieilles filles*, who might bear them two or three children instead of six or eight' (quoted by Van de Walle 1972, p. 137). There were indeed legal or quasi-legal marriage restrictions in several parts of Europe, notably the Swiss cantons and German states (Knodel 1967), but more usually the marital pattern derived from customs and norms rooted in the community, however unconsciously, as means of avoiding acute demographic pressure.

Where available land was not fully settled, as in eastern Europe, the restrictive pattern of late marriage and low fertility was not present, although Tilly (1978) suggests that an additional factor here was the early proletarianization of the rural population on great estates, so that peasant inheritance concern was not present. In the Finnmark area of northern Norway early marriage and high fertility in the early nineteenth century was essentially due to land availability in an area made habit-able by the newly introduced potato. 'To it came those who wanted to marry, yet could not find the means to do so in the southern part of the country' (Drake 1969, p. 87).

Despite the plausibility of marriage-inheritance theory, one must appreciate that the relationships between land inheritance, marriage and fertility were essentially dynamic, even in pre-industrial Europe. Time-series data show repeatedly that in times of plenty – good harvests or, as Drake (1969) has shown for parts of Norway, the arrival of herring shoals – there is a swing to younger marriage and higher fertility. A similar effect seems to have been achieved by technologically induced increases in agricultural productivity, as in parts of Brtiain and the Netherlands during the Agricultural Revolution. The effect of mortality on the relationships is much more controversial. The conventional view (Ohlin 1961, Habbakuk 1971) is that periods of high mortality open up new places on the land, thus promoting younger marriage and higher fertility. On the other hand, periods of high mortality involve foetal deaths, deaths of women of reproductive age and an impairment of fecundity (the physiological capability of women to bear children), all of which must depress subsequent birth levels. The problem can partly be resolved by an appreciation of the differing time-lags involved and of the precise measures of fertility adopted.

The relevance of marriage-inheritance theory declines wherever new employment opportunities, detached from land inheritance, become available to Europe's peasantry. In several villages in the East Midlands of England, Chambers (1965) and Levine (1974) recognize the stimulus to younger marriage and higher fertility given by the development of intensive rural industries in the eighteenth century. Gaunt (1976) notes that communities supported by a mix of farming and iron ore mining had particularly high fertility in seventeenth and eighteenth century Sweden, clearly reflecting manpower demand. Similarly Braun (1978) recognizes, partly by analysing spatially disaggregated data, that proto-industrialization through the development of cottage textile industries in the countryside around Zurich in the eighteenth century led to earlier marriage, more universal marriage and higher overall fertility. He shows that peasants were traditionally reluctant to divide their holdings among several sons, but the growth of alternative or supplementary industrial employment undermined the traditional normative obstacles to early marriage and farm division.

The widespread fertility fall in pre-industrial Europe is thus generally attributed to a distinctive, socially regulated marriage pattern. In addition, there is evidence from several parts of Europe for some degree of voluntary fertility control within marriage. One can speculate on the means adopted – *coitus interuptus*, folk abortion, sheaths of linen or animal intestines – but the demographic evidence from some reconstitution studies is clear enough. Levels of achieved fertility fluctuate over time and space and invariably fall well below the estimated biological maximum (probably 10–12 births for the average early-married woman). Van de Walle and Knodel (1980) argue that such fluctuations reflect physiological, nutritional and social factors like variable breastfeeding customs, rather than conscious birth control. Nevertheless, schedules of age-specific marital fertility sometimes show a marked reduction after thirty years of age, when desired family size may have been achieved, invariably indicating the practice of individual fertility control. Not only is this recognizable in high-status groups like the French aristocracy (Levy and Henry 1960) and the Geneva bourgeoisie (Henry 1956), but also, more importantly, in some peasant communities. A good example is provided by Wrigley's reconstruction of vital rates in the Devon village of Colyton (Tables 4.2 and 4.3). Note, in particular, the dip in marital fertility in the second half of the seventeenth century, attributed by Wrigley to sharply worsening economic conditions.

Table 4.2   *Mean completed family size in Colyton, England*

| | Age at marriage | | |
	15–24	25–29	30–39
1560–1629	7·3	5·7	2·7
1646–1719	5·0	3·3	1·7
1720–1769	5·8	3·8	2·4
1770–1837	7·3	4·5	3·2

Source: Wrigley (1966b), table 11

Table 4.3   *Age-specific marital fertility rates (per 1000), Colyton, England, 1647–1719*

15–19	20–24	25–29	30–34	35–39	40–44	45–49
500	346	395	272	182	104	20

Source: Wrigley (1966b), table 4

Clearly our accumulating knowledge of the pre-modern transition has demolished the once prevalent view that a shift from uncontrolled to controlled fertility came only with appreciable development and urbanization. It is now being suggested that pre-industrial Europe had developed a homeostatic demographic regime (D.S. Smith 1977) – a self-regulating system which very roughly matched procreation in the community to the carrying capacity of the environment.

The modern transition

It is possible to argue that the achievement of significant fertility reduction in northwestern Europe preceding significant socio-economic development is a refutation of demographic transition theory. But it is more generally held that this is not a serious problem for acceptability, provided that fertility drops considerably after effective development begins. This condition is met in nearly all European countries, in a manner typified by Sweden and Denmark (Figure 4.1). Here the crude birth rates of about 30–33 per 1000 achieved in the pre-modern transition are further and appreciably lowered in response to modernization forces gathering momentum in Scandinavia from the late nineteenth century.

It must, however, be emphasized that the fertility response to socio-economic development in nineteenth- and early twentieth-century Europe was by no means

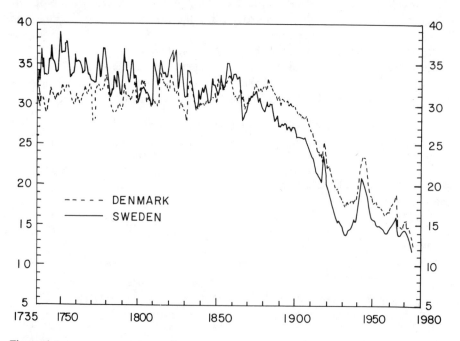

Figure 4.1
Crude birth rates in Sweden and Denmark, 1735-1976
Sources: Bogue (1969), figure 3-4; Matthiessen (1972), figure 1; UN *Demographic Yearbooks*

simple and uniform. It has proved impossible to determine anything like a threshold of development at which significant fertility decline commences. Van de Walle and Knodel (1967) attempted this task by considering indicators of development in 16 European countries at the time they commenced modern fertility decline – the date at which an index of marital fertility, during a sustained period of decline, fell to 10 percent below its highest level. They were confounded by the results: about 1800 for France compared with the early 1890s for Germany and England and Wales, where the pace and extent of industrialization and urbanization had been much more dramatic; 1894 for Scotland, when 13 percent of the male labour force was in agriculture, compared with 1910 for Finland, when the equivalent figure was 66 percent; 1908 for Austria, when the literacy rate in the adult population was 79 percent, compared with 1912 and only 40 percent in Bulgaria. They concluded, not unnaturally, that there was little in the statistical record for Europe to confirm the existence of an association between the beginning of fertility decline and any specific threshold of economic and social development.

One of the prime confounding factors is that in several parts of Europe fertility actually increased, albeit temporarily, at the beginning of industrialization. We have noted this effect with the growth of cottage industries in the eighteenth century, and similarly in the early years of nineteenth-century industrialization the effect of new employment opportunities on fertility seems to have been mediated through a relaxation of inhibitive marital customs. Data from the 1861 census reveal that the five counties of England with the youngest mean age at first marriage of women born 1826–1841 and married 1841–1861 were the rapidly industrializing counties of Durham, Staffordshire, Northampton, Lancashire and Yorkshire West Riding, while the five counties at the other end of the marriage-age spectrum were essentially rural – Somerset, Berkshire, Shropshire, Hereford and Rutland (Crafts 1978).

Coalmining areas, in particular, seem to show this fertility increase. Wrigley (1961) has identified several such areas in Europe, while British examples are provided by South Wales and Durham (Table 4.4). Friedlander (1973) and Haines (1977) demonstrate that the higher fertility of mining areas was due not only to early marriage but also to high marital fertility. This would be stimulated by the

Table 4.4 *Gross reproduction rate (per woman) in three predominantly coalmining and heavy industrial counties, England and Wales, 1851–1911.*

	1851	1861	1871	1881	1891	1911
Glamorgan	2·35	2·56	2·69	2·61	2·57	2·08
Monmouth	2·32	2·50	2·70	2·55	2·53	2·07
Durham	2·58	2·73	2·98	2·75	2·57	2·08
England and Wales	2·22	2·28	2·35	2·30	2·01	1·42

Source: Friedlander (1973–1974), table 3, By permission of The University of Chicago Press, © 1973 by The University of Chicago

lack of female employment opportunities, particularly after 1842 legislation forbidding underground work by women, and by the nature and health risks of mining which curtailed the effective working life of miners, thereby creating a need for unmarried working sons to support the family.

Population geographers should be particularly interested in the cartographic method adopted by Coale (1969) to clarify the links between European fertility declines and development. On the basis of assiduously collated data for more than 700 areas within Europe (excluding only the Southeast), he produced maps of overall fertility, marital fertility and proportion of females married in the child-bearing ages, all for the year 1900, which is close to the median date for the onset of significant fertility decline in Europe's national populations. The specialized indices used for the three maps need not be described fully here, except to say that they attempt a standardization for age in the absence of detailed age-specific fertility statistics.* The resultant patterns (simplified in Figures 4.2, 4.3 and 4.4) give an absorbing but complex snapshot of spatial fertility conditions at one critical moment in time.

Although Hajnal's western European marriage pattern of late marriage and widespread celibacy was breaking down in the nineteenth century, Figure 4.2 confirms the importance still at 1900 of his Leningrad to Trieste divide, with the highest incidence of marriage being in Hungary, Poland and the non-Baltic provinces of Russia. High rates are also found in southern Spain, where the Moorish element in Spanish cultural tradition is somewhat fancifully cited by Coale, and in parts of France, where an unusually early decline in marital fertility had enabled the lifting of normative restrictions on marriage. At the other end of the scale, Ireland reveals its well-known marital response to the famines of the mid-century. A precarious population-resources balance may also account for low marriage incidence in the Scottish highlands.

The most striking feature of the marital fertility pattern (Figure 4.3) is the remarkable low fertility throughout France, Brittany alone excepted. Even more remarkable is the fact that fertility in this largely rural country had fallen consistently from the very beginning of the nineteenth century. As early as the 1801–1810 decade crude birth rates below 25 per 1000 had been reached by the five departments of Normandy, and a dozen other departments recorded rates of 25–29 per 1000 (Van de Walle 1978). An often-cited reason has been the inheritance provisions of the 1804 Civil Code which, in line with the egalitarian philosophy of the

---

* The index of marital fertility for any area is constructed from:
(a) vital statistics records of the number of legitimate births to married women in that area during a particular period
(b) census data of the number of women in that area in each age group
(c) a known age-specific fertility schedule of a population with extraordinarily high fertility – Hutterite women in North Dakota married in the 1920s.
The index is calculated by comparing the actual number of legitimate births in the particular area and period with the number that would be expected if married women there were experiencing the Hutterite age-specific fertility schedule.

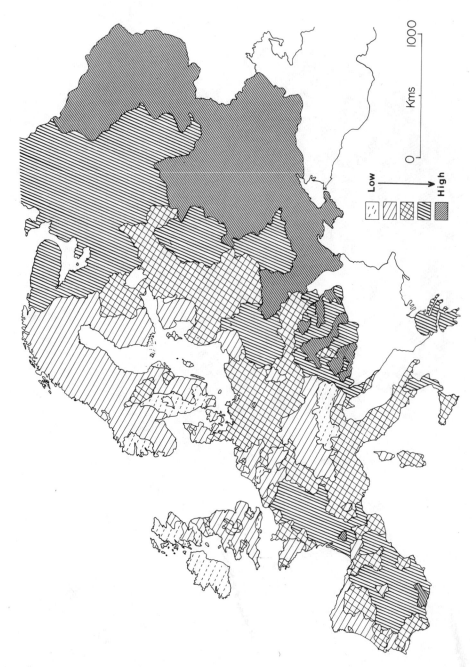

Figure 4.2
Index of proportion married among women of child-bearing age, 1900
Source: simplified from Coale (1969), map 1.   By permission of The University of Michigan
Press, © 1969 by The University of Michigan.

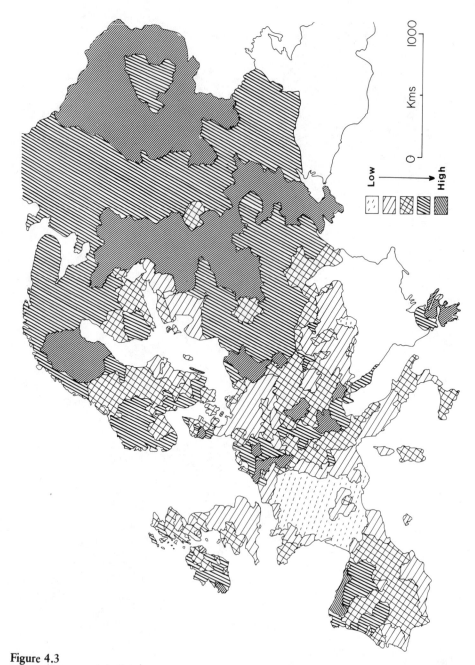

Figure 4.3
Index of marital fertility, 1900
Source: simplified from Coale (1969), map 2.   By permission of The University of Michigan
Press, © 1969 by The University of Michigan.

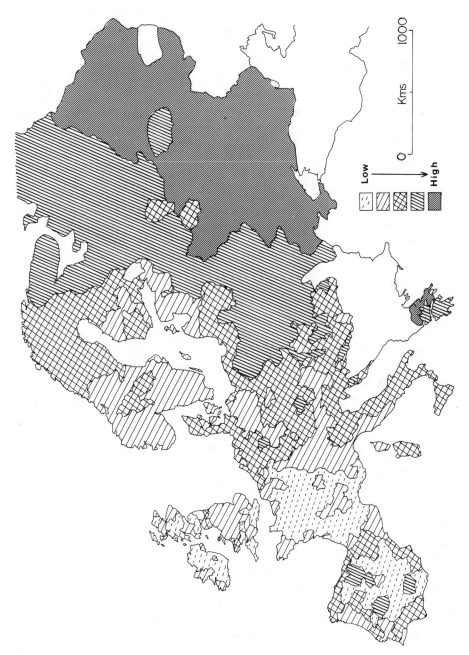

Figure 4.4
Index of overall fertility, 1900
Source: simplified from Coale (1969), map 3.   By permission of The University of Michigan Press, © 1969 by The University of Michigan.

Revolution, required Frenchmen to divide the bulk of their property equally between their children. It is argued that the peasantry adopted small families as a conscious mean of avoiding excessive fragmentation of holdings. This explanation is now recognized, at best, as simplistic. Hermalin and Van de Walle (1977) show that primogeniture was by no means universal before the Revolution and that inheritance practices remained diverse and often contrary to the spirit of the Code throughout the nineteenth century. They attempt to analyse by multivariate statistical methods the relationship between inheritance pattern and demographic characteristics in a series of cross-sections, using departments as the units of analysis, but their results are inconclusive.

Van de Walle (1978) also uses departmental data in a series of correlations for various years in the nineteenth century between indicators of fertility, mortality and rural wealth. He achieves some progress, by finding, for example, that the poorest areas with high mortality, like Brittany, preserve relatively high fertility, but he again concludes (p. 288) that 'France will remain the tantalising puzzle.' At the most general level of explanation, one can suggest that there seems to have been a unique combination in rural France of the need for, and the knowledge of, contraception within marriage. Compared with other parts of western Europe, agricultural improvements were slow to develop, the supply of unused land was restricted, industrialization was retarded, and emigration was made difficult by the loss of colonies. There was thus a clear need for fertility restraint among the peasantry to avoid demographic crises. At the same time, the means of achieving this were more readily available and acceptable in France, partly because its nobility had long been European leaders in the practice of contraception and partly because the Revolution had promoted rational attitudes towards the control of one's destiny.

Even if one excludes France as a very special case, it is still difficult to interpret the pattern of Figure 4.3 in relation to levels of regional economic development. One can find some support for the expected inverse relationship – low marital fertility, for example, in Catalonia, Piedmont-Liguria and the Stockholm area, and high marital fertility in Ireland, Greece, Poland and Russia. Yet major anomalies occur, like low fertility in the rural southern provinces of Hungary, which Demeny (1972) attempts with difficulty to explain, and high fertility throughout Belgium and the Netherlands. Van de Walle and Knodel (1980) speculate that the key to understanding the spatial pattern is to be found less in socio-economic forces than in the partly, but not completely, related socio-cultural changes in female status, secularization and individual aspirations, all of which are difficult to measure.

The map of overall fertility (Figure 4.4) shows essentially the combined effect of nuptiality (Figure 4.2) and marital fertility (Figure 4.3). High values for both components ensure very high overall fertility in Greece and in many parts of eastern Europe, particularly in Russia. The same pattern is shown to a lesser extent in Spain. Elsewhere in western and northern Europe there is a fairly uniform pattern of low or modest overall fertility, although it is often derived very differently – in the case of Ireland, for example, from low nuptiality and high marital fertility and in the case of Aquitane from high nuptiality and low marital fertility.

It should be appreciated that the transition in Europe from high fertility in traditional agrarian societies to low fertility in modernized societies, while a universal feature, has been accomplished in different ways and at different rates of progress. A useful scheme summarizing the most critical aspects of the transition has been provided by Matras (1965). He identifies four strategies of family formation:

	Uncontrolled Fertility	Controlled Fertility
Early Marriage	A	B
Late Marriage	C	D

Strategy A is present in parts of the Third World today and characterized the whole of Europe up until the sixteenth century, when Strategy C was adopted in northwestern Europe to form its pre-modern transition. The transition C to B in this area constitutes the modern transition. There is no doubt about the general move to younger marriage, as Figure 4.5 demonstrates, but the transition from C to B could have been accomplished via A or D. In some industrial areas a path via A may well have been followed, but the more common passage was through the intermediate stage D in which marital fertility was now controlled but marriage remained late. In this way early marriage was made possible by substituting fertility control within marriage for delayed marriage and celibacy as the prime means of restraining population growth. Individual, rational control over fertility had replaced the unconscious control exerted by society norms. Thus the distinctive and repressive western European marriage pattern disappeared when it was no longer necessary. In Europe to the east of Hajnal's Leningrad-Trieste divide the move was directly from A to B, although generally delayed until the early decades of this century.

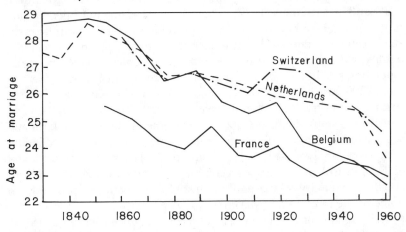

Figure 4.5
Mean age at first marriage for females in four European countries, 1830-1960
Source: Van de Walle (1972), figure 1

The transition outside Europe

In the developed countries of North America, Australasia and Japan the progress to low controlled fertility provides interesting comparisons and contrasts to European experience.

In North America there is no equivalent to western Europe's pre-modern transition achieved through delayed marriage. In the United States the very high fertility rates up to the beginning of the nineteenth century are commonly attributed to ready availability of land in a frontier nation. Coale and Zelnick (1963) estimate that in 1800 the crude birth rate was 55 per 1000 and the total fertility rate 7.0 per woman. There then ensued a long period of fertility decline until the 1940s. The crude birth rate fell to about 43 per 1000 in 1850, 30 per 1000 in 1900 and 18 per 1000 in 1940, with the equivalent figures for the total fertility rate being 5.2, 3.2 and 2.0. That part of the decline from the late nineteenth-century is explicable in terms of increasing industrialization, urbanization and general modernization – standard demographic transition theory – but the earlier nineteenth-century decline in an essentially agricultural country is more intriguing. The popular modern explanation (e.g., Easterlin 1976a) is that, as the nation's agricultural land filled up, farmers became increasingly concerned about their children's ability to acquire good farmland; hence they began to limit family size. Empirical evidence supports this view. Yasuba (1961) found that in the first half of the nineteenth century state and territory birth rates were strongly correlated negatively to population densities, suggesting that in the older settled areas relative scarcity of land contributed to fertility decline, while in the frontier regions of the West the availability of free or cheap land maintained high fertility. These conclusions are confirmed by more sophisticated regression analyses undertaken by Forster and Tucker (1972).

A similar relationship between fertility and the density and nature of agricultural settlement is found by McGinnis (1977) to have been operating in Upper Canada (the southern part of contemporary Ontario) in the mid-nineteenth century. On the basis of data from 55 counties he demonstrates a strong inverse correlation between fertility, measured by child-woman ratios, and population density, measured by population size in relation to maximum acreage ever cultivated. He also uses data from 1200 farm households, extracted from manuscript returns of census enumerators, to demonstrate that fertility levels were at their highest in the most recently settled townships. In such frontier environments not only is farmland likely to be available to the subsequent generation but, in addition, 'Surrounding oneself with a large family is a rational response to the generally hazardous and risky life of the more isolated settlers. As a community grows up, people are able to depend upon the community at large and even institutions organised specifically to shoulder some of the risk of life' (McGinnis 1977, p. 208).

In Australasia significant decline in marital fertility commenced in the 1880s, with a remarkable uniformity of timing and rate of decline exhibited by the individual Australian states and New Zealand (E. F. Jones 1971). Despite considerable geographical isolation of states from one another, their common cultural heritage and common experiences led to very similar patterns of change in reproductive behaviour, thus supporting the adjustment rather than the diffusion basis of demographic transition theory.

In pre-industrial Japan, as in Europe, there is now clear evidence from an accumulating series of local studies that fertility levels were both socially and individually controlled to combat population pressure in subsistence agrarian societies with few opportunities for territorial expansion. Hanley (1977) shows that age at marriage was late and that significant proportions of women never married. She also demonstrates strong evidence for fertility control within marriage. Women typically terminated child-bearing in their early- or mid-thirties after achieving an average family size of about three children. Such modest family sizes were regulated not only by fertility control, notably through abortion, but also by widespread resort to infanticide and child adoption. Adoptions were used negatively to divest families of excess children and positively to compensate for child deaths and, in particular, to ensure the existence of male heirs.

Japanese demographic evolution is also reminiscent of parts of Europe in that fertility almost certainly rose under the initial impact of economic modernization from the mid-nineteenth century. Thus Taeuber (1958, p. 55) concludes: 'The Japanese experience supports the hypothesis that it is the transitional society that manifests the highest fertility.' She also considers (p. 55) 'the possibility that the fertility controls of an ancient society may decline simultaneously with the increase in the controls of an industrial society. If so, there may be a considerable period in which the demographic transition involves a change in the class incidence of family limitation but not in its total amount.' Certainly for a long time the overall decline in Japanese fertility was modest (crude birth rates of about 38 per 1000 in the 1880s, 30 per 1000 in the 1930s and 33 per 1000 in the late 1940s), bearing in mind the rapid pace of industrialization and urbanization. This has been explained by both Taeuber (1958) and Wilkinson (1967) in terms of the retarded pace of social as opposed to economic transformation. They cite the maintenance of a paternalistic labour situation and a traditional family-centred social organization which left cultural milieu and values virtually unchanged.

Japanese resistance to the small-family ideal finally crumbled in the 1950s, when in a single decade the crude birth rate was halved, providing the most concentrated fertility reduction ever achieved in the world. This may be interpreted as the inevitable accompaniment of further modernization, but a special instigating factor was the desperate demographic plight of Japan immediately following the Second World War. At a time of economic chaos and national demoralization the country had to absorb seven million Japanese from its lost empire and cope with a natural increase surge brought about by the rapid response of the death rate to medical and public health programmes. There was an immediate and widespread desire to limit family size in all social classes, and the prime means adopted was abortion, made available by the state on liberal grounds in 1948.

Post-transition trends

Demographic transition theory provides an adequate general explanation for the demographic evolution of developed countries until well into this century, and in particular for the sustained fertility fall which had lowered total fertility rates by the 1930s to between 1.5 and 2.0 births per woman, some way below generation-replacement levels. But in the last four decades, in the period aptly characterized by Campbell (1974) as 'beyond the demographic transition', there have been appreciable fluctuations in fertility in developed countries, as Figures 4.1 and 4.6 demonstrate. Although these fluctuations have been remarkably consistent from one country to another, they have rarely been predicted by demographers and they have defied attempts at definitive retrospective explanation.

It is possible to argue that these fluctuations are entirely compatible with demographic transition theory, in that the postwar fertility increases, as measured by period indices, are a response to temporary changes in the timing of births and marriages, with no appreciable impact on the long-term relationship between modernization and fertility reduction. According to this view, the fertility falls throughout the developed world from the mid-1960s reflect a return to normality after the exceptional postwar baby boom caused partly by the making up of marriages and births postponed during the war and partly by a general trend towards younger age at marriage, at least until about 1960. In England and Wales, for example, the married proportion of women aged twenty–twenty-four rose from 34 percent in 1939 to 59 percent in 1961, since when it has remained fairly constant, although declining somewhat in the 1970s to 55 percent in 1977.

More elaborate explanatory approaches have centred on variants of the basic economic theory of fertility (Becker 1960). The central part of the theory is that demand for children is determined by a household's attempt to maximize satisfaction by balancing its subjective tastes (the intensity of desire for children relative to goods and services) against the constraints and opportunities imposed by resources (largely income) and costs (monetary, time and effort). Thus the demand for children can be expected to vary directly with a couple's tastes or preferences and with its available resources, and inversely with expected costs.

Much attention has been focused on the resources or income factor, because of an apparent contradiction to the theory posed by the well-known secular association between growing affluence and falling fertility. But Weintraub (1962), Adelman (1963) and Heer (1966) show by international cross-sectional analysis that, when controls are instituted for factors like infant mortality and educational attainment, there is a positive relationship between fertility and national income per head. Moreover, time-series data have been used to demonstrate that the relationship in the *short-term* between income and both marriage and fertility is positive. Evidence to this effect from pre-industrial and nineteenth-century Europe presented earlier in this chapter is confirmed by the work of Kirk (1942), Galbraith and Thomas (1941) and Silver (1965) on the relationship between business cycles and demographic trends in Germany and the United States in the twentieth century.

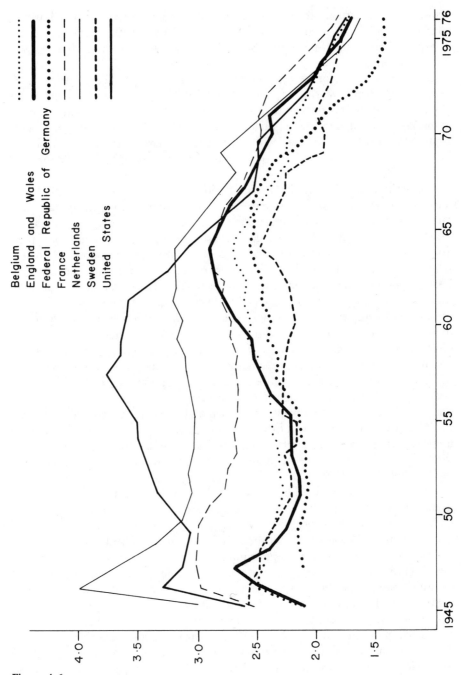

Belgium ....
England and Wales ━━━━━
Federal Republic of Germany ●●●●●●●
France ─────
Netherlands ──────
Sweden ─ ─ ─ ─
United States ━━━━━

Figure 4.6
Total fertility rates (per woman) in selected developed countries, 1945-1976

They find that marriages and births increase following an improvement of business conditions and decline when business falls away. Economic fluctuations can thus be expected to advance or postpone births, but their effect on ultimate family size is more problematical.

The income effect on fertility helps to explain the enhanced fertility levels between the Second World War and the mid-1960s, since there were appreciable and continuous rises in per capita income in most developed countries at that time, in marked contrast to the depressed levels of the 1930s. One can also argue that the fertility falls of the 1960s and 1970s are to some extent a consequence of slower income growth and growing economic insecurity, expressed in inflation and unemployment.

It is in the work of Easterlin (1968, 1976b, 1978) that the economic theory of fertility has been most widely developed and most successfully operationalized in an interpretation of fertility fluctuations. He argues that the critical determinant of a couple's demand for children is the relationship between their resources and their aspirations for consumption of goods and services. If their resources are scarce relative to their aspirations, they will be more reluctant to have additional children. Easterlin suggests that a major influence on aspirations is the standard of consumption that young adults have inculcated from the households in which they were raised. For example, young couples brought up by parents experiencing a low income and low material standard of living tend, in turn, to have low aspirations concerning their own consumption of goods and services. He argues that this was an important cause of the postwar baby boom, in that young couples had only modest consumption aspirations because of their upbringing in the Depression years of the 1930s. Consequently they felt they could afford several children, particularly in an era of buoyant labour demand and general prosperity. But the reverse pattern became evident by the late 1960s, when young couples had greatly increased aspirations for material consumption fashioned by their upbringing in the prosperous 1950s; hence the preference for goods and services over children in the late 1960s and 1970s.

Similar reasoning was used by Banks (1954) to explain the initiation of modern fertility reduction in England in the 1880s. He observes that the English middle classes were relatively prosperous between about 1850 and 1870, but a major depression in 1873 was the harbinger of several lean years. Middle-class incomes did not fall in real terms, but opportunities narrowed and the rapid growth of incomes ceased. Since, however, the aspirations of middle-class families continued to grow, parents perceived a worsening of their economic situation and thus restricted their family size.

Easterlin has also identified another important cyclical influence on the relationship between resources and aspirations. This is the echo effect of fertility on the age structure of the male working population. He demonstrates that the low fertility of the 1930s reduced the proportion of younger to older workers in the late 1940s and the 1950s, so that the consequent labour demand for young workers ensured a high level of prosperity (resources) for potential parents. The resultant high fertility led in turn to a flooding of the job market with young workers in the 1960s and 1970s, so that the relative prosperity of the child-bearing cohort was undermined. The age structure of the working population is not, of course, the only influence on the relative prosperity of the child-bearing cohort, but it does seem to exert an important cyclical influence, as Figures 4.7 and 4.8 demonstrate. In these graphs the waves or swings in fertility in the United States and England and Wales relate very closely to an index of labour force age structure. An important inference from the graphs is that fertility rates might well start to climb in the 1980s, but Easterlin does recognize that while the goodness-of-fit between fertility and age structure over the 1940–1970 period is impressive in the United States, England and Wales, Australia and Canada, it is much less so in several countries of continental Europe.

Readers will appreciate that this explanatory account of fertility fluctuations has concentrated on elements embraced by the economic theory of fertility. There are, of course, additional influences at work, which can be incorporated with varying degrees of difficulty into a costs, resources and tastes framework. The increasing participation of women in the labour force has often been cited as a contributory

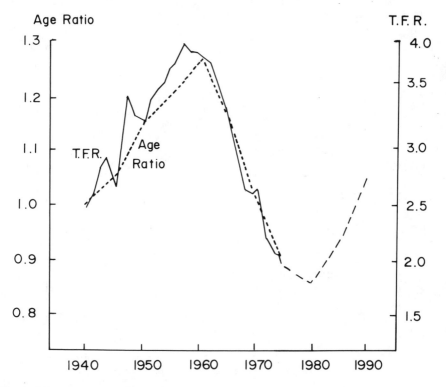

Figure 4.7
United States: total fertility rate (per woman), 1940-1975, and actual and projected ratio of males aged 35-64 to males aged 15-34
Source: Easterlin (1976b)

factor to modern fertility declines, and clearly this can be regarded as a cost constraint on family building – the income foregone in child-rearing. Other influences, like the role in fertility reduction of the feminist movement and of the conservation and zero population growth lobbies, can possibly be incorporated as influencing tastes. But the more liberal provision of legal abortion facilities and improved contraceptive technology, notably the widespread adoption of the oral pill from the mid-1960s, can hardly be incorporated in the economic theory of fertility since they do not influence demand for children. In any case, the significance of their role in fertility reduction is problematical. Some have argued (e.g., Westoff 1975) that the decline in unwanted births resulting from more widespread use of more effective birth control practices has been a major factor in fertility decline in some developed countries since the mid-1960s. On the other hand, a historical perspective reveals that knowledge of, and access to, what might be regarded as at any time the more modern forms of birth control have never been important independent influences on fertility. Attitudes and values towards child-bearing have always been the critical factor. The limited influence of birth control

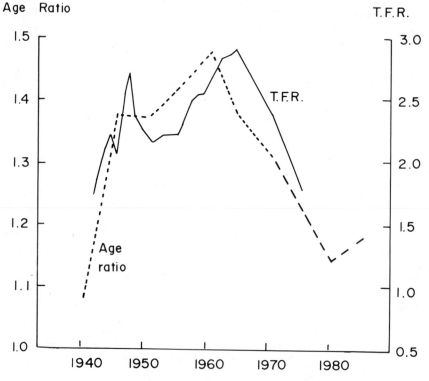

Figure 4.8
England and Wales: total fertility rate (per woman), 1940-1975, and actual and projected ratio of males aged 35-64 to males aged 15-34
Source: Easterlin and Condran (1976), figure 5

technology can be inferred from the wide range of traditional and modern methods used in several developed countries in the early 1970s (Table 4.5). All of these countries were experiencing pronounced fertility decline, but were achieving it by the use of very different methods. In particular, one should note the heavy reliance in some countries on primitive methods like withdrawal.

The remarkably consistent pattern of post-transition fertility fluctuations in Western developed countries has not been followed by the USSR and eastern Europe. Andorka (1978) has emphasized the diversity of trends within this area. In the rather less developed countries of Yugoslavia and Poland, appreciable and sustained declines in total fertility rates (from about 3.5 births per woman in the early 1950s to 2.2 in the early 1970s) can be explained reasonably adequately in terms of general modernization, i.e., demographic transition theory. In the USSR, fertility did not begin to decline significantly until after 1960, with its Asian regions being particularly resistant, but in Hungary, Czechoslovakia, East Germany, Bulgaria and Rumania pronounced fertility reduction in the 1950s had brought about the lowest fertility levels in the world during the 1960s. In 1962, for example, the total fertility rate in Hungary was 1.8 births per woman, when the United States rate was still 3.5. Particular factors cited have been the housing shortages associated with intensive urbanward migration, and also the wide availability of government abortions from the mid-1950s to promote maternal welfare and female employment. In these countries there has been no further secular reduction in fertility in the 1970s, enabling many developed Western countries to overtake them in fertility reduction. There have been short-term fluctuations, some of which can be related to government policies in the field of abortion provision and family allowances. The most spectacular, although short-lived, example was the doubling of the Rumanian total fertility rate from 1.9 births per woman in 1966 to 3.7 in 1967, consequent upon a reversal of previously permissive abortion laws.

Table 4.5   Percentage distribution of contraceptors by main method used, revealed by 1970–1972 social surveys

	Denmark	Finland	USA	France	Czecho-slovakia
IUD	4	4	9	2	14
Pill	37	26	41	17	4
Condoms	30	40	17	12	19
Diaphragm	9	–	7	1	–
Withdrawal	7	21	3	52	52
Rhythm	2	1	8	14	3
Other	11	8	16	2	8
Total	100	100	100	100	100

Source: Economic Commission for Europe (1976)

Differential fertility

Sociologists have studied in great detail the ways in which fertility varies within developed societies by social patterning based on variables like class, income and religion. It might be argued that population geographers, on the other hand, should be more interested in the fashioning of spatial fertility variations by ecological patterning. Yet such patterning is itself largely the product of particular spatial mixes of social factors. Thus the attributes of an area which fashion its fertility level are essentially those discussed in sociological literature as differential fertility, so that they are of central interest to population geographers.

The essence of differential fertility is that within national societies there exist social groupings with particular norms and values concerning family size. These groupings overlap, since they can be based on one or several variables, making it analytically difficult to assess the impact of specific variables.

The significance of fertility differentials varies over time, particularly in relation to stage of demographic development. This is why differential fertility figures prominently in demographic transition theory, since fertility decline is regarded as starting in particular social groups and then diffusing throughout society, with time-lags due to group differences in values and attitudes and in birth control practices. Therefore, as the demographic transition begins, fertility differentials are at their widest. As the transition progresses, differentials can be expected to diminish and possibly disappear in post-transition societies of the modern world. Yet the evidence presented here is that fertility differentials are remarkably persistent, fully warranting the contemporary attention of population geographers.

The major variables in differential fertility will now be reviewed, followed by a consideration of how such variables have been incorporated by population geographers in spatial analyses of fertility.

Social class

In the major period of fertility decline in developed countries between the 1880s and the 1930s there emerged a marked negative relationship between social class and fertility. This was because small-family norms and the practice of effective birth control were first adopted in higher status groups, before being diffused down the class gradient. But as diffusion nears completion in contemporary societies, there has been a narrowing of differentials, and even some inversion in the higher status groups. In other words, a U-shaped pattern has emerged, with the lowest fertility now being found in groups of intermediate status (Figure 4.9 and Table 4.6). Members of these groups (Social Classes II and IIIN in the British classification – managers, teachers, clerks, etc.) are expected to conform to bourgeois standards of dress, housing and material possessions, but since they have progressive salary scales they have only modest incomes during the family-building period of their life-cycles. Thus, accordingly to the economic theory of fertility, their resources (and consequently their fertility) are restrained in a way not experienced by the more affluent professional groups or by manual workers whose maximum

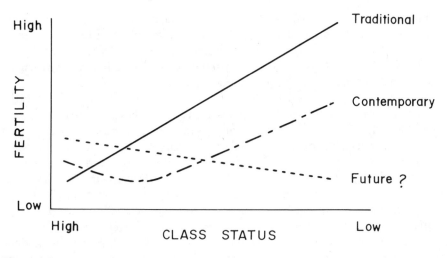

Figure 4.9
Relationship between fertility and class status in developed countries

earning power is achieved in early manhood.

Recent evidence suggests that differentials continue to narrow. Between 1970 and 1975 the number of legitimate live births in England and Wales by social class of husband fell by only 4 percent in Social Classes I and II but by 33 percent in Classes IV and V, with only a marginal contribution to this disparity being made by changes in the size and distribution of the population at risk through social mobility and other factors (Pearce and Britton 1977). This is why there has been some speculation that the future relationship between class and fertility might very well be a postive one (Figure 4.9). It is, however, hard to imagine that the lowest status groups will not retain their relatively high fertility. Such groups constitute what some have termed an 'underclass', exhibiting in life-styles a 'culture of poverty' (Lewis 1959), embracing attitudes of fatalism, apathy, lack of long-range planning and the like which ensure the maintenance of high fertility and high mortality. A useful case study in this area is that by Askham (1975) of fertility motivation and behaviour among working-class families in Aberdeen.

Table 4.6   Average family size for women married once only (before 45) by social class* of husband and duration of marriage, England and Wales, 1971

	I	II	IIIN	IIIM	IV	V	All
10–14 years	2·23	2·12	1·99	2·28	2·30	2·56	2·24
15–19 years	2·25	2·17	2·00	2·34	2·37	2·66	2·29

* For definition of social classes, see, p. 53
Source: 1971 Census of Population, *Fertility Tables*

Two components of social class which are thought to contribute particularly strongly to fertility differentials are educational attainment and family income. Using data from the 1-in-a-100 Public Use Sample census tapes in the United States, Rindfuss and Sweet (1977) have demonstrated that fertility differentials by female educational attainment are both appreciable and persistent (Figure 4.10). One factor is likely to be the tendency for later marriage among more highly educated women. Another concerns the tastes or preferences of such women, in that they are more likely to have major interests and commitments outside family life. Then again, more educated couples are likely to be more efficient family planners.

The income variable is more complex to interpret. According to the basic economic theory of fertility, one should expect a positive relationship between fertility and family income, whether income is measured currently or in terms of long-term income prospects (Easterlin's 'potential income'); in other words, better-off couples can afford, and are likely to achieve, larger families. In reality, however, fertility usually varies inversely with income – 'the rich get richer and the poor get children'. Becker (1960) felt able to resolve the anomaly by pointing to the differing abilities of groups to match desired fertility with achieved fertility. He argued that, when contraceptive efficiency in a population is extremely low or extremely high, fertility does respond to income in the predicted fashion. Thus the positive relationship between income and fertility has been found both among pre-transition Polish peasants (Stys 1957) and among those members of a surveyed

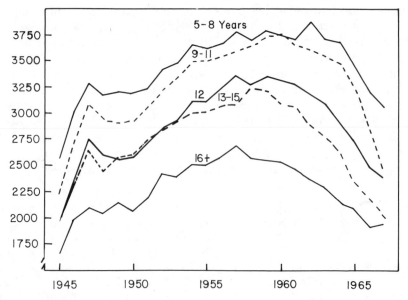

Figure 4.10
Total fertility rates (per 1000) in five education groups, based on number of years spent by women in full-time education: United States, 1945-1967
Source: Rindfuss and Sweet (1977), figure 3-1.   By permission of Academic Press, Inc.

population in Indianapolis who admitted to being completely successful in controlling the number and spacing of their children (Kiser and Whelpton 1953). Another explanation of the anomaly is that income is correlated with other fertility-influencing variables like education and urbanization, so that the generally low fertility of high-status groups is due to high educational attainment and urban life-style, *despite* a high-income level. Some demographers do not accept these arguments and insist like Blake (1968) that babies are not consumer durables; there is something qualitatively different between the decision to have a child and the decision to purchase a new car or washing machine.

Perhaps the most acceptable expression of the income effect on fertility is in the so-called relative income hypothesis (D. Freedman 1963). This suggests that fertility is positively related to relative income (the relationship between a person's income and that of his peer group in terms of age, education, class, residence, etc.). Thus the more affluent a couple within its reference group, the higher will be its fertility.

Female employment

It is often argued that participation by women in the labour force makes demands on time and energy at the expense of child-raising, thereby accounting for the inverse relationship consistently found within developed countries between fertility level and proportion of married women working; this is perhaps one reason for the relatively low fertility often found in textile areas. But it is far from proven that participation in the labour force influences fertility more than the reverse (Terry 1973). It must be recognized that women drop out of employment because they have children, and that some women seek employment because of subfecundity or sterility in themselves or their partners.

Much depends also on the nature of employment. The conflict between roles of mother and worker is most acute in the case of full-time, career-structured employment outside the home. There is less incompatibility when employment is part-time or based on the family home. This is how Federici (1968) accounts for the lack of any relationship between female employment and fertility in agricultural southern Italy, in contrast to the normal inverse relationship found in urban and industrial northern Italy.

Religion

Within Western developed countries the fertility of Roman Catholics is invariably higher than that of Protestants because of differences between the two socio-religious groups in both practice of birth control and in desired family size. The proscription by the Roman Catholic Church on methods of birth control other than abstinence and the rhythm method is well known, although survey data have revealed sharp rises in the proportion of Catholic women deviating from the birth control teaching of their church – from 30 percent of American women aged twenty–twenty-four in 1955 to 78 percent in 1970 (Westoff and Bumpass 1973). More important is thought to be the higher value attached to a larger family in

Catholic doctrine than in Protestant teaching, which tends to emphasize more the quality rather than the quantity of children.

Protestantism itself covers a wide spectrum of denominations, and there is plenty of evidence (e.g., Ryder and Westoff 1971) to show that the more fundamentalist groups like Mormons, Nazarenes, Pentecostals and Jehovah's Witnesses in the United States have fertility levels as high as Catholics. It is significant that the Mormon state of Utah exhibits by far the highest fertility rate of American states. In 1976 its crude birth rate of 29.3 per 1000 was double the national rate of 14.7 per 1000, despite its population being heavily city-based – a factor which would normally inhibit high fertility.

It has sometimes been argued (e.g., Petersen 1969) that in Western societies religion does not have a significant independent effect on fertility, in so far as fertility differences between religious groups are essentially due to the differing compositions of these groups by occupation, education and the like. While Protestants have a socio-economic structure close to the national average, Catholics are over-represented in low-status groups, and Jews, who have the lowest fertility of all, are over-represented in high-status urban groups. Yet whenever attempts are made to standardize for socio-economic structure (Freedman, Whelpton and Smit 1961, Lenski 1961, Compton 1978), the Protestant-Catholic fertility differential does survive, not least because the normal inverse relationship between fertility and class structure does not occur among Catholics; higher status Catholics, it seems, are more likely to heed church advice on family size.

Although some demographers (Westoff 1975, Jones and Westoff 1979) are predicting the imminent disappearance of the Catholic-Protestant fertility differential in the United States, some of the more refined surveys of fertility intentions suggest otherwise. Coombs (1979) has developed a new measure of family-size preference from a short series of survey questions. He recognizes that when individuals give a stated preference that is discrete and fixed, they may, in fact, be selecting one number out of a range of acceptable possibilities. For example, two people may select three children as a first preference, but if one picks two and then one as second and third choices, and the other chooses four and then five, then the preferences underlying their first choice of three are very different. The problem is confounded by preferences for the sex of children. Accordingly, Coombs has developed a scale (IN–1 to IN–7) which measures a respondent's underlying preference or bias towards family size. From 1973 survey data in the United States (Table 4.7), he shows that being Catholic contributes to an underlying preference for a larger family, particularly if both husband and wife are Catholic. Where only the husband is Catholic, the wife's preferences are about the same as in wholly non-Catholic families.

A provocative hypothesis is that Catholic fertility will be particularly elevated in those societies in which Catholics constitute an appreciable minority (van Heek 1956, Day 1968). In such circumstances there may well be a stricter adherence to basic Catholic principles and, particularly if there is a feeling of discrimination, there might be an incentive to increase the demographic strength of one's group

Table 4.7   Percentage distribution of family-size preference (measured by IN-scale 1–7)* by social characteristics: married women, 15–44, United States, 1973

	Small family ——————— Large family				
	IN 1–2	3	4	5	IN 6–7
Religion of husband and wife					
Both Catholic	14	15	25	25	21
Wife only Catholic	23	19	25	19	15
Husband only Catholic	29	22	24	16	9
Neither Catholic	29	21	25	14	11
Ethnicity of wife					
Spanish origin	14	14	27	18	27
All other	26	20	24	17	13
Race of wife					
Black	35	15	19	15	17
White	24	20	25	17	13

* In IN number does not indicate the number of children preferred; it is a scale number indicating place on a continuum from small to large family-size preference.
Source: Coombs (1979), table 2

within the national community. This is how Day explains that fertility is higher in the important Catholic minorities in the United Kingdom, Switzerland, the Netherlands, the United States, Canada, Australia and New Zealand than in the Catholic majorities of France, Belgium, Luxembourg, Italy and Austria.

An expression of this theory at work in the contemporary world is surely to be found in Northern Ireland, where there is active hostility between the Protestant and Catholic communities. At the 1971 census Catholics comprised 37 percent of the country's total population, and in the same year their total fertility rate of 4140 per 1000 was a remarkable 50 percent higher than the equivalent rate of 2760 per 1000 among Protestants (Compton 1976). Compton shows that a projection of growth in the two communities, based purely on fertility and mortality schedules of the early 1970s, would lead to a Roman Catholic majority in Northern Ireland by 2011, although if one takes recognition of the greater susceptibility of Catholics to emigration on the basis of the 1961–1971 records, such a majority would be delayed until 2031. The social and political implications are immense.

Canada provides another intriguing test case, where the French-speaking, almost entirely Catholic population of Quebec comprises just over one-quarter of Canada's population. Perhaps nowhere in the world was the Catholic large-family ideal more effectively realized, since it was reinforced by nationalist propaganda of the *revanche des bercaux* type. It was the high fertility of French Canadians that ensured their political survival in face of a flood of English-speaking immigrants. But in recent times there has been a startling turnabout. Provincial fertility rates indicate that Quebec's premier position was already being eroded in the 1930s and that from about 1960 Quebec has consistently shown the *lowest* provincial fertility in Canada; in 1974, for example, its total fertility rate of 1657 per 1000 (compared with the national rate of 1875 per 1000) was far below replacement level. It is easier to chart than to explain this dramatic reversal (Long 1970, Beaujot 1978), but it can be argued that it does not necessarily invalidate the van Heek–Day hypothesis. This is because French-speaking Catholics, although comprising an appreciable minority within Canada, do comprise a large majority within Quebec, where there is already considerable autonomy within a federal state and where there are insistent demands for secession.

Urbanization

Among the most stable and persistent of fertility differentials has been the inverse relationship between urbanization and fertility, at least from the early stages of demographic transition when urban social conditions proved more conducive than those in the countryside for innovations like small-family preferences and modern birth control practices. Figure 4.11 shows the persistence of the urban–rural fertility differential in the United States up to 1970, while another example is provided by total fertility rates within Hungary in 1974: Budapest – 1797 per 1000, other urban centres – 2178 per 1000, villages – 2627 per 1000 (Andorka 1978, p.283). The differential seems to be maintained above all by the higher costs of raising and educating children in urban areas.

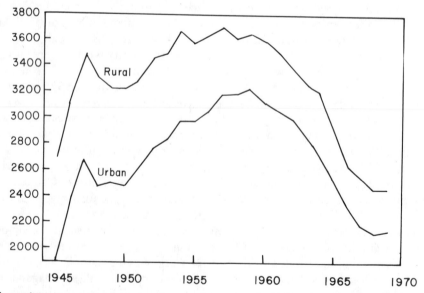

Figure 4.11
Total fertility rates (per 1000) for white rural and urban women: United States, 1945-1969
Source: Rindfuss and Sweet (1977), figure 7-1.   By permission of Academic Press, Inc.

Ethnicity

The only way in which the biological attribute of ethnic or racial group could possibly affect fertility is through fecundity, and there is simply no evidence for this. But since different ethnic groups within a country are likely to occupy different social situations, whether or not caused by discrimination, their fertility levels are likely to vary.

The plural nature of society in the United States provides an excellent context for studying this differential. Figure 4.12 depicts fertility levels for six American ethnic groups between 1955 and 1969. The pervasiveness of trends is a striking feature, suggesting that all six groups are responding to similar sets of stimuli. There has been some narrowing of differentials over the period, particularly between blacks and whites, but there is no evidence of substantial convergence. It can be argued that these differentials are simply the result of socio-economic differences between the groups, although attempts to test this hypothesis by controlling for factors like income and education have been inconclusive and even contradictory (Goldscheider and Uhlenberg 1969, Kennedy 1973, Roberts and Lee 1974).

Relevant to this problem are survey studies of family-size preferences. Ryder and Westoff (1971) report that in 1965 American blacks desired slightly less children than American whites (3.2 compared with 3.3 for married women with husband present), but that the expected number of children was greater for blacks (4.0 compared with 3.3); the preference for slightly smaller families among blacks than whites is confirmed by 1973 survey data (Table 4.7). On the basis of such findings,

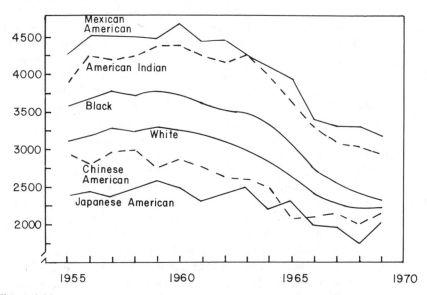

Figure 4.12
Total fertility rates (per 1000) for six ethnic groups: United States, 1955-1969
Source: Rindfuss and Sweet (1977), figure 5-1.   By permission of Academic Press, Inc.

Westoff (1975) and Weller (1979) consider that the higher fertility of blacks is caused by a higher proportion of unwanted births, so that with more effective family planning a convergence of black and white marital fertility is imminent. There is no doubt that among the most highly educated females fertility has for some time been lower among blacks (Rindfuss and Sweet 1977, figure 5.3).

Spatial analyses

A spatial perspective may well be the central concern of geographical analysis in population and other fields, but this is no justification for inferring that spatial analyses of fertility are the distinctive preserve of population geographers. There has, in fact, been considerable use by demographers of territorially disaggregated data in their attempts to understand the factors which influence fertility. The goal of such work is often to throw light on the dynamic relations between fertility decline and socio-economic change, particularly when time-series data are lacking, although Janowitz (1973) and Shin (1976-1977) are among those who have emphasized that cross-sectionally observed relationships between variables are not necessarily applicable to longitudinal inter-relations.

Reference has already been made to the way in which cross-sectional data have been profitably subjected to cartographic methods (Braun 1978, Coale 1969) and to statistical analysis (Yasuba 1961, Forster and Tucker 1972, McGinnis 1977, Van de Walle 1978). Additional work by nongeographers in this field is discussed extensively by Andorka (1978, chapter 4.3). He cites several works which profit-ably expose regional data to multivariate analysis. A Polish study of early 1960s' data reveals a positive relationship of fertility to both per capita income and its growth rate, but only when other aspects of modernization are controlled through the calculation of partial correlation coefficients. A Dutch study derives multiple correlation coefficients of 0.71 (1960 data) and 0.68 (1967 data) between fertility and a set of five socio-economic variables for 129 regions of the Netherlands. The most important variables were the percentages of population belonging to the Roman Catholic and Orthodox Reformed (Calvinist) Churches – socio-religious groups which have resisted more than others small-family norms.

A further example is drawn from Andorka's own research. After conventional regression analysis using 1960 census data for 191 districts of Hungary, in which he derived a multiple correlation coefficient of 0.68 between the total fertility rate and a set of four development indicators, he closely examined the pattern of residuals (deviations of individual units from the overall regression line). A sys-tematic pattern emerged, whereby the Northeast of the country revealed a higher than predicted fertility, while the reverse pattern was found in the agriculturally underdeveloped South. There are no obvious additional variables, derived from differential fertility theory, to explain these regional anomalies, which also seem to have existed at earlier periods. Andorka could provide only the most tentative hypotheses to explain how these traditions of low fertility in the South and relatively high fertility in the Northeast had developed independently of the modernization pattern.

It is clear, then, that some demographers have made detailed spatial studies of fertility, invariably with a view to testing hypotheses on the relationship between fertility and socio-economic factors. Such studies complement much more numerous studies using time-series data for national units and social survey data for individuals. There is, however, an interpretation problem associated with territorial data known as the ecological fallacy (W.S. Robinson 1950, Duncan et al. 1961, chapter 3). The essence is that one cannot crudely infer behaviour relating to individuals from aggregate population data relating to places. Andorka (1978) provides a good example from 1930 regional data in Hungary. In both bivariate and multivariate analysis there was a significant positive correlation between fertility and the percentage of Protestant population. But it would be premature to conclude on the basis of these results that Protestants had a higher fertility than the rest of the population. In fact, Protestants had the *lower* fertility in each region, the point being that in predominantly Protestant regions *each* denominational group had higher fertility. Much has been made of the ecological fallacy in sociological literature, but examples like the Hungarian one are rare, and by way of balance readers can be referred to a study by Duncan (1964) which, in assessing the relationship between fertility and house rents in an American city, found a very close accordance in results between an analysis using census tract data and one using individual survey data. He concludes (p.88): 'This exploration, therefore, seems to bolster our confidence in the general validity of the findings of studies in differential fertility where areal variation was the sole source of information on socio-economic differentials.'

From this short review it is obvious that population geography cannot claim spatial analysis of fertility as its own preserve, yet its practioners have made significant contributions. It is often impossible to distinguish between the work of demographers and population geographers in such analyses, but there is a tendency for the former to use an understanding of the spatial pattern as a means to an end, often to test hypotheses within the field of differential fertility. Population geographers, on the other hand, centre their interest on the spatial pattern itself and its subsequent elucidation. Their basic interpretative approach is to regard spatial differentials in fertility as being reducible to the spatially clustered effects of the variables recognized in differential fertility.

As in so many fields of geography, traditional cartographic methods have been supplemented, and in some cases supplanted, by statistical analyses of varying degrees of sophistication. An excellent example of the traditional approach is provided by Heenan (1967) in his consideration of the evolving spatial pattern of fertility in South Island, New Zealand. The portrayal and description of fertility patterns are meticulous, but interpretations are tentative. Much of the explanatory evidence, notably on the religious composition of the population, is presented in map form, so that there are subjectivity problems in comparing patterns.

Methodological evolution is illustrated by Compton's study (1978b) of the spatial pattern of fertility in Northern Ireland. For the province as a whole, and separately for Belfast, he maps two indices of fertility by electoral wards. One is a period measure, the general marital fertility rate (legitimate children born in the year 1970-1971 per 1000 ever-married women aged fifteen–forty-nine), while the other is a cohort measure, completed family size (children ever born to 100 ever-married women aged fifty–fifty-nine in 1971). Correlation analysis aids the interpretation of the resultant patterns. The correlations by ward between fertility and religious denomination (expressed as the percentage of Roman Catholics in the population, derived from a voluntary question in the 1971 census) are impressively high, despite the lower marriage rate of Catholics in the prime child-bearing age group of twenty–twenty-nine years. Compton notes that the positive correlations are stronger for completed family size ($r = 0.73$ for Northern Ireland and 0.80 for Belfast) than for current marital fertility (0.68 and 0.50 respectively), suggesting that there might be a weakening over time of the relationship, particularly in Belfast. He also notes statistically significant positive relationships between fertility and Social Classes IV and V, after controlling for religious denomination. A similar spatial analysis of fertility in the Republic of Ireland (Coward 1978) indicates that the pattern of overall fertility is the outcome of two very different component patterns – those of nuptiality (highest in the West) and marital fertility (highest in the East).

A more complex reliance on statistical methods in a geographical study of fertility is provided by M. G. Wilson (1978b) in his multivariate analysis of small-area data for the Australian City of Wollongong. The mapped pattern of child-woman ratios for 137 districts is difficult to interpret, but multiple regression analysis reveals that variations in age and marital status within the fifteen–forty-four female population (structural or compositional variables) account for almost 70 percent of the variation in the obviously not completely standardized measure of fertility, while the addition of three socio-economic variables (the incidence of male 'blue-collar' workers, the work status of married females and the prevalence of apartment-dwelling households) raises the explanatory power to almost 80 percent. Ideally, of course, measures of fertility should be free of structural effects, so that the role of socio-economic variables can be more readily assessed, but analysts often have no alternative to the child-woman ratio because, as in the Wollongong study, birth registration data may not be available for small area populations. It is sometimes desirable, prior to regression analysis, to collapse the set of independent variables into composite dimensions by means of factor analysis, with the resulting sets of factor scores being employed in the analysis. This is recommended when the original variables are appreciably intercorrelated. An example is provided by M. G. Wilson (1971b) in his entirely statistical examination of the spatial dimension of reproduction in the Australian state of Victoria.

A particularly refined geographical analysis of fertility is provided by M. G. Wilson (1978a) through his use of rich data from the Fertility Tables of the 1971 Census of Scotland to compute a fertility index which takes account not only of female age and marital status but also of female age at, and duration of, marriage. The resultant spatial pattern is cartographically difficult to interpret (Figure 4.13), since high fertility embraces several of the rural Highlands and Islands counties as well as Glasgow and its urban-industrial hinterland, while low fertility characterizes rural counties in southern and northeastern Scotland as well as the cities of Aberdeen, Dundee and Edinburgh. But the use of just two independent variables in regression analysis accounts for almost half of the fertility variation ($r = 0.68$, $r^2 = 0.46$). The two variables are the proportion of married females aged fifteen–forty-four employed outside agriculture, and the proportion of all marriages celebrated

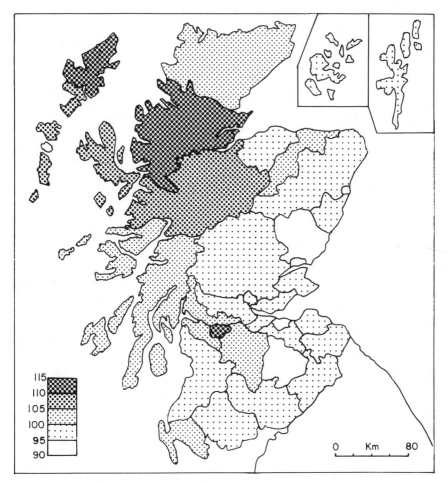

Figure 4.13
Standardized cumulative marital fertility ratios, Scotland, 1971; the ratio is described on p. 94
Source: M.G. Wilson (1978b), figure 1

in the Roman Catholic Church; note, for example, figures for the latter variable of 24.7 percent in Glasgow in 1972, compared to 4.0 percent in Aberdeen, 8.6 percent in Edinburgh and 15.9 percent in Dundee. Wilson extends his analysis by disaggregating cumulative fertility by marriage cohort, but the cartographic and statistical patterns of overall cumulative fertility are clearly discernible in the individual cohorts, suggesting a deeply ingrained and temporally persistent spatial pattern of fertility and associated social topography. It may be concluded that studies such as this indicate that intergroup and interarea differentials in fertility are still alive in post-transition societies, despite their long predicted demise as part of the process of demographic convergence.

CHAPTER 5

FERTILITY PATTERNS: LESS DEVELOPED COUNTRIES

Throughout the Third World fertility rates were high until about 1960, with the vast majority of countries estimated to have crude birth rates of 40-50 per 1000 and total fertility rates of 5500-7500 per 1000. High as these rates are, they are well below biological maxima, indicating the widespread presence of cultural restraints on fertility even in quite unmodernized societies. For example, among the Yoruba in Nigeria it is estimated that the average woman experiences sexual relations for less than half of her fecund married life; post-natal sexual abstinence often extends to three years, well exceeding the period of lactation (Caldwell and Caldwell 1977). Similarly in rural India, when a woman's daughter or daughter-in-law gives birth to a child, she often develops a 'grandmother complex' and attempts to be sexually passive (Mandelbaum 1974). Nevertheless, there is very little evidence, outside Japan, for the sort of pre-modern transition which had lowered fertility rates in northwestern Europe in the seventeenth and eighteenth centuries.

Although the data record is fragmentary, it is probable that as recently as the middle of this century a fairly uniform pattern of fertility characterized the two-thirds of the world's population inhabiting the less developed countries. Fertility variations between countries were almost certainly slight, and within countries there was probably only modest variation by social or spatial grouping. This is in marked contrast to the pattern of mortality, which was responding actively but variably by the 1950s both to socio-economic development and to programmes of imported health technology.

Fertility increases

Some developing countries may even have witnessed slight increases of fertility in the 1940s and 1950s in parts of South America (Collver 1965) and the Caribbean–Central American region (Byrne 1972), and more recently and probably more substantially in sub-Saharan Africa (Valentine and Revson 1979, Romaniuk 1980). In some cases the increases may well have been illusory, reflecting improvements in birth registration systems. In other cases, genuine although modest increases have been attributed to three major factors: widow remarriage, increased stability of sexual unions and improved health. The first factor has been cited by Srinivasan et al. (1978) as contributing to the maintenance of high fertility in the Indian state of Karnataka (formerly Mysore) between 1950 and 1975, despite some modernization and appreciable family planning programme effort. Remarriage of widows, uncommon in the past, is now socially acceptable in much of India.

Increased stability of sexual unions seems to have been particularly important in the Caribbean region, long characterized by an informal polygamous mating system embracing several types of socially accepted nonmarital as well as marital unions. Opinions differ as to the effect of nonmarital unions on fertility. It can be argued that women in such unions may well feel impelled to have children to make the relationship more permanent and that men are unlikely to show sexual restraint when they are not strictly responsible for their offspring. Nevertheless, the favoured demographic view (G. Roberts 1955, Blake 1961, Stycos 1968, Nag 1971) is that fertility is lower in less stable unions, essentially because sexual activity is reduced in the often extensive periods between unions; but for an alternative view, supported by Barbados survey data, see Ebanks et al. (1974).

The effect on fertility of mortality reduction and general health improvements is also controversial (for recent reviews, see Preston 1978, and C. Taylor et al. 1976, although there does seem to be a distinction between short-term positive and long-term negative effects. In the short term, although the improved survival of infants reduces the risk of pregnancy because of continued breastfeeding, fertility is likely to be enhanced (Arriaga 1970) because married couples survive longer as child-producing units, because foetal mortality is reduced and because the fecundity of women is increased as venereal disease, malaria and deficiency diseases like pellagra recede. Attention has recently been drawn (McFalls 1979) to many parts of intertropical Africa where in non-contracepting societies between 20 and 50 percent of women above fifty years of age have never borne children. Major factors cited are chronic undernutrition, rampant, untreated disease, and the side-effects of abortion and female circumcision. The complex spatial incidence of such factors may well underlie the surprisingly substantial spatial variation in total fertility rates for sub-Saharan Africa estimated and mapped by Adegbola (1977); other factors could be the variable pattern of breastfeeding practices and of spouse separation consequent upon temporary migration.

But the long-term effect of mortality improvement is to reduce fertility. In India, under conditions of fairly high mortality, it has been estimated (Berg 1974) that a family must have 6.3 children to be 95 percent sure that one son survives to the father's sixty-fifth birthday – an important consideration in the absence of a national social security system. Mortality improvements lessen the need for 'insurance' births, although it is doubtful that individuals are capable of making a conscious, rational adjustment in fertility behaviour to changes in survivorship conditions. Pebley et al. (1979) suggest, on the basis of a Guatemala survey, that mortality declines must occur over two generations to make a significant impact on a woman's desire for additional children. There is more agreement that improvements in survival reduce fertility by altering community fertility norms and by disrupting social and economic structures, like land inheritance systems, designed for low levels of child survivorship.

Fertility reduction: international variations

Until about 1960 there was little sign of any fertility reduction in the Third World associated with incipient modernization. Even when fertility falls were recognized in the 1960s in countries like Singapore, Barbados and Taiwan, it was generally felt that these were the result of special circumstances operating in, from a global point of view, demographically insignificant countries. By the mid-1970s, however, the widespread nature of continuing fertility falls in the Third World is thought to have become an established feature (Table 5.1), even encompassing several of the most populous countries which have traditionally been regarded as potential seedbeds for population-based catastrophes, notably China, India, Indonesia and Egypt.

Table 5.1   Crude birth rate in less developed countries, 1950–1975, by continent and most populous countries

	Crude birth rate (per 1000)				Percentage Change	
	1950–1955	1960	1965	1975	1950–1955 to 1965	1965 to 1975
Africa	49	48	48	46	−1	− 4
Nigeria	49	50	50	49	+1	− 1
Egypt	45	44	42	35	−6	−17
Ethiopia	51	51	50	49	−2	− 2
The Americas	42	41	41	36	−3	−14
Brazil	41	39	42	38	+2	−10
Mexico	47	45	44	40	−6	− 9
Colombia	46	45	44	33	−5	−25
Asia and the Pacific	42	40	41	35	−4	−15
China	37	31	34	26	−9	−24
India	42	44	43	36	+1	−16
Indonesia	45	47	46	40	+2	−13

Source: Mauldin (1978), table 1

One cannot, however, be absolutely confident about the extent of fertility reduction, essentially because birth figures recorded in the majority of less developed countries are reliable only within wide ranges. The major agencies which collect, evaluate and adjust such figures to produce estimated birth rates are the UN Statistical Office, the US Bureau of Census, the Population Council, and the UN Population Division. But Cavanaugh (1979) demonstrates that there are often appreciable differences between their estimates, so much so that if one compared the lowest estimate for 1965 with the highest estimate for 1974 in each of 33 selected less developed countries, about one-half of the countries would actually show *increased* crude birth rates between 1965 and 1974. Therefore, 'Using various rates from different sources . . . it is possible to "prove" that a given country's rate has greatly declined, declined only moderately, has stayed the same or has increased depending on what one wants to "prove" (Cavanaugh 1979, p.292). It may well be that the estimates of birth rate reduction given in Table 5.1 err somewhat on the optimistic side. A major session of the 1979 meeting of the Population Association of America was devoted to a lively debate on the extent of recent world fertility decline, stimulated by the widely publicized estimate of Bogue and Tsui (1978) that the world's total fertility rate declined from 4.6 to 4.1 births per woman between 1968 and 1975. In the debate Thomas Frejka of the Population Council argued that the estimated fertility declines in India, Pakistan and Bangladesh were nonexistent, while in Indonesia the decline was about half of the 29 percent estimated by Bogue and Tsui.

During this modern period of probable but somewhat indeterminate fertility reduction, appreciable spatial differences in fertility seem to have opened up in the Third World. It will be the major purpose of this chapter to examine such differences, at both inter-country and intra-country levels.

The basis of variation

Demographic transition theory would suggest that fertility variations between less developed countries are simply the result of different levels of development. Yet this theory is predicated on essentially European demographic experience, and there is a good deal of controversy as to its applicability in the Third World.

Figure 5.1 depicts the relationship in the late 1970s between the crude birth rate and the most widely used and readily available indicator of development, gross national product per capita, for developed and less developed countries. There is clearly an overall pattern of declining natality as economic well-being increases, just as transition theory predicts, but the relationship is curvilinear. This suggests that the relationship is relatively weak *within* both the less developed and the developed countries. Therefore, at low levels of development, increases in per capita product may well have little impact on fertility level. Only after a threshold of development has been achieved does fertility seem to respond inversely to development.

But to measure development in terms of just one component is, of course, undesirable. Not only does GNP per capita ignore the often variable and demographically important distribution of income within a society, but there are a host of other social and economic variables which contribute to the development or modernization dimension.

There are also two broad groups of factors, largely but not entirely independent of development, which might be expected to have some formative influence on the variable pattern of fertility in the Third World. First, there are broad cultural forces which might elevate fertility in pro-natalist Catholic and Islamic societies, particularly when the traditional subordination of women in the latter (Kirk 1966) is reinforced as in the late 1970s by the political ascendancy of religious fundamentalists in Pakistan, Iran and other parts of western Asia; conversely, Chinese and Chinese-related ethnic groups may be more likely to reduce fertility because of their pragmatic response to changing conditions (Taeuber 1965). Then there is the internationally variable impact of family planning programmes. Their impact is partly a function of development and cultural factors, but there are also independent influences at work, such as differential external stimulus and funding.

Appreciable literature and numerous technical analyses have been devoted in the last two decades to the problem of disentangling the interactive effects on Third

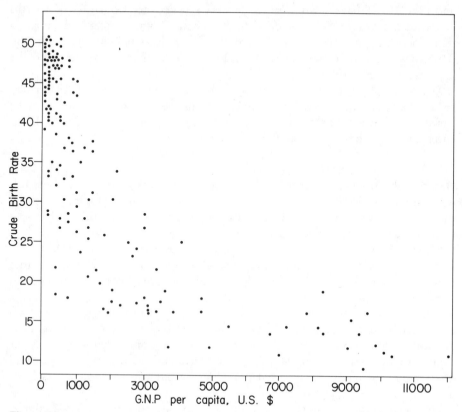

Figure 5.1
Crude birth rate by Gross National Product per capita, 150 countries,* 1976-1978
Source: data from Population Reference Bureau, *World Population Data Sheet, 1980*
*see Table 2.4

World fertility of development, cultural background and family planning intervention programmes. But at the macro-level of international variations, despite the
intrinsic geographical nature of the problem, there appears to have been no work
by population geographers. The most common studies are cross-sectional regression analyses, using countries as units of analysis, that employ a fertility measure as
the dependent variable and several modernization indicators as independent variables. There are obvious problems of analysis and interpretation, not always
confronted openly by practitioners, stemming from the unreliability of crude data,
particularly on births. Moreover, cross-sectional studies reveal associations, rather
than causes as such, so that one must beware of attaching significance to theoretically unsound relationships. Consider, for example, the way in which De Castro
(1952) used the statistically impressive inverse relationship between national fertility and protein consumption to suggest that hunger and protein deficiency stimulate sexual activity and production of female hormones – a view refuted by
physiologists.

Cross-sectional studies, which will now be reviewed selectively, may be divided conveniently into those using pre-and post-1970 data. Generally it is only among the latter that family planning programme variables have been incorporated, as a response to their growing strength and likely influence.

Studies of pre-1970 data

As early as 1950 Latin American nations with more modern socio-economic characteristics were more likely to exhibit lower fertility. Stycos (1968) was able to demonstrate correlations of -0.61 and -0.80 between mid-century crude birth rates and levels of literacy and urbanization respectively, but the correlation between crude birth rates and GNP per capita was only -0.26, suggesting that within a fairly narrow development range (Latin America in 1950) there are more important modernization influences on fertility level than GNP per capita. Objections might be raised to the use of crude birth rate as the dependent variable in this and other studies, since its level is influenced by age structure as well as by fertility behaviour. But for nations with high fertility experience in the immediate past there are not likely to be significant differences in age structure, and by its nature the crude birth rate is much less liable to age-structure distortion than is the crude death rate. In any case, the data necessary for more refined indices are simply not available in the majority of less developed countries; even the crude birth rate has often to be estimated from census data and sample registration.

Using 1960–1964 data, Kirk (1971) examined natality-modernization relationships within three broadly homogeneous cultural regions of the less developed world: Latin America, Islamic countries and southern Asia. The relationships were much stronger within each of the groups than for less developed countries as a whole, suggesting that gross cultural differences, however crudely defined, are significant influences on fertility. For the 25 Latin American countries, modernization variables of urbanization, literacy, nonagricultural employment, life expectancy, and telephone, newspaper and hospital provision gave individual correlations with the crude birth rate of between -0.68 and -0.94, so that collectively these measures accounted for as much as 90 percent of the variance in birth rates. Associations for the other two regions were lower, and the best fits of natality to modernization were achieved with rather different independent variables: education in the Islamic nations and GNP per capita in southern Asia.

Support for the cultural region approach is provided by Janowitz (1971) in a study of gross reproduction rates and modernization variables in 57 developed and less developed countries about 1960. She found that use of five regional dummy variables considerably enhanced the predictive power of her regression model.

A problem in all multivariate regression analysis is that of multicollinearity. When there is appreciable intercorrelation among the independent variables, as there invariably is within the modernization package, it becomes difficult to assess the relative importance of individual variables. This problem was clearly recognized by Oechsli and Kirk (1974–1975) in their analysis of crude birth rate variation among 25 Latin American and Caribbean countries in 1962 and 1970. In place of several individual indicators of development, they adopt an overall index, which is an equal-weighted average of ten socio-economic indicators commonly used in fertility analysis. The method of index construction is to standardize indicators by giving a mean of zero and a standard deviation of one to each indicator's data set; then the average of the ten standardized indicator values for any particular country is its development index.

Figure 5.2 indicates a close relationship in 1962 between birth rate and development index. The relationship can be best represented by the beginning of a declining logistic curve, which accounts for more than 80 percent of the variance. But conterminous, unlagged variables may not be the best way of relating natality to development, since transition theory suggests that the values and attitudes governing family size take some time to respond to a changing social environment. Accordingly, Oechsli and Kirk proceed to adopt a lag of about eight years, relating 1970 birth rates to 1962 development index values (Figure 5.3). It is clear from a comparison of the two graphs that the use of lags improves the goodness of fit; the mean-square deviations around the curves are 17.0 and 9.9 points for unlagged and lagged cases respectively.

In cross-sectional analyses one must always beware of glibly deducing temporal changes from cross-sectional data. Each country is, in fact, 'on its own trajectory through time and the development process. The cross-section picture can be generalized to the probable time series only if there are great similarities in the trajectories of the countries through time and modernization' (Oechsli and Kirk 1974–1975, p.409). Recognizing this objection, S.E. Beaver (1975) employed a pooled cross-sectional and longitudinal multivariate analysis of fertility and modernization for a set of 24 countries in Latin America and the Caribbean over the 1950–1970 period. Each country at a given time was treated as a separate observation, and since four time periods were used this resulted in a total of 96 (4 x 24) observations. Seven independent variables, all of them indicators of modernization and most of them lagged seven–ten years before natality, together accounted statistically for 65 percent of the variance in standardized birth rate and 77 percent of that in crude birth rate.

Beaver justifiably regards his analysis as providing strong empirical support for the theory of demographic transition. But, more distinctively, he also draws attention to the significant role of cultural factors, unrelated to development, in explaining the pattern of residuals – that part of natality variance 'unexplained' by the regression model. By adopting a cultural-racial grouping of countries, he finds that the European countries (Argentina, Uruguay, Cuba and Puerto Rico) and the African-East Indian countries of the Caribbean tend to have lower natality than predicted by the regression model. On the other hand, the mestizo countries of mainly Amerindian racial background but with some mixture of European ancestry (Mexico, Peru, Venezuela, El Salvador and Honduras) have higher than predicted natality. The Amerindian countries (Bolivia, Equador, Guatemala and Paraguay) show only slight departures, in no systematic direction, from predicted levels.

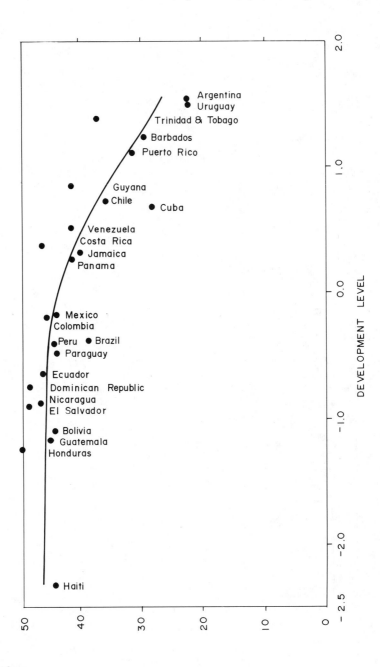

Figure 5.2
Crude birth rate (per 1000) by development index (see text), Latin American and Caribbean countries, 1962
Source: Oeschli and Kirk (1974-1975), figure 2.   By permission of The University of Chicago Press, © 1975 by The University of Chicago.

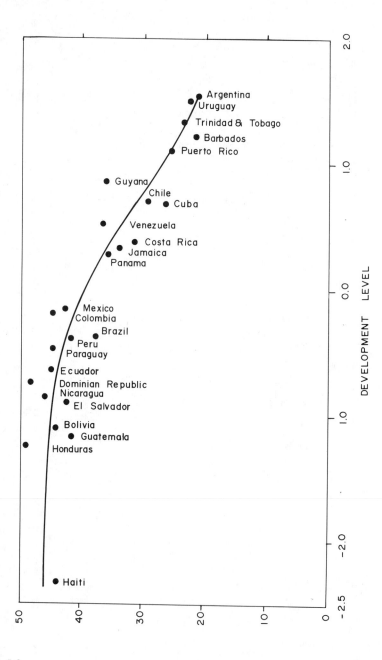

Figure 5.3
Crude birth rate (per 1000), 1970, by development index, 1962, for Latin American and Caribbean countries
Source: Oeschli and Kirk (1974-1975), figure 3. By permission of The University of Chicago Press, © 1975 by The University of Chicago.

Beaver suggests that differences between the groups in family structure and sex roles hold the key to interpretation. Southern European countries, which supplied the bulk of European immigrants to Latin America, subscribed to chauvinistic sex roles, with a strong ideal of male dominance and very different standards of sexual behaviour for men and women. On the other hand, nuclear families were stable and the kinship system exerted fairly strict controls over sexual relations and marriage. In the mestizo countries the chauvinism of southern Europe becomes what is popularly termed *machismo*. But having adopted the sexual ideals of southern Europe, these societies lack the social controls to restrain the resulting behaviour, since the social structure of the indigenous Amerindian society has been disrupted. Many births are illegitimate, and even married men may have few obligations to their wives. In the African–East Indian countries illegitimacy is also common, but the southern European pattern of sex roles is absent. Fertility reduction is promoted here by the instability of sexual unions and by the greater freedom women enjoy to engage in many activities, including fertility control. Beaver's study, therefore, confirms the view that cultural background can facilitate or delay demographic change independently of socio-economic development.

Development versus family planning programmes

The new variable incorporated in modern studies of Third World fertility reduction is family planning programme effort. The origins and growth of such programmes will be discussed in a subsequent chapter on population policies, but their differential impact on the Third World may now be considered.

There has been considerable debate among both academics and policy-makers as to the relative roles of development and family planning programmes in promoting recent fertility falls in much of the Third World. Substantial claims – from what has been irreverently dubbed 'the condom school of thought' – have been made for intervention programmes, in so far as fertility may be regarded as a function of both demand and supply factors: demand factors that determine the motivation for fertility control and supply factors that provide the information, goods and services to effect that control. It has been suggested that there is often a close temporal, and therefore functional, relationship between growth of programme effort and decline of fertility. In addition, World Fertility Survey data for ten developing countries in 1974–1976 show: that high proportions of women at all socio-economic levels want no more children, including large proportions among rural, poor and uneducated women; that there is a huge unmet demand for fertility control services; and that level of development is not a dominant factor in determining desire for fertility control (Brackett et al. 1979). It is acknowledged that these findings do not support classical demographic transition theory.

On the other hand, it was quickly recognized (Davis 1967, Hauser 1967) that some of the early claims made for programme influence in Taiwan, Singapore, Hong Kong and the like failed to control adequately for continuing modernization. In Taiwan, for example, the proportion of women aged twenty–twenty-four who had attained a junior high school level of education rose from 24 per cent in 1966 to

54 per cent in 1974 (Schultz 1980). Demeny (1974, p.158) expresses a common sceptical view: 'The power of family planning programs to achieve more than limited demographic objectives . . . is questionable. Since people can be expected to find the means to control fertility if they want to, and since without such a desire the availability of . . . contraceptive technology is inconsequential, it is unlikely that family planning can do much more than accelerate a process that should occur in any case.' Extending this argument, programmes may arise only to satisfy the motivation that development itself creates, so that 'policy success, where it can be claimed, usually turns out to refer to a marginal acceleration of a change already underway' (McNicoll 1978, p.96). Moreover, it is development which provides the necessary infrastructural capability (communication networks, health centres, administrative skills, etc.) for launching a strong programme effort.

A plausible compromise view is that 'a program tends to have the greatest impact at medium stages of development; at lower stages the motivation for smaller families, which is a consequence of development, is not great, and at later stages the natality decline will take place regardless of the program. In the middle ranges an active family-planning program diffuses birth control more rapidly than otherwise would be the case' (Oechsli and Kirk 1974–1975, pp.416–417).

A natality model
Clearly, the development, cultural and programme influences on fertility behaviour are deeply interwoven, so that it is very difficult, and perhaps technically impossible, to untangle inter-relationships in a complex biosocial system so as to apportion degree of influence with any precision. Yet statistical attempts have been made. A useful introduction to these is provided by a model (Figure 5.4) which attempts to identify component influences on natality in less developed countries and to specify relationships between the components. It effectively summarizes much of our previous discussion.

Analysis of 1965–1975 changes
The most comprehensive recent cross-sectional study is probably that of Mauldin and Berelson (1978), which analyses the correlates of fertility decline in 94 developing countries for the 1965–1975 period. They initially decompose changes in crude birth rate into three components: changes effected through age structure, marriage patterns and marital fertility.

Age structure
When fertility begins to decline in a high fertility country, the proportion of children in the population decreases but the proportion of females of child-bearing age increases. This, in itself, should increase the crude birth rate, except in those countries experiencing appreciable emigration of young adults. Several such exceptions are found in the Caribbean region where Ebanks et al. (1975) estimate that the age- and sex-selective emigration accounts for almost 20 percent of the crude birth rate decline in Barbados between 1956 and 1970.

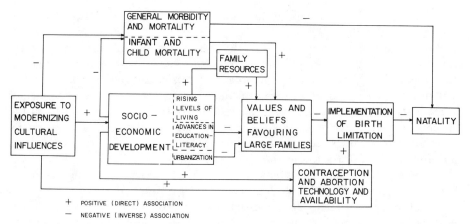

Figure 5.4
Causal diagram of influences on natality with particular reference to less developed countries. Reverse relationships and weak relationships are not shown. An example of a reverse relationship is how high infant mortality may reflect, through neglect and abuse of children, parental reaction to high natality generally and unwanted births specifically; such a relationship has been postulated for both pre-industrial Europe (Van de Walle and Knodel 1980) and contemporary Latin America (Scrimshaw 1978).
Source: adapted from S.E. Beaver (1975), figure 4-1

Marriage patterns
In so far as almost all births in most developing countries are to married women, changes in age at marriage can be expected to influence the number of births. The data in Table 5.2 indicate that in many developing countries there was a trend towards later marriage in the 1960s. In a few cases this reflects legislation instituting a minimum age at marriage and banning polygomy, and in the case of China it is widely reported that later marriage has been strongly exhorted as a central plank in the government's population policy. But, more typically, later marriage seems to accompany socio-economic development, with a particularly important role being

Table 5.2   Percentage of females never married, selected less developed countries, around 1960 and 1970

	No. of countries	15–19 age group 1960	1970	20–24 age group 1960	1970
Africa	6	56	69	16	25
Asia and the Pacific	20	65	73	24	33

Figures are not given for the Americas because of the preponderance in several countries of nonmarital, consensual unions
Source: Mauldin (1978), table 6

played by the increasing education, employment and general status of women (Duza and Baldwin 1977).

But at individual community levels the reasons promoting later marriage are invariably more complex, and indeed more interesting, than glib references to 'development' suggest. For example, in a modernizing Sri Lankan village, where parent-arranged marriages are the norm and where nearly 45 percent of women of reproductive age were unmarried in 1976, marriage delays are dictated in the higher socio-economic groups by the prestige parents obtain by offering in marriage a daughter who is provided not only with the traditional dowry but also with an education and at least potential employability (Tilakaratne 1978).

The important role of age at marriage in natality reduction is implied in the age-specific pattern of fertility decline in developing countries, bearing in mind that early contraceptive practice for child-spacing is infrequent in such societies. Tsui and Bogue (1978, table 6) estimate that 73 percent of the decline in the total fertility rate for Asia (excluding USSR and Japan) from 5330 per 1000 in 1968 to 4490 per 1000 in 1975 was concentrated in the fifteen–twenty-nine age groups.

Marital fertility
A decline in marital fertility reflects above all changing values and attitudes towards child-bearing and family size, uninfluenced by the structural factors of age and marital composition.

To decompose crude birth rate change into its three component parts, one needs data on age- and marital-specific birth rates which are only available in a minority of developing countries. The pattern revealed by such data is, however, illuminating (Table 5.3). It is clear that changes in marital structure have more than compensated for increases in the proportion of women of reproductive age, while,

Table 5.3   *Components of crude birth rate decline in selected less developed countries*

		Crude birth rate			Percent of decline due to:		
		Beginning	End	% change	Age structure	Marriage pattern	Marital fertility
Fiji	1966–1975	36	28	−22	−21	29	93
S. Korea	1966–1974	35	25	−28	0	9	91
Mauritius	1962–1972	38	24	−36	−25	53	72
Singapore	1957–1970	43	22	−48	−13	53	60
Sri Lanka	1963–1971	34	30	−13	−42	89	53
Taiwan	1965–1975	32	23	−28	−42	49	93
Thailand	1965–1975	42	37	−12	−22	19	103
Turkey	1960–1975	45	32	−29	8	23	69

Source: Mauldin and Berelson (1978), table 5

in addition, there have been appreciable reductions in marital fertility. This pattern may not, of course, be entirely typical of the less developed world, since the countries in Table 5.3 have experienced well above-average modernization and fertility decline.

The analytical kernel of the Mauldin-Berelson study is a series of correlations for 94 developing countries between crude birth rate change, 1965–1975, and variables measuring modernization level and family planning programme effort about 1970. Seven standard variables were selected to represent the education, health, economic and urbanization dimensions of modernization, while programme effort was measured by an index developed by Lapham and Mauldin (1972). Fifteen programme criteria contribute to this index (e.g., public statements by leaders, use of mass media, availability of contraceptive supplies, presence of home-visiting fieldworkers); each criterion is scored on a 0–2 range, so that index scores for countries can extend from 0 to 30.

The correlations are presented in Table 5.4. Predictably there is appreciable intercorrelation among the modernization variables, and programme effort is also correlated, although to a lesser extent, with the modernization variables. Crude birth rate change is correlated significantly with all modernization variables apart from GNP per capita, but none of these associations reaches the 0.89 level of correlation between crude birth rate change and programme effort. The modernization variables in combination achieve a multiple correlation coefficient of 0.81 with crude birth rate change, thus accounting statistically for 66 percent of the latter's variance (coefficient of determination = r^2 = 0.66). Although substantial, this is well below the r^2 of 0.78 achieved by the programme variable alone. When

Table 5.4 Coefficients of correlation between selected variables, 94 developing countries, around 1970

	1	2	3	4	5	6	7	8	9
1. Adult literacy	1·00								
2. School enrolment	·80	1·00							
3. Life expectancy	·87	·76	1·00						
4. Infant mortality rate	−·78	−·71	−·86	1·00					
5. Nonagricultural male employment	·65	·73	·80	−·73	1·00				
6. GNP per capita	·23	·38	·40	−·37	·62	1·00			
7. Urbanization	·45	·58	·58	−·54	·78	·57	1·00		
8. Family planning programme effort	·64	·52	·70	−·64	·52	·07	·32	1·00	
9. Crude birth rate change (1965–1975)	·70	·60	·76	−·71	·61	·13	·42	·89	1·00

Source: Mauldin and Berelson (1978), pp. 99, 104, 105

the modernization and programme variables are considered together, the r² value rises to 0.83. The addition, therefore, of the programme effort variable to the set of modernization variables raises the 'explanation' of variance in crude birth rate decline from 66 percent to 83 percent.

These findings are confirmed, even to the extent of remarkably similar r² values, when the 1965–1975 crude birth rate decline is regressed against:

(i) changes in modernization variables, 1960–1970, and programme effort, 1970–1972.
(ii) modernization variables, 1960 (for lag effect), and programme effort, 1970–1972

With respect to the 'development versus family planning' debate, Mauldin and Berelson conclude that the joint impact is more effective than either alone, and that programme effort makes a substantial difference, not merely a trivial one. On the basis of their analyses they tentatively apportion 'credit' for recent declines in Third World crude birth rates along the lines indicated in Table 5.5.

Another cross-sectional study confirms the findings of Mauldin and Berelson. In accounting for 1968–1975 changes in estimated total fertility rates of 89 less developed countries, Tsui and Bogue (1978, p.32) conclude: 'From an analytical point of view, the model's performance is good, but the important implication is not the amount of total explanation rendered by the model but the verification of family planning's independent effect on birth rates. Having allowed other factors to reign freely in explaining 1975 fertility levels, we find that, by including family planning effort last, it is able to make an independent and significant impact on 1975 fertility levels.'

Table 5.5   Estimated decomposition, by percentage, of recent decline in Third World crude birth rates

	Age structure	Marital patterns	Marital fertility	Total
Modernization level		25	35–40	60–65
Policy effort				
family planning			15–20	15–20
legal sanctions and organized pressure		5–10		5–10
Consequences of earlier demographic trends	−5 to −10			−5 to −10
Unknown		5–10	10–15	15–25
Total	−5 to −10	35–45	60–75	100 (approx.)

Source: Mauldin and Berelson (1978), p. 123

Having considered overall relationships in less developed countries between fertility and associative factors, it is now of interest to observe how closely individual countries conform to the overall pattern. Table 5.6 presents this information in an economical manner. The vertical axis represents an index of modernization calculated, by means of country rankings, from the seven modernization variables specified in Table 5.4. It may be regarded as measuring motivational readiness for fertility reduction. The horizontal axis represents strength of family planning programmes, with the earlier described 0–30 scale divided into groups of 0 (none), 1–9 (weak), 10–19 (moderate) and 20+ (strong). One can ignore initially the birth rate decline figures and concentrate on the relationship between modernization and programme strength. That a relationship exists is confirmed by the clustering of countries in the four cells along the diagonal from top left to bottom right. But countries to the left of these cells all have stronger family planning programmes than their modernization level would suggest: China, North Vietnam, India, Indonesia, etc. Conversely, countries to the right have weaker than predicted programmes. Particularly anomalous are the high modernization countries with no or weak programme effort. Although discussion of international differences in programme commitment will be postponed until the chapter on population policies, it may be observed that these highly anomalous countries fall almost entirely into two groups, Islamic and Latin American, where pro-natalist elements have resisted fertility regulation policies.

Considering now mean declines in birth rate by cell, there are fairly clear gradients both by row and column, showing the graded influence of both modernization and programme effort. One might note, however, that at the high modernization level, there is virtually no differential impact on natality between moderate and strong programmes, but at the lower-middle level of modernization, there are appreciable differences in natality reduction between weak, moderate and strong programme countries. This would seem to confirm the view, quoted on page 138, of Oechsli and Kirk.

Finally, within each cell there is remarkable uniformity in the size of birth rate decline, the only anomalies being Iran, Egypt and Turkey. The overall pattern of Table 5.6 is, therefore, a clear demonstration of essential regularity in recent fertility declines in the Third World.

Association and cause: cautionary observations

Social scientists have long been aware of the dangers of inferring cause from association, even when a theoretically reasonable hypothesis for a causal relationship is available. One must beware of interaction effects, such as those illustrated in Figure 5.5. Many cross-sectional studies of fertility make an implicit assumption that fertility level at any given time is influenced by current or earlier levels of development. This is theoretically reasonable, but one should appreciate that development level is itself fashioned in part by earlier fertility levels. This is what some demographers mean when they talk about a vicious circle in which poverty and high fertility can sustain each other. Another interaction effect, difficult to

Table 5.6   *1965–1975 crude birth rate decline (percent) by modernization level and family planning programme effort: 94 developing countries*

Modernization level	Programme effort							
	Strong		Moderate		Weak		None	
High	Singapore	40	Cuba	40	Venezuela	11	Korea, North	5
	Hong Kong	36	Chile	29	Brazil	10	Kuwait	5
	Korea, South	32	Trinidad and		Mexico	9	Peru	2
	Barbados	31	Tobago	29	Paraguay	6	Lebanon	2
	Taiwan	30	Colombia	25			Jordan	1
	Mauritius	29	Panama	22			Libya	−1
	Costa Rica	29						
	Fiji	22						
	Jamaica	21						
	Mean	30	Mean	29	Mean	9	Mean	3
Upper Middle	China	24	Malaysia	26	Egypt	17	Mongolia	9
			Tunisia	24	Turkey	16	Syria	4
			Thailand	23	Honduras	7	Zambia	−2
			Dominican		Nicaragua	7	Congo	−2
			Republic	21	Zaire	6		
			Philippines	19	Algeria	4		
			Sri Lanka	18	Guatemala	4		
			El Salvador	13	Morocco	2		
			Iran	2	Ghana	2		
					Ecuador	0		
					Iraq	0		
	Mean	24	Mean	18	Mean	6	Mean	2
Lower Middle	Vietnam, North	23	India	16	Papua		Angola	4
			Indonesia	13	New Guinea	5	Cameroon	3
					Pakistan	1	Burma	3
					Bolivia	1	Yemen,	
					Nigeria	1	P.D.R. of	3
					Kenya	0	Mozambique	2
					Liberia	0	Khmer/	
					Haiti	0	Kampuchea	2
					Uganda	−4	Ivory Coast	1
							Saudi Arabia	0
							Vietnam, South	0
							Madagascar	0
							Lesotho	−4
	Mean	23	Mean	14	Mean	1	Mean	1
Low					Tanzania	5	Laos	5
					Dahomey	3	Central African	
					Bangladesh	2	Republic	5
					Sudan	0	Malawi	5
					Nepal	−1	Bhutan	3
					Mali	−1	Ethiopia	2
					Afghanistan	−2	Guinea	2
							Chad	2
							Togo	2
							Upper Volta	1
							Yemen	1
							Niger	1
							Burundi	1
							Sierra Leone	0
							Mauritania	0
							Rwanda	0
							Somalia	0
					Mean	1	Mean	2

Source: Mauldin and Berelson (1978), table 12

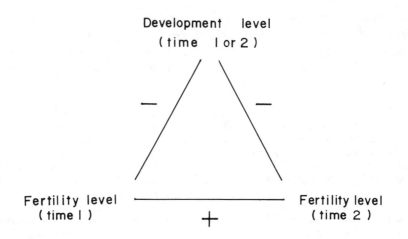

Figure 5.5
Fertility and development relationships over time

disentangle statistically, is the way in which modernization creates an infrastructural capability which may then be used to promote a strong programme effort.

The association-causation-interaction argument is well put by Oechsli and Kirk (1974–1975, p.403): 'We can say that modernisation, at some level, is associated with a given mortality level, as we can say that the birth rate tends to stay high until some critical level of development is reached and then tends to decline as development proceeds, but we cannot say that development "causes" declining birth and death rates; rather, certain patterns of change in these vital rates are part of the process of development. . . . Thus, the theoretical basis for the present study avoids attempts to outline specific causal chains and, instead, proceeding from the postulate that development is an orderly holistic process with some empirically determinable consistencies, attempts to fit changes in birth and death rates into the process.'

Finally, it should be appreciated that modernization or development variables may be better regarded, not as the fundamental determinants of fertility behaviour, but rather as surface, identifiable expressions, or causal surrogates, of decision making. It may be regretted, therefore, that 'much more emphasis is given to the study of aggregate linkages between variables such as education or income distribution and fertility than on the detailed mechanisms that may be at work' (McNicoll 1978, p.83). Continued emphasis on determinants of fertility at an aggregate level may detract attention from the structures that govern them, so that the complexity of fertility behaviour response to environmental change is masked.

A simple but telling illustration of the need to dig deeper than level of modernization and programme effort to really *understand* why recent fertility declines have varied among societies has been provided by Hawthorn (1978) in a comparison of China, Taiwan and India. Each entered its modern political history in the late 1940s with high mortality and fertility and a large, impoverished and exploited rural population. By the late 1970s, however, in China and Taiwan (with crude birth rates of about 22 and 24 per 1000 respectively) fertility had fallen as far and as fast as in any large population outside Japan, whereas in India (crude birth rate of 35 per 1000) the decline has been retarded and modest. Hawthorn explains the recent demographic differences in these terms:

> The first and most obvious difference between China, Taiwan and India is that two are inhabited by Chinese and one is not. What effects this may have had, independently of any associated differences of social organisation, are not known. A second difference is that unlike the two Chinas India has been crippled by trying to take democracy seriously. This had led the Congress party . . . to accede to the interests of the dominant groups in the countryside, to allow them low taxes and effective freedom from real agrarian reform in return for delivering the votes. A third difference related to this, is that whereas for different reasons and in different ways the two Chinas (Taiwan, by putting a low and effective ceiling on landholding, increasing the proportion of owners and successfully encouraging a large amount of non-agricultural activity in rural areas, the People's Republic by eventually abolishing private landholding and guaranteeing a decent subsistence in a consequently collectivised agriculture) have each created a relatively secure present and a relatively predictable future for a majority of rural people, India has not. One consequence of this has been to make poor rural Indians more persistently dependent upon the economic and social security provided by kin. A fourth difference is that China and to a lesser extent Taiwan have brought more unmarried and married women into gainful employment outside the home. A fifth difference is that in China and to a lesser extent Taiwan, family planning and the means of improving child health have been made readily available to people in rural areas and connected to the supply of other services, whereas in India, they have not.
>
> (Hawthorn 1978, pp. 15–16)

Although these comparisons are at the most general level, they do make the point that political and social structures can appreciably influence fertility levels in ways not necessarily related to the standard modernization process, thereby underlining criticism of much population-and-development literature which pays 'little more than lip service to the distinctiveness of cultural and institutional settings' (McNicoll 1978, p.84).

Hawthorn concludes (p.17) that 'for the analysis . . . of the conditions, correlates, causes and consequences of different rates of fertility in poor societies . . . it seems more illuminating to concentrate on relatively particular political, economic and social histories than on trying to refine more abstract and general (and spuriously precise) theoretical models.' This is, of course, a controversial conclusion. It runs somewhat against the tenor of discussion in this chapter, which has emphasized the essential regularity, at the most general level, of recent fertility trends in the Third World.

Variations within countries

Since international variations in Third World fertility can be interpreted fairly convincingly through the interaction of modernization, family planning programmes and cultural-political structures, it appears logical to cite their differential impact as controlling spatial patterns of fertility within less developed countries. One cannot, however, take this as read, since social science literature constantly warns of pitfalls in transferring findings from one scale of analysis to another.

Modernization

Most studies do, in fact, find a fairly close relationship between a country's modernization surface and its spatial pattern of fertility. An instructive example is provided by Brazil, well known for its spectacular internal contrasts in development. For the country as a whole there was a decline of about 8 percent in the total fertility rate between the 1930s and the 1960s, but Figure 5.6 indicates that this was concentrated entirely in the more developed regions of the extreme south and the

Figure 5.6
Estimated total fertility rates (per woman) in regions of Brazil, 1930-1940 (first figure) and 1960-1970 (second figure)
Source: data from Moreira et al. (1978), table 2

hinterlands of São Paulo and Rio de Janeiro. There were actual increases of fertility in the 'outback' regions of Amazonia, Mato Grosso and the Northeast – a not uncommon demographic response to initial socio-economic improvement. Another factor may have been the way in which an expanding frontier situation in Amazonia, Mato Grosso and the newest coffee-growing state of Parana stimulated large families in much the same way as in nineteenth-century North America.

The most common spatial expression of modernization and fertility relationships in Third World countries is in urban-rural contrasts. After a review of Latin American cross-sectional studies, Stycos (1978, p.41) states: 'In so far as any single variable is consistently related to lower fertility levels, it is urbanization.' In this context urbanization can best be regarded not as an independent modernization component but as a spatial concentration of modernizing forces like employment diversification, income growth, education provision and female employment. Indeed, in a multivariate study of 74 areal units of Puerto Rico, it was found that in each of three periods between 1950 and 1970 an urbanization variable had no significant relationship to fertility when industrialization and female education variables were controlled (Albuquerque et al. 1976).

In the very early stages of modernization Third World cities do not always exhibit lower fertility levels than their rural hinterlands, as studies in India, Egypt, Mexico and Zaire have shown (W. C. Robinson 1961, Abu-Lughod 1964, Zarate 1967, Romaniuk 1980); and in Malawi the total fertility rate in 1971–1972 was estimated from a sample registration of the African population to be 7.7 children per woman in urban areas and 6.5 in rural areas (Malawi Population Survey 1973). First-generation peasant migrants to the city do not necessarily adopt new ideals of family size since 'continued ruralization of cities in the Third World and concomitant subsistence urbanization raises serious doubts as to whether ecological residential shifts presage reduced fertility in the absence of a fundamental restructuring of the social and economic order' (Albuquerque 1976, p.55).

But there is no doubt that in the majority of contemporary Third World countries fertility rates are lowest in the large urban areas. For example, in 1975–1976 the crude birth rate in the rural areas of El Salvador was estimated at 49 per 1000, compared with 34 per 1000 in metropolitan San Salvador (Morris et al. 1979), and in Paraguay estimated rates for the rural areas and Greater Asuncion were 49 and 24 per 1000 respectively (Morris et al. 1978). The quality of data on which such estimates are made may well be suspect, being based as they are on sample surveys conducted in often difficult conditions, but there can be no questioning of the Taiwanese data (Table 5.7), derived from what is widely regarded as a model system of data recording for over 330 township-level administrative divisions.

It is tempting to attribute the reduced fertility in urban areas simply to the way in which various facets of modernization promote smaller family norms. But the important structural role of marriage composition must also be considered. In Sri Lanka, for example, the mean age at marriage for females in the city of Colombo was 24.7 years in 1971, compared with 23.5 years in the country as a whole (Tilakaratne 1978), while in Paraguay only 48 percent of women aged

Table 5.7   Total fertility rates (per 1000), Taiwan, 1965–1975

	Cities	Urban townships	Rural townships
1965	4167	4806	5344
1970	3627	3971	4363
1975	2549	2892	3235

Source: Te-Hsiung Sun et al. (1978), table 25

fifteen–forty-nine in Asuncion were in marital unions in 1977, compared with 64 percent outside the capital (Morris et al. 1978).

Marriage data by settlement grouping from Taiwan are particularly revealing (Table 5.8). They show a consistent urban-rural gradient in proportion married for all three age groups and for both 1961 and 1969. The trend towards later marriage is also evident in that decade in all settlement groups (see Table 5.3 for its impact on the country's crude birth rate). When marital structure is controlled (in the final three columns of Table 5.8), the expected urban-rural gradient in fertility is found only in the twenty-five–twenty-nine (and subsequent) age groups. As to reasons for delayed urban marriages, one can cite the roles of female employment, female education and socially disruptive rural-urban migration. This is a common pattern, but it is not universal; in Puerto Rico, for example, correlation analysis shows no inverse relationship between female proportion married and degree of urbanization among 74 areal units in 1950, 1960 or 1970 (Albuquerque et al. 1976).

Many studies of fertility variation within Third World countries employ a macro-level approach and invariably demonstrate, often through multivariate analysis of areal data (Hermalin 1975), the co-existence of fertility decline and modernization. But in terms of actual causal relationships, the role of moderniza-

Table 5.8   Proportions of females married and marital fertility rates by cities, urban townships and rural townships, Taiwan, 1961 and 1969

		% of females currently married			Marital fertility rate per 1000		
		15–19	20–24	25–29	15–19	20–24	25–29
1961	Cities	12·5	56·0	85·1	408	445	358
	Urban	11·2	59·6	90·0	375	404	387
	Rural	13·3	64·0	92·3	331	395	394
1969	Cities	7·3	47·0	83·8	523	460	322
	Urban	7·4	50·4	88·6	514	486	343
	Rural	9·4	57·7	92·6	470	475	350

Source: Hermalin (1972), table 4

tion appears somewhat abstract. To appreciate the real mechanisms at work, detailed observation of particular communities is required. A good example is the 1975 study by Das Gupta of a village 15 miles from Delhi which had been the scene of an earlier sociological study in 1953. Many changes had taken place in the village between these dates. Subsistence agriculture had given way to cash cropping, and the village had become integrated into a wider economy. There was a much greater dependence on outside income, particularly from employment in Delhi. New schools and a health centre had been built, electricity introduced, and a proper road built to give direct access and a new bus service to Delhi. It is observed that different caste-based groups within the village have reacted quite differently in their fertility behaviour response to these modernization changes, and in particular to external employment opportunities: 'The upper strata find it easier to secure the better paid permanent jobs, simply because they are in a position to meet the heavy but necessary investment in education and bribes. The volume of investment thus required puts a premium on lower fertility and helps to explain the increasing interest among this group to limit their family size.

'Of the lower strata, only some have struggled to make these investments and thereby managed to get a foothold on the upward spiral to economic success. However, the bulk of the poorer strata cannot afford such heavy expenditure and have to rely on their traditional village occupations and casual jobs for their subsistence. These people hope to maximise their potential income by having large numbers of children, which in turn makes it increasingly difficult for them to get on to the upward spiral' (Das Gupta 1977, p.119).

It is evident then that fertility behaviour of individuals is guided by the norms of the groups to which they belong. Such groups exist at all levels, embracing nations, urban and rural divisions of nations, and even castes within individual villages.

Family planning programmes

'The idea that a family-planning program can bring fertility decline to a country without social and economic modernisation . . . is not even plausible, much less proven' (Davis 1970, p.30). This is a categorical rejection by an eminent demographer of the demographic impact of early programmes, a view that has persisted in a significant section of the demographic fraternity: 'Disillusionment with conventional family planning programmes as the main policy instrument with which to induce fertility declines is already widespread, as the evidence accumulates of their limited coverage and low demographic effectiveness' (Repetto 1978, p.37). Nevertheless, the current concensus view among population analysts, derived from macro-studies of the Mauldin-Berelson type and micro-level KAP surveys (knowledge, attitude and practice of family planning), is that programme effort can, and often does, play an important role over and above that of modernization in promoting fertility reduction. If programme effort does exert an influence in fertility, then the particular spatial pattern of programme input (clinics, fieldworkers, media messages) can be expected to contribute to spatial variations in fertility level.

The most fundamental spatial division within Third World countries, as far as fertility is concerned, is that between cities and rural areas. But does an urban bias exist within family planning programmes, and, if so, does it contribute significantly to lower fertility in cities? There can be little doubt of the metropolitan dominance within family planning programmes, particularly in their early stages. Programme input is attracted to larger cities partly by the relatively receptive environment created there by modernizing influences and partly by the logistical advantages for promotion offered by a compact population and urban media (cinemas, television, newspapers, posters, etc.). A useful demonstration of this spatial bias is provided by a distribution map (Figure 5.7) of family planning field studies, meeting certain

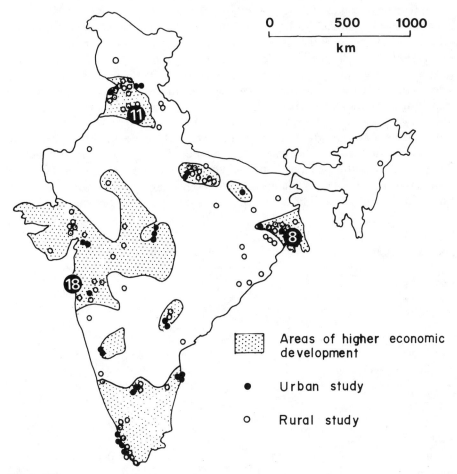

Figure 5.7
India: location of family planning field studies, 1966-1972, and areas of higher economic development
Source: Blaikie (1975), figure 7.1

criteria of importance, undertaken in India between 1966 and 1972. Of a total of 144 studies, 79 (55 percent) were located in large towns or cities, which as a group comprise less than 20 percent of the country's population. Moreover, Figure 5.7 indicates that there were very few studies, urban or rural, in the less developed regions.

It is sometimes argued (Baldwin and Ford 1976, Brackett et al. 1978) that the desire for smaller families is widespread in rural areas, and that what is lacking to achieve significant fertility reduction there is the provision of contraceptive knowledge and supplies. This argument is invariably based on surveys of attitudes towards family size, which suggest (Table 5.9) that the majority of rural women want no more children, that there is no systematic difference between them and urban women in this wish, and that desired family size is only modestly lower in urban areas. One should, however, treat such data with the greatest caution (for a critical consideration of the predictive validity of stated reproductive intentions, see Westoff and Ryder, 1977). In fact, a salutory antidote to the above argument is provided by KAP survey data from Taiwan between 1965 and 1976 (Table 5.10). These show that there has been no convergence in preferred family size among social strata, defined on the basis of education and urbanization, despite appreciable convergence in contraceptive knowledge. Thus in a society where appreciable modernization and programme effort have ensured very wide diffusion of contraceptive awareness and practice, the rural population and the least educated population still desire the larger families. What is being suggested here is that major programme effort in family planning would not achieve the considerable demographic impact in the rural areas of fairly unmodernized societies that some have

Table 5.9   Attitudes towards family size among currently married women in urban and rural areas of selected less developed countries, 1974–1976

	Percentage of women wanting no more children		Mean number of children wanted	
	Urban	Rural	Urban	Rural
Colombia	60	64	3·9	4·5
Dominican Republic	39	50	4·4	5·1
Fiji	54	47	3·9	4·3
South Korea	71	73	3·0	3·6
Malaysia	49	40	4·0	4·6
Pakistan	54	47	3·9	4·3
Panama	60	66	4·0	4·6
Sri Lanka	64	61	3·5	4·0
Thailand	45	59	3·4	3·7

Source: World Fertility Survey data from Brackett et al. (1978), tables 6 and 11

Table 5.10   Preferred number of children and practice of contraception among married women aged 22–39 by two modernization indicators, Taiwan, 1965–1976

	Preferred number of children			Percentage ever prac- tised contraception		
	1965	1970	1976	1965	1970	1976
Education						
None	4·1	4·0	3·4	19	51	78
Primary	3·9	3·8	2·9	32	54	73
Junior high	3·6	3·3	2·6	51	71	80
Senior high or more	3·2	3·0	2·3	60	79	78
Urbanization						
Rural township	4·2	3·9	3·2	21	48	73
Urban township	3·9	3·8	3·1	26	54	72
Small city	3·8	3·6	2·7	32	62	78
Large city	3·7	3·5	2·7	43	69	81

Source: Te-Hsiung Sun et al. (1978), table 9

claimed, but this is not to deny the need to counter the urban bias of existing programmes.

Attention can now be devoted to more narrowly spatial considerations, notably the way in which distance from programme input affects contraceptive behaviour and fertility performance. There is no doubt that this important spatial dimension has been scantily treated in the otherwise 'information overload' literature on programme evaluation. This is, of course, an eminently geographical field of interest, and it is pleasing to be able to refer to three relevant case studies, all with important policy implications, conducted by geographers.

A Chilean metropolitan fringe

Fuller (1974) examines the importance of distance between residence and clinic in the practice of contraception, compared with the influence of socio-economic variables traditionally employed by population analysts in studies of differential fertility. The setting is a lower class, nonagricultural community of some 40,000 population on the fringes of Santiago, and served by a single family planning clinic. It is demonstrated that several variables are correlated with birth control practice, but when the influence of the spatial variation of these correlates has been extracted, the distance variable emerges as the single most powerful discriminator between users and nonusers of contraceptive techniques.

Rural India

The study by Blaikie (1975) in northern Bihar has been described by a respected reviewer as 'arguably the best detailed account of the workings of a less successful family planning programme' (Hawthorn 1978, p.15). Using both survey and ecological data, Blaikie considers the relevance of spatial diffusion theory, particularly diffusion from innovation hearths, to understanding the spatial pattern of family planning acceptance. He finds that the 'neighbourhood effect' (the effect of physical distance on the amount of contact between innovators and recipients) is of little importance. At a micro-regional scale, in an area of about 50 square kilometres, the correlation coefficient between family planning knowledge and distance from family planning facility was only -0.01 for females. The female information network, in particular, is highly restricted both spatially and socially and is inaccessible to central-node extension methods.

It is caste, literacy and existing family size, rather than distance, that seem to determine the take-up of family planning in northern Bihar. This leads Blaikie to observe (p.138) that 'the functional reasons which make a particular innovation attractive or feasible at all are not constant from one decision-maker to another and often vary over space in a non-random manner.' Geographers should beware, therefore, of their intuitive bias towards the importance of contagious effects and the distance-decay function. The basic spatial diffusion models tend to be little more than information diffusion models which cater inadequately for differential resistance to innovation adoption imposed by cultural factors. Hawthorn (1978, p.442) observes that such models 'may work among uncomplicated populations of small and ambitious farmers in lowland Sweden or the American midwest. They do not work in the tangled human landscapes of India.'

Barbados

By means of cartographic and statistical cross-sectional analyses for 1960 and 1970, H. R. Jones (1977) examines the spatial impact on fertility reduction of the western hemisphere's most successful family planning programme. By 1960 the programme had barely begun, but by 1970 about a quarter of women of child-bearing age had been enrolled, and an indeterminate, but presumably substantial, proportion of women were practising contraception at that time outside the programme. The concurrence of programme build-up with the 1960–1970 inter-censal period provides a rare opportunity to make a 'before-and-after programme' study of fertility patterns, although significant changes in the island's socio-economic structure were conterminously occurring as a monocultural sugar growing and processing economy was being transformed by the growth of tourism and government employment into a tertiary or service-based economy; between 1960 and 1970, for example, the proportion of working population engaged in agriculture declined from 25 to 15 percent. The combination of an active family planning programme and continuing modernization was responsible for the total fertility rate falling from 4.3 per woman in 1955–1960 to 2.3 in 1970.

Figure 5.8 depicts the 1960 pre-programme pattern of fertility for 28 areas aggregated from 340 census enumeration districts to ensure statistical reliability of cross-sectional data in a country whose total population was only 235,000 in 1970. The index of fertility used is the child-woman ratio, with the conventional 0–5

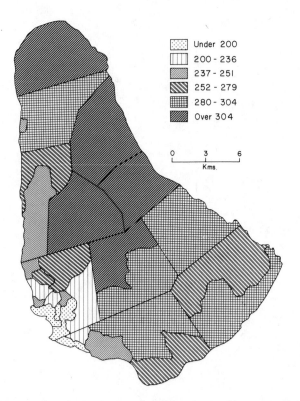

Figure 5.8
Number of children under 2 years of age per 1000 females aged 15-44 years, Barbados, 1960
Source: H.R. Jones (1977), figure 1

enumerator amended to 0–2 to make the index more temporally incisive. More refined indices cannot be adopted because of the unavailability of annual data on births for areas smaller than the 11 parishes of the island.

A comparison of Figure 5.8 and 5.9 suggests that the 1960 fertility pattern may be interpreted through the ecological theory of metropolitan dominance, by which cities exert an organizing influence on the social structure of their hinterlands by the diffusion of urban norms and values, so that gradient patterns in socio-economic characteristics are established. The lowest fertility rates are clearly in and around Bridgetown, with intermediate rates in the suburban coastal extensions to Speightstown and Oistins. The close relationship between 1960 fertility and urban-based modernization can be demonstrated statistically. Modernization is represented by the proportion of male working population in 1960 in white collar jobs. For the 28 areal units the correlation coefficient is −0.91, so that the degree of 'explanation' of spatial variation of fertility by a single measure of modernization can be regarded as 83 percent.

The subsequent spatial impact of the family planning programme now needs to be considered, since clinic and fieldwork activities are obviously subject to spatial

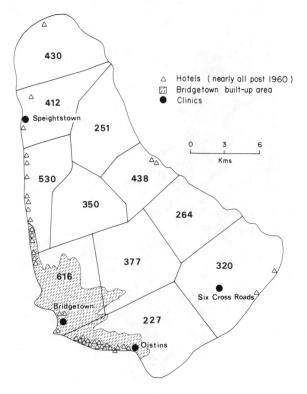

Figure 5.9
Selected features of settlement and of family planning activities in Barbados. The figure in
each parish refers to the number of women (per 1000 women aged 15-44 in 1970) contacted
by fieldworkers of Barbados Family Planning Association in an eighteen-month period,
1970-1971.
Source: data from Barbados Family Planning Association

concentration. Figure 5.9 shows the location of the four clinics where contraceptive
advice and supplies are available daily, and also the density of fieldwork by parish
for the limited period for which data are available. An outstanding feature is the
high concentration of field activity in the Bridgetown-centred parish of St. Michael,
which also has the crucial headquarters clinic and, of course, a range of modernizing influences.

The 1970 spatial pattern of fertility is depicted in Figure 5.10. Despite widespread and appreciable reduction of fertility in the 1960–1970 decade, there has
been little reduction in degree of regional variation; the coefficient of variation
$[(\sigma/\bar{x}) \times 100]$ in the ratios was 17.2 in 1960 and 15.4 in 1970. Although the
regional pattern appears broadly similar for both dates, there are differences, and
these might be attributable to the programme's spatial impact. The single index of
modernization which proved so powerful in interpreting the 1960 fertility pattern
now accounts for well under half of the 1970 fertility variation ($r^2 = 0.44$). Other
modernization and demographic structure variables were incorporated in the

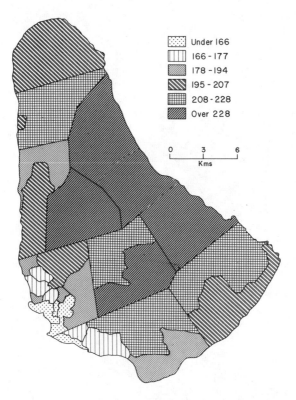

Figure 5.10
Number of children under 2 years of age per 1000 females aged 15-44 years, Barbados, 1970
Source: H.R. Jones (1977), figure 3

analysis, and after being reduced to three uncorrelated independent variables by principal components analysis, a regression with 1970 fertility levels as the dependent variable produced an r^2 value of 0.62. This is a substantial level of explanation, yet it falls well below the r^2 of 0.83 achieved by just one modernization variable in 1960.

In examining the pattern of 1970 residuals (Figure 5.11), one can certainly discern the spatial role of the family planning programme. The areas of significant positive residuals, where the regression equation overestimates 1970 fertility levels, are all close to clinics, while the parishes of highest fieldwork density generally show positive residuals.

There are policy implications stemming from the concentration of family planning activity in Barbados in the areas of greatest accessibility and modernization, notably in the Bridgetown metropolitan area, where programme activity reinforces the ongoing influence on fertility reduction of modernization. Organizational changes in the fieldwork programme are likely to accentuate rather than diminish these differentials, as effort since 1970 has been concentrated less on traditional domestic visits in outlying rural areas and more on large employment sites, with the

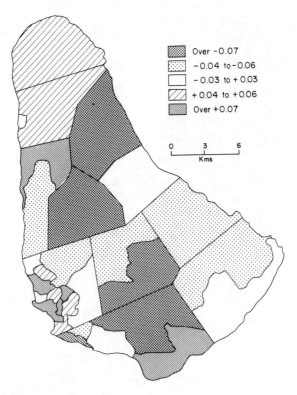

Figure 5.11
Residuals from regression of 1970 fertility levels on modernization and demographic
structure variables in Barbados
Source: H.R. Jones (1977), figure 4.

object of achieving higher contact rates. Inevitably this has accentuated the programme's urban bias, since the major employment sites are concentrated in
Bridgetown and obviously draw the bulk of their labour from the adjacent urban
population.

Clearly, important regional differentials in fertility do exist in an island as small
as Barbados, and metropolitan dominance in family planning activity contributes
actively to their maintenance. This suggests a need for some spatial reallocation of
programme resources within the island, along the lines of the somewhat exceptional but generally successful South Korean family planning programme where
programme input has always been concentrated in rural areas (Foreit et al. 1980).

CHAPTER 6

POPULATION GROWTH: PATTERNS, THEORIES, PROBLEMS

Having examined mortality and fertility separately, it is now appropriate to consider their interactive contribution to overall population growth through natural increase. The fascinating story of world population growth is how a few thousand wanderers a million of so years ago grew into today's billions of inhabitants of cities, towns and villages. The story comprises a long era of almost imperceptible growth, and a brief modern period of rapid expansion.

Homo sapiens is thought to have become distinct from its hominid predecessors about a million years ago. Between then and the beginning of agriculture and domestication of animals about 8000 BC, the average rate of population growth can be very roughly estimated at about 0.00001 percent per annum, so that in this 99 percent of man's history the population had increased to a mere 5–10 million (the number which anthropologists estimate as being capable of support by hunting and gathering cultures). After the establishment of agriculture and sedentary communities, the world's population grew to about 300 million by AD 1 and 800 million by 1750, but still the average growth rate was well below 0.1 percent per annum (Dumond 1975).

The modern period of rapid population growth may be regarded as starting about 1750 (Figure 6.1). Average annual growth rates climbed to about 0.5 percent between 1750 and 1900, 0.8 percent in the first half of this century, 1.7 percent between 1950 and 1970, and 2.0 percent in the 1970s (Coale 1974). In this minute period of human history the world's population has quintupled, from 0.8 billion in 1750 to 4.4 billion in 1980. Thus in less than 0.1 percent of man's history has occurred more than 80 percent of the increase in human numbers.

The modern period of population growth is clearly a transitory episode. If the growth rate of the 1970s were to be maintained, the population would double every 35 years or so, so that in 500 years there would be standing room only on the earth's surface. Simple arithmetic, therefore, shows that a return to a growth rate much nearer zero than 2.0 percent per annum is inevitable, but whether this will be achieved through lower birth rates or higher death rates, or some combination of

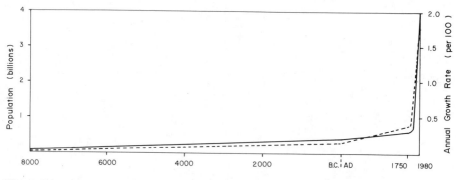

Figure 6.1
Growth of the world's human population in size (broken line) and in annual growth rate (continuous line)
Source: Coale (1974), p. 42. Copyright © (1974) by Scientific American, Inc.

both, is the great imponderable. The most plausible scenarios must surely be based on an understanding of the past interaction of mortality, fertility, resources and culture. In effect, the past must serve as our laboratory.

Pre-industrial demographic trends

The very slow population growth up to the eighteenth century was due to limits imposed by the carrying capacity of the environment in relation to levels of material culture. This has given rise to the concept of a ceiling of population, which is relatively unchanging for hunting and gathering cultures but which can rise from time to time in improving agricultural societies. These arguments have been criticized on the basis of their deterministic and somewhat static assumptions, yet they do retain conceptual utility.

Mortality checks

Traditionally it has been thought that population growth was regulated and maintained at subceiling levels by variable mortality. Early Malthusian theory is of this type. Malthus, in his first *Essay on the Principle of Population* (1798), argued that the power of the population to increase was greater than that of the earth to produce subsistence. He illustrated the differential by suggesting that population, when unchecked, tends to grow in a geometrical ratio (2,4,8,16,32), doubling perhaps every 25 years, whereas food supply at best increases arithmetically (2,3,4,5,6). Therefore, to maintain a balance between population and food supply, population growth is inevitably checked by:

a 'Misery' – the positive checks of famine, disease and war
b 'Vice' – abortion, sexual perversion and infanticide
c 'Moral Restraint' – the preventive checks of sexual abstinence and late marriage.

Only in the later editions of his essay did Malthus think that 'moral restraint' (broadened now to include, at least implicitly, contraception) could be in any way effective. His earlier views, which constitute classical Malthusian theory, posit the mortality-inducing positive checks as the fundamental regulators of population growth. They are exemplified by the demographic crises or catastrophes that historical demographers have identified in pre-industrial Europe.

Fertility checks

Only fairly recently has there been an awareness that a population equilibrium, at or some way below a ceiling level, may have been maintained in pre-industrial societies by different combinations of fertility and mortality (Figure 6.2). Three arguments can be used to suggest that fertility within pre-industrial societies varied both temporally and spatially, was invariably well below reproductive potential, and was at times a more important regulator of growth than mortality.

(i) Social conventions can be observed in some bird and animal populations to regulate fertility so that excessive population pressure on limited resources, and

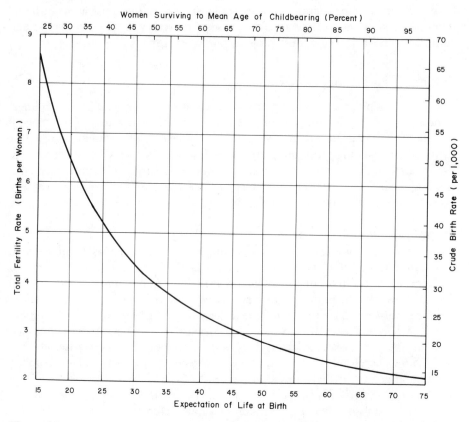

Figure 6.2
The maintenance of a nonmigrating population at a constant size by different combinations of fertility and mortality. If, for example, the birth rate was 50 per 1000, then life expectancy at birth would have been about 20 years, one-third of all women would have survived to mean child-bearing age, and these survivors would have averaged some 6.5 births.
Source: Coale (1974), p. 45. Copyright © (1974) by Scientific American, Inc.

therefore the extreme rigours of Darwinian natural selection, are avoided (Wynne-Edwards 1962, 1965). For example 'in birds which nest in colonies, such as storks and rooks, the number of nesting sites in the colony may be restricted by convention. Only those birds can breed which establish tenure upon one of the nesting sites. To secure a good site is evidence of high rank in the hierarchical society. Those lowest in the hierarchy, though sexually mature, may be unable to gain a site and so be prevented from breeding. The number of breeding pairs thus remains constant from year to year and the pressure upon the food supplies of the territory belonging to members of a rookery does not rise as it might if there were no social controls upon breeding' (Wrigley 1967, p.192).

(ii) Anthropological studies of successful hunting and gathering societies suggest that their population densities are consistently lower than the normal carrying capacity of their environment, that their populations remain at a near stationary level, and that there is a margin of child-bearing potential above fertility level; this margin is controlled by conventions to effect birth spacing.

Particularly rich and revealing demographic information has been collected from a population of !Kung Bushmen who were still practising a hunting and gathering economy in the 1960s in the Kalahari Desert of southern Africa (Lee and DeVore 1976, Howell 1979). Expectancy of life at birth has been calculated from childbirth histories to be about 33 years. If this had been accompanied by natality levels common in today's less developed countries, there would have been a population explosion. Instead, the completed family size of women surviving to the end of the child-bearing period was only about five – just sufficient to produce a stationary or very slowly growing population.

How was this modest family size achieved in a technologically primitive society? One should never underestimate the role of subfecundity under conditions of poor health and undernutrition (Frisch 1975), but more emphasis is placed on deliberate child-spacing in order to accommodate activities necessary for hunting and gathering peoples, and to provide for the nutrition of the very young. Since mothers need to be mobile, not only between camps but also in daily food gathering, they are unable to carry more than a single child on hip or back. Moreover, foods soft enough to permit the early weaning of infants are often unavailable to hunting and gathering peoples, so that infants often have to be breastfed for three–four years. The needs for appreciable birth intervals are clear, but the methods used are not. In addition to post-birth sexual abstinence, *coitus interuptus* and abortion, there may well be a contraceptive effect from the severe calorie drain of prolonged breastfeeding, in that there is insufficient body fat for ovulation to take place. Infanticide may also have contributed significantly to child-spacing (although not, of course, to birth-spacing), as it did among the Australian aborigines (Krzywicki 1934).

The low fertility of the nomadic !Kung contradicts traditional theories that the size of hunter-gatherer populations was limited solely by high mortality rates. !Kung population size remained stable essentially because there were so few children born. When the !Kung become sedentary, their birth intervals drop by a third. There is no longer the need to 'travel light' in term of material possessions and young children, and infants can be weaned much sooner by giving them grain meal and cows' milk.

One should beware of making wide inferences from studies of limited populations, but demographic studies of groups like the nomadic and sedentary !Kung have certainly led to new perspectives on population growth in Palaeolithic and Neolithic times. It may well be that with the beginnings of agriculture there were *increases* of both mortality and fertility. Concentration of population in villages could be expected to promote the transmission of diseases, and there was always vulnerability to crop failure. Thus 'the greater population attained by the agriculturists is correctly attributed to an enhanced supply of food, but the appealing inference that reduced mortality was responsible for this acceleration of growth is not necessarily justified' (Coale 1974, p.21).

One should also note that the causative relationship between the Neolithic Revolution and population growth is a matter of some controversy. Traditionally it has been assumed (e.g., Childe 1936) that the adoption of an agricultural economy led to subsequent population growth, but some (notably Cohen 1977) argue that population growth came first, and was the cause, not the result, of the Neolithic. More generally, Clark (1967) and Boserup (1965, 1975) argue that population growth is the stimulating cause of agricultural change, following 'a long-established if minor tradition in economic writing which argues that not only does population growth cause economic improvement but that without such a spur human society would remain culturally and economically stagnant' (Grigg 1979, p.64).

(iii) There is abundant evidence (see Chapter 4) that in the 200 or 300 years preceding industrialization the population growth of agricultural communities in western Europe and Japan was regulated not so much by mortality as by the fertility effects of an oppressive marital pattern. Age-specific marital fertility was high, but the majority of women married late or not at all.

A homeostatic regime
Homeostasis may be defined as the tendency for the internal evironment of the body to remain constant in spite of varying external conditions. It has been argued convincingly (D. S. Smith 1977, Corsini 1977) that homeostatic demographic patterns characterize pre-industrial populations, in that demographic variables tend to check each other to maintain an equilibrium. Any disequilibrium between population growth and resources tends to generate a correcting or homeostatic response. Classic Malthusian theory describes such a response, in terms of positive checks on population growth, but we have seen that fertility variations can play the same regulatory role.

If one accepts the homeostatic theory of counterbalancing demographic forces, then the demographic diversity among pre-industrial populations becomes easier to reconcile. Differences in mortality, marital structure and marital fertility did not generate equivalent differences in population increase. The rate of natural increase was clearly more constant than the individual components of population changes, so that 'the whole of the population engine of early modern Europe makes considerably more sense than any of its parts examined in isolation' (D. S. Smith 1977, p.43).

The demographic transition and the demographic cycle

A general description, although not a complete explanation, of changing rates of mortality, fertility and natural increase in the more developed countries of the world since the eighteenth century is provided by demographic transition theory. This posits a particular pattern of demographic change as accompanying a nation's progression from a largely rural, agrarian and illiterate society to a dominantly urban, industrial and literate one. During the course of this progression, which is regarded to all intents and purposes as irreversible, there are major reductions in both fertility and mortality, so much so that in the past two centuries average life expectancy in developed countries has doubled and standardized fertility halved.

If fertility and mortality declines had been concurrent, population growth in developed countries would have been fairly modest, as was uniquely the case in France where there had been exceptionally early fertility decline in a dominantly agrarian society. But elsewhere in the developed world mortality decline preceded fertility decline by about a century, leading to the replacement of a demographic steady state by the population explosion of nineteenth-century Europe and North America. In some cases there may have been a slight increase of fertility at the beginning of industrialization, further accentuating population growth in the transition.

Figure 6.3 provides a schematic representation of the standard demographic transition. Note how in pre-industrial societies the birth rate is relatively constant, while the death rate fluctuates from year to year in response to epidemics and variable food supply. After the transition the roles are reversed: the death rate remains constant while fertility oscillates in relation to cultural and economic forces not yet fully understood. An actual example (Figure 6.4) is provided by Denmark, one of the few countries with reasonably reliable demographic data before the nineteenth century. Its population growth from about 1 million in 1800 to 5 million in 1975 (despite appreciable emigration to North America) is clearly due to the lag of about a century between the onsets of fairly regular mortality decline (1790) and fertility decline (1890). Superimposed on Figure 6.4 is the

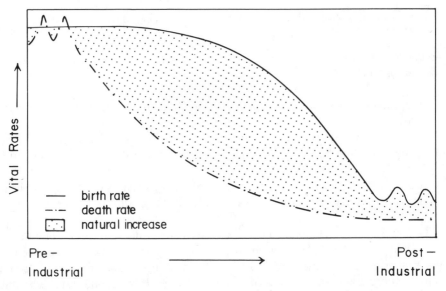

Figure 6.3
The standard demographic transition

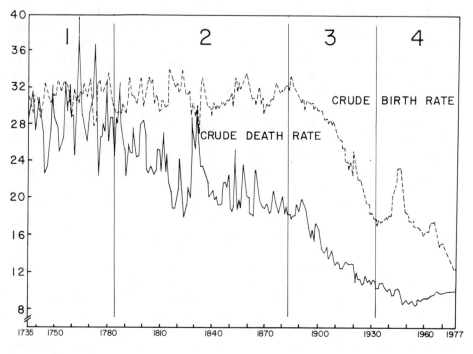

Figure 6.4
Crude birth rates and death rates in Denmark, 1735-1977, and stages of the demographic cycle
Source: birth rates and death rates from Matthiessen (1972), figure 1, and UN
Demographic Yearbooks

sequence of stages in population growth which some demographers have termed the demographic cycle:

1   High stationary stage, with high fertility and high mortality providing very little growth
2   Early expanding stage, with high fertility and declining mortality
3   Late expanding stage, with declining fertility but still significant population growth
4   Low stationary stage, with fertility and mortality levelling out to re-establish a fairly stationary population, thus completing the cycle.

This cycle can be recognized clearly in the Danish data, although population growth in the fourth stage has been greater than in most countries of northwestern Europe. By extrapolating from 1930s' trends in countries like France and Britain, some demographers suggested a fifth stage in the cycle – a senile stage, when the birth rate would fall consistently below the death rate, causing population decrease. Postwar elevation of birth rates seemed to have discounted this, but major fertility falls in the 1960s and 1970s have brought about a situation of natural decrease in some recent years in Austria, West Germany, East Germany, Sweden and Luxembourg. There is, however, little evidence to suggest that this might be a long-term pattern; if anything, the evidence (e.g., Easterlin 1976) favours fertility increases in the 1980s. Periods of slight population decrease, if interspersed with periods of increase, are quite compatible with a stage 4 – low stationary – situation.

The patterns of demographic transition and demographic cycle can be recognized clearly enough in developed countries, but the way in which they are derived from the social and economic changes associated with development or modernization is a more complex matter. We have reviewed in previous chapters the separate responses of mortality and fertility to socio-economic change. All that needs to be repeated here is that there has been a good deal of variety between and within developed countries in such demographic responses. In particular, no threshold levels of development can be identified for the initiation of regular fertility decline. This has led some to question and even reject the validity of demographic transition theory (e.g., Goldscheider 1971). Yet surely a certain degree of inconsistency can be accommodated within such a sweeping macro-historical theory? At high levels of generality the demographic transition does provide an effective generalization of much of the world's demographic history. From such a model one should not expect useful averages. There is no 'typical' period of time needed for the transition, no 'typical' lag in fertility reduction, and no 'typical' level of urbanization, literacy or wealth to initiate fertility reduction.

Before proceeding to assess the relevance of demographic transition theory in less developed countries, it is useful at this stage to consider a theory which provides a broad rationale for the demographic transition.

Theory of demographic regulation

This optimistic theory asserts that 'modern man is able to foresee demographic catastrophe long before it arrives and takes adaptive action long before it is forced on him by the brute forces of nature' (Bogue 1969, p.53). Emphasis is thus placed on man's unique position as a highly flexible and adaptable creature, capable, in particular, of curtailing his fertility when mortality reduction (a universally valued goal) causes population to grow faster than the environment's ability to sustain it.

In such circumstances a society has to regain control of its growth, so that the regulation of fertility becomes identified with group, as well as individual, welfare. It is not a straightforward automatic response, but embraces the entire process of social change whereby a solution in terms of behavioural norms must be devised, diffused and widely adopted.

The theory is based, therefore, on an underlying functionalist assumption that societies strive to maintain an equilibrium. To some extent it is an expression of homeostasis or auto-regulation, although there may well be an appreciable time-lag and consequent population growth during the adjustment, because of cultural inertia; such inertia will vary from society to society.

The demographic transition and less developed countries

For some time it has been fashionable to deny the applicability of demographic transition theory to the Third World. It is emphasized that imported medical and public health technology has drastically cut mortality, but has not been accompanied by the significant modernization changes necessary to promote fertility reduction from the high levels permitted by a pattern of early and near-universal marriage never experienced in pre-industrial Europe. It is shown that the resultant population growth rates of 3.5 to 2.0 percent per annum, with populations doubling every 20–35 years, far exceeded growth in any of Europe's nineteenth-century transitions.

Yet there are clear relationships in the Third World between levels of development or modernization and levels of mortality and fertility, as Chapters 2 and 5 have demonstrated. The more developed countries have, on the whole, experienced the greatest mortality declines and the beginnings of fertility reduction. It has been observed that in Latin America 'as in Europe, the broadest implications of transition theory do materialise: birth rates are falling in the countries that are relatively developed and have low mortality . . . also as in Europe, natality tends to fluctuate in the predecline period' (S. E. Beaver 1975, p.146).

But although the early stages of demographic transition may be observed in the Third World, there is no assurance that the later stages will replicate European experience and achieve, through fertility regulation, environmentally sustainable population levels (the other regulation method widely used by European societies – mass emigration to the New World – is unrealistic in today's socio-political climate).

Proponents of demographic regulation as a universal theory suggest optimistically that the necessary rapid fertility regulation can be achieved in the Third World. They point out that latecomers to the transition process, notably Germany, southern and eastern Europe and Japan, have all experienced a concentrated and accelerated fertility decline; that, contrary to some views, the pace of modernization in many Third World countries is actually more rapid than in nineteenth-century Europe; and that governments are now prepared and have the capability to promote policies of fertility regulation. There are others who maintain that high fertility is so institutionally interwoven with the entire cultural fabric of less developed countries that its reduction is an intractable problem. The demographic history of the next two or three generations will therefore be of crucial importance and, to scholars, great fascination (Freeman and Jahoda 1978). No one can be confident of his preferred scenario.

Global growth problems

In the last two decades in affluent Western countries there has been a huge surge of concern by scholars and general public, although somewhat less by governments, about global population growth and its associated problems. This can be related to four factors.

(i) Population growth has reached an unprecedented level, with the world's population doubling every 35–45 years, raising ever more vividly the spectre of 'standing room only'. At no point in their demographic transitions did European nations experience the growth in population-related demand for basic necessities that now confronts today's less developed countries. Medium variant population projections published in 1979 by the UN Population Division and by the US Census Bureau suggest that the world's population will have grown from about 4.1 billion in 1975 to 6.2 billion in 2000; the major assumption of the projections is that the current (1980) annual growth rate of about 1.7 percent will drop to about 1.5 percent by 2000. A staggering 90 percent of the population increase will occur in the less developed countries, which comprised 68 percent of the world's population in 1950, 73 percent in 1979 and a likely 78 percent in 2000.

(ii) The snowballing role of population momentum has become more widely appreciated. An analogy is the momentum of a speeding train that cannot be brought to an immediate halt even with full application of brakes. An enormous momentum for growth has been created by the very young age structure of today's less developed countries, the legacy of high fertility in the immediate past. Even if replacement levels of fertility were reached in the developed world by 1980 and in the less developed countries by 2000 (very optimistic assumptions), the world's population would still expand to 8 billion. In fact, many demographers think it unlikely that stabilization will occur before a level of 10 billion or so is reached about a century from now.

(iii) The publication in 1962 of Rachel Carson's *Silent Spring*, highlighting the decimation of wildlife by pesticides like DDT, set off major concern in the developed world about environmental deterioration. Well-publicized episodes like the Torrey Canyon and other oilspills, Minimata Bay mercury poisoning, Lake Erie fish kills, defoliation in Vietnam and desertification in the Sahel have fuelled this concern about man's ability to contain pollution and effectively husband life-support systems. The concern expressed itself in the formation and rapid growth of pressure groups like the Conservation Society, Friends of the Earth and Zero Population Growth, and in major world conferences like the 1972 Stockholm meeting on the Human Environment and the 1974 World Food Conference and World Population Conference.

The role of population growth in environmental management is expressed in a simple equation:

$$I = PF$$

where I is the total impact of a society on the ecosystem, P is population size, and F is impact per capita (Ehrlich and Ehrlich 1972, p.259). Some scientists like Barry Commoner have argued that F is the more critical factor, embracing life-style and particularly consumption patterns, but there is little doubt that when P and F increase simultaneously, as has generally been the case in the modern world, the effect on I can be massive.

(iv) Recent decades have seen a growing awareness not only that problems of population growth, food supply, dwindling natural resources, pollution, under-employment and the like are essentially global in nature, but also that they are intimately and intricately inter-related; therein lies the field of modern human ecology.

It is obvious, then, that discussion of global population growth problems can only be meaningful within a wider, system-related context. Attitudes have tended to polarize into standpoints which can be termed Malthusian pessimism and technological optimism.

Malthusian pessimism

The fundamental thesis of Malthus that population tends to outstrip resources and therefore is invariably checked by 'misery' was widely scorned until fairly recently. The demographic and economic history of Europe in the nineteenth and early twentieth centuries seemed to disprove him, since the standard of living, despite unprecedented population growth, continued to climb. More recently it has been appreciated that Europe's population at that time was being supported not only by its internal resources, but also by the New World's provision of food and industrial raw materials and its absorption of Europe's surplus population. At a *global* level, taking a long-term perspective, the Malthusian thesis is not discredited.

In the 1960s and 1970s photographs taken from outer space have provided a salutary reminder that the earth is like a spaceship. It has limited resources aboard, so that the human population cannot expand its numbers and resource demands indefinitely, or spaceship Earth would simply run out of fuel, food and other vital support systems. Fears and indeed forecasts of a global eco-catastrophe became common, even fashionable, in literature (*The Population Bomb, Born to Starve, The Hungry Future, End to Affluence, People: An Endangered Species*). Perhaps the arch-prophet of doom has been the American biologist Paul Ehrlich (1971, 1972), haunted by the apocalyptic fear that spaceship Earth would be blown up by its internal population bomb: that mankind would breed itself into oblivion. In much-quoted phrases he asserted that the battle to feed all of humanity was over and that hundreds of millions of people would starve to death in the 1970s and 1980s.

The high-water mark of modern Malthusianism was reached with the publication of *The Limits to Growth* (Meadows et al. 1972) – a landmark book which, love it or hate it, admire it or ridicule it, has commanded world-wide attention and debate. Its mode of commissioning was indicative of the late 1960s and early 1970s mood of ecological concern. An informal international association with a restricted, prestigious membership, the self-styled Club of Rome, had embarked on a breathtakingly ambitious undertaking, nothing less than a *Project on the Predicament of Mankind*. It had been impressed by the system dynamics work undertaken by Jay Forrester (1971) and his colleagues at the Massachusetts Institute of Technology, so that model-based work was commissioned on the global interaction of five basic factors that determine and, it was presumed, ultimately limit growth – population, agricultural production, natural resources, industrial production and pollution.

The basis of the simulation work conducted in *The Limits to Growth* study was a series of calculated or assumed relationships between the five basic factors and their component elements. Given these relationships, computer runs were made to project recent trends into the future. These runs invariably spell out disaster, since one cannot indefinitely accommodate exponential (geometric) growth in a finite system. Sooner or later, negative feedback loops of famine, pollution and resource depletion result in a system overshoot and collapse. Stripped of jargon, these are, of course, the positive checks of Malthus.

Figure 6.5 is the 'standard' run, based on the projection of historical growth values and the assumption that there is a 250-year supply of nonrenewable resources at 1970 usage rates. The system collapses disastrously well before 2100, as is the case with subsequent runs using what the study team regards as even the most optimistic assumptions about resource expansion, pollution control and fertility reduction. Such assumptions prolong the period of population and industrial growth, but cannot remove the eventual limits to growth.

The social advocacy of the study and its supporters is clear. Since unlimited growth in a finite world is impossible, two other options are left: an unthinkable nature-imposed limitation of growth, involving massive famine, disease, pollution and the like, or a self-imposed limitation – an extension of the preventive checks of Malthus to embrace birth control programmes, capital shifts from manufacturing to agriculture, environmental management, and the adoption of ecologically harmonious life-styles.

The Limits to Growth was favourably received by many biologists and ecologists well versed in the exponential growth of animal and plant populations up to a critical environmental 'carrying capacity'. But reviews by social scientists have generally been harsh (Cole et al. 1973, W. C. Robinson 1974, McGinnis 1974), with the major criticism being summed up by the old computer maxim: Garbage In, Garbage Out. In other words, computer studies are only as good as the quality of information and assumptions adopted. For many economists, the assumptions about future resource availability do not adequately take into account the way in which the market system provides incentives for substitution, recycling and new extractive methods; for example, wood was once a major source of fuel, but when supplies became scarce near cities, it was collected from ever greater distances, so that the cost rose and substitution by coal was stimulated. But the major criticism has centred on the lack of sociological insight in a study carried out essentially by systems engineers: 'Its utter lack of sociological content has yielded a model of a world that no-one knows. It is a world without social heterogeneity. . . . Thus all nations, all people move to a catastrophe or harmony at an identical pace. There are no haves and have nots simultaneously. There are no differences in demographic transition' (McGinnis 1974, p.299).

Mesarovic and Pestel (1974) have provided a more refined simulation study, again commissioned by the Club of Rome, which takes into account at least some

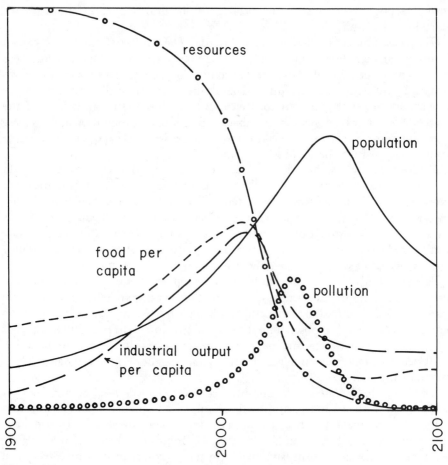

Figure 6.5
The Limits to Growth: world model standard run. The standard run assumes no major change in the relationships that have historically governed the development of the world interaction system, and all plotted variables follow historical values from 1900 to 1970. Food, industrial output and population grow exponentially until rapidly diminishing resources brake industrial growth. Population growth is finally halted by a rise in the death rate due to decreased food and medical services.
Source: figure 35 from *The Limits to Growth: A Report for the Club of Rome's Project on the Predicament of Mankind*, by D.H. Meadows, D.C. Meadows, J. Randers and W. Behrens. A Potomac Associates Book published by Universe Books, New York, 1972.

of the criticisms of *The Limits to Growth*. They recognize diversity within the greater world system, and by regional disaggregation show that catastrophes or collapses can occur in different regions, for different reasons, at different times. The food-population balance in southern Asia is examined in detail. They show that under what they regard as very optimistic assumptions for agricultural land expansion, fertilizer input and fertility reduction, the food crises in the region will worsen, so that early in the next century, in order to stave off catastrophe, the region would have to import some 500 million tons of grain a year. Even if this were available, the cost and logistics of shipping and internal distribution are staggering. It is at the regional level, then, that the Malthusian scenario of catastrophe is at its most convincing; it would seem to accord to reality in the famines of the 1970s in Bangladesh, Bihar, Kampuchea, Ethiopia and the Sahel.

Technological optimism

In assessments of mankind's survival prospects, the arguments of Malthusian doom-mongers are opposed by the 'technical fix cheer-mongers'. Their views are neatly represented in a poem, 'The Technologist's Reply to a Conservationist's Lament', written by the American economist Kenneth Boulding.

> Man's potential is quite terrific
> You can't go back to the Neolithic.
> The cream is there for us to skim it
> Knowledge is power and the sky's the limit.
> Every mouth has hands to feed it.
> Food is found when people need it.
> All we need is found in granite
> Once we have the men to plan it.
> Yeast and algae give us meat,
> Soil is almost obsolete.
> Men can grow to pastures greener
> Till all the earth is Pasadena.
>
> Moral:
> Man's a nuisance, Man's a crackpot.
> But only man can hit the jackpot.
>
> (A. Chisholm 1972, p.31)

Faith is thus put in man's innate ability to adapt, invent, substitute and recycle, so that a breathing space is provided until the Third World populations complete their demographic transitions.

Some of the more strident claims of the technical fix standpoint have been made by the futurologist Herman Kahn, director of the Hudson Institute. He argues (Kahn et al. 1976) that wealth inevitably trickles down to the poor, so that within a few decades everyone on earth will be rich by contemporary standards. He maintains that with current and quasi-current technology the earth can support over 15 billion people at per capita incomes well in excess of the current United States average. The world, he argues, will never run out of resources, since the entire planet is composed of minerals. There would be a steady state of substitution and recycling – an 'Age of Substitutability' (Goeller and Weinberg 1976). The technological optimists also maintain that the social advocacy of The Limits to Growth causes more problems than it solves: 'A failure to maintain economic growth means continued poverty, deprivation, disease, squalor, degradation, and slavery to soul-destroying toil for countless millions of the world's population' (Beckerman 1974, p.9).

Both the Malthusian and the technical fix viewpoints have been savagely mauled by radical economists and Marxists on the grounds that they both ignore the critically important social organization of production, distribution and consumption. It has been observed that only the poor go hungry, that scarcity is engineered for profit maximization by capitalism and that 'povery is due to maldistribution of resources both internationally and within nations and not to the physical limits of producing the resources themselves' (Sandbach 1978, p.27). A much-quoted case is Brazil, where considerable growth in GNP per capita is not thought to have benefited the vast bulk of the population, because the benefits of growth have been siphoned off by powerful local élites; there has been no trickling down of benefits to the landless rural poor and the shanty-town dwellers.

Recent trends in population–food balance

The preoccupation of mankind has always been to obtain enough food, the basic life-support resource. This is less evident in the developed world, where only about one-fifth of disposable income is spent on food, but in many Third World countries the proportion is between 60 and 90 percent. It is instructive to review recent trends in world food production against a backcloth of rival Malthusian and technical fix paradigms for the future relationship between population and resources.

At a global or macro-regional scale the evidence suggests that the population–food balance has improved significantly during the 1970s. Despite unprecedented population growth, global food production per head of population increased by a healthy 6 percent between about 1970 and 1978 (Table 6.1). Yet this global success was achieved essentially through considerable production increases in the developed countries, since in Latin America and the Far East (excluding China) per capita increases were only modest, while in Africa there was a significant worsening of the food–population balance. Moreover, there have been particular years, notably 1972, when per capita food production fell appreciably in many parts of the world. It needs little imagination to appreciate the potentially disastrous famine consequences of two or three bad years like 1972 occurring in a row.

The food scarcities in 1972 were caused by drought in southern Asia and many parts of Africa; by the failure of the Peruvian anchovy catch, creating extra demand for alternative sources of protein like soya beans; and by massive grain purchases, consequent upon harvest failure, by the Russians. The USSR became the world's largest importer of grain, purchasing a total of 30 million tons (net) in 1972 and 1973, compared with net exports of 9 million tons in 1970 and 1971. These commercial purchases quickly exhausted accumulated grain reserves in North America, so that as the 'Kansas cathedrals' emptied, charitable famine relief became increasingly difficult in southern Asia and Africa. By the end of 1973 world

Table 6.1 Indices of food production per capita

	1969–1971	1972	1973	1974	1975	1976	1977	1978
World	100	99	102	102	103	103	104	106
Developed market economies:								
North America	100	102	103	103	109	112	114	114
Western Europe	100	100	104	108	106	106	107	111
Oceania	100	100	111	103	111	116	111	124
Developing market economies:								
Africa	100	97	92	96	93	94	90	91
Latin America	100	98	98	101	102	104	105	105
Far East	100	95	101	96	102	103	103	103
Centrally planned economies:								
Asia*	100	101	104	106	108	109	109	110
Europe and USSR	100	101	113	110	108	111	111	117

* China, North Korea, Vietnam
Source: UN *Statistical Yearbook 1978*, table 7

grain reserves had fallen to their lowest level in two decades, equivalent to less than a 30-day supply.

Useful preliminary discussions of the geography of hunger have been provided by Learmonth (1978) and Dando (1980). Learmonth suggests that there are traditional famine tracts, which lie mainly in areas of low to moderate rainfall with high variability, peopled by sedentary subsistence cultivators. At these climatic margins of agriculture, a series of drought years may cause human disaster on a massive scale, particularly in those countries whose ports, internal communications and administrative systems cannot cope with appreciable food transfers, whether derived internally or externally. The areas periodically afflicted are the margins of the Old World deserts from Africa north and south of the Sahara to central Asia and northwestern China, as well as parts of India and northeastern Brazil. Commercial farmers operating in similar climatic environments, like Australian stockfarmers and American wheatfarmers, may well encounter periodic financial hardship, but rarely famine, although one should never forget the Dust Bowl disaster of the 1930s in the American Great Plains. Learmonth also discusses the world distribution of kwashiorkor, a protein-deficiency disease, reminding us that hunger and malnutrition are much more widespread in the Third World than actual famine. Most people in the less developed countries are condemned 'to a monotonous, low-quality diet, consisting mainly of cereal grains or tubers and other starchy roots. For the poorest 20 percent of the population the diet falls below the physiological requirement for a normally active, healthy person' (Revelle 1974, p.165).

The precarious balance between food and population in the Third World would not be so potentially catastrophic if the huge potential food surpluses of North America and western Europe could be made available readily to counter Third World famine and malnutrition. Among the growing demands from Third World countries for a New International Economic Order (Anell and Nygren 1980), to regulate their relationship with developed countries on what they regard as a fairer basis, has been that for an internationally managed world food bank. This would comprise food grain stores for famine relief, fertilizers to enable crop production to be quickly boosted in critical regions, reserves of land for putting under the plough in emergencies, technical information to promote better yields, and stores of crop genes to enable new varieties to quickly replace those stricken by pests or fungi.

That this has not occurred has been explained by some in terms of the political and financial expediency practised by Western governments and Western agribusiness, thereby emphasizing the institutional 'Achilles heel' of the technical fix argument. 'The fact that food is a basic human necessity does not mean that it is universally thought of as a basic human right. For a limited number of agents in a position to call most of the shots, food is nothing more than a series of commodities on which money can be made' (S. George 1976, p.139). Thus it is that food production in developed countries is related to monetary market demand and not to the real needs of human beings: 'If US farm policy over the past half century can be thought of as having a theme, it has been to prevent productivity from driving down prices. . . . From Soil Bank to Public Law 480 to drowning baby pigs, little that might elevate prices has not been tried' (Poleman 1975, p.513). Much the same could be said of the common agricultural policy of the EEC, designed to enhance the incomes of its own farmers to the extent of creating butter mountains and wine lakes at the expense of any alleviation of food deficits in the Third World.

The wastefulness of Western agriculture is also expressed in its emphasis on livestock products, since cattle, sheep, pigs and poultry consume four to seven times as much food energy as they provide in their edible products. This has provoked an outraged eminent agronomist to exclaim: 'The rich white man, with his overconsumption of meat and his lack of generosity for poor people, behaves like a veritable cannibal – an indirect cannibal. By consuming meat, which wastes the grain that could have saved them, last year we ate the children of the Sahel, Ethiopia and Bangladesh' (Dumont 1974).

A strong case has also been made out (S. George 1976, Omvedt 1975, Sinha 1976) for the way in which Western governments exploit rather than alleviate food deficits in the Third World. The following remarks from two *liberal* American politicians speak for themselves:

> Before people can do anything they have got to eat. And if you are looking for a way to get people to lean on you and to be dependent on you, in terms of their cooperation with you, it seems to me that food dependence would be terrific (Hubert Humphrey, Hearings of the Senate Agriculture and Forestry Committee 1957, p.129).

> The great food markets of the future are the very areas where vast numbers of people are learning through Food for Peace to eat American produce. The people we assist today will become our customers tomorrow (George McGovern 1964, pp.24–25).

A former US Agriculture Secretary, Earl Butz, has been quoted (*Nation's Business*, June 1973) as saying: 'Food is a weapon. It is now one of the principal tools in our negotiating kit.' It is well known, for example, that the American initiatives in the Middle East in the 1970s have been dependent on the provision of vast quantities of wheat to Egypt. Tarrant (1980), in a useful attempt by a geographer to relate food aid, mainly supplied on a bilateral basis by the United States, to food need between 1974 and 1976, recognizes one group of less developed countries (Cyprus, South Korea, Chile, Egypt and Jordan) where aid on a per capita basis appears generous. The political significance of these countries to the United States at that time is obvious enough. In contrast, he points to many countries, particularly in the Sahel, whose food aid in relation to their critical food deficits is as slight as is their international strategic significance.

Given these obstacles to effective food transfer from the food-rich West to the hungry countries, what are the prospects for agricultural development within the Third World itself? First, it needs to be said that after two decades when Third World development programmes were dominated by grandiose project investment in manufacturing, communications and other infrastructural services, the 1970s have seen a salutary emphasis on the rural sector which embraces the bulk of the population, and certainly of the poor. The fashionable current priority for agricultural development is even shown by the capitalist world's largest and most powerful lending institution, the International Bank for Reconstruction and Development (the World Bank).

A technical fix solution to Third World population–food problems is still widely canvassed, largely on the grounds that there is scope under current technology for doubling the amount of cultivated land in the Third World, especially in Africa and Latin America, and that there is considerable potential for raising the low yields per acre to something like current Japanese levels. At its most naïve, West-is-Best level this view is well represented by T. Lynn Smith (1976, p.45): 'By about 1930 this system [of Western mechanized agriculture] had become the most modern and effective of all the ways of getting products from the soil. In it the tractor and its associated implements, along with the automobile and the motor truck, the gasoline engine, and electrically driven machines for milking, grinding feed, powering feed belts, and so on, are the core components. . . . This mechanised way of farming is the portal through which Colombia's agriculture is entering the twentieth century, and in the years immediately ahead the chances are that its adoption and spread will enable the production of food, feed and fiber to spurt out ahead in the race with the rapidly growing population. . . . In brief, an entire mechanised way of farming is readily available for installation at any place where the necessary financing may be provided.'

But the great bulk of recent development literature is insistent that Western-type agriculture is at best inappropriate and at worst catastrophic in Third World settings. It is profligate in use of fossil-fuel energy (Leach 1976), and its labour productivity emphasis makes little sense in countries whose one really abundant resource is people. Even the breeding in the West of high-yielding wheat and rice varieties and the wide distribution from the mid-1960s of the new 'miracle' seeds and their associated packages of growing methods in many Third World countries, notably Mexico, India, Pakistan and the Philippines, have been a somewhat mixed blessing (Frankel 1971, King 1974, Griffin 1974, UN Research Institute for Social Development 1974). This so-called Green Revolution has certainly increased marketable surpluses, important for the growing millions of urban consumers, but it has also exacerbated inequalities between rich and poor regions and rich and poor farmers. It has benefited a small, politically powerful élite of large, rich and literate farmers at the expense of the majority of peasants who are unable to afford, and sometimes to understand, the package of fertilizers, pesticides and water input necessary for the successful adoption of the new varieties.

There is a growing consensus that the food problems of the Third World can be alleviated more by social and political reform than by technical innovation. The 'trickle down' theory of development, which has selectively and, some would argue, exclusively favoured large landowners, industrialists and urban workers, is giving way, at least among development advisers, to a 'basic needs' philosophy, whereby development strategies attempt to satisfy the fundamental, but modest needs of the bulk of the population, who are essentially the rural poor. There may be a place for so-called intermediate technology, which supplements rather than replaces agricultural labour. There is certainly place for the provision of agricultural credit at equitable interest rates, since only a small élite minority of Third World farmers have access to state or bank credit. The typical Third World peasant borrower is left to the far from tender mercies of village usurers and their extortionate interest rates.

But the most fundamental rural development need is now thought to be access to land. 'The task of raising yields . . . must confront the attitudes and institutions that have so long held these rural societies stagnant. Most important is to change "the relation between man and the land", creating the possibilities and the incentives for a man to work more, to work harder and more efficiently and to invest whatever he can lay his hands on to improve the land, in the first instance his own labor. This is the essence of the demand for a well-planned land and tenancy reform. Such reform has been on the agenda in all underdeveloped countries; with only a few exceptions it has been botched' (Myrdal 1974, p.178). The exceptions, where land redistribution, often accompanied by the establishment of co-operatives, has played an important part in raising rural living standards, include the market economies of Japan, Taiwan and South Korea. Among socialist countries, China's recent success in feeding its huge population has been attributed above all to the ways in which land is farmed collectively, not for a distant state bureaucracy but for the local commune; the agricultural workforce thus has a strong collective stake in its own productivity.

The case of China emphasizes that hunger is not simply caused by population pressure. Before the 1949 revolution, with a population of less than 300 million, but with a feudal, landlord-dominated countryside, this was indeed the *China, Land of Famine* depicted by Mallory. But by 1980, with a population exceeding 900 million, recurrent and widespread famine is a thing of the past. One might argue, therefore, that hunger is not caused by population pressure on limited resources but by inadequate socio-political structures.

CHAPTER 7

POPULATION POLICIES

Recognizing that social and economic problems may be caused or aggravated by particular levels of population growth, governments at various stages in the twentieth century have intervened in an attempt to regulate the dynamics of population growth. Strictly defined, population policies are those 'policies explicitly adopted by governments for their presumed demographic consequences' (Berelson 1974, p.6), although the ultimate aim of demographic manipulation is the achievement of primary goals like the enhancement of national security and of economic and social welfare. There is little scope for any manipulation of the death rate to achieve demographic ends, and although government control of immigration has become an important element in regulation of population growth in a few countries like Australia and Canada, it is political intervention in fertility that forms the core of most population policies. This chapter will discuss only population policies concerning the level and growth of national populations. No competent geographer would ignore, as some demographers have done, government policies on population redistribution, but these can be discussed more appropriately in the following chapters on migration.

A straightforward distinction can be made between the pro-natalist policies adopted by several, but by no means the majority of developed countries, and the anti-natalist policies adopted by an increasing number of Third World countries.

Pro-natalist policies

These have been adopted in some European countries (Glass 1967, Berelson 1974) in response to the fertility troughs reached in the 1930s and the 1970s. A pro-natalist policy can embrace two major strategies: first, restrictions on access of couples to methods of fertility control; and second, a more positive attempt to influence attitudes to child-bearing through the provision of financial incentives and the creation of a moral climate approving of large families.

Perhaps the most explicit pro-natalist policies have been those pursued by Fascist regimes in the 1930s. The major elements in the Nazi programme in Germany were: the criminal prosecution of induced abortions; the suppression of contraceptive information; a tax on unmarried adults; a marriage loan to young couples which could be partly written off by·having children; family allowances, tax concessions and housing preferences for large families; and intensive propaganda on the building of a master race. The number of marriages and births did increase dramatically. The crude birth rate rose from 14.7 (per 1000) in 1933, when the Nazis came to power, to 18.0 in 1934 and 19.7 in 1938. But, in addition to the influence of population policy measures, there was the undoubted stimulus given to fertility by falling unemployment and growing national self-confidence. Moreover, most of the increase in births came from first births, suggesting that parents were encouraged to have their children sooner, but not necessarily in larger numbers. This tends to be a common feature of pro-natalist policies – an immediate elevation of period fertility measures, but little effect on completed family size.

In Fascist Italy, similar pro-natalist measures were introduced from 1926, but with little impact even on period measures. Other European countries where pro-natalist policies were widely discussed and variably implemented in response to the 1930s fertility trough were Belgium, Sweden, the United Kingdom and France. The interactive coincidence of stagnant economies and stagnant populations was a source of concern to many analysts (Myrdal and Myrdal 1934, Spengler 1938, Reddaway 1939), and Royal Commissions to advise on population problems were established in Sweden and the United Kingdom. Little was done in Britain other than the institution of family allowances, but in Sweden a conscious attempt was made to adopt an essentially democratic and egalitarian population policy (G. Myrdal 1940, A. Myrdal 1945). The guiding principles have been that the burden of national demographic replacement should be spread over the whole population, that individuals should be free to decide on the number of their children, and that quality of children should not be sacrificed to quantity. Therefore, liberal access to abortion and other birth control means has been provided, as well as a wide range of financial and social benefits for families with children.

But it was France that exhibited the greatest government concern about low fertility, the outcome of an exceptional demographic history in which fertility had declined continuously from as early as the late eighteenth century and in which there was a mortality toll of over 1 million men during the First World War. Between 1800 and 1940 the populations of Britain, Germany, Belgium and the Netherlands had grown between two and three times, but that of France by only 50 percent. Its military humiliations by Germany were widely attributed to differential growth rates of population. Accordingly, in 1920 a law was enacted prohibiting not only induced abortion, but also the sale of contraceptives and propaganda for birth control; only from 1967 have the various provisions of this law been repealed, although they had long been disregarded. Commissions on births were established in all *départments*, and a series of financial incentives to families with children was introduced, culminating in the *Code de Famille* of 1939. Family allowances and a *salaire unique* paid to mothers remaining at home have been appreciably higher than comparable allowances in other countries, to the extent that in the 1950s they comprised, for a three-child family, more than the average wage. Again it is difficult to assess the demographic effect of these measures and the pro-natalist atmosphere that they generated. The major problem is that fertility increased in all developed countries in the 1940s, regardless of the presence of pro-natalist policies, but it must be said that the increases were particularly marked in France (Figure 4.6). Calot and Hecht (1978) speculate that legislative measures may have raised French fertility by some 10 percent.

These, then, have been the major government responses to the demographic stagnation of the 1930s. They may not comprise formal population policies ('there is in France no population policy if we mean by that a set of co-ordinated laws aimed at reaching some demographic goals', Bourgeois-Pichat 1974, p.546). Rather they should be regarded as 'mild ideologies and piecemeal programs leaning towards pro-natalism' (Stycos 1977, p.103). Moreover, governments in many developed countries found the arena of population regulation an altogether too sensitive area for government intervention. In the United States, for example, President Eisenhower declared in a 1959 presidential news conference: 'I cannot imagine anything more emphatically a subject that is not a proper political or governmental activity or function or responsibility. This government has not, and will not as long as I am here, have a positive political doctrine in its programme that has to do with this problem on birth control. That's not our business' (quoted in Nam and Gustavus 1976, p.135).

Little was heard of pro-natalism in the 1950s and 1960s as fertility rates climbed to well above generation-replacement levels throughout the developed world. Indeed, there was growing concern in the Western world about the pressure of growing populations on limited resources. The Commission on Population Growth and the American Future (1972, p.7) reported that 'the time has come to challenge the tradition that population growth is desirable: What was unintended may turn out to be unwanted, in the society as in the family.'

But the widespread and appreciable fertility falls of the 1970s (Figure 4.6) have rekindled fears of population decline in several developed countries. By 1976 six countries (Austria, Belgium, East Germany, West Germany, Luxembourg and the United Kingdom) were at the stage of zero or negative population growth, with the crude death rate equal to or above the crude birth rate, and there were as many as 26 countries, accounting for a quarter of the world's population, with net reproduction rates of 1.10 or less (Figure 7.1). However, in many of these countries the age structure resulting from past patterns of fertility and immigration can be expected to produce further population increase for some decades to come, even if generation-replacement rates remain at or below unity.

It is in the socialist countries of eastern Europe that modern pro-natalism has been most evident and, indeed, most successful. In the mid-1960s these countries were exhibiting the world's lowest crude birth rates (15–16 per 1000), giving rise to considerable government concern about the future adequacy of labour force numbers. Some governments (Hungary and Czechoslovakia) responded with packages of measures to moderately restrict what had hitherto been very liberal access to abortion and, more importantly, to provide significant financial incentives to families with children. Particular emphasis was given to supporting working mothers by maternity leave, job protection and child-care allowances. Fertility does seem to have responded, and the crude birth rates in eastern Europe in the late 1970s of about 17–18 per 1000 (apart from East Germany) have been well above those in western Europe.

The *cause célébre* of East European population policies has been Rumania, where a remarkable degree of government coercion has been used to achieve fertility goals. The crude birth rate had fallen to 14 per 1000 in 1966, and state-provided abortion had become the dominant method of fertility control; the number of abortions per 100 live births rose from 30 in 1958 to a staggering 408 in 1965, accounting for about 80 percent of all conceptions (Berelson 1979). The

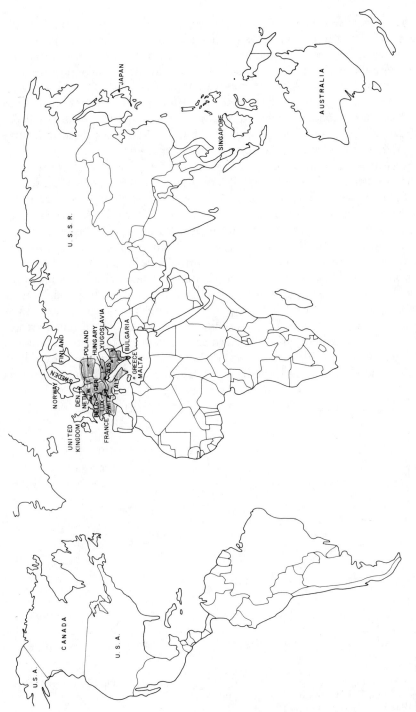

Figure 7.1
Countries with net reproduction rates per woman of 1.10 or less, 1976
Source: Day (1978), pp.2 and 7. By permission of Population Reference Bureau, Inc.

government response was a 1966 decree making abortion legally available only under very restrictive conditions and stopping the importation of birth control pills and intra-uterine devices. Thus the dominant means of fertility control was suddenly withdrawn, without any provision for, indeed the disencouragement of, viable substitutes. Fertility levels responded immediately and dramatically, with the crude birth rate almost doubling to 27 per 1000 in 1967. But as fertility has fallen subsequently, some commentators (e.g., Teitelbaum 1972, Andorka 1978) have tended to view the 1967 surge as a minor blip on the fertility curve, indicative of the inability of governments to significantly alter fertility trends.

But Berelson (1979) argues convincingly that the fertility effects of the 1967 Rumanian measures were still being felt a decade later, that there was no sign of fertility falling to its 1966 level, and that there would be a positive echo effect on fertility in the 1990s. Some of his evidence is shown in Figure 7.2, where the average birth rate of five East European countries is used as a plausible estimate of Rumania's rate in the absence of 1967 legislation. Rumania's policy, therefore, can be regarded as successful in that population targets have been met, but there have been serious costs. These include the frustration of parental choice, an increased maternal death toll from illegal abortion, and the dislocation in education, housing and employment as the 1967–1970 bulge moves through the age groups. A similar dislocation – not so extreme and temporally concentrated, but of much greater magnitude – is occurring in many Western countries as the postwar baby-boom cohort passes through its life-cycle (Bouvier 1980). Maternity wards that expanded rapidly to cope with soaring births in the 1950s were left with empty beds as

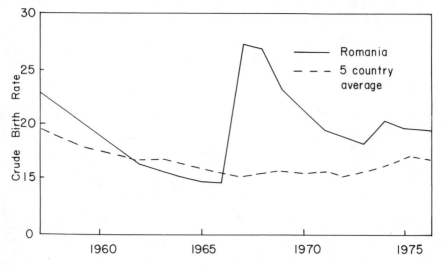

Figure 7.2
Trends in crude birth rate (per 1000), 1957-1976: Romania and average of Bulgaria, Czechoslovakia, East Germany, Hungary and Poland
Source: Berelson (1979), figure 1

'baby-boom' gave way to 'baby-bust' from the mid-1960s. A similar story, staggered over time, can be seen in primary schools, secondary schools and, now, universities.

Outside eastern Europe government response to the subreplacement levels of fertility reached in several developed countries in the 1970s has been somewhat muted. The implications of stationary or slightly declining populations have been widely considered (Sauvy 1976, Spengler 1975, 1978, Day 1978, Council of Europe 1978), in an atmosphere generally free from 1930s-type alarmist fears for national security and virility. Technological advances in armaments and in manufacturing and service industries have undermined the crude size role of military and labour manpower, so that the traditional view of a country's security, economic power and international prestige being a function of its population size is discredited.

Greater attention is being given to evolving age structure than to actual size of populations. Consider, for example, the 1978 medium-variant population projection of the Swedish Central Bureau of Statistics (Table 7.1) which typifies the demographic situation in western Europe. Under this projection the country's population of 8.2 million in 1977 would rise to 8.4 million in 1986, but then fall to 8.3 million in 2000 and 7.8 million in 2025. The proportion of population of working age would increase up to the end of the century, as the appreciable 1945–1965 birth cohorts enter and then form the core of the labour force. Not until next century would there be a worsening of the overall dependency burden (essentially the ratio of children and retired to the working population). One needs to consider, however, the composition of the dependency burden, since there is a greater cost of maintaining the elderly (pensions, health care and social services) than children and youths (health care and education). Table 7.1 shows clearly that dependency will become increasingly concentrated in the older age groups, at a time when the family unit seems increasingly ill adapted to shoulder the burden of

Table 7.1   *Percentage age distribution of the population of Sweden*

	1950	1977	2000*	2025*
0–14	23·4	20·4	18·1	16·8
15–64	66·3	63·9	65·5	63·1
65+	10·3	15·7	16·4	20·0
Total	100·0	100·0	100·0	100·0

* Assumptions: (1) 1977 age-specific death rates, except for slight declines among men over 80 and women over 50.
(2) annual net immigration of 10,000 until 1985, and of zero thereafter.
(3) total fertility rate to increase from 1·64 in 1977 to 1·80 in 1985, thereafter remaining constant.

Source: Gendell (1979), table 2, By permission of the Population Reference Bureau, Inc.

the aged; hence the likelihood of an ever-growing public sector involvement and a reallocation of national resources – the so-called greying of national budgets – not least because of the growing electoral power of the elderly. Already there is concern for the actuarial viability of pension funds. Inflation has savagely eroded the value of accumulated pension funds, while the ratio of contributors to benefactors steadily worsens. In the United States the ratio of persons paying Social Security Payroll Taxes to beneficiaries aged 65 and over was 5.1 to 1 in 1960, but is likely, under current domographic projections, to be merely 2.1 to 1 by 2030 (Bouvier 1980, Figure 9).

It seems, therefore, that the major response of Western governments to any extensive period of subreplacement fertility will be in institutional mechanisms within the broad field of economic and social policies. Recent fertility trends have clearly been the outcome of changing norms within society, and governments are likely to concentrate more on adjustments to the consequences of such changes than on probably vain attempts to influence the norms which dictate them.

Governments are reluctant to infringe what is widely regarded as a basic human right to decide freely the number and spacing of one's children, so that the only acceptable pro-natalist policy is an increasing socialization of the costs of children, which can be justified on the grounds of social justice alone (Eversley 1980). For example, a recent survey in France indicated that the most widely supported of many possible pro-natalist measures were those which would make it easier for mothers to combine family responsibilities with a job (Calot and Hecht 1978).

Finally, by adopting an alternative perspective, it is possible to argue 'that governments should welcome the prospect of a temporarily declining or stationary population, since it indicates that the wishes of the population are essentially in accordance with what would seem to be desirable from a global point of view' (Van de Kaa 1978, p.228). This remark is made significantly by a Dutch demographer, since the Netherlands, with its high population density, dependence on external resources and recent history of high fertility, is now possibly the only developed country to be concerned about excessive population growth.

Anti-natalist policies

Origin and growth
The first government to formally support a family planning programme with the aim of reducing national fertility was India in 1952, but such was the lack of government-perceived urgency throughout the Third World that by 1964 similar national programmes had been established only in Pakistan, South Korea, Fiji and China. It was the mid-1960s that witnessed a surge of fertility regulation policies, as a response to several factors:

(i) Publication of results from the 1960 round of censuses revealed higher rates of population growth than had been expected, particularly in Latin America.

(ii) In 1965 and 1966 the monsoon rains failed in large parts of the Indian subcontinent, causing severe food shortages and widespread concern about the fragility of the population–resources balance. Major famines were averted only by heavy grain shipments on concessional terms from the United States.

(iii) Development economists became strongly influenced by Coale's and Hoover's work (1958) on the mathematical modelling of the Indian economy under different fertility assumptions. Projections over a 30-year period suggested that per capita income could be 40 percent lower under the high, compared with the low, assumption. This was also the time when Rostow's stages model of economic growth (1960) held sway in development thinking orthodoxy. The critical 'take-off' stage of a national economy into self-sustained growth required a level of savings and productive investment that high population growth rates seemed to inhibit.

(iv) The development in the early 1960s of oral contraceptives and intra-uterine devices and their acceptance by lower status groups in pilot studies encouraged development planners for the first time to believe that Third World fertility rates could be regulated by intervention policies. A parallel was naïvely drawn with the role of imported medical and public health technology in reducing death rates.

(v) There emerged, particularly through the work of Enke (1966, 1967), the economic concept of value of births averted by family planning programmes. Development planners and donor agencies were seduced by arguments that the value of permanently preventing a birth in a typical Afro-Asian country could be about $250 (largely health and education costs), against an actual achievement cost of some $1 per year per participant. Thus it was that in 1965 President Lyndon Johnson urged a United Nations audience: 'Let us act on the fact that less than five dollars invested in population control is worth a hundred dollars invested in economic growth', and in the same year a United States senator advocated family planning programmes 'to prevent American aid from being poured down a rat-hole' (both quoted by Stycos 1971a, p.115). Such financial estimates may well have been wide of the mark, but there can be little doubt of the essentially modest cost of family planning programmes. In the mid-1970s the highest programme expenditure in a representative group of 28 less developed countries was merely $1.3 per person per year in Mauritius (Nortman 1977).

A significant impetus was thus given in the mid-1960s to the formation and external funding of national family planning programmes in the Third World. In 1962 Sweden was the first developed country to earmark a major part of its foreign aid programme to birth control; in 1964 a Population Office was established within the US Agency for International Development, and AID missions in Latin America were advised to consider population programmes as a priority area; and in 1965 the United Nations began to provide advisory services to family planning programmes. By 1976 as many as 63 countries in the less developed world, embracing 92 percent of its population, had launched their own programmes or endorsed those of private groups like the International Planned Parenthood Federation. In about half of the programmes the aim is clearly to reduce fertility in the interest of national development planning, while in the others family planning is supported essentially on grounds of health, human rights and family welfare, regardless of any national demographic impact. It is remarkable how in the space of one generation Third World governments have shifted from almost universal indifference or condemnation of family planning to almost universal approval or acceptance today.

Global pattern

Population geographers should be particularly interested in the overall global pattern of government stances on family planning. Figure 7.3 shows that in Asia, under conditions of very large populations and high densities, the great majority of governments are committed to a reduction in population growth rate. African nations on the whole have yet to develop official anti-natalist positions. Their high death rates, international and tribal tensions, and low modernization levels clearly deter the adoption, let alone the implementation, of anti-natalist policies. Egypt is the major exception, showing essentially Asian characteristics.

Latin America is an enigma in governmental response to population growth. The majority of its governments have come, fairly late in the day, to support family planning activities on essentially humanitarian grounds, largely to lessen the excesses of back-street abortions and child abandonment. But despite possessing for some decades the world's highest rates of population growth, the continent has very few governments prepared to back anti-natalist policies. One potent contributory factor is the widespread cult of *machismo*. Another is the pattern of settlement, which provides vast areas of sparsely peopled 'outback' of popularly perceived development potential, even though the bulk of the population lives under conditions of high density and even congestion. Then there is the suspicion that United States imperialism has been imposing birth control as a means of limiting the emerging power of Latin America. This may be regarded as a further expression of exploitative dependency theory (Frank 1969), with the international family planning movement viewed as a CIA wolf in sheep's clothing. Finally there is the role of the Roman Catholic Church in its general pro-natalist stance and its specific disapproval of 'artificial' forms of birth control. There is a good deal of survey evidence that at the level of individual behaviour the Church's pronouncements on birth control are widely disregarded, but in the political arena the Church's influence on government decision-makers is often crucial (Stycos 1971b).

Scepticism and opposition

Although family planning programmes have been an integral part of the development package orthodoxy preached by Western advisers for almost two decades, the appropriateness and effectiveness of their role continues to be severely questioned. The basic assumption of many programme planners that members of traditional societies desire smaller families but, in the absence of modern contraceptive knowledge and supplies, are unable to realize these desires, has come under increasing fire. The point has been put simply but powerfully by the president of the World Bank:

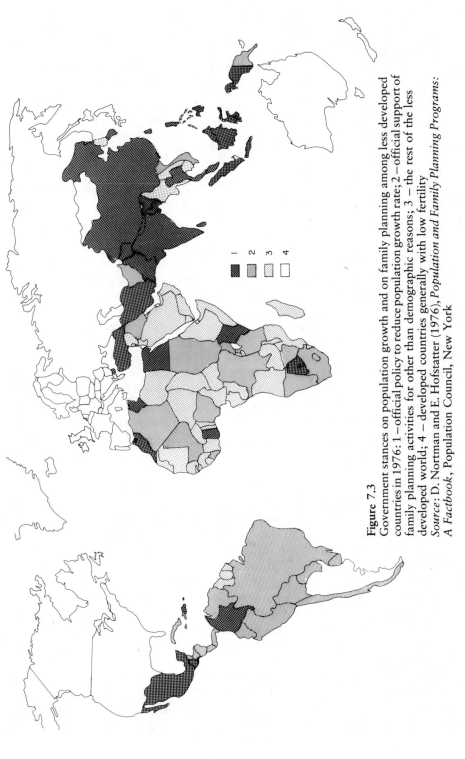

Figure 7.3
Government stances on population growth and on family planning among less developed countries in 1976: 1 – official policy to reduce population growth rate; 2 – official support of family planning activities for other than demographic reasons; 3 – the rest of the less developed world; 4 – developed countries generally with low fertility
Source: D. Nortman and E. Hofstatter (1976), *Population and Family Planning Programs: A Factbook*, Population Council, New York

It is the poor, as a generality, who have the most children. And it is the poorest countries, as a generality, that have the highest birth rates.

But it is a mistake to think that the poor have children mindlessly, or without purpose, or – in the light of their own personal value systems – irresponsibly.

Quite the contrary.

The poor, by the very fact of their poverty, have little margin for error. The very precariousness of their existence habituates them to be cautious. They may be illiterate. They are seldom foolhardy. To survive at all they are forced to be shrewd. . . .

. . . Poor people have large families for many reasons. But the point is they do have reasons. Reasons of security for their old age. Reasons about additional help on the land. Reasons concerning the cultural preference for sons. Reasons related to the laws of inheritance. Reasons dictated by traditional religious behaviour. And reasons of personal pride. (McNamara 1977, p.170)

Some of these points have been demonstrated very clearly by Mamdani (1972) in the context of a Punjab village which had failed to respond to an intensive family planning campaign. A water carrier, mistaking Mamdani for a family planner who had contacted him some years ago, remarked: 'You were trying to convince me in 1960 that I shouldn't have any more sons. Now, you see, I have six sons and two daughters and I sit at home in leisure. They are grown up and they bring me money. . . . You told me I was a poor man and couldn't support a large family. Now you see, because of my large family, I am a rich man' (Mamdani 1972, p.109).

There is thus an increasing appreciation of the distinction between macro- and micro-consequences of high fertility. At a society level high fertility invariably entails high net costs, but at a family level net costs are likely to be low, and there may even be net benefits. This has become 'a source of some ambivalence in donor attitudes and local policymaker attitudes towards family planning programmes, which some interpret as vaguely coercive; if poor families benefit from large numbers of childen, why persuade them to limit their fertility?' (Birdsall 1977, p.84).

Opposition to the prominence of family planning programmes in development strategies has also developed at a government level. Socialist states are influenced by Marxist doctrine which declares that overpopulation, as a maladjustment of the social system, is found only in the capitalist world; it can be solved only by the reorganization of society into a 'collective mode of production' where the 'productive forces of the people would increase more rapidly than their numbers'. This has prevented some Third World socialist states with obvious problems of population pressure (Cuba, Vietnam, Burma and North Korea) from endorsing policies specifically to reduce population growth rates (Figure 7.3). On the other hand, China has shown an essentially pragmatic response to its massive demographic problems, enabling its government to pursue one of the world's most vigorous and successful policies of fertility reduction.

More than anything, it was the 1974 World Population Conference at Bucharest that brought population issues generally, and Third World family planning programmes specifically, into a world-wide political arena. Western representatives were taken aback by the often savage critcism of their intervention policies in the

Third World. The West was accused of placing too much emphasis in development strategies on the population problem generally and on birth control specifically, and far too little on the promotion of social and economic progress; if population policies had a role to play, they would have to be integrated into broader development programmes. Representatives of Third World governments called repeatedly, not for family planning programmes as the basic means of getting out of their poverty trap, but for 'a new international economic order' based on greater justice and equality in international systems of trade, banking, migration and information flow. They argued that high fertility was not the cause of their poverty and development problems, but the result. The point was driven home with catch phrases like: 'The best contraceptive is development'; 'Take care of the people, and population will take care of itself'; 'To practise family planning, you first of all have to have something to lose'. Emphasis in the West on 'the world population problem' obviously persuaded some Third World governments that they were being asked to deal with someone else's problems, and they were quick to retort that the greatest threat to the world's ecological balance was the profligacy and overconsumption of the West ('one American baby will consume in its lifetime 50 times more of the world's resources than an Indian baby').

The plan of action that finally emerged from the Conference was far from the strong, unequivocal commitment to fertility reduction programmes that Western delegates had canvassed. The watered-down plan went little further than emphasizing the sovereignty of nations to determine their own population policies and recommending that governments should make available the information and facilities to enable couples to achieve their desired family size.

The most recent setback to anti-natalist policies has been the growing political strength of Islamic conservatism. The acceptance of fertility regulation in Islamic societies has been retarded traditionally, not by any fundamental theological objections, but essentially by the code of ethics, morality and behaviour which enshrines male dominance (Kirk 1967). The family is patriarchal, descent is through the father's line, sons inherit the bulk of the family's wealth, and men can take up to four wives. Female education is neglected, and since a woman's place is emphatically in the home she is spared any conflict between motherhood and outside employment. Modern contraception is commonly seen as a threat to the traditional power structures of the family, especially the domination of wives and daughters. In Bangladesh, for example, 'the majority of the country's 600,000 imams and muezzins and the 66,000 teachers in madrasas [Islamic schools] have been strongly opposed to family planning. . . . In a country where newspapers and radios do not reach the rural majority, the weekly meeting at the mosque is still a powerful channel of opinion moulding' (*People* 1979, 4, p.14).

Family planning movements have, therefore, always encountered difficulties in the Islamic world, but these have been exacerbated, particularly in Pakistan and Iran, by the modern Islamic revival. In Pakistan the movement towards greater conformity with Islamic law has reportedly resulted in the suspension of family planning promotion and a ban on press publicity of population issues (*Intercom*

March 1979). In Iran the 1979 revolution abruptly reversed the Shah's attempt to establish a Western-style, industrial, secular state encouraging female employment, equal rights in marriage and liberal access to contraceptive and abortion services. The right of women to work without their husband's consent has been removed; the testimony of two women is now required to equal that of one man; the minimum age of marriage has been lowered from 18 to 15 years for women, and from 21 to 18 years for men; access to sterilization and abortion on social grounds has been withdrawn; the pill and IUDs have been removed from government programmes; family planning clinics have been closed, and many of their workers charged with anti-Muslim activities. Protests from feminist groups in urban Iran have been vociferous, and one wonders if the government's hard-line stance against women's rights and reproductive freedom can be maintained.

Modern policy emphasis

Largely as a response to the criticism of, and the difficulties faced by, the earlier family planning programmes, there has been a growing awareness of the need to restructure programmes. In conformity with modern thinking on development strategy, more attention is now given to political and sociological factors, thereby broadening the perspective of programmes from largely supply systems organized and executed technocratically by medical workers and demographers. Five major changes in emphasis may be identified. Only the first of these embraces the supply side; the other changes relate to motivation, recognizing rather belatedly that family planning works only for those who want it and that fertility behaviour can never be divorced from its socio-economic context.

(i) The early programmes were highly centralized, clinic based, and catered almost exclusively for better educated, more literate and higher income urban groups; such policies were defended on the grounds of cost-effectiveness and the need to establish programmes where they had the best chance of success. But the principal policy challenge today is to design and implement strategies that will reach the less privileged, rural and illiterate people who form the majority in most less developed countries. There is a greater emphasis on so-called community-based programmes, in which established commercial channels may be used for supply distribution and local fieldworkers for a whole range of extension services. The family planning role in China of the 'barefoot doctors' has been particularly notable; one of the seven chapters in their handbook is devoted to family planning, emphasizing motivation and late marriage as well as contraceptive methods.

But the very real difficulties facing rural extension programmes have been demonstrated clearly and unequivocally in Blaikie's study (1972) of northern Bihar: 'Many FP workers have little knowledge of the village life they have firmly turned their backs on. They are faced with a suspicious target population, who can (and do) put forward cogent reasons for not taking up FP. Strategies of avoidance, derision, and sometimes open confrontation, make the work extremely difficult' (p.82). 'FP workers simply do not bother to go far from their homes. Male FP workers are supposed to make twenty "night-halts" a month in villages in their allocated zone to ensure that the more remote villages are not neglected. Although their monthly "tour diaries" dutifully show that this regulation has been fulfilled, it is common knowledge that most invent their diaries in the same place in which they have spent most of the month – at home' (p.75). 'Muzaffarpur District . . . is supposed to have a special FP doctor for each Block. . . . Only 27 out of 40 sanctioned posts are filled. Reputedly, Patna [the state capital of Bihar] has about 300 underemployed or unemployed doctors who are unwilling to take up rural appointments' (p.133).

(ii) There is growing awareness of the need to restructure social institutions as the fundamental means of reducing fertility, although specific programmes in this field are still rare. McNicoll (1978, pp.95–96) has outlined the problem: 'The felt need to do something to curtail rapid population growth combined with reluctance or inability to embark on any thorough-going restructing of local institutions, forms the setting for "mainstream" population planning. . . . And institutional reforms involving matters such as land tenure, inheritance or local taxation, come up sharply against entrenched interests once they are given any bite.'

One institutional restructing that is much discussed, and which seems to have been accomplished successfully in China, is the enhancement of the status of women through laws governing marriage, divorce and inheritance and through greater access to education and employment. Another is the state provision of social security in old age, to undermine one of the props of the large family norm. Another, and much more politically contentious, is the more equitable distribution of resources and opportunities within societies: 'Nations in which only a small élite constitutes the modern sector while the majority of the population continues to live at the subsistence level and to maintain its traditional way of life are not likely to experience reduced national fertility as readily as those countries which bring about mass participation in the development process' (Rich 1973, p.9).

The income inequalities in most less developed countries are well known: 'Typically, the upper 20% of the population receives 55% of the national income, and the lowest 20% receives 5%' (McNamara 1977, p.167). In such societies 'development' as measured by GNP growth frequently benefits the few and bypasses the many, so that for fertility reduction the pattern of development is at least as important as its crude pace. Repetto (1978) has shown that fertility has fallen more in countries where income distribution has improved (Costa Rica, Sri Lanka, Taiwan) than in those where it has not (Brazil, India, Puerto Rico). Kocher (1973), Bhattacharyya (1975) and Flegg (1979) provide similar findings. Repetto concludes (p.37) that 'redistributive measures and a selective strategy of growth designed to raise the incomes of the relatively poor would be more successful in lowering the rate of population growth than the present mix of development policies.' The point is put more graphically by S. George (1976, p.63): 'the best way to go about it [reducing fertility] is not to distribute condoms and IUDs and hope for the best, but to give people effective land reform and more income.'

(iii) Governments can intervene, through their tax, welfare and other policies, to change the balance of incentives and disincentives bearing on fertility behaviour.

The most explicit case of intervention to transfer the cost of fertility to those generating it is in Singapore, where Prime Minister Lee Kuan Yew pointed out in 1970: 'Beyond three children, the costs of subsidised housing, socialised medicine, and free education should be transferred to the parent' (quoted in McNamara 1977, p.171). Accordingly, the highest priorities in the allocation of scarce housing are given to those with two or less children, income tax relief is restricted to the first three children, paid maternity leave is granted for only two confinements, and charges in maternity hospitals rise for each successive birth (Anderson et al. 1977).

Some of these measures may be regarded as punitive, and they have rarely been adopted elsewhere. But a similar restriction on tax relief was introduced in South Korea in 1975, while in China a system of rewards and concessions was introduced in 1979 for couples who limit themselves to a single child; such couples are favoured in the allocation of urban housing, the granting of plots for private farming, the size of grain rations and the ancillary charges made for schooling.

(iv) Coercion, using the power of the state to overcome the resistance of individuals, has been adopted *in extremis*, with variable success, in a few anti-natalist policies. Controlling age at marriage for demographic reasons may be regarded as coercive. In China couples are 'strongly encouraged' not to marry before the ages of twenty-four for females and twenty-six for males. Compare this with the situation in Bangladesh, where the 1975–1976 World Fertility Survey recorded a median age at marriage for women over thirty of 12.5 years, rising to only 15.0 years for those in the fifteen–nineteen age group.

In India a 1976 amendment to civil service conduct rules stipulated that civil servants should ensure that the number of their children did not exceed three. In the same year the state of Maharashtra, of which Bombay is the capital, actually passed a compulsory sterilization bill for couples with over three children, although it never became law because the country's president refused to sign it (Nortman 1977). But it was alleged coercion in the national vasectomy programme (accusations of beggars and youths being rounded up to meet sterilization quotas) that led to the 1977 electoral defeat of Mrs. Gandhi's Congress Party after 30 years in office. Rarely, if ever, can a population policy have had such dramatic, nondemographic impact.

(v) The need to mobilize community interests in the support of family planning programmes is now more widely appreciated. The problem is to convince the population in general, and community leaders in particular, that the fertility behaviour of individuals does have a very real public impact, not least upon the local community. There is nothing revolutionary in this, since historical demographers have shown that in pre-industrial Europe and Japan social pressures at village level often regulated the fertility behaviour of individuals to ensure that the demands of growing populations did not outstrip local resources.

The contemporary Third World provides two outstanding examples of how an anti-natalist social consensus seems to have been successfully developed. In China 'the whole administrative, economic, and social infrastructure of the country, from the highest level down to the smallest rural community and urban neighbourhood association, takes on the task of instilling the advocated marriage and family planning patterns' (Nortman 1977, p. 28). 'At every level of every organisation there is a member responsible for family planning: the woman in the factory is propagandised not only by one of her fellows in the work unit [around 15 people] under the overall guidance of the union or the Women's Federation, but by her street committee or courtyard orderly. . . . Individuals see their fertility plans as an integral part of the plan for their area, affecting not only the birth rates but how the community's funds can be deployed and what priorities will have to be for the future' (Kane 1977, p. 217). It is widely thought that the ready implementation of goals is a function of China's unique socio-political system, but Chen (1975) has described how several elements of China's planned birth programme are capable of transference.

Certainly in the Indonesian island of Bali family planning has been made very much a community affair, focused on the lowest level self-help organization, the *banjar* or hamlet. Key members of Bali's 3500 *banjars* were lobbied by family planning personnel, so that promotion of family planning came to figure prominently in the monthly meetings of household heads on community affairs. Hull et al. (1977) describe how maps are displayed in the *banjar* halls, with houses of IUD-users outlined in blue, pill-users in red and condom-users in green. They also indicate that a good deal of the agricultural land is worked collectively, undermining the basic need of a peasant family to increase its labour force by child-bearing. Bali reportedly now has the lowest fertility in Indonesia, its total fertility rate having fallen from an estimated 5.8 children per woman in 1967–1971 to 3.8 in 1976, when 38 percent of the island's married women of child-bearing age were using modern contraception (Hull et al. 1977, p. 24).

It seems clear then that anti-natalist policies are most likely to succeed when the interests of individuals and societies can be brought into congruence, so that the fertility behaviour of individuals contributes to, rather than detracts from, the improvement of common welfare.

CHAPTER 8

INTERNAL MIGRATION

Who moves? Where to and from? Why? And with what consequences for the areas of origin and destination? These are the questions that have sustained a huge literature in the social sciences on migration; for recent bibliographic surveys, see Welch (1970), Greenwood (1975) and Short (1979). Convention distinguishes migration within countries (internal migration) from migration between countries (international migration). The distinction is not simply one of scale. More fundamental is the extent of government intervention in the migration process – appreciable in the case of international migration in this century.

The important role of migration in population change is manifest when one considers that a community can gain population only through births and in-migration, and can lose population only through deaths and out-migration. Within countries the differences between communities in both birth and death rates tend to be smaller than differences in migration rates, so that the principal mechanism of internal population redistribution is migration. This has become particularly evident in the 1970s with the reduction of mortality and fertility differentials and the establishment of quasi-zero population growth conditions in many developed countries. The wider social significance of migration derives from its cause-and-effect relationship with social transformation. Every country that has undergone modernization has simultaneously experienced a major redistribution of its population.

Disciplinary approaches

Among formal demographers there has been remarkably little primary interest in migration, reflecting their lack of concern for spatial, as opposed to temporal, perspectives. Even in the field of spatial demographic accounting, where migration is considered as part of a system of stocks and flows, demographers have stood back in favour of planners, regional scientists and geographers (Rogers 1968, Alonso 1973, Rees and Wilson 1977). The approach of economists to migration is typically macro-analytical, using aggregate data to consider migration as an adjustment to labour market mechanisms. Sociologists have relied more on field survey data and have focused their interest on migration differentials, motivation of migrants, the relationship between physical and social mobility, and the adaptation of migrants to host societies.

Migration, as a spatial re-allocation of human resources, is of central interest to the spatially oriented discipline of geography, particularly with the modern emphasis in human geography on spatial processes and spatial interaction. Among the demographic components of change, it is certainly migration rather than mortality or fertility that has attracted most analytical attention by population geographers. Earlier descriptive work on migration patterns has given way to the interpretation of such patterns through statistical analyses of covarying factors. It is pleasing to report that geographical work on migration has not simply and slavishly adopted methods and theory from other disciplines, but has contributed important and distinctive insights. This is perhaps best seen in the behavioural work on intra-urban movement, where the geographer's long experience in the handling of small area as well as survey data has stood him in good stead. The growing concern in geographical work with policy implications is also very evident in migration studies. Redistribution of population was selected as the central theme for the 1976–1980 term of the International Geographical Union Commission on Population Geography, and two international conferences were devoted to this theme in 1978 (International Geographical Union 1978a, 1978b).

What is migration? Temporal and spatial dimensions

Of the three major components of population change, migration is the most difficult to conceptualize and measure. The definition of birth and death, at least for statistical purposes, is clear cut, but migration is 'a physical and social transaction, not just an unequivocal biological event' (Zelinsky 1971, p. 223). The fact that a migrant is a person who travels 'is the only unambiguous element in the entire subject' (Barclay 1958, p. 243).

The term *mobility* is the most general concept in the field. *Spatial mobility*, embracing all sorts of territorial movements, should be distinguished from *social mobility*, a term extensively used by sociologists for changes in socio-economic status. But all forms of spatial mobility cannot be regarded as migration. Of the four categories shown in a simple typology of spatial mobility (Table 8.1), only category D would universally be accepted as migration. Category A largely comprises commuters, involving no change in residence. Category B includes the movement of seasonal or temporary workers, some seasonally nomadic pastoral groups, and also students moving termly between family home and college; such movements are often designated as *circulation*, which covers 'a great variety of movements, usually short-term, repetitive, or cyclical in character, but all having in common the lack of any declared intention of a permanent or long-lasting change in residence' (Zelinsky 1971, p. 226). Category C embraces, above all, intra-urban residential relocation, the dominant category of residential movement within countries. The Current Population Survey of the US Bureau of Census reveals that 48 percent of the population over five years of age changed residence between 1970 and 1975, and that 45 percent of these 'movers' had simply relocated within the same metropolitan area. Similarly, the 1977 General Household Survey in Britain reveals that 60 percent of all moves of residence within the twelve months preceding the survey were of under five miles.

Table 8.1   *A classification of spatial movements of population*

	Recurrent	Nonrecurrent
Local	A	C
Extra-local	B	D

Source: Duncan (1959), p. 699

Whether or not intra-urban residential movement should be regarded as migration is a moot point. There are those like Lee (1966, p. 49) who define migration broadly 'as a permanent or semi-permanent change of residence. No restriction is placed upon the distance of the move.' More typically a distinction is drawn between local movers and migrants by the erection of migration-defining boundaries. Thus Bogue (1959, p. 489) reserves the term migration 'for those changes of residence that involve a complete change and readjustment of the community affiliations of the individual. In the process of changing his community of residence, the migrant tends simultaneously to change his employers, friends, neighbours, parish membership, and many other social and economic ties. The local mover, by contrast, may simply move across the street to a house a few blocks away. Very likely he retains his same job, breaks no community ties, and maintains most of his informal social relationships.' Many analysts have found this distinction intuitively attractive, although it does raise thorny questions about the nature, areal extent and hierarchical ordering of communities.

The crossing of a civil boundary of some kind is a crude means, and often in terms of data availability the only means, of distinguishing a migrant from a local mover. In many countries there are three levels of territorial unit whose boundaries may be used: large provinces or regions, intermediate counties or districts, and minor townships, parishes, wards or communes. In most cases the migration-defining boundaries adopted are those of the intermediate units – a compromise between too gross and too detailed extremes. It is essential, therefore, that in any published study of migration care should be taken to define the precise nature of spatial mobility that is to be classified as migration, with a clear specification of both temporal and spatial criteria.

Geographers have emphasized that migration numbers and rates are strongly influenced by the size, shape and internal population distribution of the areal units employed in migration analysis (Kulldorff 1955, Willis 1972). The larger and more compact an area, the fewer will be its migrants and the greater its internal movers, other things being equal. A concentration of population around the centre of the unit has a similar effect (Figure 8.1). The point is significant because the areas commonly adopted for migration tabulations vary widely in size, shape and population distribution. Although this seems obvious to practitioners of a spatially oriented discipline, it has not prevented misleading comparisons being made elsewhere, as in the following statement: 'In the United States . . . annual interstate mobility [affects] about 3% of the population. Annual rates of inter-regional mobility [are] for Italy, $\frac{1}{2}$%; West Germany, 1.8%; and for France, 1.0%. . . . These figures suggest that the recent rate of rather more than 2% in England and Wales falls short of the American rate, but is greater than the rate for a number of other European countries' (*Ministry of Labour Gazette* August 1967, p. 620, quoted by Weeden 1973, p. 46).

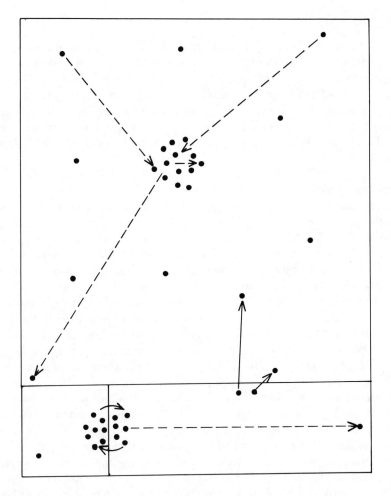

Figure 8.1
The effect of areal size, shape and population distribution on the classification of spatial
mobility as migration (continuous line) or local movement (broken line)

Data sources

'Just as in physical and biological sciences theory cannot develop without experimentation, in social sciences there can be no development without a systematic observation of social events' (Elizaga 1972, p. 127). 'In any society, knowledge and understanding of migration patterns is largely determined by the quality and detail of the data available and, only after that, by the precision of the analytical approach and the insight of the theoretical concepts employed' (Woods 1979, p. 196). Therein lies the justification for a fairly extensive review of data sources on migration.

Population registers

The most detailed, yet comprehensive, migration data are usually provided in those countries which maintain population registers; they include the Scandinavian countries, West Germany, the Netherlands, Japan and most eastern European countries (UN Dept. of Economic and Social Affairs, 1970). The recording at a local level of demographic events like migration may be a primary purpose of some registers, as in Sweden (Hofsten 1966), or may simply be a by-product of registration for security or a range of administrative reasons, as in Japan (Kono 1971).

The spatial organization and tabulation of registration data varies. Some record files are arranged by place of birth, others by place of residence, and others by place of residence of the family head. Only in some countries are the data from local registers aggregated regionally, so that 'the real difficulty in developing adequate models [of migration] from population register data may well end up being the overabundance rather than the lack of data. Disaggregation is not a totally unmixed blessing since it creates more and more statistics, and the need for some summary organisation becomes imperative' (Clark and Moore 1978, p. 274). But the outstanding merit of population registers is that they generally record all migrations, even of chronic movers, as well as the accompanying socio-economic characteristics of migrants. The richness of register data may be illustrated by Ginsberg's study (1978) of time intervals between residential moves in Norway. His data file covered all men aged sixteen–sixty-seven in 1971 resident in Norway throughout the period 1965–1971. The month, year, regional origin and regional destination of each move within this population could be recorded, as well as the age, marital status, income, wealth and employment of the mover in 1970.

Social researchers have often made pleas for the introduction of population registers in countries like Britain where migration data have been notoriously deficient. Strong opposition has focused on possible infringements of individual liberties, so that it was only under the exceptional circumstances of the Second World War and its immediate aftermath that a national register operated in Britain. Every civilian then possessed an identity card and ration book, and all changes of residence other than temporary or strictly local ones had to be reported to the local registration office. The data are of only limited analytical value (Newton and Jefferey 1951, Rowntree 1957) because of the disruption of normal population movements at that time.

Population censuses

A national census is the only other source of migration data covering the whole population, although unlike a continuous registration system it is tied to particular dates and can only provide a 'snapshot' of an essentially dynamic phenomenon. Several forms of migration data may be provided by, or calculated from, national censuses (Rees 1977).

Net Migration

The balance between in- and out-migration can be estimated by indirect, residual methods for administrative areas which are areally stable between censuses.

By the so-called vital statistics method, net migration during an intercensal period may be obtained as a balance between total population change and natural increase:

$$M_n = (P_{t+n} - P_t) - (B_n - D_n)$$

where M is the net migration during the intercensal period n; P_t and P_{t+n} are the total populations at two successive censuses; and B_n, D_n are the total births and deaths during the intercensal period. This method can only provide an estimate of net migration, because registration systems do not distinguish births and deaths in the original population from those among migrants. More critically, an emphasis on net movement can give a misleading impression of the migration process, since the balance between a migration stream and its counterstream is invariably small. There are no such beings as 'net migrants'; rather, there are people who arrive at places and people who leave them, often almost cancelling each other out in aggregate terms. Nevertheless, in the absence of more detailed data, net migration estimates do provide valuable insights into the nature of population growth and decline, and can give some indication of the comparative 'attractiveness' of areas at particular periods. Consider, for example, Figure 8.2, one of a series of maps used by Lawton to demonstrate the spatial nature of population growth in England and Wales between 1851 and 1911, and also Figure 8.3 for a more recent spatial pattern of intercensal net migration.

An alternative method of estimating intercensal net migration is the survival ratio method. A breakdown of the population by age and sex at successive censuses is needed, as well as survival ratios, usually obtained from national life-tables:

$$M_{An} = (A_{t+n}) - (A_t.S_A)$$

where M_{An} is the estimated net migration of a cohort A over the intercensal period n; A is an age and sex cohort at the beginning (A_t) and at the end (A_{t+n}) of the period; S_A is the estimated survival ratio for cohort A – the proportion of persons from that cohort who can be expected to survive to the next census. The advantage of the method is that it enables net migration to be assessed for segments of the population as well as, by aggregation of cohort data, for the population as a whole.

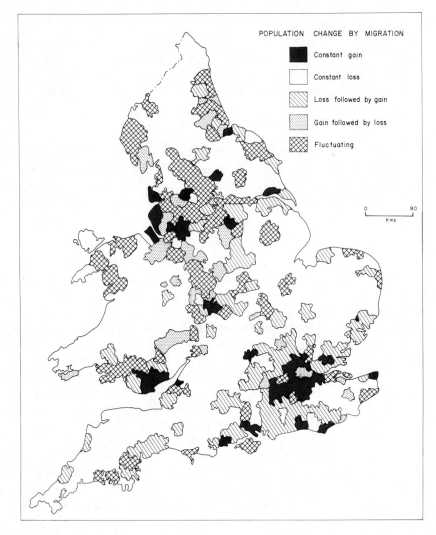

Figure 8.2
Migration trends, 1851-1911, by registration districts. Five types of trend are derived from
the sequence of six net intercensal migrations.
Source: Lawton (1968), figure 6

A net outflow of population throughout the period characterizes the rural areas, with no
apparent distinction between the livestock farming areas of the North and West and the
cereal farming areas of East Anglia. Comparatively few urban areas exhibit migration gains
in every decade. Rather, there is a distinction between those with migration gains followed
by losses (the inner parts of conurbations and some of the older industrial areas in Durham,
Lancashire, Yorkshire and the Black Country) and those with migration losses followed by
gains (suburban areas, particularly around London, and the newer industrial towns of
southern England and the East Midlands). Thus, 'already, it would seem, the cradle areas of
the industrial revolution were reflecting in population trends the slowing down in their
economic growth: the drift to the south-east had begun' (Lawton 1968, p.62).

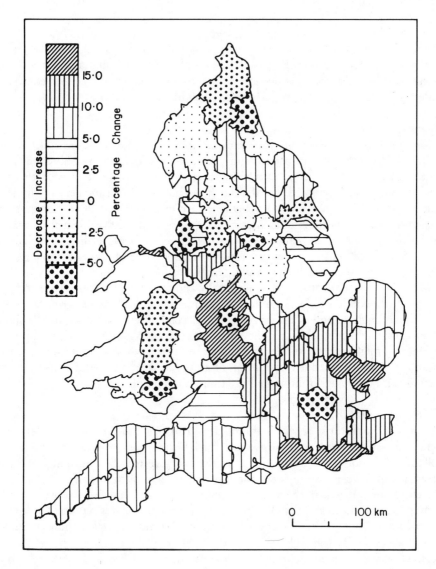

Figure 8.3
Population change by net migration, 1961-1971, by Economic Planning Region
subdivisions
Source: Champion (1970), figure 3
   The pattern is dominated by centrifugal movement from the conurbations – particularly
marked in the Southeast and the Midlands, but discernible elsewhere despite the coarseness
of spatial division; in the Northwest, for example, net migration losses in Liverpool and
Manchester are complemented by gains in South Cheshire, Northeast Wales and the line of
the M6 motorway. There has been an accelerated influx of elderly people to the retirement
coasts of Sussex, North Wales, the Fylde, Norfolk, Devon and Cornwall (Law and Warnes
1977), while in much of northern England and parts of Wales a combination of rural
depopulation and industrial stagnation contributes to net out-migration.

One example of its use in population geography is the way in which House (1965) estimated 1951–1961 net migration by sex and quinary age group for local authorities in northeastern England. But an awareness of spatial variations in mortality should lead one to question the assumption that survival ratios based on national life-tables can be properly applied to local populations.

Birthplace data
Before the introduction of direct census questions on migration (from 1940 in the United States and 1961 in Britain) birthplace data provided the only means of assessing the overall spatial pattern of migration flows. A data matrix by origin and destination can be assembled for 'lifetime' flows between birth and census enumeration. But multiple and return movements are excluded, as are movements of nonsurvivors, and the individual 'lifetime' migrations could have taken place at any time from one day to 100 years before census enumeration. Nevertheless, such data have been used extensively, but cautiously, by population geographers to identify basic migration streams (for example, see Figure 8.4).

More sophisticated, although conceptually and statistically hazardous, attempts to use birthplace data to estimate net intercensal migration between pairs of counties in England and Wales have been undertaken by Friedlander and Roshier (1966) and Baines (1972). But in their attempts to estimate intercensal, as opposed to lifetime, migration flows they are forced to make several assumptions (as, for example, on the initial age distribution of a migrant group to which survivorship factors can be applied) that some may find unacceptable.

Enumerators' returns
The manuscript returns of census enumerators can yield a rich harvest of migration data to researchers prepared to engage in the laborious task of data extraction and collation (Lawton 1978), although confidentiality restrictions normally prevent access to more recent censuses – in the case of Britain to those later than 1881. It is, therefore, the censuses of the mid-nineteenth century that have seen most research activity on migration at a detailed local scale. One approach is represented by the way in which Pooley (1977), using a 10 percent systematic sample of households in Liverpool in 1871, was able to display the different distributions in the city of persons born in Ireland, Scotland, Wales and the rest of England; clear relationships could be drawn with the city's social topography.

More ambitious have been attempts to monitor residential mobility by using the techniques of historic record linkage (Wrigley 1972, 1973) to trace individuals between successive censuses by means of city directories, rate books and the like. North American studies include those on Boston (Knights 1971) and Hamilton (Katz 1976), while comparable work in Britain embraces Leicester (Pritchard 1976), Huddersfield (Dennis 1979) and Liverpool (Lawton and Pooley 1976, Pooley 1979). Not only is it possible to trace the spatial and temporal pattern of residential movement, at least within the community under study, but individual movements can also be matched with census data on occupation, age, marital

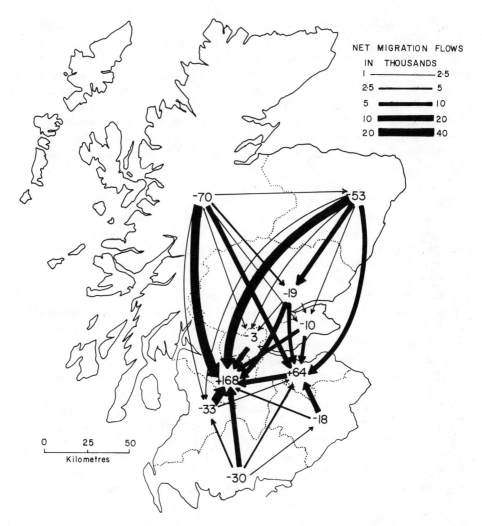

Figure 8.4
Net 'lifetime' migration between Scottish regions on the basis of place of birth and place of
enumeration data at the 1901 census. The figure shown for each region is the overall balance
in thousands. The pattern is dominated by inflows to the manufacturing, mining and urban
belt of central Scotland.
Source: simplified from Osborne (1958), figure 5

status, etc. In this way it is possible to compare the propensity and pattern of
movement among different demographic or social groups. One must, however,
always consider the problems of representativeness when a high proportion of a
sample of households drawn from a particular census cannot be traced subsequently. This was the case with 54 percent of Pooley's sample of 2446 households
in Liverpool, the reasons being mortality, movement out of the city, and inability to

trace households within the city; it appears, for example, that low-status house-holds and Welsh-born persons were under-represented in traced movers, in the former case because of poorer coverage of lower status streets and multi-occupied dwellings in the city directories, and in the latter case because of difficulties of tracing those with common surnames like Jones and Davies. Nevertheless, the potential richness of this fairly recently exploited source of migration data is illustrated in Figure 8.5A, where the moves of 19 heads of household from one street in Liverpool are traced over the 1871–1881 decade. It is probably only from rare personal diaries (Figure 8.5B) that more detailed information on individual moves can be made available for nineteenth-century migration.

Direct questions on migration

Such questions are still rare in national censuses, even in developed countries. They provide data on one or all of: duration of residence, place of previous residence, and place of residence at a fixed prior date (in the case of recent censuses in Britain and the United States one and/or five years before census day). Valuable informa-tion is thus provided on migration flows and, through cross-tabulation with other census data, on the correlates of migration, but the information is incomplete and sometimes unreliable. In British censuses (Welch 1971) someone who moves more than once during the one- or five-year period is recorded once only, and migrants under one year (or five years) of age at census day are ignored, since only persons alive at both census day and the earlier specified date are considered. There is also the problem of chance variation when, as in recent British censuses, migration information is collected from, or processed for, a 10 percent sample of the popula-tion. The problem here is that migration is a sparse or minority event, and is also subject to clustering, in that people often move or stay in family groups. As a response to this sampling error problem, which is particularly evident in sparsely peopled rural areas, it is intended that 1981 British census migration data will be processed at a 100 percent level, although high coding costs permit only one migration question – on place of residence one year before census day.

Partial registers

In most countries there are quasi-registers of population which provide direct or indirect data on migration for considerable segments of the population. Such registers include electoral lists, social or health insurance registers, local authority housing lists, public utility files, tax registers, school rolls and factory employee records, although not all are freely accessible to researchers. A few examples can be given to illustrate their use in migration studies.

In France everyone whose name appears on the electoral lists has a *fiche* or card which is classified by his commune of birth and gives details of date of birth and occupation. Each time an elector changes his commune of usual residence, it is recorded in the *fichier*. For various periods the Institut National de la Statistique et des Études Démographiques has aggregated and published the migrational infor-mation by *départements* and settlement types. The centralized data have been

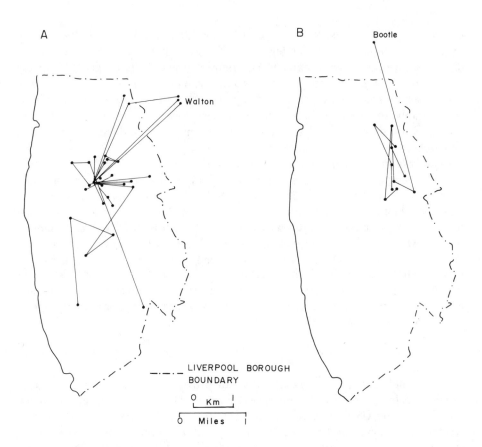

Figure 8.5
A: Individual moves from Virgil Street, Liverpool, 1871-1881
Although some evidence is provided of suburban movement from an inner-city
working-class area, the major feature is the short distance over which most moves occurred,
78 percent being under 1.6km.
B: Residential mobility of David Brindley, Liverpool, 1882-1890, as recorded in his diary.
This further illustrates the closely circumscribed area within which working-class people
moved in Victorian cities. The diary records Brindley's community attachment to that part
of Liverpool within which he moved, largely, it seems, in association with life-cycle stages.
All his homes were rented, facilitating frequent movement.
Source: Pooley (1979), figure 5

extensively analysed (e.g., Croze 1956), and the *fichiers* of individual communes
have supported localized migration studies (e.g., Bravard 1957).
    In Britain the National Health Service covers virtually the whole population, and
whenever anyone changes his or her doctor, this is recorded, together with any
associated change of address. If a movement transcends the boundary of an area
health authority, a record is kept on a central register. Studies of inter-area migrant
flows within Scotland using these centralized data have been conducted by Hol-

lingsworth (1970) and H.R. Jones (1970), while Rees and Rees (1977) show, by reference to the upper Afan Valley in South Wales, that intra-area flows can be derived from registers held at area level. Comprehensive as these registers are, they do not cover the few private patients, and they can only identify those changes of address which accompany a change of doctor, so that short-distance moves will be considerably underenumerated in NHS registers. Researchers must also consider problems posed by the variable time-lag between migration and registration with a new doctor.

A study of intra-urban migration in Glasgow (Forbes et al. 1978) illustrates the use of housing registers in migration studies. About 60 percent of the city's housing is rented within the public sector, where centralized housing files provide information, including previous address, on all tenants. This information was assembled for all movers into public housing in 1974. Similar information was collected for moving owner-occupiers, in this case from the Register of Sasines (National Land Register). The only moving households excluded from the study were those in the private rented sector, which then accounted for about 20 percent of Glasgow's housing stock. Since all addresses were grid-referenced, opportunities were readily available for the spatial analysis of in- and out-movement on the basis of 100-metre or 1-kilometre squares (Figure 8.6).

Social surveys

National multipurpose sample surveys can provide migration data at regular intervals. A long-established example is the Current Population Survey conducted monthly by the US Bureau of Census. Questions in the survey on duration of residence, frequency and distance of moves, and life-cycle timing of moves have formed the basis of important migration studies (e.g., Taeuber et al. 1968), as have similar questions in the Census Bureau's Annual Housing Survey (Long and Hansen 1979). A British equivalent, since 1971, is the annual General Household Survey of some 15,000 households. Occasionally there may be national surveys devoted exclusively to migration – for example, the British labour mobility survey of Harris and Clausen (1966).

There is a plethora of ad hoc migration surveys, fairly restricted in geographical coverage and sample size, where detailed interviews are conducted with known migrants and occasionally, for control purposes, nonmigrants. Although data are collected retrospectively, with all the problems of recall and post-event rationalization, detailed information does emerge on the characteristics of migrants, on the circumstances of their movement and, less satisfactorily, on a reconstruction of their decision making.

But how is a sample frame or enumeration list of migrants constituted in countries not operating population registers? In Britain the annually revised electoral lists for small areas are often used in a preliminary screening process (Rees and Rees 1977, Johnson et al. 1974). New names on electoral lists may well be in-migrants; but they could also be persons who had just reached voting age, or had

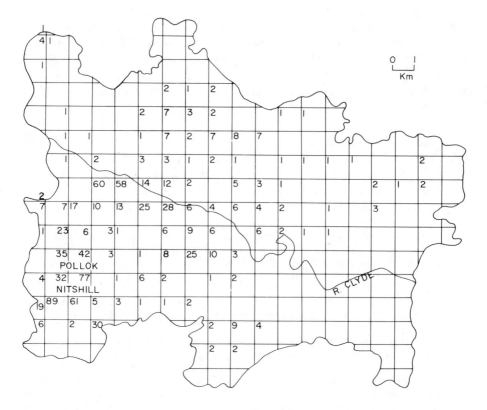

Figure 8.6
Migration field within Glasgow of in-migration households to the Pollock and Nitshill public housing estate during 1974. The number of households originating in each square kilometre is shown.
Source: Forbes et al. (1979), figure 31

changed their name on marriage, or had been mistakenly omitted from the previous register. Much easier to identify are very particular migrant groups – coalminers (R. Taylor 1969), farmers (Nalson 1968, Sublett 1975), managers (House et al. 1968), university graduates (Mackay 1969), new town residents (H. R. Jones 1976), and employees of relocated firms (Mann 1973).

Macro-analytical models

Within migration theory a significant division exists between, on the one hand, the models of explanation derived from social physics which interpret aggregate behaviour as the outcome of impersonal macroscopic laws and, on the other hand, micro-analytic perspectives which examine individual migrant behaviour as the expression of decision making which need not be economically or spatially rational.

A common theme of the macro-analytical migration models is the search for regularities which are capable of mathematical expression. The models generally have an ecological basis in that migration is measured between areas, and explanation is based on the environmental and community context of migration flows. Yet the emphasis is on universal explanation through principles which are independent of specific situations or embrace all of them.

The classical gravity model

The first formal statement of the critical role of population size and distance in fashioning migration patterns was made by Ravenstein (1885) in his 'laws' of migration which he derived from an analysis, using census birthplace data, of intercounty movements within Britain in the nineteenth century:

1 ... the great body of our migrants only proceed a short distance and ... there takes place consequently a universal shifting or displacement of the population, which produces 'currents of migration' setting in the direction of the great centres of commerce and industry which absorb the migrants. ...

2 It is the natural outcome of this movement of migration, limited in range, but universal throughout the country, that the process of absorption would go on in the following manner:
   The inhabitants of the country immediately surrounding a town of rapid growth, flock into it; the gaps thus left in the rural population are filled up by migrants from more remote districts, until the attractive force of one of our rapidly growing cities makes its influence felt, step by step, to the most remote corner of the kingdom. Migrants enumerated in a certain centre of absorption will consequently grow less with the distance proportionately to the native population which furnishes them. ...

3 The process of dispersion is the inverse of that of absorption, and exhibits similar features.

4 Each main current of migration produces a compensating countercurrent.

5 Migrants proceeding long distances generally go by preference to one of the great centres of commerce and industry. (Ravenstein 1885, pp. 198–199)

In the 1930s and 1940s the roles of population size and distance in determining interaction of all sorts became formalized in what have become known as gravity models. They are based on Newton's Law of Universal Gravitation, which states that two bodies in the universe attract each other in proportion to the product of their masses and inversely as the square of the distance between them. Of course, people are not molecules, but they may be regarded as predictable in their aggregate behaviour on the basis of mathematical probability.

Zipf's P/D hypothesis (1946, 1949) is representative of the classic gravity model of social interaction pioneered also by W.J. Reilly, E.C. Young, J.Q. Stewart and W. Warntz (Carrothers 1956). Zipf regarded the movement of goods, information and people within the social system as an expression of his 'principle of least effort', whereby intercommunity movement is such as to minimize the total work of the system. He expressed the amount of movement (M) between any two communities (*i* and *j*) as being directly proportional to the product of their populations (P) and inversely proportional to the shortest transportation distance between them (D):

$$M_{ij} = k \; \frac{P_i \cdot P_j}{D_{ij}} \qquad \text{(k is the proportionality constant)} \; .$$

In the case of migration, the formula has an intuitive reasonableness. Population size, at origin, is an acceptable index of people anxious to move and, at destination, of opportunities available. Similarly, distance deters migration because of the difficulties and expense of travelling, the wish to maintain social contacts at place of origin, and the limited information available on long-distance opportunities. Consider, for example, the flows of migrants to and from Birmingham in 1965–1966 (Figures 8.7 and 8.8). The migrant linkages with Birmingham are dominated either by adjacent areas (Coventry, Worcester, Kidderminster) or by more distant but populous areas (London, Manchester, Liverpool, Leeds, Newcastle). The flow patterns also illustrate the finding of Olsson (1965) that the size of a migration stream is more highly correlated with the size of its own counterstream than with any demographic, spatial or economic variables.

Several attempts have been made in migration research at a more precise specification, through differential weighting, of the P/D relationship. It is now widely agreed that the impact of distance is not uniform, so that its relationship to migration is only rarely the simple inverse one specified in Zipf's formula. In order to fit different sets of migration data, exponential values have been adopted for D ranging from 0.4 to 3.0 (Hagerstrand 1957). The lower values generally apply at the more advanced stages of economic development, when the frictional drag of distance is less powerful, so that migration fields are extensive and have gentle gradients. Anderson (1955) suggests that the distance exponent is a variable which is inversely related to population size. Likewise, Olsson (1965) considers that sensitivity to distance diminishes with an increase in the hierarchical order of both origin and destination settlement. Stewart (1960) also suggests that there may be circumstances in which the P component in the formula should be raised to a power above unity, specifically at those stages of development when big cities exert a disproportionate pull on migrants.

Modified gravity models

With time, the simple physical analogies of the gravity model have been qualified. In particular, the population size variables have been replaced or supplemented by largely economic variables designed to capture the relative drawing power or comparative advantage of areas (Lowry 1966). A typical example is the expanded gravity model used by Rogers (1967) in his 'successful' analysis of inter-regional migration in California ($r^2 = 0.92$).

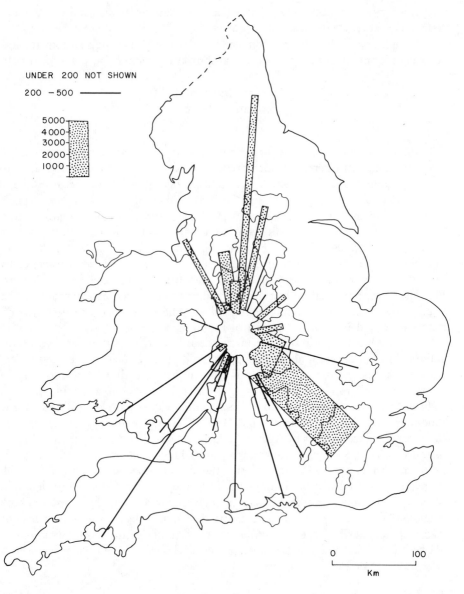

UNDER 200 NOT SHOWN

200 – 500 ——————

5000
4000
3000
2000
1000

Figure 8.7
In-migration to Birmingham Standard Metropolitan Labour Area from other SMLAs,
1965-1966, recorded by 1966 census. Boundaries are shown only for those SMLAs
contributing over 200 migrants.
Source: Johnson, Salt and Wood (1974), figure 4.4

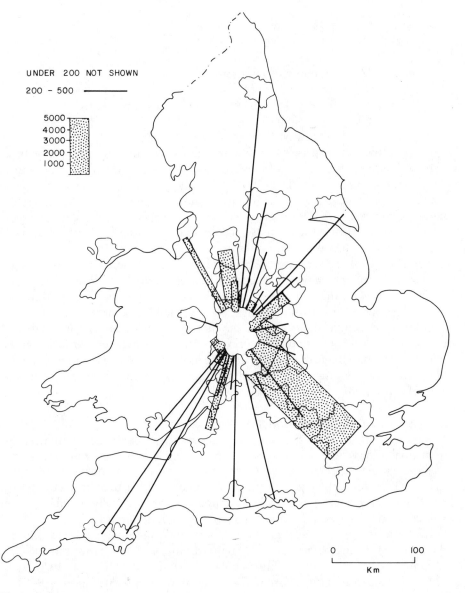

UNDER 200 NOT SHOWN

200 – 500 ————

5000
4000
3000
2000
1000

0   100
     Km

Figure 8.8
Out-migration from Birmingham Standard Metropolitan Labour Area to other SMLAs,
1965-1966, recorded by 1966 census. Boundaries are shown only for those SMLAs receiving
over 200 migrants.
Source: Johnson, Salt and Wood (1974), figure 4.5

$$M_{ij} = k \left[\frac{U_i}{U_j} \cdot \frac{WS_j}{WS_i} \cdot \frac{LF_i.LF_j}{D_{ij}} \right]$$

where M_{ij} = number of migrants from i to j
 U = civilian unemployment rate
 LF = labour force eligibles (i.e., of working age)
 WS = per capita income
 D_{ij} = highway distance between i and j.

It may come as a surprise to learn that in tests of models of this type the basic gravity components usually account for by far the greater part of migration variation. For example, in Masser's (1970) analysis of migration between English conurbations an r^2 of 0.91 was obtained from operationalizing a simple gravity model, compared with 0.95 from an extended model of the Lowry-Rogers type. This is largely because the emphasis in these models is on absolute numbers of migrants, rather than migration rates.

Another variation (Hagerstrand 1957) adopts as a functional measure of population size the number of personal contacts between areas of origin and destination at the beginning of the migration period, thereby recognizing the critical importance of friends and relatives in lubricating migration flows through the provision of information, initial housing and the like. A common proxy for number of personal contacts is the amount of previous migration between particular areas, but this raises the charge that a good fit in the model may simply reflect a constancy of migration-regulating conditions, rather than any functional role of 'the friends and relatives multiplier'.

Intervening opportunity models

It was in 1940 that Stouffer, an American social psychologist, introduced his influential 'intervening opportunities' hypothesis. He argued that linear distance was less important a determinant of migration patterns than the nature of space; that distance should be regarded in socio-economic rather than geometric terms; and that because migration is costly, socially as well as financially, a mobile person will cease to move when he encounters an appropriate opportunity.

His basic hypothesis was that 'the number of persons going a given distance is directly proportional to the number of opportunities at that distance and inversely proportional to the number of intervening opportunities' (Stouffer 1940, p. 846). This may be expressed in a formula – using the version of Strodbeck (1949)

$$y = k \frac{\Delta x}{x}$$

where y is the expected number of migrants from a place to a particular concentric zone or distance band around that place, Δx is the number of opportunities within this band, and x is the number of opportunities intervening between origin and midway into the band in question.

An operational example is given in Table 8.2, where detailed data from the Swedish population register are used to 'predict', restrospectively (!), the numbers of migrants moving from one parish to ten surrounding zones. The formula is used to distribute between the zones the known total number of out-migrants (801). The measure of opportunities, in-migration from all origins during the period under study, corresponds with measures adopted in several other tests of Stouffer's formula (Bright and Thomas 1941, Isbell 1944, Strodbeck 1949). The actual opportunities to prospective migrants could be housing, employment or environment; they are the kind that have attracted migrants and are measured by them. This is a neat way of avoiding a direct specification of opportunities, which could

Table 8.2   *Stouffer's intervening opportunity theory applied to out-migration from the parish of Vittsjö, Sweden, 1946–1950*

Zone (measured by distance of parish centres from Vittsjö)	Total in-migration			Expected number of migrants from Vittsjö	Observed number of migrants from Vittsjö
	per zone Δx	intervening x	$\dfrac{\Delta x}{x}$	$k\,\dfrac{\Delta x}{x}$	O
1. Adjacent parishes	4,104	2,052	2·00	251·5	167
2. 10–20km	1,636	4,922	0·33	41·5	33
3. 20–30km	24,156	17,818	1·36	171·0	203
4. 30–40km	19,160	39,476	0·49	61·6	43
5. 40–50km	35,596	66,854	0·53	66·7	58
6. 50–60km	48,549	108,927	0·45	56·6	69
7. 60–70km	82,141	174,272	0·47	59·1	96
8. 70–80km	55,719	243,202	0·23	28·9	41
9. 80–90km	26,849	284,486	0·09	11·3	11
10. 90–100km	158,803	337,312	0·42	52·8	80
(The proportionality constant			$\sum 6·37$	$\sum 801·0$	$\sum 801$

$$k = \frac{\sum O}{\sum \dfrac{\Delta x}{x}}\ )$$

An example can illustrate how intervening in-migrations (opportunities) are calculated. For zone 3, the number is derived by summing Δx (zone 1), Δx (zone 2) and $\frac{1}{2}\Delta x$ (zone 3).

Source: Hagerstrand (1957), table 5.3

never be comprehensive, but it does pose conceptual and technical problems. Circularity is present when migration from the particular origin under study (Vittsjö in Table 8.2) comprises part of the measured opportunities in surrounding bands (Table 8.2 does, however, indicate the very limited double counting involved in this instance). Another problem is that in-migration only represents opportunities or vacancies filled, so that in areas of economic buoyancy and employment expansion it will invariably underestimate opportunities available.

In 1960 Stouffer refined his 'intervening opportunities' model. He had been concerned with the operational inflexibility of the original model in that it could only cope with migration flows from a given centre to surrounding distance bands. He also came to realize that the take-up of opportunities in place B by inhabitants of place A through migration is inversely proportional not only to the opportunites intervening between A and B but also, as a further recognition of the variability of space, to the number of competing migrants from elsewhere. His refined formula takes the following form (using the version of Galle and Taueber, 1966):

$$y = k \, \frac{X_O \, . \, X_I}{X_B \, . \, X_C}$$

where, during a particular period

y = the number of migrants from City 1 to City 2
X_O = all out-migrants from City 1
X_I = opportunities in City 2, measured by total in-migrants
X_B = opportunities intervening between Cities 1 and 2, measured by total in-migrants to a circle having as its diameter the distance from City 2 to City 1 (Figure 8.9)
X_C = migrants potentially competing for opportunities in City 2, measured by total out-migrants from all Cities within a circle having as its centre City 2 and as its radius the distance from City 2 to City 1 (Figure 8.9).

Exponents for the terms in the formula can be determined empirically to improve the flexibility and goodness of fit of the model.

Application of the formula to 116 intercity migration streams in the United States, for 1935–1940 (Stouffer 1960) and 1955–1960 (Galle and Taueber 1966), produces r^2 'explanations' of more than 90 percent of the migration variance. Although the major contribution is made by the $X_O . X_I$ size effect, both intervening opportunities and competing migrants make independent and roughly equal contributions to the model's predictive utility. Another test of the model has been by Jansen and King (1968) on intercounty migration in Belgium. Here the formula performed well only *within* the French and Flemish linguistic regions, emphasizing important cultural constraints on migration.

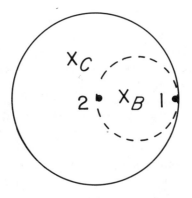

Figure 8.9
Schematic representations of the areas (circles) relevant to intervening opportunities (X_B) and competing migrants (X_C) for a migration flow between City 1 and City 2 according to Stouffer's refined 'intervening opportunities' formula

Multiple regression models

Resource to such models has dominated aggregate migration analyses in the 1960s and 1970s. In the basic single-equation model the dependent variable is some measure of migration (gross or net, absolute or population-standardized) for an area, while the hypothesized independent (predictor) variables comprise a selection of demographic, social and economic variables.

The flexibility of the multiple regression model is its great attraction. Several of the variables from gravity and intervening opportunity models may be adopted in multiple regression analyses (indeed, the Lowry-Rogers modified gravity model was operationalized in its original form in this way). But the range of possible independent variables extends well beyond these to embrace demographic, occupational, environmental and other measures. The flexibility is such that different sets of independent variables may be used for different sets of migration data; a variable offering a high degree of 'explanation' in one application may not be adopted in another. Such flexibility does have a cost, in that reliance is often placed more on ad hoc empiricism than on plausible theory: 'The proliferation of aggregative multiple regression analyses has had more the character of intelligent treatment of data than the testing of theoretically derived hypotheses' (Margolis 1977, p.41).

The choice of independent variables rests a good deal on an appreciation of differential migration propensities. The most important variables determining these propensities are:

Age
This is the most important characteristic known to distinguish migrants from nonmigrants. Indeed, D. Thomas (1938), in a classic review of migration differentials, concluded that the only differential which stood up to several contexts was that young adults were more migratory than other groups. This reflects the

demands generated in the expansionist phases of both family and career life-cycles, as well as the generally positive relationship which exists between a person's age and community attachment. Residential movement is clearly associated with marriage and family growth, while the more speculative forms of labour migration more readily attract those without major family commitments and without the seniority, job security and pension rights derived from extensive employment in a single firm; older workers may also experience discrimination against them in hiring policies.

Figure 8.10 provides a typical example of age-specific migration probabilities, with the high mobility of young adults and their preschool offspring being clearly demonstrated. The higher peak for females in the fifteen–twenty-five age range reflects their greater tendency to move on marriage (Ogden 1980), as well as their more spatially concentrated, essentially urban, employment opportunities.

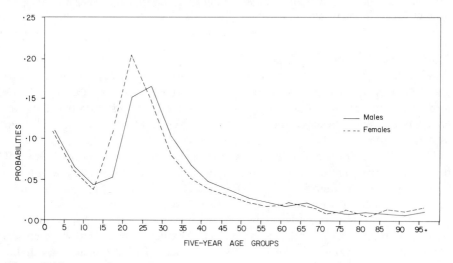

Figure 8.10
Age-specific probability of migrating, Sweden, 1966
Source: Woods (1979), figure 7.4.   Based on data from Shryock and Siegel (1976), p.400

Socio-economic status
In societies like that of nineteenth-century Britain it appears that the most mobile elements in the population have been the lower status social groups unencumbered by possessions and with ready access to rented housing and to lodging opportunities (Redford 1926, Pooley 1979). But in contemporary developed countries there is overwhelming evidence that the more skilled, better educated and higher income groups have the greatest propensity to migrate, especially over longer distances. A few examples may be cited. Ladinsky (1967) reports that 30 percent of male professional, technical and kindred workers, compared with only 16 percent of the total male employed population, made an intercounty move of residence

between the 1955 and 1960 censuses in the United States; for interstate moves the respective figures are 11 percent and 5 percent. In a sample study of labour in-migrants to four British cities in 1971, Johnson et al. (1974) found that 41 percent of migrants were in the managerial and professional groups, although these groups comprised only 17 percent of the employed population of the four cities. The 1977 General Household Survey in Britain records that 15 percent of professional workers had made at least one inter-regional move over the previous five years, compared with only 4 percent of unskilled manual workers.

The higher status groups have the ability and training to obtain and analyse many information sources on jobs and housing over a wide geographical area. But although the labour market for higher status jobs is territorially a wide one, it is often a small one in terms of actual jobs available, so that changing an employer will often entail mobility of the 'spiralist' type – 'The progressive ascent of the specialists of different skills through a series of higher positions in one or more hierarchical structures, and the concomitant residential mobility through a number of communities at one or more steps during the ascent, forms a characteristic combination of social and spatial mobility' (W. Watson 1964, p.147). Higher status workers are well able to bear the financial costs of moving, although they are often reimbursed by employers, and they have ready access to private housing through their credit-worthiness with building societies.

Not all the higher status groups have high rates of spatial mobility. Ladinsky (1967) shows that the self-employed professions – doctors, dentists, lawyers, architects, accountants, etc. – require appreciable investments in capital equipment and the building up over several years of clientéles, so that mobility is restricted. In contrast, there is a migratory élite of white collar workers comprising high-level managerial and technical staff encouraged to move among the branches of large, multilocational government and private organizations (McKay and Whitelaw 1977).

At the other end of the migration propensity spectrum, unskilled workers scan much more restricted horizons for job opportunities. For them there is no equivalent of the *Sunday Times* or *Observer* which provide nationwide coverage in Britain of job opportunities in a wide range of professional occupations; nor do they have specialized journals like those in teaching, law and medicine with extensive coverages of vacancies. Because their kinds of jobs are widely available spatially, there is often no requirement or incentive for the unskilled to make long-distance moves. Their lower incomes and lower mobility allowances make the financial costs of migration a significant deterrent, while their access to housing in a new area is restricted by the difficulties faced by incomers, as opposed to long-term residents, in aquiring rented public or private housing. They are also less socialized than the middle classes in modes of adaptation to new environments.

Past migration experience
It is now widely recognized that migration potential is functionally related to migration experience, in that in-migrants to a community are more likely to

become out-migrants than are long-term residents (Morrison 1967, McGinnis 1968, Land 1969).

Migration is thus not unlike sinning – once done, it is easier to do again! The theoretical justification is that personal and community bonds deter migration and that these bonds gain in strength with increasing duration of residence (Zimmer 1955, Toney 1976).

Migrant stock

Hagerstrand (1957), Nelson (1959) and Greenwood (1970) are among those who have incorporated measures of personal contacts between areas in migration models which give high levels of explanation. Their necessarily indirect measures are based on past migration or birthplace data. There is, however, a fundamental difficulty in including such a 'migrant stock' measure as an independent variable in regression analyses: both past and present migration are likely to have been influenced by socio-economic conditions which are fairly constant over time. In other words, one of the independent variables, past migration, is likely to be influenced strongly by several of the others; multicollinearity of a particularly severe form could be present. Thus Vedder and Gallaway (1970, p.480) state that they 'know of no satisfactory means of quantifying friends and relatives in a fashion which would not result in a tautology being created in our [regression] analysis'.

Areal attractiveness

Multiple regression models often include measures not only, as above, of the population's propensity to migrate, but also of the environmental attractiveness of areas. Greenwood (1970) and Gober-Meyers (1978) include a temperature variable in their analyses of interstate migration in the United States, on the grounds that, other things being equal, a warm winter climate will attract migrants, especially retirees, to states like Florida, Arizona, New Mexico and California. About 5 percent of household heads moving between American states in the 12 months preceding the 1974–1976 Annual Housing Survey indicated a change of climate as their main reason for moving (Long and Hansen 1979). More commonly adopted in migration regression analyses are measures of economic performance and opportunites like per capita income and unemployment rate (Oliver 1965, Jack 1971, Weeden 1973, McNabb 1979). It should be noted that the invariably positive correlation found both temporally and spatially between rates of unemployment and out-migration is not due to high mobility among the unemployed themselves (they are, in fact, relatively immobile), but to the way in which poor employment prospects encourage the younger, better educated and trained workers to leave.

Analytical problems

The use of migration data in multiple regression analyses does pose some distinctive conceptual and operational problems. Since migration is a flow responding to variables operating at some earlier period, it is often desirable to lag some of the variables (Greenwood 1970), although this is often not possible with census data. A striking example can be drawn from a time-series regression of net migration from Scotland to England and Wales, 1954-1968, on relative unemployment in the two countries. The regression accounted for only 26 percent of total variation in migration with no lags applied, but for 85 percent with a one-year lag (Scottish Economic Planning Board 1970).

Another problem concerns the choice of areal units, particularly if one wishes to exclude short-distance residential movement from the analysis. A partial solution has been to compile the relevant data sets for city regions (Fielding 1971) or geographical labour markets (Flowerdew and Salt 1979). These units are defined by employment and journey-to-work criteria and encompass within them the great bulk of intra-urban moves.

There has also been a growing awareness (e.g., Greenwood 1975) that most multiple regression studies of migration regard inter-regional migration purely as a response to socio-economic conditions, while ignoring the important promotional role of migration in socio-economic change. A conceptually sounder approach than the single-equation regression model is the use of a system of simultaneous equations in which migration and socio-economic change are regarded as interdependent. For example, in an analysis of interstate migration and economic growth in the United States between 1965 and 1970, Gober-Meyers (1978) adopts a study model comprising a set of three equations simultaneously determined. The three dependent variables are net migration, growth in per capita income and change in population composition.

Probabilistic models
The previous groups of models are characterized by a deterministic approach, involving a specification of the relationship between migration and its explanatory variables. They are generally ill suited to forecasting, because of the difficulty of predicting values for the independent variables. Probabilistic models of migration, on the other hand, are specifically designed for forecasting migration flows, but only under restrictive assumptions. Such models generally apply Markov Chain methods to a matrix representation of a migration system in which known interarea flows are represented by transition probabilities. Assuming, somewhat unrealistically, a constancy of such probabilities over time, future patterns of migration may be predicted (Rogers 1966, Compton 1969, Joseph 1975). Woods (1979, p.189) sums up well: 'Markov Chain models are essentially of a descriptive and at best exploratory nature. Their function is not to interpret reality, but to let it change along pre-determined lines.'

Micro-analytical perspectives and models

Several of the models discussed in the previous section give adequate statistical explanation for the volume, distance and direction of migration flows by submitting aggregate data to macroscopic analysis. Such models are essentially structural in nature, dealing with measurable entities and establishing mathematical descriptions of apparent relationships. They provide only a highly aggregated explanation of migration flows, so that the motives of migrants have to be inferred, not always satisfactorily, from the objective structural determinants.

As a reaction to the impersonal, mechanistic nature of such models, growing attention has been paid to the decision-making process among individual movers and occasionally, for control purposes, of stayers. A migration pattern is, after all, a composite expression of the aspirations, needs and perceptions of real persons; and mobility behaviour is one of several means by which individuals can seek well-being or utility maximization. The focus, therefore, of micro-analytical migration models is on the behaviour of individuals rather than on the characteristics of places and populations, and there is a ready recognition that prospective migrants may perceive and respond to environments with varying degrees of rationality. Compared with macro-analytical models, the behavioural migration models deal with people rather than places, and processes rather than patterns, while their more loosely framed and conceptual nature makes them more flexible, but less precise. Having said this, there is little analytical value in considering every household to be unique in the way it responds to environmental stimuli. Analytical progress can be achieved only through some degree of generalization, although 'the question arises as to what level of disaggregation is acceptable for the assumptions of within-group behavioural homogeneity' (Clark and Moore 1978, p.4).

Some micro-modelling landmarks
The first detailed study of the migration process was that of Rossi (1955) on intra-urban residential mobility in Philadelphia. He concluded that the major process involved was the way in which families adjusted their housing to the needs which arise at specific stages of the life-cycle. Table 8.3 is an attempt to model the relationships between residential mobility, urban structure and life-cycle stage.

Table 8.3 Housing needs associated with different stages of the life-cycle for urban, middle-class, American families in the private housing market

	Life-cycle stage	Housing needs/aspirations
1	pre-child	cheap, central city apartment
2	child-bearing	renting of single family dwelling close to apartment zone
3	child-rearing	ownership of relatively new suburban home
4	child-launching	as in 3, or move to higher status area
5	post-child	residential stability
6	later life	institution/apartment/live with children

Source: Abu-Lughod, Foley and Winnick (1960) and Short (1978)

One should also note the important migration role of household formation and dissolution; about one-quarter of US households that relocated in 1972-1973 had a change of head of household during the year, involving separation, divorce, death or new household formation (Quigley and Weinberg 1977).

Lee (1966) sees the migration process as involving sets of perceived factors relating to origin and destination, and a set of intervening obstacles (Figure 8.11). The sets of factors and obstacles will vary among individuals in relation to life-cycle, socio-economic and personality characteristics.

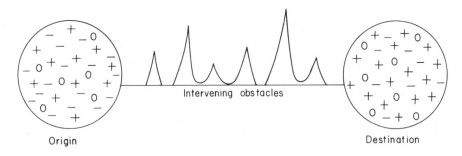

Origin   Destination

Figure 8.11
Origin and destination factors and intervening obstacles in migration. Attracting factors are shown as +, repelling factors as −, and neutral factors as 0.
Source: Lee (1966), p.48

Germani (1965) regards migration as the outcome of objective factors working within a normative and psychological context. His objective factors are the characteristics of potential places of origin and destination, and the nature of the contact between them. The normative context embraces the norms, beliefs and values of the society at origin, and the psychological context takes into account the attitudes and expectations of specific individuals.

Wolpert (1965, 1966) conceives of migration behaviour as embracing, above all, the evaluation of place utilities. These measure a person's level of satisfaction with respect to particular locations within that limited portion of the environment – his action space – that is relevant to his decision behaviour. He shows that the evolution of a person's action space over time is associated with a complex of institutional and social forces.

Brown and Moore (1970) suggests that the migration process comprises two major phases. The first involves the development of a state of dissatisfaction or stress, which can be reduced by an adjustment of needs, by a restructuring of the environment or by migration. Given a desire to migrate, the second phase involves the evaluation of place utilities within the household's search space.

These are some of the more influential frameworks which have been proposed for an effective understanding of the migration process. They form the basis of a simple model represented schematically in Figure 8.12.

A *simple model*

Emphasis is given in Figure 8.12 to a developmental or biographic analysis of action to explain behaviour in terms of a sequence of stages along an extended time-line. In the migration context, such a longitudinal approach embraces a stayer-mover option at each major stage of development and considers what Wentholt (1961, p.219) has called 'the total migration situation of each migrant'.

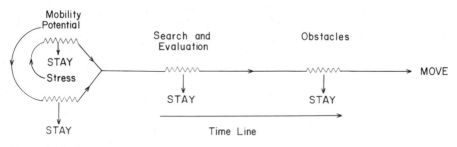

Figure 8.12
A longitudinal representation of the migration process

Whether a high mobility potential or the reaching of a threshold of stress merits chronological primacy appears to be an insoluble problem of the chicken-and-egg type. They interact so intimately that stress is not simply a function of objective characteristics like inadequate housing, unsatisfactory employment or environmental decay; it also reflects the ability to consider escape from such conditions by migration. Persons with low migration potential (determined partly by age, socio-economic status, etc.) could well rationalize the same features which others find objectionable.

It is also possible to conceive of mobility intentions being pursued by people of high mobility potential – the so-called chronic movers – quite independently of any significant level of stress. Morrison (1973) suggests that the population may be regarded as a continuum of migratory potential. At one end are the highly mobile households with low decision thresholds (needing very little stress to make them move), while at the other end are the virtually immobile households with high decision thresholds (Figure 8.13). In a study of out-migration from several mining villages in Durham, R. Taylor (1969, 1979) distinguishes 'a sense of dislocation' among would-be migrants from 'a sense of belonging' among stayers.

Given a decision to seriously contemplate migration, the next step is to search for and evaluate relocation possibilities. Silk (1971) has identified a sequence in basic search behaviour: goal specification, procedure selection, and information gathering. Geographers are particularly interested in the spatial parameters of information gathering, termed 'awareness space' by Brown and Moore (1970). Such space can be divided into 'activity space', where information is obtained by direct observation on a regular, often day-to-day basis, and 'indirect contact space', where information is derived from more general forms of communication like

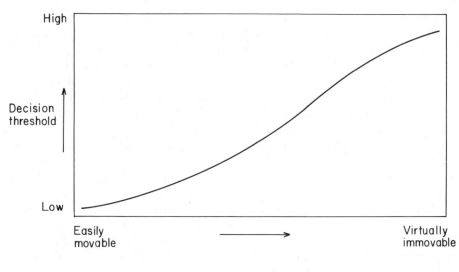

High

Decision
threshold

Low

Easily
movable

Virtually
immovable

Figure 8.13
A continuum of household-moving potential
Source: Short (1978), figure 5

relatives, acquaintances and mass media. For many low-status groups the 'indirect contact space' may be highly constrained, in contrast to groups of communicators like university teachers, who travel and telephone extensively, attend conferences, consult a wide range of colleagues and follow several professional publications. Another division in information gathering is between the use of formal channels such as newspapers, estate agents and manpower agencies, and of informal contacts like friends, relatives and workmates.

Search behaviour rarely operates optimally. Herbert (1973) and Barrett (1974) in their empirical studies of residential mobility within Swansea and Toronto both report that searching is not a thorough, systematic process; not infrequently it consists of a fairly casual consideration of a few vacancies within a familiar and fairly restricted area.

If an evaluation of the place utilities thrown up by search behaviour leads to a desire to move, there are still several obstacles to be surmounted before migration can take place. Some of these, like physical distance and family ties, may already have been operational at earlier stages in the migration process, but others now emerge for the first time. There are sometimes institutional barriers like the quotas and stringent selection procedures that have been increasingly applied to international migration in this century; likewise, there were the poor relief Settlement Laws of eighteenth-century England which led Adam Smith to declare that 'it is often more difficult for a poor man to pass the artificial boundary of a parish than an arm of the sea or a ridge of high mountains'.

But the major obstacles to internal migration in the modern world concern the operation, and particularly the rigidities, of the housing market. In Britain the decline of privately rented housing, with its traditional ease of entry and rapid turnover, has clearly restricted mobility, as has the provision within this sector of controlled rents for existing tenants. Owner-occupiers are sometimes inhibited from moving from economically depressed areas like the South Wales valleys by the difficulties of selling their houses when demand is low, and by the higher house prices in more prosperous areas. There is also the 'gatekeeping' role of estate agents and building societies, as they direct certain types of clients towards or away from particular parts of a city (Boddy 1976, Williams 1978).

But, above all, it is the allocation policies for public rented housing which make lower income groups much less mobile in Britain than their American counterparts. Such housing comprises about one-third of the country's housing stock, but rises to nearly two-thirds in cities like Glasgow and Dundee. In their allocation of tenancies, local authorities often discriminate against incomers by a length of residence qualification which one human geographer has described as 'bizzarre, to say the least. To acquire such subsidised housing one has to be on the town housing authority's waiting list; but to get on that list one has to already reside in that town! The consequences for migration can be easily deduced' (Cox 1972, p.66). Not until 1980 did central government put pressure on local authorities to ease such restrictions in the interest of labour mobility. Furthermore, there are often restrictions on movement *within* the public housing sector of a local authority, as P. Taylor (1979) has highlighted in a study of 'difficult to let, difficult to live in, and difficult to get out of' estates in Killingworth. All this suggests that 'individual household decisions [on residential mobility] are made in a decision-making environment, hierarchically structured by the central and local state, financial institutions and estate agents' (Short 1979, p.434).

Operationalizing behavioural models

The basic model should specify the factors which might induce or inhibit a particular action – migration in the case of Figure 8.12. An accounting scheme embracing various facets of these factors may then be developed, so that it can be translated into a data collection guide, which is invariably an interview schedule. On the basis of the survey data analysis (H. R. Jones 1974, in the case of Figure 8.12), the preliminary model can be verified, modified or rejected. Some have regarded migration as being well suited to this type of analysis. It possesses 'a definite locus in time, involving a fairly uniform sequence of acts. The structural orderliness of residential shifts helps movers to reconstruct the sequence of events and feelings which made up the act of moving' (Rossi 1955, p.457).

Nevertheless there are several dimensions of the migration process that pose difficulties to analysts. The recurrent problem, as in all behavioural studies, is the acquisition of good quality data. Most commonly, data are collected from cross-sectional, retrospective interviews with migrants who are successful in the sense that they have at least remained at their destination long enough to be detected by researchers. There tends to be little information on those who contemplate migration, but eventually stay, or those who move but return quickly, or on the really chronic movers. Information from retrospective surveys is also subject to error from recall and from post-event rationalization. This certainly applies to reconstructions of decision making, and even to more objective 'life history' information.

The alternative strategy of monitoring actual and potential migration situations of individuals as they evolve over an extensive time period by means of longitudinal studies is arduous and hazardous. There are serious methodological problems in asking people about something they have not done, and there are also 'problems of reaching sufficient depth in an interview situation: the topic is such as to demand a long interview – probably repeated at several time intervals – and such goodwill in response may be difficult to obtain in a situation where point and purpose is not obvious to the layman' (Herbert 1973, p.44).

The one thing that should be obvious from this review is that a simple survey question – 'Why did you migrate?' – cannot, by itself, be expected to elicit meaningful answers. This is because several factors are involved in any move, because migrants find difficulty in recalling and articulating their thinking at the time of migration, and, most importantly, because the question can be answered at several levels of generalization. Reference, therefore, in migration surveys to 'employment reasons', 'housing reasons', 'environmental reasons' and the like are very crude summaries of complex behavioural situations. They have greatest credibility when a funnelling approach is adopted in interviews, in which the total migration context is explored before the respondent is requested to sum up by indicating the most important reasons for his move.

A systems approach

The strategies and methodologies devised to explain migration have been highly varied, and it has proved particularly difficult to integrate the macro- and micro-analytical perspectives into a successful grand model. One widely acknowledged attempt has been Mabogunje's conceptualization of the problem within the framework of general systems theory. He considers rural-urban migration, with particular reference to Africa, as 'a circular, interdependent, progressively complex, and self-modifying system in which the effect of changes in one part can be traced through the whole of the system' (Mabogunje 1970, p.16). In his specification of the complex of interacting elements, particular emphasis is given to the social, economic, political and technological environments. While such emphasis is salutary at a conceptual level, there are, nevertheless, enormous operational problems in specifying, and certainly in measuring, such all-embracing contexts.

Migration in developed countries: government attitudes and policies

An equilibriating or cumulative process?

In neoclassical *laissez-faire* equilibrium theory, migration is regarded as an adjustment mechanism which directs the spatial economy to a state of equilibrium. It is seen as enabling people to respond to changing spatial patterns of economic opportunities, so as to achieve a more optimal pattern of labour allocation. The theory is that migration, stimulated by inter-regional disparities in unemployment, labour vacancies and wage rates, eventually destroys such disparities by siphoning off surplus labour in some areas and eliminating labour shortages in others. As an apparent corrector of imbalances, migration might therefore seem to merit government approval, particularly since, at the level of individual welfare, migration has traditionally been an important vehicle of social mobility; consider, for example, how cityward migration from rural areas has given people access to the training needed for high-income urban employment.

But the more sophisticated monitoring of regional economies in the last few decades has shown that migration is very far from the ideal homeostatic process that equilibrium theory suggests. There is abundant evidence that migration may very well maintain, and even accentuate, the inter-regional disparities of which it is initially a function. Drawing on Keynesian theory, G. Myrdal (1957) and Hirschman (1958) were among the first to demonstrate this systematically, particularly with the cumulative causation model which shows how areas consolidate initial economic advantage through inter-regional flows of goods, finance, information and people.

Subsequent workers have elaborated the self-perpetuating nature of migration (Thirlwall 1966, Muth 1971, Greenwood 1973). They emphasize the essential interdependence between supply of and demand for labour; thus an influx of migrants will increase demand for local goods and services, create more jobs and draw in more migrants, while the opposite, downward spiral process operates in areas of net out-migration. Then there is the selective nature of migration, with migrants drawn disproportionately from the younger, more skilled and more ambitious elements in the labour force, which further increases the productivity and employment-generation potential of areas of in-migration at the expense of areas of out-migration. More than anything, it is the unrealistic assumption of labour as a homogeneous factor that discredits the equilibriating role of migration as an economic adjustment mechanism.

The destabilizing role of migration can be observed particularly clearly in the poorer and more remote upland areas of Europe. Initially, rural exodus reduces population pressure by creating a more tolerable relationship between population numbers and resources, but because of its self-perpetuating nature, migration may proceed eventually to undermine the demographic and economic health of the community (White 1980). So many young men may leave that the agricultural land cannot be worked effectively, and the population may fall below the level necessary to support vital community services like shops, churches, schools and doctors. Beaujeu-Garnier (1966) talks of a vitality threshold, a level of population below which decline becomes irreversible. An extreme example is the remote Scottish island of St. Kilda, where demographic seepage over generations finally toppled it over the threshold of survival, leading to the state evacuation of its debilitated and demoralized population in 1930.

Planned deconcentration

Very few countries have adopted explicit and coherent policies on population redistribution, but in the last few decades fairly amorphous policies have evolved in several developed countries to counteract, or at least restrain, the cumulative economic and population growth of favoured metropolitan areas like Greater London and Greater Paris at the expense of peripheral regions (Klaassen and Drewe 1973, Sundquist 1975, Vanhove and Klaassen 1980). A case for government intervention can be made on several grounds (McCrone 1969): economically, there is concern for the underuse of social capital stock and infrastructure in areas of net out-migration and for the inflationary effects on housing and other sectors in areas of appreciable net in-migration; socially, there is concern for the debilitation and possible disintegration of some communities, particularly when culturally distinctive societies such as rural Wales and rural Brittany are at risk; and, strategically, there are obvious disadvantages in large concentrations of industry and population.

Government attempts to promote deconcentration have operated not so much through specific migration policies s through more general planning policies. These attempt to restrain the physical and industrial growth of metropolitan core regions and to encourage growth in the peripheral regions by the provision of financial and infrastructural incentives for job creation. In Britain, for example, some elements of this 'carrot-and-stick' policy have included: government restrictions on manufacturing and office growth in the Southeast through the withholding of industrial development certificates and office development permits; a package of incentives (grants, loans, tax concessions, industrial premises) for job creation in development areas; and, at an intraregional scale, the luring of population from congested inner cities to a range of New Towns and Expanded Towns where public housing and new jobs have been provided.

But *within* the more depressed regions in Britain and elsewhere, central and regional authorities have tended to promote a concentration of employment opportunities and population at what are thought to be the more favoured locations. This accords with 'growth pole' orthodoxy of the 1950s and 1960s which held that injections of regional aid could achieve most impact through spatial concentration and that 'ripples of growth' would emanate from the favoured centres.

A policy of intraregional concentration can occasionally lead governments into active policies of population redistribution. Such has been the case in Newfoundland, where the population of small remote communities has been encouraged to leave by resettlement grants and by conscious government policy not to improve, and in some cases to withdraw, services like schooling and road maintenance (Hoggart 1979). Between 1954 and 1976 as many as 27,000 people had been 'assisted' to move to centres which were thought to offer better economic opportunities and improved access to social services. Of the island's 1200 settlements in the 1950s, some 250 had been evacuated by 1976 (Staveley 1978).

Centripetal forces

Spontaneous deconcentration   *U . K . urban sprawl*

A spillover of central city populations into the suburbs and then into the rural
fringe or exurbia has been a common feature of migration in developed countries
for several decades. The driving force has been the search for superior residential
environments permitted by greater affluence and by the ability of modern transportation systems to cope with commuting. Figure 8.14 provides a composite picture
of such metropolitan redistribution of population within Britain between 1966 and
1971; it also demonstrates how each migration stream has an important counterstream, even at this intrametropolitan scale, as Ravenstein maintained almost a
century ago.

What is new in the 1970s in many developed countries is a deconcentration of
population not simply from conurbations into their immediate hinterlands, but
from many metropolitan regions as a whole into the more peripheral regions of the
country. Figure 8.15 provides fairly consistent evidence from six countries where
appreciable net in-migration to their metropolitan regions in the 1950s and early
1960s had disappeared by the mid-1970s, often giving way to net out-migration. It
is important to realize that these metropolitan regions were consciously defined to
be 'large enough to contain all conceivable spillover of population from their

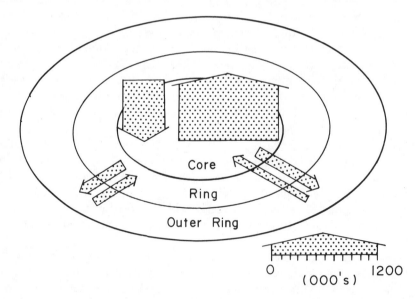

Figure 8.14
Interzonal migration within British metropolitan labour areas, 1966-1971. Metropolitan
cores comprise local authorities with employment of over 20,000. Metropolitan rings
comprise local authorities with more than 15 percent of their employed population
commuting to the core. Outer metropolitan rings comprise all other contiguous local
authorities having more of their employed population commuting to a particular core than
to any other. Between them the three zones account for 95 percent of Britain's population.
Source: Kennett (1980), figure 7.4

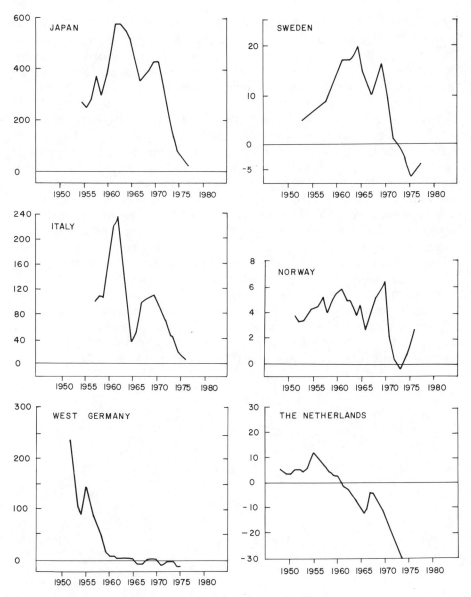

Figure 8.15
Annual net internal migration (in thousands) into metropolitan regions
Japan: Tokkaido (Kanto, Kinki, Tokai)
Sweden: Greater Stockholm, Greater Malmo, Greater Göteborg
Italy: Northwest (Piemonte, Valle d'Aosta, Liguria, Lombardia)
Norway: Østlandet
West Germany: Ruhr and Rhine Valley States
Netherlands: West (Ranstad Holland)
Source: Vining and Kontuly (1978), figures 1-4, 6 and 8

central cities. That is, we have purposefully over bounded these regions in anticipation of the objection that the decline of migration into the major metropolitan regions is simply an extension of their "functional fields" beyond their official boundaries. Thus in most countries, the core region contains between 20 and 30 percent of the territories of those countries, a much larger area than is commonly assigned them' (Vining and Kontuly 1977, p.50).

Further evidence is provided from the United States, where the largest metropolitan areas – those with over 2 million people – lost just over 2 million people through net out-migration from 1970 to 1976, in contrast to a net in-migration of just under 2 million in the 1960s. From a regional perspective, both the Northeast and North-central regions lost population by migration between 1970 and 1975 to both the West and South (Figure 8.16). The pull of the West is not unexpected, despite the recession in California in the early 1970s, but the turn around in the migration balance of the South is remarkable. From being a rural reservoir of migrants to the northern cities, the South has now become the primary destination for migrants within the United States. By 1977 every state in the South was showing net in-migration (Current Population Survey data), and for the South as a whole there was a net in-migration of young and old, blacks and whites, and poor and affluent (Long and Hansen 1979). And why? The residential attractions of Florida for the wealthy and retired are considerable, but more important has been the addition of 430,000 manufacturing jobs in the South between 1970 and 1976, compared with losses of 770,000 and 185,000 respectively in the Northeast and

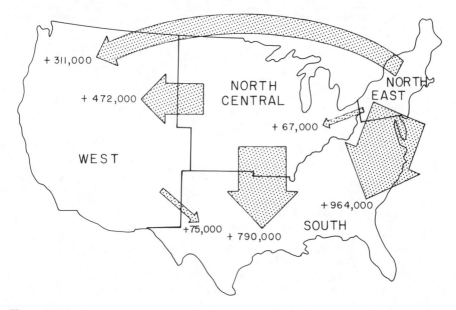

Figure 8.16
Inter-regional net migration flows, United States, 1970-1975
Source: Biggar (1979), figure 2.   By permission of Population Reference Bureau, Inc.

North-central regions (Biggar 1979). This modern industrial attractiveness of the South has been explained with particular reference to the availability and cost of energy, water, land and labour (Breckenfeld 1977), while Berry (1980, p.18) emphasizes that 'the time-eliminating properties of long-distance communication and the space-spanning capacities of the new communication technologies are combining to concoct a solvent that has dissolved the agglomeration advantages of the industrial metropolis.'

It is not just jobs, but also disenchantment with big city living that has drawn migrants from the New Yorks, Detroits and Chicagos of the North into the rural areas (Zelinsky 1978), small towns and smaller metropolitan areas of the South and West: 'Higher crime rates, traffic congestion and the hassle of commuting, and the day-to-day aggravation of having to deal with surly waitresses and cabbies, and the suffocating crush of unsmiling humanity have discounted to some degree the opportunities for upward social mobility and cultural advantages of the great Northern metropolitan centres' (Biggar 1979, p.26). It seems clear that noneconomic quality of life considerations have been playing a greater role in migration motivation in the more affluent countries in recent years (Svart 1976).

Inter-regional population dispersal has occurred in countries both with (Sweden, Italy, Netherlands) and without (Japan, USA) strong deconcentration policies, which suggests that the vital factor is the diseconomies of metropolitan scale which set in inexorably at an advanced stage in economic development. Naturally this has led to a growing criticism of deconcentration policies. It is argued that deconcentration will occur regardless of government intervention, and that such intervention can exacerbate some of the problems which are now known to accompany decon-centration. The major problem is once again the selective nature of out-migration, so that metropolitan cores are left with more than their fair share of the old, the sick, the unskilled, the unemployed and the alienated (Berry 1980, Frey 1980). At the same time, the rating revenue of city authorities falls, making it ever more difficult to maintain community services (Eversley 1972, Bradford and Kelejian 1973, Stone 1978). One response in Britain has been that government promotion of deconcentration, at both inter- and intra-regional scales, has been considerably dampened from the mid-1970s, as more attention and resources are given to the problems of the inner cities (Keeble 1977); and local government reorganization in Britain in the mid-1970s went some way to creating authorities which integrate low-revenue/high-cost cities with their wealthy commuting hinterlands.

Assistance to migrants

Governments in several developed countries provide financial aid to certain categories of labour migrants, partly to lubricate the labour market and partly to enhance individual welfare. The Canadian Manpower Mobility Program is one example (Kosinski 1978) and the Employment Transfer Scheme in Britain is another. Under the latter scheme, a worker who is unemployed or liable to redundancy can receive financial support to move beyond daily travelling distance of his existing home so as to take up employment in a new area. With increasing unemployment and increasing grants for travel, rehousing and settling in, the number of workers moving annually under the Employment Transfer Scheme rose from 6,000 – 8,000 in the early 1970s to over 26,000 in 1977-1978 (Johnson and Salt 1978), when such government-assisted migration became, for the first time, a significant element in national labour migration.

The regional pattern of recent assisted migration in Britain is shown in Figure 8.17. About one-third of all transferees moved within their own region, particularly notable being the movement from the extreme North and West of Scotland to oil-related job opportunities in northeastern Scotland. But the all-dominant movement is from the North and West of the country to the South, particularly to London. Therein is the root of the apparent inconsistency between a regional policy that has attempted to move jobs to the peripheral regions ('work to the workers'), and a migration scheme which encourages people to move in the very opposite direction ('workers to the work'), with the usual multiplier effects on regional employment. In defence of government policy, it can be argued that the Employment Transfer Scheme provides immediate, short-term benefits to individuals, while overall regional policy aims at long-term restructuring of regional economies.

Government assistance to labour migration has also been criticized on the grounds that it exacerbates the drain of young and skilled workers from the peripheral regions. In an examination of Employment Transfer Scheme movers within and from Scotland, Beaumont (1976, 1977) confirmed the appreciable over-representation of young workers, but his data also suggested that the unskilled were just as likely to move as the skilled; in fact, 68 percent of his sample were sales workers and unskilled or semiskilled manual workers. He also found that almost 70 percent of his sample would have migrated even without assistance, and that the wastage rate (return migration after a very short period) was extremely high. In terms of cost effectiveness, he concluded that assistance should be concentrated on groups which most needed assistance in moving – the married, the older and the lesser skilled unemployed.

A case can also be made out for the better integration in Britain of migration policies and housing policies (Johnson et al. 1974). Only in the New Towns and in the Key Workers Scheme (where financial aid and council housing are provided for incomers to key manufacturing jobs in expanding firms in development areas) is in-migration linked formally to the provision of employment and housing. Elsewhere, there are several policies of central and local government which inhibit migration, however desirable such policies may be on other grounds. They do this by the residential qualifications usually needed for the allocation of council houses, by the rent controls in the private sector which encourage existing tenants to sit

Figure 8.17 (right)
Assisted labour migration, 1977-1978; principal transfers under Employment Transfer Scheme
Source: Johnson and Salt (1978), figure 1

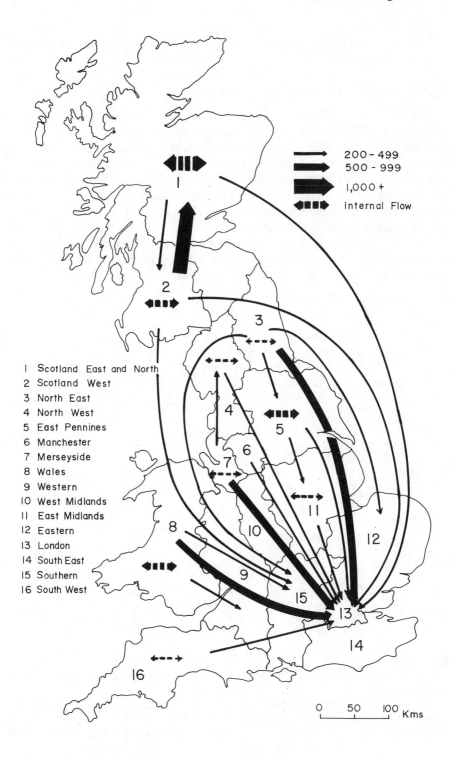

200 - 499
500 - 999
1,000 +
Internal Flow

1   Scotland East and North
2   Scotland West
3   North East
4   North West
5   East Pennines
6   Manchester
7   Merseyside
8   Wales
9   Western
10 West Midlands
11 East Midlands
12 Eastern
13 London
14 South East
15 Southern
16 South West

0   50   100 Kms

tight, and by the large lump sum payments often made under the Redundancy Payments Scheme.

Migration within less developed countries

Despite the huge range of societies and environments within the less developed realm, it is possible to discern 'definite, patterned regularities in the growth of personal mobility through space-time during recent history, and these regularities comprise an essential component of the modernisation process'; in particular, 'a transition from a relatively sessile condition of severely limited physical and social mobility toward much higher rates of such movement always occurs as a community experience the process of modernisation' (Zelinsky 1971, pp. 221-222). These statements form the basis of Zelinsky's five-stage mobility transition (Figure 8.18) which he sees as paralleling (and interacting with) the vital or demographic transition. His work provides a rare example of a population geographer's use of space-time awareness to formulate a valuable and distinctive overview of some

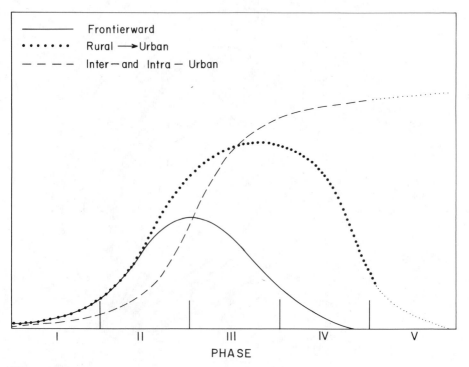

Figure 8.18
A schematic representation of how levels of different forms of mobility vary by stage of modernization.
Phases: I, the pre-modern traditional society; II, the early transitional society; III, the late transitional society; IV, the advanced society; V, a future super-advanced society.
Source: Zelinsky (1971), figure 2.   By permission of the American Geographical Society.

important links between development theory and demography – links which have been further clarified within population geography by Pryor (1971, 1975).

Traditional immobility

Zelinsky's phase 1 of the mobility transition is the premodern, traditional society, with conditions characteristic of medieval Europe and much of the less developed world prior to extensive penetration by European institutions in this century. Given the subsistence nature of the economy, the strength of local social ties, poorly developed communications, sharply circumscribed awareness space and minimal disposable incomes, it is hardly surprising that territorial mobility, barring disaster, was highly restricted (Figure 8.18). Zelinsky demonstrates this with census birthplace data from countries like India, Taiwan and Ceylon in the first half of this century.

Frontierward movement

An important demographic feature of Zelinsky's phase II (early transitional society) is the growing rate of natural increase, as mortality falls while fertility remains high and sometimes increases. The resultant population pressure can be regarded as pushing population into relatively unsettled areas of agricultural potential often found on a state's perimeter. Such pioneering frontierward movement embraces various mixes of spontaneity and government promotion. Examples may be drawn from the movement of New Englanders into the Midwest in the early nineteenth century, of Japanese colonists into the northern island of Hokkaido in the early twentieth century, and, more recently, of Brazilians to the Amazonian frontier and of Javanese and Filipinos to the outer islands of Indonesia and the Philippines. Frontierward movement is often a surprisingly robust competitor to urbanward movement in the early transitional phase, partly because 'the transfer to a comparably rudimentary economy in a far locality might mean less dislocation in social space than transfer to a nearby city' (Zelinsky 1971, p.232).

Rural to urban migration: dualism and dependency models

As Figure 8.18 demonstrates, this becomes the dominant form of territorial and social mobility during Zelinsky's early transitional stage, when the onset of modernization is expressed in a growing rate of natural increase, the beginnings of economic transformation, the provision of modern communications and a general rise in material expectations.

The scale of urbanward movement in the Third World in recent decades has been immense (UN Population Division 1975, Beier 1976). Between 1950 and 1975 Third World cities absorbed 35 percent of the *global* population increase, and UN projections suggest that these cities are likely to absorb just over half of the 1975–2000 increase. In 1975, for the first time in world history, a majority of the world's urban population was to be found in the less developed countries, and by 2000 the proportion is expected to reach two-thirds. The urban population will then comprise 41 percent of the total population of less developed countries, compared to 16 percent in 1950 (Figure 8.19). Startling figures can be given for individual cities. Mexico City grew from 2.9 million in 1950 to 10.9 million in 1975, with an annual average growth rate of 5.4 percent; by the year 2000, under an assumed annual growth rate of 4.4 percent, this population would reach 31.6 million, making it easily the world's largest city.

The preponderance of rural-origin migration as a component of urban growth characterizes the early stages of rapid urbanization. Later, natural increase within the city becomes an increasingly dominant contributor, reflecting the particularly young age structure which in-migration creates and the diminishing proportion (although not absolute number) of rural population. In Rio de Janeiro, for example, net in-migration from all origins accounted for about 75 percent of the 1920–1950 population growth, 55 percent of the 1950–1960 growth, and 43 percent of the 1960–1970 growth (Martine 1972); equivalent figures for São Paulo are 71 percent (1940–1950) and 58 percent (1950–1960) (Hogan and Berlinck 1976).

The way in which modernization promotes rural-to-urban migration as a spatial and sectoral redeployment of human resources can now be considered in relation to general theories of development and modernization. A model of dualism, or the co-existence within a national society of two largely separate sectors or systems – the traditional sector and an expanding modern sector – has been widely adopted in studies of Third World economic development. The traditional sector is seen as subsistence based, pre-capitalist, of low productivity and technologically backward, in contrast to the technologically advanced and productive modern sector

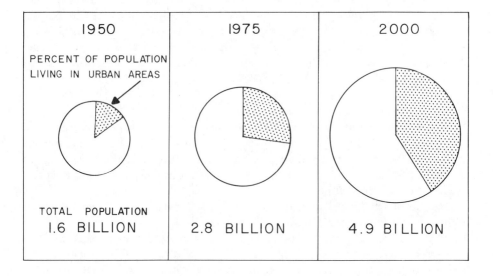

Figure 8.19
Growth of urban population and total population of less developed countries, 1950-2000
Source: Beier (1976), figure 1.   By permission of the Population Reference Bureau, Inc.

which concentrates industrial development, modern government services and material advancement generally. An important linkage between the two systems is the outflow of labour from the low-productivity traditional sector, particularly when impelled by the push of falling mortality and of environmental hazards like the 1970s droughts in the Sahel and northeastern Brazil, into the expanding, materially rewarding, but spatially constricted opportunities within the modern sector. These opportunities, initally present in areas of plantation agriculture and mining created by European investment and organization, have become increasingly concentrated in the large urban centres, particularly the primate cities which have commandeered the great bulk of modern manufacturing investment and centralized government services. In the early days of modern sector development there is evidence of forced labour transfer from the traditional sector, but a more potent and durable cause of population movement has been the cash needs, particularly for taxes and rising material aspirations, generated by the development of a money economy.

Some of the value judgements underpinning the classic, essentially Eurocentric, dual economy model, in particular the implication that desirable development is generated within and diffused from an expanding modern sector, have been attacked in recent Marxian analyses of labour migration (e.g., Amin 1974). It is argued that the realities of the world political economy are such that traditional, community-based modes of production in the Third World are transformed by Western capitalist penetration, operating through its colonial metropolitan beach-heads, into conditions of dependency and *under*development (Griffin 1969, Frank 1971), one of the strongest manifestations of which is labour migration. Whichever interpretation one prefers (the issues are well summarized for geographers in relation to sub-Saharan migration by Swindell, 1979), it is clear that 'internal migration is a manifestation of the progressive and cumulative incorporation of provincial areas into the dominant national urban economy' (Roberts 1978, p.98).

There are some important features which distinguish rural-to-urban migration in the Third World from its counterpart in developed countries.

Primate city dominance
In most Third World countries a metropolis-periphery model is the basis of spatial inequalities, and the all-dominant target of migration is the national metropolis, where the concentration of modern sector activity has created hyper-urbanization of striking proportions. Bangkok is perhaps the most primate city of any country in the world. Containing just over half of Thailand's urban population, it accounted for almost two-thirds of all urban growth in the country during the 1960s (Goldstein et al. 1976); its population in 1960 was already 26 times that of the second largest city, but by 1978 this had risen to over 45 times (Lightfoot 1979). Another example is provided by Tunisia, where the major net migration flows within the country between 1969 and 1975 can be seen to concentrate heavily on the city of Tunis (Figure 8.20); net flows to other large settlements like Sousse and Sfax have been small. However, it is likely that primacy will decline in the more modernized

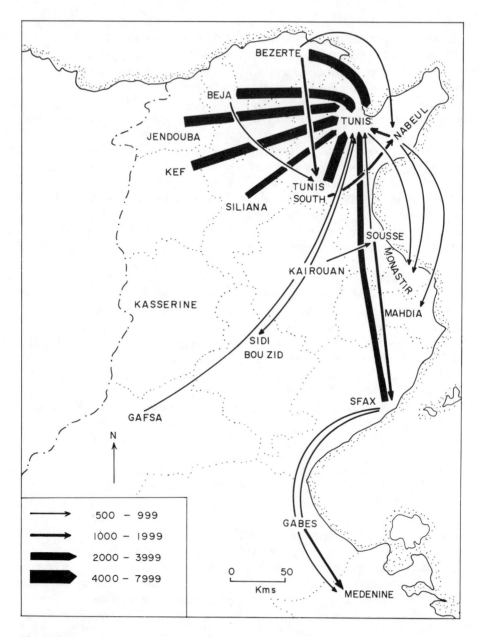

Figure 8.20
Net migration between administrative divisions of Tunisia, 1969-1975
Source: Findlay and Findlay (1980), figure 1

Third World countries, partly because the extent of in-migration required to maintain very high growth rates in the very largest cities is increasingly unlikely, and partly because there is evidence of the onset, as in developed countries, of diseconomies of scale (B. Roberts 1978).

Circulation

This term now denotes a variety of movements, usually short-term and repetitive, when there is no intention of any long-lasting change of residence. The term was used with this meaning by Mitchell (1959) in a study of sub-Saharan migration, and it has been widely applied by geographers to similar movements throughout the tropics (Gould and Prothero 1975, Chapman 1978).

A very simple form of circulatory migration had been observed in areas where a markedly seasonal climatic regime, notably in the monsoonal lands of West Africa and Southeast Asia, allows migration to be integrated with the annual agricultural cycle (Prothero 1965, Ng 1975, Lightfoot 1979). After the main harvest migrants leave for the cities, where construction employment is at its height in the dry season, and they return to plough, plant and weed their farms at the onset of the rainy season. They thus maximize their returns from both the subsistence and the monetary economies. This simple seasonal linkage between town and country has been supplemented by other forms of circulation in which in-migrants to the city may remain for periods of between a few weeks and several years before returning, temporally or permanently, to their rural origin. Even in these disparate cases there is some seasonal control, since departure from, and re-entry to, rural areas is often timed in relation to the agricultural cycle (Mitchell 1969).

It is clear then that many in-migrants to Third World cities exhibit a dual identity as townsfolk and countryfolk; they are urban dwellers loyal to a rural home. They may be forced out of the countryside by monetary and sometimes educational needs, but they are drawn back intermittently by community relationships. Gugler (1969, p.146) shows that throughout sub-Saharan Africa 'urban dwellers regularly visit their rural homes where they make gifts, find wives, maintain land rights, build houses, intend to retire eventually, want to be buried; they receive gifts in return, offer hospitality to visitors from home, and help new arrivals in town.'

Mitchell emphasizes the importance of life-cycle stage in determining patterns of circulation, and a typical sequence of events affecting the migratory behaviour of an individual is set out schematically in Figure 8.21. He sees the basic cause of labour circulation as 'the separation of the places where the opportunities for earning money exist and the places where a person's major social and personal ties and obligations are located' (Mitchell 1969, p.175).

Circulation of this type is less common in Latin America essentially because there are fewer land ties binding urban populations to their rural origins (B. Roberts 1978). This reflects the long-established dominance of large estates, whose peons, share-croppers and tenants are being increasingly transformed through the capitalization of agriculture into a rural proletariat which has little individual, family or community stake in the land (Greaves 1972, Lopes 1978, Buksmann 1980).

Age (yrs)	*Pressures operating while in rural areas*	*Pressures operating while in urban centres*

18   Normal expectation to start work. Economic pressures, especially to acquire marriage payment. School
20   fees for younger siblings.

Obligation to parents, especially agricultural, and interest in marriage.

25   Pressures from parents-in-law and wife and young family.

Need to maintain agricultural production – and necessity of visiting wife and children and building a house for them.

30   Rising costs of growing family, especially school fees, taxation.

Kinship obligations to ageing parents and parents-in-law. Responsibilities in connection with sisters – need to repair houses
35   and maintain agriculture.

Purchase of cattle and acquisition of farm equipment. Alternatively,
40   accumulation of capital for rural enterprises.

Greater difficulty of re-employment if job is lost. Loss of housing if means of support disappears. Succession to position of authority in rural system –
45   especially if father is dead. Eldest son about to make his first trip to
50   town.

Figure 8.21
Representation of a labour migrant career
Source: Mitchell (1969), figure 3.   By permission of Cambridge University Press.

Urban underemployment

Inflow of migrants has far exceeded the employment-absorptive capacity of Third World cities, creating massive problems of urban unemployment and particularly of underemployment. Riddell (1978) has shown that the urban population growth rate of about 7 percent per annum in West Africa in recent years has been double the growth rate in modern sector employment, while Bairoch (1973) demonstrates that the percentage of Third World population living in urban areas considerably exceeds the percentage of active population employed in manufacturing, in sharp contrast to the earlier development experience of European countries. The growing numbers of 'marginal' urban dwellers survive through the 'trickling down' of modern sector wages into the ever-expanding 'informal' or 'unregulated' sector of activities like shoe shining, laundering, barbering, street vending, begging, prostitution and theft. Under free market conditions one might expect the labour surplus to force down modern sector wages, but this is often prevented by minimum wage legislation and by the growing sensitivity of multinational corporations to their internal and international reputations.

Incomers to the urban informal sector may well be worse off, in real terms, than if they had stayed in the rural economy (Gugler 1975). But *some* in-migrants are widely known to have been highly successful, so that incomers are prepared to play an urban employment lottery game. 'There is a considerable element of chance in this game because much of the hiring is haphazard. And the game is very serious: rural income is foregone, costs are incurred in migration, severe hardship is experienced in urban employment. But new migrants keep joining in the "gold rush" prospecting for urban employment'. (Gugler 1976, p.192). Economists have argued that migrants will continue to move cityward as long as their *expected* income there is greater than their rural income. The expected urban income may be defined as the product of a modern sector income and the probability of gaining a job in that sector (Harris and Todaro 1970, D. W. Jones 1975).

One effect of urban labour surpluses has been to modify the role of labour circulation. Migrants still maintain strong ties with their rural origins, but they are more reluctant to make periodic returns of long duration, because of the difficulty of regaining urban employment. Migration to the cities is therefore becoming more permanent, with the urban worker more commonly being joined by his family.

Interurban migration

When a large proportion of a country's population lives in urban areas (in most Latin American countries this is now well over 50 percent), it is natural that interurban migration should replace rural-urban migration as the dominant form of internal migration. Survey data show that as early as the 1960s two-thirds of recent in-migrants to Santiago, and one-half of those to Lima, were coming from urban places of over 5000 population; less than one-tenth of in-migrants to each city came from localities with under 1000 population (Elizaga 1972). In Tunisia, moves between urban areas accounted for 27 percent of all moves recorded in the 1966 census, but for 50 percent of those recorded a decade later; over the same period the proportion of moves from rural to urban areas fell from 36 percent of the total to 19 percent (Findlay and Findlay 1980).

Because empirical investigation has been sporadic, there has been a good deal of speculation (reviewed by Gilbert and Sollis 1979) about the nature of interurban migration within a settlement hierarchy. Figure 8.22 shows diagrammatically how intermediate urban centres can play various roles in the general displacement of rural population towards the biggest cities. In 'direct' and 'step' migration, the rural out-migrant makes his way, either directly or by means of an intermediate stay in a lower order urban centre, to the large city. In the case of 'fill-in' migration, an individual moves from a small to a large city, thereby creating a vacuum in the smaller centre which is filled by someone moving from an adjacent rural area. This time-sequence is reversed in the 'push-out' version, when rural incomers compete to such an extent with the indigenous population of small towns that some townsfolk decide to move to a large city in pursuit of better opportunities. Obviously the 'fill-in' and 'push-out' forms of migration can take place *within* any grade of the settlement hierarchy, and not simply between grades as depicted in Figure 8.22. It has also been argued (Kemper 1971) that there is an intergenerational form of 'step' migration in that parents may move from rural areas to small cities, and their children may move on later to a large city.

Recent evidence from four Asian cities (Speare and Goldstein 1978) suggests that metropolitan in-migrants with an urban origin adjust better to metropolitan labour

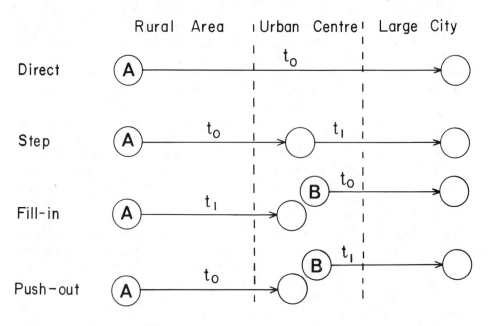

Figure 8.22
Basic forms of migration within a simple settlement hierarchy
Source: Gilbert and Sollis (1979)

and housing markets than their counterparts moving directly from rural areas; they are also likely to be more innovative and possess higher aspirations for upward social mobility (Tirasawat 1978). This reflects the reduced 'cultural distance' in interurban migration, as well as the generally higher educational qualifications and technical skills of interurban migrants. There is concern that smaller towns may be losing their more enterprising and better qualified inhabitants, while attracting less skilled rural incomers. Gilbert and Sollis (1979) suggest that this hypothesis of migration flows inducing a net debilitative effect on small towns merits particularly careful investigation in the context of Latin America, where there is a well-known lack of dynamism in towns of this size.

Policy considerations

Capital cities doubling in size every decade would impose burdens on even the most affluent developed countries, but for some time such growth has been the norm in Third World environments of low and severely stretched resources. Inevitable results have been growing unemployment and underemployment, mushrooming shanty towns of squatters on the urban periphery or in gullies, swamps and hillsides within the city, and grossly overextended systems of transport, water and sanitation provision (Davis 1975, Dwyer 1975, Beier 1976, Lloyd 1979). Many of these social costs of cityward migration are simply not recognized in the balance of costs and opportunities considered by individual migrants, but they are of central concern to government decision-makers – not least because of the way in which they forment social and political unrest through an 'explosion of despair' when great deprivation and conspicuous consumption are juxtaposed within the confines of the city (Sween and Clignet 1969, Cohen 1974, Gutkind 1975).

A few governments have attempted to turn back the cityward tide through the direction, and sometimes the coercion, of migrants. For some time up to 1978 people were removed from Tanzanian cities unless they could prove they were in employment (*Economist*, March 11, 1978). In Tunisia, *Centres d'acceuil et d'orientation* were set up in cities in the late 1970s in order to redirect poorly integrated migrants to their regions of origin (Findlay and Findlay 1980). A very special, sinister case was the enforced removal of much of the urban population of Cambodia under the Khmer Rouge regime. Within the context of tropical Africa, Gugler (1976) has proposed that recruitment for major job vacancies in the cities should be shifted to the rural areas; employees in the regulated sector, both public and private, should be required to recruit through rural-located labour exchanges, although provision would obviously have to be made for the urban born and reared. The point of this proposal is that it would reduce the speculative inflow of labour which presently 'queues' for limited job opportunities. But the essential weakness of all these policies and proposals is that they attempt to treat outward symptoms rather than basic causes.

More fundamental policies are those which try to redress the spatial imbalance of opportunities within countries. Governments do have the power to reduce metropolitan bias and induce rural development through investment and taxation policies. Consider, for example, how the role of government as the biggest employer in most Third World countries permits the possibility of job decentralization from metropolis to nodes at lower levels in the urban hierarchy, thereby providing intervening opportunity alternatives to migrants. There is also the somewhat special case of national capitals being relocated in more central but less developed parts of their countries (e.g., Brazil, Malawi, Nigeria).

Rural development in itself does not necessarily restrain cityward migration, since the provision of modern transportation and particularly of education often accelerates rural exodus because of broadening horizons, rising material aspirations and a growing contempt for rural life (Bryant et al. 1978, Bell 1980). But where the commitment to rural development and nonurbanized industrialization has been very strong, notably in China in the 1960s and early 1970s (although not in the late 1970s' reversion to a more conventional Western-style economic transformation), it seems that metropolitan growth can be reduced to manageable proportions. Another special case is the villagization programme introduced in Tanzania in 1967 as a specifically socialist development policy to transform the rural social and economic structure through population collectivization. Several million people have been moved and resettled in the new *ujamaa* villages in an attempt to stimulate collective ownership, the provision of basic amenities and a more rational distribution of population in relation to land resources (Hirst 1977, Thomas 1978, Mwansasu 1979). But in the majority of Third World countries the spatial disparities created under colonialism are perpetuated and even reinforced by post-independence governments furthering the interests of the élite groups that they represent (Leys 1975, Lipton 1977, Riddell 1978).

CHAPTER 9

INTERNATIONAL MIGRATION

The distinction between internal and international migration reflects the compartmentalization of the modern world into sovereign states and its effect on the recording of territorial mobility. Clearly, many features of migration are common to internal and international movements – the roles of spatial inequalities, distance decay, selectivity, decision making, self-perpetuation, counterstreams and the like – but the extent of national government intervention and control does add a distinctive dimension to international migration. This dimension has become increasingly dominant in the modern world, as the following spatio-temporal study of the evolution of international migration will demonstrate. Another important difference is the greater change in socio-cultural environment involved in moving from one country to another, with all the implications, spatial as well as social, for migrant adaptation and assimilation.

Origins

At early periods, when national territories were only loosely defined, the distinction between internal and international migration is meaningless. A more appropriate distinction is that between short- and long-distance movement. Davis (1974) argues that it was the rise of town-based, quasi-literate civilizations in the Near East and Mediterranean regions that initiated a significant level of long-distance migration through the technological inequalities between territorial groups. The civilized core regions drew peasants and artisans from their immediate hinterlands, and also so-called barbarians from the periphery and beyond. Movements of the latter were of two types. First, there was the slave labour captured in successful military campaigns like those of Imperial Rome in North Africa, Gaul, Britain and the Rhine frontier. At the height of the Roman Empire, the city of Rome had a population variously estimated at between 300,000 and 2 million (Hollingsworth 1969), of which between one-quarter and one-third are thought to have been slaves. It is hardly surprising that a proposal to make slaves wear distinctive dress in Rome was rejected on the grounds that it would be too dangerous to let them see how numerous they were. Plinny the Younger is known to have possessed 500 slaves between his town house and country estates, and any Roman who could muster less than eight slaves was of very little account (Cunliffe 1978). The majority of slaves were employed in arduous or menial occupations like pyramid building in Egypt, silver mining in Greece and domestic service in Rome, although some skilled trades were also a slave preserve, like the Greek tutors of wealthy Roman households.

Second, there were the periodic surges of horse-riding warrior nomads from the throbbing pulse of interior Asia into its wealthier and more civilized fringes. A wavelike pattern of tribes pushing their neighbours before them can often be identified, with the outer ripples finding expression in such conquering invasions as of the Hittites into Anatolia, the Scythians into Egypt, the Aryans into the Indus cities, the Huns, Goths and Vandals into the Roman Empire, the Seljuk Turks into Persia, the Mongols into China and Asia Minor, and the Ottoman Turks into the

Balkans. Not dissimilar movements were those of the Angles, Saxons, Jutes and Vikings into Britain.

European expansion overseas

By about the seventeenth century long-distance migrations throughout the world began to comprise a single network organized in the interests of the politically and economically dominant states of northwestern Europe. The voyages of discovery and subsequent reconnaissance had opened European eyes to the possibilities of exploiting the New World, but the manner of exploitation, and hence the associated migration patterns, varied in relation to the particular physical and cultural environment encountered and to the particular European origin of the colonizers. Two environments stand out in terms of the amount of international migration that was stimulated.

The first type, comprising sparsely peopled, tropical and subtropical coastlands, was quickly exploited, because of maritime accessibility and the potential provided by warm, humid climates for the production of exotic crops. Thus, in the coastlands of the Caribbean and of the Americas from Virginia to Brazil, Europeans organized the commercial production of cotton, sugar, tobacco, coffee, tea, spices, indigo and rice. In the absence of any significant indigenous population, large quantities of cheap labour had to be imported. Initially, European labour was used under an indenture system, whereby an individual would contract to work for an employer abroad for a fixed number of years in exchange for his passage and subsistence, and at the end of his term he could become a free settler. But since Europeans were poorly equipped to work in such climates and since the numbers coming forward under a basically oppressive recruitment system were always limited, plantation managers quickly resorted to slave labour from Africa, the first cargo of slaves arriving in Virginia, for example, in 1619. The number of slaves leaving Africa has been estimated as 11–12 million, with a mortality toll during the voyages of about one-tenth to one-quarter (Curtin 1969).

With the abolition of slavery during the nineteenth century, British and Dutch colonialists substituted a semi-slave trade in indentured labour from the huge population and poverty reservoirs of Asia, especially India and China, where it was not difficult to recruit men willing to tolerate a period of hard labour abroad at a low wage; often the only alternative was starvation. There were appreciable flows to Guyana and Trinidad, but the major destinations were the new zones of plantation agriculture in Malaya, Sumatra, Ceylon, Fiji, Hawaii, Natal, East Africa and Mauritius. Coolie labour was also imported extensively for tin mining in Malaya and Sumatra and for railway construction in East Africa and California. Not all of these international movements within and from Asia were confined to indentured labourers, and, in addition, many labourers remained at their destinations on the expiry of their contracts, often to enter and eventually dominate many sectors of commerce. Hence, by the time that barriers were placed on immigrant contract labour early in this century, because of growing tensions at destination between immigrant and native workers and because of government concern at origin about notorious abuses of the system, major external pools of ethnic Chinese and Indians had been created, whose growth by natural increase provides substantial minorities in many countries today (Table 9.1).

Table 9.1   Estimated number of ethnic Chinese in selected Asian countries about 1970

	Number ('000)	% of total population
Thailand	4930	14
Indonesia	4800	4
Malaysia	3600	34
S. Vietnam	2660	15
Singapore	2200	98
Cambodia	2000	30
Burma	500	2

Source: Bouvier (1977), table 1, By permission of the Population Reference Bureau, Inc.

The second type of New World environment to attract European investment and settlement was the sparsely peopled, temperate zone grassland and deciduous woodland, environmentally well suited to established European technologies, agricultural practices and settlement patterns. The huge outpouring from Europe to such environments in the Americas, South Africa, Australia and New Zealand constitutes the most important migratory movement in human history, embracing some 55–60 million emigrants from Europe between 1820 and 1930, or about one-fifth of Europe's population at the beginning of the period. But for as much as three centuries after discovery, these lands had received a mere trickle of settlers. The earliest colonial powers, Spain and Portugal, had consciously discouraged permanent migration as they sought to plunder their possessions for luxuries and precious metals, while the Dutch, French and British encouraged only as many settlers as seemed required to consolidate their territorial claims. Demographic pressures within Europe were rarely acute before the nineteenth century, and 'few people were so poor or so persecuted that they wanted to transfer to a wild area to live under subsistence conditions and battle savages' (Davis 1974, p.97). Such distant lands were considered fit for military and commercial adventurers, deported criminals, paupers, political and religious dissidents, but hardly for the decent ordinary citizen. Hence by 1800 the white population of the United States had barely exceeded 4 million, and as late as 1840 there were less than 200,000 Europeans in Australia and a mere 2,000 in New Zealand.

What then were the factors that opened the emigrant floodgates in the decades following the Napoleonic Wars? These can be readily appreciated by reference to the simple push-pull-intervening obstacles conceptualization of migration (Figure 8.11).

Push factors

Demographic pressures built up in eighteenth- and nineteenth-century Europe as mortality rates fell with the onset of modernization. The resultant dislocation of agricultural and social systems involved severe rural congestion, farm subdivision and landlessness at a time when industrial growth was often insufficient to absorb surplus rural population; in fact, in the early stages of industrialization, mechanization often led to severe unemployment among domestic and handicraft workers. Rural employment problems were exacerbated where a transformation of farming structures involved land consolidation and tenant eviction, as in the British enclosure movement generally and the notorious highland clearances specifically.

The role of emigration as a safety-valve to European population growth can be illustrated by the total of 750,000 emigrants from Norway and 1,100,000 from Sweden between 1840 and 1914, the equivalent of 40 percent and 25 percent respectively of each country's natural increase during that period (Grigg 1980). But the most spectacular, although atypical, example of blood-letting is Ireland. The population of the country had increased from 5 million in 1800 to almost 8.5 million by 1845, only to drop by nearly 2 million to the 1851 figure of 6.5 million. Some 800,000 are thought to have died of disease and starvation, and a further million emigrated, during the fateful five years following the ravages of potato blight in 1846 (Cousens 1960).

Pull factors

Complementing land hunger in Europe was the lure of virgin lands in the New World, by now tamed by the pioneers. Particularly attractive environmentally to agriculturists were the humus-rich grasslands and deciduous or mixed woodlands of the North American interior, the South American pampas, the South African veld and large parts of New South Wales, Victoria and New Zealand. These areas were sparsely peopled and barely exploited agriculturally by their indigenous populations, and an additional inducement in most, although not all, areas was a liberal government policy of public land distribution at little or no financial cost to bona fide settlers. For example, the Homestead Acts in the United States and Canada in 1862 and 1872 respectively offered to settlers, for a nominal fee of $10, title to a quarter section (160 acres) of public land after five years' residence and farming.

Intervening obstacles

Major deterrents to overseas migration are often an unawareness of opportunities and the physical, financial and social hardships encountered in any long-distance movement; but both deterrents receded significantly in the nineteenth century. Knowledge of the new continents was enhanced by the development throughout Europe of pamphlets, newspapers and postal services, and once a significant movement had been initiated, information transmission through a friends-and-relatives network was assured.

Before the nineteenth century oceanic voyages were long and arduous with the typical transatlantic crossing taking two months and a considerable mortality toll of passengers. Sailing vessels were improved early in the nineteenth century, but, more important, they were replaced by steamships from the middle of the century, with their greater space, speed and safety standards. Transport developments on land were equally important. Railways carried emigrants to the ports of embarkation – a vital consideration in continental Europe – and they were also instrumental in opening up the New World interiors.

The transatlantic shipping companies and American transcontinental railway companies lubricated intercontinental migration in another, more positive way. They drummed up business for themselves by their extensive promotional activities within Europe: they recruited for employers, they extended credit for fares and land purchase, and they widely propagandized the virtues of the new lands. A common poster was that of an American ploughman turning up piles of coined dollars, and the exaggerated claims of one railway company, the Northern Pacific, led to its territory being derided as 'the Banana Belt'.

One way in which obstacles to overseas migration can be eased is government promotion and assistance at origin, but there is little evidence of this in nineteenth-century Europe where *laissez-faire* policies held sway and where both business and military interests favoured the retention of large populations. In Britain the question of government assistance to emigrants was widely debated, and strongly advocated by parliamentary committees examining poverty in Scotland and Ireland, but proposals were always rejected (Cowan 1961), except in the case of particular groups like retired and discharged soldiers. The proper role of the British government was thought to lie in a general overseeing of emigration through the Emigration Commissioners, the Poor Law Commissioners and emigration agents in overseas ports, so that any financial assistance to British emigrants was left to parish authorities, philanthropic societies, landlords and emigration societies funded by public subscription. Such assisted emigrants never exceeded one-tenth of all British emigrants (Guillet 1963).

Immigration into the United States

The United States has been the dominant destination in the overseas expansion of European population, attracting a gross immigration of some 35 million Europeans between 1820 and 1930, or almost two-thirds of European exodus at that time. The United States has proved more attractive than alternative destinations in its relative proximity to Europe, in its rich endowment of agricultural and mineral resources, and in the way its political and social institutions have promoted ready assimilation and social mobility among at least European immigrants. In this last respect, South American destinations were particularly disfavoured by the master-and-man relationship of aristocratic landowner and powerless tenant which was the legacy of Spanish and Portuguese colonial regimes. In Brazil and

Argentina tenancy conditions were such that landlords were able to commandeer a good deal of the cash crop profits, as well as all of the increased land values consequent upon settlement expansion.

The era of appreciable, unrestricted entry to the United States is traditionally divided into three periods. Up until 1820, when the federal government began to keep immigration statistics, immigration was slight and was largely from Britain. At the first federal census in 1790 persons of English descent accounted for 61 percent of the population, with a further 18 percent being of Scottish and Irish descent. The only other significant European groups were the Germans in Pennsylvania, the Dutch in New York and the Swedes in Delaware (Thomlinson 1965).

The period from the 1820s to the 1880s is known as the 'old migration'. Immigration increased rapidly as canals and railroads opened up the interior, bringing in their wake waves of pioneer settlers. The origins of immigrants widened, particularly to include appreciable numbers of Germans and Scandinavians (Table 9.2), but 95 percent of all immigrants still came from northern and western Europe. Clearly it was not the poorest and most congested countries of Europe that led the way in emigration, and even within famine-ridden Ireland it was not the most destitute western regions that showed the highest regional rates of emigration (Figure 9.1). This indicates the importance of information provision, transportation facilities and private means in stimulating long-distance migration, over and above simple spatial inequalities.

During the 1880s, the 'old' gave way to the 'new migration'. Immigration from much of northwestern Europe subsided as fertility began to fall and as manufacturing employment expanded; indeed, Germany became a country of net immigra-

Table 9.2   *Number of immigrants in thousands to the United States by selected origins, 1820–1930*

	All countries	England & Wales and Scotland	Ireland	Germany	Scandi-navia	Russia & Baltic States	Italy
1820–1829	127	26	50	4	–	–	–
1830–1839	537	73	170	124	2	–	1
1840–1849	1427	217	655	384	13	–	–
1850–1859	2814	444	1029	975	25	–	8
1860–1869	2081	532	427	723	96	1	9
1870–1879	2741	577	422	750	208	34	45
1880–1889	5247	810	673	1444	672	182	267
1890–1899	3693	328	404	578	391	449	602
1900–1909	8202	469	344	327	488	1500	1930
1910–1919	6346	371	166	174	238	1106	1229
1920–1929	4294	337	206	386	205	87	527

Source: US Bureau of the Census (1960), Series C88–114

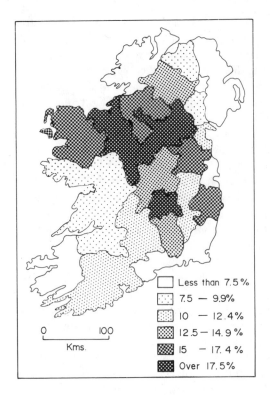

Figure 9.1
Emigration during the Irish famine, 1846-1851, as a percentage of the 1841 population
Source: Cousens (1960), figure 1

tion. The zone of heaviest emigration had now shifted to southern and eastern Europe, particularly Italy, Greece, Austria-Hungary, Russia and Poland (Table 9.2), where the spread of emigration fever was closely related to the progress of fundamental economic, social and demographic changes across Europe from the Northwest to the South and East. Everywhere, incipient economic development, transportation improvements, better knowledge of opportunities abroad, falling mortality and accelerating population growth were followed by a surge of emigration.

The 'new migration' differed from the 'old' not only in being bigger and coming from a different set of European origins, but in being dominantly directed towards the cities. By the end of the century the spread of the agricultural frontier right across the United States meant that little good land was freely available, but manufacturing and commercial growth was creating major labour demands in the rapidly expanding cities.

Urban ecological studies show that the influx of the 'new' immigrants to American cities usually took the form of spatial segregation, in which enclaves like the

Greektowns and Little Sicilies became established in the poorer neighbourhoods around city centres (Yeates and Garner 1971). Such segregation was largely by immigrant preference, as a means of cushioning the impact of an alien society (MacDonald and MacDonald 1964), and in subsequent generations there were few barriers placed on dispersal. This is in marked contrast to the more recent ghetto-ization experience of blacks and Puerto Ricans, where the formative role has been played by external pressure rather than internal coherence (Morrill 1965, Rose 1971).

The smoothing of annual immigrant flows into decadal totals (Table 9.2) suggests a fairly regular rise in immigration from the low levels of the 1820s to a deluge in the early twentieth century. In fact, there were considerable annual fluctuations, involving many peaks and troughs in the intervening period. Economists have closely examined these fluctuations in relation to economic conditions generally, and business cycles specifically, on both sides of the Atlantic (Jerome 1926, D. S. Thomas 1941, B. Thomas 1954, 1972). There is general agreement that before about 1860 the best correlation is an inverse one with harvest conditions at origin – poor harvests leading to appreciable migration, and vice versa. Later, with the growing maturity of the American economy, the dominant influence becomes the business cycle at destination, with cyclical upsurges in business prosperity in the United States attracting immigrants almost regardless of conditions in Europe. More ambitious, but controversial, is the view of B. Thomas (1954, 1972) that the economies on both sides of the Atlantic underwent complementary, interdependent, but opposite *long* swings in association with capital and population flows between them; to him, the pivotal role was played by investment transfer.

Towards the end of the nineteenth century there were signs of a new era in international migration with the imposition for the first time in the United States of barriers on immigration in response to charges of 'cheap labour' and 'unfair competition'. Immigrants under the 'old migration' had occasionally met with hostility and prejudice, especially the destitute Irish, but it was generally accepted that immigration was necessary to develop the country's resources. It was the 'new migration' which caused a fundamental change in attitudes. Not only was the flood of immigrants much greater, but they were concentrated visibly in the cities and they comprised those nationalities which were thought to be more difficult to integrate – hence their branding as 'polacks', 'bohunks' and 'wops'. The first exclusions were against prostitutes, convicts, the mentally ill and persons likely to become public charges (1875 and 1882), the Chinese (1882), the Japanese (1907) and nationals of an Asiatic Barred Zone (1917). But the ultimate expression of selective immigration control was embodied in the Quota Act of 1924, which took effect in 1929 and which continued with little modification until the mid-1960s. This limited the annual immigration from origins outside the western hemisphere to 154,000, with quotas distributed among countries in the same ratio as these countries contributed to the national origin (often through several generations) of the United States population in 1920. This was flagrant ethnic discrimination, since countries like Italy and Poland, with only short but tumultuous migration links with the United States, were granted derisory annual quotas of 6,000 compared with 66,000 for Britain and 26,000 for Germany. The countries of northwestern Europe never filled their quotas, and this, together with economic depression, actually led to a small net outflow of aliens from the United States during the 1930s.

Forced migrations

World War I heralded the rebirth of forced migration, but unlike the earlier movements of slaves to the Mediterranean empires and to the colonial economies of the Americas, the force was now normally applied by the sending country rather than the receiving one, and in the cause of ethnic and ideological purity rather than economic gain. Davis (1974, p.100) describes how 'two world wars, ignited by a nation obsessed with the separateness and solidarity of its own folk, were ironically ended by a legitimation of that obsession for nations in general. Under the Wilsonian banner of "national self-determination" it was all peoples, not only the Germans, who could claim folk sovereignty. Carried to its extreme, this ideal, which justified the dismemberment of the defeated German, Turkish and Austro-Hungarian empires, encouraged every minority to seek a territory of its own and every colony to seek "independence".' Between 1950 and 1975 the number of independent countries tripled, and the wars and revolutions which accompanied these changes created millions of displaced persons and refugees. A refugee is defined by the United Nations as 'an individual who owing to well-founded fear of being persecuted for reasons of race, religion, nationality, membership of a particular social group or political opinion, is outside the country of his nationality and is unable, or owing to such fears, unwilling to avail himself of the protection of that country' (quoted by Gould 1974, p.413). One characteristic of forced migration that is demographically significant is that the normal selectivity in the migration process by age, sex, skill and ambition is lacking, since whole communities are normally uprooted.

Just a few examples will be mentioned. Over a million Russians were dispersed and left stranded in adjacent parts of Europe as a result of the 1917 revolution and the subsequent civil war; over 300,000 Armenians fled from persecution associated with the rise of Turkish nationalism in the 1920s; more than a million refugees, mostly Jews, left Germany in the 1930s to escape Nazi persecution; some 18 million people in central and eastern Europe moved across international frontiers through flight, expulsion, transfer or population exchange in the three years following World War II (Kulischer 1948, Kosiński 1970); the 1947 partition led to some 6–7 million Muslims leaving India for Pakistan, and about the same number of Hindus and Sikhs moving in the other direction; the flight of Arabs on the proclamation of the state of Israel in 1948 has led to a Palestinian refugee force of some 1.5 million (Barakat 1973), and the Korean War of the early 1950s led to an exodus of about 4 million people from North to South Korea. Davis (1974) estimates that the grand total of forced international migrations between 1913 and

1968 amounted to 71 million, which is higher by at least 10 million than those who left Europe of their own free will in the great transoceanic migrations between 1820 and 1930. And the number of refugees continues to escalate, with the most recent mass movements being in the Ethiopia-Somalia and the Vietnam-Kampuchea-Thailand areas.

Modern permanent settlement immigration

Apart from forced movements, immigration has become focused into the developed countries, with the less developed countries of southern Europe, Africa, Asia and Latin America replacing Europe as the major supply of emigrants. A broad distinction can be made between the theoretically temporary, migrant labour movements to northwestern Europe and the Middle East, and permanent settlement immigration to the still uncrowded countries of North America and Oceania.

Net permanent settlement immigration to the world's four major receiving countries amounted to over 12 million between 1950 and 1974: 8.3 million to the United States, 2.2 million to Canada, 1.9 million to Australia and 0.2 million to New Zealand. Relative to population size, the annual rate of entry into the United States was about 2 per 1000, compared with rates of 4–6 per 1000 in the other three countries (Department of Employment and Immigration, Canada, 1979). But entry rates have diminished since 1975 with the economic downturn initiated by rising oil prices.

All four immigration countries have responded in some degree to Third World demands, consequent upon growing population pressures, for less discriminatory immigration policies, so that formal ethnic quotas or preferences were discarded in the United States in 1965, in Canada in 1962 and 1967, and in Australia in 1973, in favour of preferences based on family reunion and on labour market skills. Thus, in the United States immigrants from Asia rose from 7 percent of the total inflow in 1965 to 35 percent in 1976, when the Third World contribution as a whole was 77 percent. One consequence has been the charge that scarce development skills, which are costly to produce, are being lost to the Third World by a highly selective 'brain drain' (Glaser 1978). In Haiti, for example, a report of the United States Agency for International Development (1973) indicated that extensive emigration of health professionals had left only one doctor and one nurse for every 12,000 people. On the other hand, some Third World countries, notably India, exhibit a 'brain overflow' situation, in that university education has expanded well beyond the economy's absorptive capacity for graduates. There is also some criticism within immigration countries of large entries of physicians and other professionals from Third World countries on the grounds that it allows inadequacies in the indigenous system of professional training to be perpetuated. In the United States, for example, there are more Filipino than black doctors – a sorry indictment of the country's medical education system (Bouvier 1977).

Canada: a representative case study

In a world of growing population pressure, Canada has been one of a small handful of countries to maintain an expansionist immigration policy into the 1970s. Traditionally its governments, both Liberal and Conservative, have been convinced that the benefits of immigration generally outweigh the costs, at least for a huge, resource-rich country with one of the world's lowest population densities. A larger population has been actively sought as a means of achieving economies of scale – in resource development, manufacturing and provision of public services – and also as a means of consolidating national sovereignty in a continent dominated demographically by the United States. Yet in recent years the immigration issue has become more controversial, so that major government efforts were made in the mid-1970s to encourage a national public debate on the policy options available, through the publication of a four-volume discussion document, the *Green Paper on Immigration*, and through the establishment of a parliamentary committee on immigration policy to receive briefs and hold public meetings throughout Canada. This debate culminated in the passing of a new Immigration Act by the Canadian Parliament in 1977.

In recent decades the pattern of Canadian immigration has been fashioned dominantly by economic opportunities within Canada (Green 1976, H. R. Jones 1979). Thus Figure 9.2 reveals a generally inverse relationship between Canadian unemployment rates and immigration totals, a relationship dependent partly on prospective immigrants' assessment of the Canadian labour market, particularly through advice from friends and relatives within Canada, and partly on conscious regulation of inflow by immigration officials – the so-called 'tap on-tap off' policy. The one exceptional year when the relationship breaks down is 1957, when a dramatic surge in immigration reflected the Suez crisis and the Hungarian revolution.

This relatively simple pattern of cyclical fluctuations in immigration totals does, however, mask significant changes over time in the composition of the immigrant flow. These changes must be interpreted in relation to evolving immigration policies, which have made the pattern of immigrant selection from the late 1970s very different from that of the 1950s. The most fundamental change has been that specific manpower requirements have replaced geographic origin as the dominant selection criterion. Between 1954 and 1958, 94 percent of Canada's immigrants came from Europe and the United States, but growing objections arose to a selection system of preferred nationalities, with particular pressures being exerted by newly independent Commonwealth countries. Canada responded with new immigration regulations in 1962 and 1967 which went a long way towards establishing a universally applicable selection policy based on education, training and skills. Accordingly, for the 1974–1978 period, 51 percent of all immigrants came from countries outside Europe and the United States, despite the built-in momentum of the traditional migration pattern to maintain itself through the sponsorship of relatives and through the distribution of Canadian immigration offices abroad.

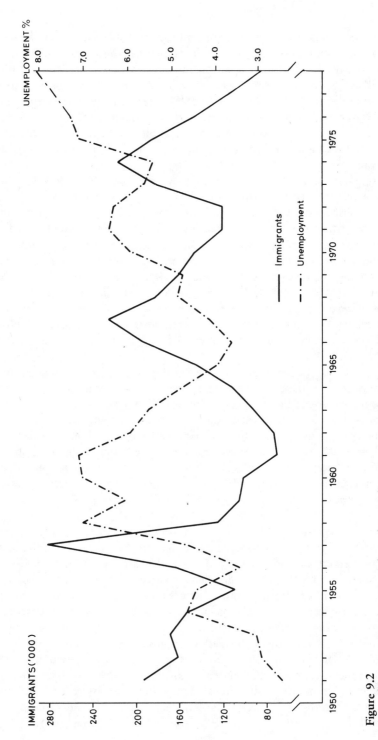

Figure 9.2
Annual immigration into Canada and annual average unemployment rate (number
unemployed as a percentage of labour force), 1951-1978
Source: H.R. Jones (1978), figure 1

The occupational composition of the immigrant stream has been related increasingly to labour market needs within Canada. In 1966 this relationship was formalized by the creation of a new government department, Manpower and Immigration, and in the same year a White Paper on Immigration set the tone of subsequent immigrant selection policy when it stated: 'We are not a country of virgin lands and forests waiting to be settled by anyone with a strong back and a venturesome spirit. . . . Canada has become a highly complex industrialized and urbanized society. And such a society is becoming increasingly demanding of the quality of its work force.'

Consequently, in 1967 a points-assessment scheme was introduced for prospective immigrants, largely in order to select, as objectively as possible, desirable workers. Unsponsored migrants had to receive at least 50 out of a possible 100 points for an assessment on several, largely work-related qualities (education, training, age, occupational skill, occupational demand in Canada, arranged employment, etc.). This form of selection has been maintained, although, with worsening employment prospects within Canada (Figure 9.2), a further restriction was introduced in 1975, whereby 10 points are deducted unless applicants either have already arranged employment (permission for which is only given if the national employment service confirms that there are no suitable Canadians available to take the job) or are in an occupation designated as experiencing labour shortages in Canada.

These selection procedures have altered the occupational composition of the immigrant stream so that managerial, professional and other highly trained occupations have increased at the expense of unskilled occupations within labouring, primary and service industries, although many immigrants can escape full assessment under the points system through being a refugee or having Canadian relatives. Indeed, Canada has an impressive record for relaxing its immigrant selection standards to cater on humanitarian grounds for refugees. About one-tenth of all immigrants into Canada since 1945 have been refugees, with recent examples being the entry of 6,000 Ugandan Asians in 1973–1974 and some 20,000 Indochinese in 1979.

Future immigration policy, regulated through the 1977 Immigration Act, will continue to respond to changing, government-perceived needs within Canadian society. The very need for immigration at all has come under increasing fire in recent years, as a response to rising unemployment, to problems of congestion and social friction in Toronto and some other areas of immigrant concentration, and to the rapid growth of the indigenous labour force resulting from increasing female participation rates and the coming of working age of the 1946–1964 'baby boom'. Many of the more recently established ethnic groups within Canada are fearful that the new Act will severely curtail immigration, particularly since they were unsuccessful in their attempt to persuade the government to recognize formally in the new Act the country's multicultural nature, not just its federal and bilingual character. Nevertheless, there are largely demographic considerations which are likely to maintain immigration, in the long term, at levels not dissimilar to those of recent years. In particular, the total fertility rate has plummeted from 3.9 children per woman in 1959 to 1.7 in 1978, so that the cohorts entering the labour force will diminish steadily from the early 1980s. If immigration is not maintained at a level well in excess of emigration (estimated by C. E. Taylor, 1979, at some 70,000 per annum during the 1970s), the dependency ratio would be affected adversely.

The immigration movement is thus far from doomed, but it will be tuned ever more sensitively to Canada's manpower needs, and a new departure is that annual immigration targets will be determined and publicly announced (120,000 for 1980, to include a Southeast Asian refugee intake of 27,000). Although the points system of assessment for applicants other than in the sponsored 'family class' will be maintained, less weight will be given to education levels and theoretical training, since general shortages of professional and highly trained people have been over-come by the transatlantic 'brain drain' of the 1960s and by a huge recent invest-ment in higher educational facilities within Canada.

A critical part of the immigration debate has focused on the spatial distribution of immigrants within Canada. Table 9.3 shows that Ontario has by far the greatest immigrant attraction relative to population, followed by British Columbia and Alberta, while the other Prairie Provinces, Quebec and the Maritime Provinces have little drawing power. The close relationship of this pattern to provincial variations in economic buoyancy within Canda is demonstrated in Table 9.3 by unemployment and wage-level data. A particularly sensitive problem has been the falling proportion of immigrants entering Quebec, since the traditional safeguard of Quebec's demographic, cultural and linguistic position within the confedera-tion, a high natural increase rate, has disappeared recently, to the extent that its provincial fertility rates are now the lowest in the whole of Canada. One response

Table 9.3   Percentage distribution of immigrants into Canada by intended province of destination, 1968–1976, and other provincial data

British Columbia	Alberta	Saskat-chewan	Manitoba	Ontario	Quebec	Maritimes	Yukon & N.W.T.
14·6	7·4	1·4	3·9	53·3	16·4	2·9	0·1
1971 population distribution (percent)							
10·1	7·6	4·3	4·6	35·7	27·9	9·5	0·3
Average annual unemployment, 1968–1975 (percent)							
6·7	3·7	3·4	3·9	4·4	7·7	8·8	
Average annual weekly wage, 1974–1975 ($)							
215	193	179	174	193	186	165	

Sources: Department of Manpower and Immigration, Annual Immigration Statistics, Ottawa; Canadian Statistical Review

has been that both provincial and federal efforts are being made to identify and tap promising sources of French-speaking immigrants such as West Africa; another has been the deliberate channelling of Vietnamese refugees into Quebec.

But the spatial problem that dominates all others is the concentration of immigrants in the larger metropolitan areas. Recently, more than half of all Canadian immigrants have been drawn to Toronto, Montreal and Vancouver, and 76 percent of the population increase in the Toronto metropolitan area between 1961 and 1971 was accounted for by foreigners who had immigrated in that decade and were enumerated in the city in 1971. It is now firm government policy to promote a more dispersed pattern of immigrant settlement, although few positive means exist in democratic societies to steer immigrants against prevailing population currents. The counselling of immigrants abroad as to desirable locations within Canada has become more active, an evaluation of the suitability of the intended area of residence is being incorporated in the points-assessment scheme, and consideration is being given to measures which would ensure that immigrants adhere to their stated intended area of residence, at least for several months after entry. Attempts in Britain to fashion the entry of Ugandan Asians along similar lines had little success, so that the monitoring of such dispersion programmes is just one aspect of contemporary immigration policy in Canada which should attract the professional interest of population geographers.

Migrant labour and regional labour markets

Figure 9.3 shows several parts of the world where the spatial proximity of labour-deficit countries and labour-surplus countries has given rise to a pattern of regional labour market systems, each of which embraces several countries. Seers et al. (1979) have applied the core-periphery concept to each of these systems, since the more developed, capital-rich core countries possess the power to organize labour inflows from their less developed peripheries very much in their own interests.

Europe
International labour movements within Europe had already become significant by the early decades of this century. The two important destination countries were Germany, recruiting migrants from central and eastern Europe for its rapidly expanding manufacturing industries, and France, where labour needs were created by its falling fertility, its ageing population and its wartime manpower losses. The number of foreigners in France, recruited on short-term contracts mainly from adjacent Belgium, Italy and Spain, rose from 1.4 million in 1919 to 3 million in 1930, but there was considerable enforced exodus in the subsequent depression (Power 1976).

Causes
The 1960s saw the development of a larger scale and wider network of migrant labour flows. Three major causes may be identified. First, there were the labour

Figure 9.3
Major international flows of migrant workers within regional labour markets in the 1970s

demands created by rapid economic growth in the more developed European countries. Second, the demographic echo effect of low fertility in the 1930s and early 1940s was a sluggish growth rate in the indigenous labour force of northwestern Europe – about 0.5 percent per annum in most countries in the 1960s. At the same time, population pressure was high in the Mediterranean region, where in Spain, Portugal, Yugoslavia and Greece the expansion of the labour force was about 1.0 percent per annum, and the share of the labour force in agriculture still as high as 25–40 percent in 1970; in Turkey, Algeria, Morocco and Tunisia, the pressure was even greater, with equivalent figures of over 2.0 percent per annum and 45–65 percent. Clearly there was a reserve of unemployed and underemployed labour in the peripheral countries available, and often anxious, for recruitment. Third, because of social mobility aspirations, the indigenous workers and even the registered unemployed in northwestern Europe are simply not prepared to man an increasing range of what are thought to be unpleasant menial and sometimes dangerous occupations. Thus over 90 percent of Munich's dustmen are immigrants, and even on production-line jobs the boredom factor is such that Ford at Cologne was employing 15,000 immigrants, mostly Turks, in its 1973 labour force of 33,000 (King 1976). These are the new coolies.

Forms of migration
Freedom of labour movement within the EEC is restricted to nationals of member states, of which only one, Italy, has been a traditional labour exporter; and Italy was unable to cope with EEC labour demands in the 1960s, due to the competing claims arising from economic growth in northern Italy and in adjacent Switzerland. The response within the EEC was to recruit foreign workers from other Mediterranean countries on a contract basis, normally for a year, but renewable for further prescribed periods. Bilateral labour recruitment agreements between countries became normal, as between West Germany and Italy (1955), Spain (1960), Greece (1960), Turkey (1961), Morocco (1963), Portugal (1964), Tunisia (1965) and Yugoslavia (1968). Thus it was that foreign workers in West Germany rose from about 300,000 in 1960 to a peak of about 2.6 million at the beginning of the energy crisis in September 1973 (Kuhn 1978). The number then in northwestern Europe as a whole (excluding Britain) was about 6 million, and they comprised about 30 percent of the labour force in Switzerland and Luxembourg, 10 percent in France and West Germany, 7 percent in Belgium and 3 percent in the Netherlands.

 - The ruthless self-interest of governments and employers in recruiting countries ensured that labour inflow was organized on a temporary, fixed-contract basis, that it was regulated strictly in relation to cyclical trends, and that it normally took the form of young, male, unaccompanied workers filling unskilled vacancies. The common term for migrant workers, *Gasterbeiter* or guest worker, suggests that they are there only at the invitation of their German hosts, for a short period only, and that they should be grateful for the privilege (Power 1976). Similarly, the Germans have widely used the term *Konjunkturpuffer* to describe how ready recruitment and shedding of migrant labour can be used as a buffer against the disruption of cyclical fluctuations.

Until the late 1960s the pattern of labour migration conformed broadly to that desired by the recruiting countries; for example, the modal stay for Italian migrants in Europe at that time was 6–12 months (King 1976). But as migrant workers became more familiar with conditions in host countries, the more they desired to settle there and bring their families, and perhaps return to their homeland only for holidays and retirement. Many migrant workers have succeeded in achieving more or less permanent settlement, so that by the early 1970s there was about one dependant for every migrant worker in northwestern Europe. This has been achieved despite several forms of official discouragement operating variably in host countries: the fixed-term nature of contracts; the tieing of residence rights to job possession; reduced social security benefits and political rights; remote prospects of achieving citizenship; and the need for immigrants to demonstrate an ability to provide adequate accommodation for their families.

The United Kingdom provides a special case of migrant labour inflow. Its growth rate and consequent labour demand have been sluggish in recent decades, being reflected in a small net outflow of population, primarily to the older Commonwealth countries and the United States. There has, nevertheless, been a substantial inflow of 'replacement' labour into the kinds of jobs and areas being vacated by the indigenous population. Britain's labour-supplying 'periphery' is distinctive in comprising not only the fringes of the European labour market in Ireland, Italy, Malta and Cyprus, but also the distant realms of the former British Empire in the West Indies, India and Pakistan. In the 1950s, when the populations of Commonwealth countries could migrate freely to Britain and settle permanently, the inflow showed a strong temporal association with labour market conditions in Britain (Peach 1965), and there was a substantial element of temporary migration by unaccompanied males, particularly from India and Pakistan. But, as a response to growing public disquiet, the 1962 Commonwealth Immigrants Act and subsequent restrictive legislation have transformed the nature of this immigration. The necessary work permits for independent immigrants are subject to stringent annual quotas, so that the great majority of coloured immigrants in recent years have been dependants seeking family reunion and permanent settlement.

Spatial factors

Distance is a major factor determining the spatial pattern of intercountry migration linkages within the European labour market; hence the dominant flows from Spain and Portugal to France; from Italy to Switzerland; from Yugoslavia, Greece, Italy and Turkey to Germany; from the Irish Republic to the United Kingdom; and from Finland to Sweden. In addition, the importance of traditional political connections is seen in the channelling of North African outflow into France, while a case has also been made out for a biasing of linkages through the linguistic and cultural similarities between Spain, Portugal, Italy and France (Heijke and Klaassen 1977).

The regional origin of migrant workers within the countries of southern Europe is depicted in Figure 9.4. In countries at the initial stage of emigration, Turkey and Yugoslavia in the 1960s, the outflow is concentrated in their more developed regions – Slovenia and Croatia, and the western provinces of Turkey; the role of opportunity awareness would appear to be critical, as it was in fashioning the regional pattern of European migration to the New World in the nineteenth century. In countries with a longer experience of labour migration, outflow is heaviest in areas of least development and most population pressure – Portugal north of the Tagus, Galicia, Andalucia and much of the Meseta in Spain, the Mezzogiorno in Italy, and the islands and northern mountainous regions of Greece (Tapinos 1966, Livi-Bacci and Hagmann 1971, King 1976).

The distribution of immigrants within host countries is best interpreted in relation to the immigrants' role as replacement population, attracted to job and often residential vacancies created by the upward social mobility and outward physical mobility of the indigenous population (Peach 1966). In Britain the seven major conurbations, which contain one-third of the country's population, all showed a population decrease between 1961 and 1971; yet they accounted for 63 percent of the 1971 census population born in the New Commonwealth (Peach 1975). In Sweden, the three major metropolitan regions account for 69 percent of the country's population, but 80 percent of net foreign immigration between 1975 and 1977 (Vining and Kontuly 1978); and in France, 26 percent (200,000) of the country's net foreign immigration between 1968 and 1975 was concentrated in the Paris region, which during the same period experienced a net outflow of 140,000 indigenous population (Vining and Kontuly 1978).

Turn of the tide?
From the end of 1973 one host country after another has imposed severe restrictions, and in some cases total bans, on further recruitment of foreign labour, although not of seasonal workers. The immediate cause was a looming recession induced by higher oil prices, but equally potent factors were the mounting public hostility towards immigrants and the expansion of domestic labour supply as the postwar 'baby boom' cohorts joined the workforce. It is one matter restricting recruitment, but it is quite another repatriating foreign workers and their families on either a voluntary or compulsory basis, and this has occurred on only a modest scale.

Data inadequacies bedevil all numerical estimates in this field, but Böhning (1979) suggests that the number of foreign workers in northwestern Europe (excluding the UK) has fallen from about 6 million in 1973 to about 5 million in 1979, while the number of dependants has remained fairly stable, despite much coming and going. The increased desire of migrant workers to settle permanently is shown in the contrast between the 1967 recession in Germany, when about one-quarter of all previously employed foreigners returned home, and the 1974 recession, when only about 15 percent did so (Kuhn 1978). Clearly, many guests have outstayed their welcome but refuse to pack their bags.

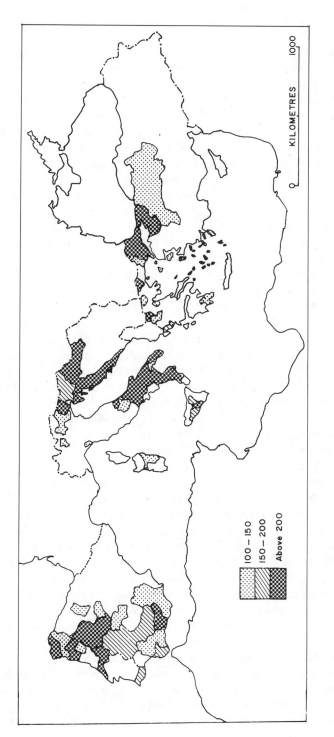

Figure 9.4
Regional pattern of emigration from countries of southern Europe, 1965-1968. Shading categories represent the percentage excess of regional over national rates.
Source: simplified from King (1976), figure 1

Costs and benefits

Any evaluation of the European migrant labour system must consider its impact on the societies at origin and destination and on the migrants themselves.

Since the system has been initiated, organized and controlled by the 'core' developed countries, it can be expected to have conveyed benefits upon them. This was outstandingly the case in the days of strictly temporary and rotational immigration when the supply of immigrant labour could be turned on and off to match the cyclical pattern of labour demand in the core countries. Entrepreneurs also benefited from the lower cost of migrant workers, since lower wage grades could be created for them and they were less resistant to methods which reorganized the labour process more profitably (Paine 1979). Guest workers were young, single (or at least unaccompanied by dependants) and of good health, since they were often subject to medical examination before acceptance. In social security terms such workers had few liabilities, and since they produced considerably more goods and services than they consumed, they also served to check inflationary forces.

During the 1970s, however, many of the distinctive features of the migrant labour system were being eroded as immigrants and their dependants increasingly sought quasi-permanent settlement. In the words of a Swiss economist quoted by Power (1976): 'We called for workers, and there came human beings.' Employers have found it more difficult to maintain job and wage differentials between immigrant and domestic labour, and much higher social infrastructual costs have had to be incurred by the state in the provision of family housing, education, health services, unemployment, sickness and compensation benefits, and pensions. In this changed situation there has been considerable discussion (Wolter 1975, Hiemenz and Schatz 1977, Paine 1979) about the likelihood of European entrepreneurs attempting to keep down production costs by locating new plant in peripheral countries where local workers could be paid even less than under the migrant labour system and where the rising social costs of that system could be avoided.

In terms of migrant welfare, a major and, some would say, intolerable cost of the migrant labour system has been family separation, invariably for periods of several months and often for several years. Family reunion in host countries is hindered not only by entrance restrictions, but also by the shortage and high cost of housing, exemplified in the spawning of *bidonville* shanty towns around the major French cities. Exploitation of immigrant labour has also been rife, as one UN report on the French building industry demonstrates. The industry 'has evolved complete networks of organization, from the recruitment of the workers in Africa to their work and their housing on building sites, sites which have all the aspects of real camps and where the laws are openly flouted: ridiculously low wages (sometimes agreed on in Africa when the employee does not have any benchmark to assess the pay offered); food and transport provided by the firm which charges excessively for its poor quality services; housing in huts; limitation of visits to certain hours, and the prohibition of women; suppresion of all rights of trade unions and political expression' (quoted by Power 1976, p.17). A particular subproletariat, notoriously susceptible to employer and landlord exploitation, is the illegal immigrants who gain entry clandestinely, or by forged papers, or by overstaying. They are vulnerable to abuse because they feel unable to complain to any legal authority. Their numbers have often been estimated conservatively at about half a million, or some 10 percent of the immigrant labour force in mainland Europe, but the current freeze on legal recruitment has boosted their numbers.

It can be argued that first-generation immigrants have migrated voluntarily, in response to even harsher conditions at origin. The dissatisfaction and resentment about working and living conditions in host countries is often greater among rootless second-generation immigrants who cannot identify with a host society which discriminates against them or with a homeland they may never have seen. This frustration has often expressed itself in so-called race riots, as in the West Indian St. Pauls district of Bristol in April 1980.

For the countries of origin, the costs and benefits of the migrant labour system are finely balanced. The fact that governments of such countries have often encouraged, organized and financially subsidized the exodus of migrant workers implies that benefits are likely to accrue to the society at origin as well as to the migrants themselves. Pressures on domestic labour markets are reduced, and valuable foreign exchange is provided by emigrant worker remittances – to the extent that such receipts in Turkey in 1973 were comparable to 90 percent of the value of the country's exports of merchandise; equivalent proportions in other countries were Portugal 62%, Greece 58%, Yugoslavia 49%, Morocco 27%, Tunisia 24%, Algeria 20%, Spain 18% and Italy 7% (Seers et al. 1979). In addition, foreign workers have been thought to return home with modern technological skills, enabling them to act as agents of innovation and forces for development; an investment in human capital has taken place.

The reality of the situation is now known to be very different. It is not coincidental that as the inflow of remittances has increased, so too have the deficits on visible trade balances. Growing familiarization with foreign consumption styles leads to disdain for domestic products and a growing dependence on expensive foreign imports. Studies of return migration, somewhat neglected as a research area by population geographers (King 1978), show time and time again (Böhning 1972, Baucic 1972, Cerase 1974, King 1976, Van Amersfoort 1978) that returning migrants are rarely bearers of initiative and generators of employment. Only a small number acquire appropriate vocational training – most are trapped in dead-end jobs – and their prime interest on return is to enhance their social status. This they attempt to achieve by disdaining manual employment, by early retirement, by the construction of a new house, by the purchase of land, a car and other consumer durables, or by the taking over of a small service establishment like a bar or taxi business. There is thus a reinforcement of the very conditions that promoted emigration in the first place. It is ironic that those migrants who are potentially most valuable for stimulating development in their home area – the minority who have secured valuable skills abroad – are the very ones who, because of successful adaptation abroad, are least likely to return. It requires a determined government campaign, as mounted by Guyana in the 1970s (Strachan 1980), to persuade highly qualified nationals to return.

There are also problems of demographic imbalance stemming from the selective nature of emigration. Many villages in southern Europe have been denuded of young men, with consequences not only for family formation and maintenance but also for agricultural production. In southern Italy, Wade (1979) has described how the agricultural workforce has become increasingly made up of women, old men and children, and the contrast between market-oriented capitalist farming on the plains and self-sufficient family farming in the hills has grown sharper. At its most acute levels, selective emigration can engender a social and economic malaise that George Bernard Shaw recognized in rural Ireland – 'a place of futility, failure and endless pointless talk'.

The common view, therefore, in the early days of the European migrant labour system, that migration, although often painful for individual migrants and their families, is a transitory phase which aids the development of the sending country, is now discredited. 'Stripped to its bare essentials, the engagement of migrants creates value added which is largely, if not exclusively, internalised in the country of employment and thus further increases its wealth and power relative to the country of origin' (Böhning 1979, p.409). Migration could thus even be regarded as a form of development aid *from* the periphery *to* the core. This is not to say that conditions at origin would be better without emigration; there is, after all, a reduction in unemployment and underemployment and a gain in income. What it does mean is that the gains from the migrant labour system have been demonstrably unequal and that a strong case can be made out for the legitimacy of compensation (Böhning 1977, 1979) within the framework of the much discussed but little implemented New International Economic Order.

North America

As the world's richest nation, the United States has been a magnet to migrants from its less developed periphery in Mexico and the Caribbean. Puerto Ricans have unrestricted access, profiting from their country's Commonwealth status in the United States, but citizens of other countries have to compete for the 120,000 quota places allotted annually since 1968 to the western hemisphere. One consequence has been an escalation in illegal immigration, achieved either by overstaying short-duration visas or simply by walking over a virtually open border with Mexico of some 2500 kilometres – the traditional swimming across the Rio Grande by 'wetbacks' has been made redundant by the depletion of the river by irrigation. The number of illegal immigrants apprehended increased sixfold between 1966 and 1975, and in the latter year they were twice as numerous as legal immigrants; more than 80 percent were Mexicans. Senior government officials claim that over 1 million aliens enter the US illegally, without apprehension, each year, but Heer (1979) has used data from the Current Population Survey of the US Bureau of Census to estimate that the *net* inflow, which is the important figure as far as job competition is concerned, is more like 100,000–200,000 annually. There cannot, of course, be illegal immigrants without illegal employers anxious to recruit cheap docile labour, and more than anything it has been the powerful agribusiness lobby that has used the threat of dearer food to thwart legislation against such rogue employers.

Reichert and Massey (1979) provide a fascinating picture of migrant labour from one Mexican village where an unusually high reliance on migration is the result of an unusually large proportion of landless families. A collection of migration histories revealed that 35 percent of the adult population had migrated temporarily to the United States in 1978, mainly to take up seasonal agricultural employment in California and Florida. Most of the migrants were holders of US resident visas, entitling them to permanent residence if they so wished, but almost one-quarter were illegal migrants. Figure 9.5 reveals that legal and illegal immigrants have very different patterns of movement, since vulnerability to detection makes it less easy for illegals to maximize their earnings by working at peak harvest times in different areas.

Southern Africa

As in other parts of the world, spatial inequalities and structural dependency are the basis of the migrant labour system, but the southern African system is unique in the way in which it has been totally dominated by host country interests for a period extending over several decades.

Foreign African workers in South Africa, all of them male and totalling more than half a million in 1971 (Protheto 1974), come mainly from Lesotho, Mozambique, Botswana, Swaziland and Malawi. They are recruited by the Witwatersrand Native Labour Association (established as long ago as 1900) for arduous and dangerous labouring in the gold mines (F. Wilson 1972, 1976). Rigid control by the South African government and employers ensures that migration is strictly temporary (one- or two-year contracts) and that there is no accompaniment of workers by their families. There has never been any prospect that the migrant worker can become a permanent settler; indeed, the migrant labour system is a buttress to apartheid.

Middle East

Just as the 1973 rise in oil prices suppressed labour demand and migrant labour recruitment in the European labour market, so it stimulated demand and recruitment in the capital-rich but labour-deficient oil states of the Middle East. By the late 1970s this had become the most active international labour market in the world, with over 2 million foreign workers being present in 1979 in the Arab OPEC countries (R.P. Shaw 1979). Table 9.4 indicates that in the group of major labour-importing countries, foreign workers comprised just over one-half of the labour force in 1975–1976, with the proportion rising to over two-thirds in Kuwait, Qatar and the United Arab Emirates.

A major data collection and investigation programme, commissioned by the International Labour Office, has recently provided a rich picture of labour movements in the Arab world (Birks and Sinclair 1977–1978, 1979). Capital inflow

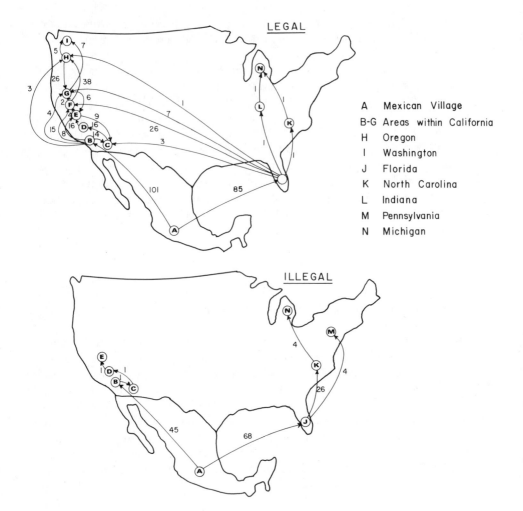

Figure 9.5
Migration routes by number of migrating units (worker and dependants) from a Mexican village to the United States in 1978.
Source: Reichert and Massey (1979), figure 1.　By permission of Population Reference Bureau, Inc.

following the oil price rises of the 1970s has stimulated a development boom in the oil states, all of them anxious to press ahead quickly with infrastructure, social services and diversification into manufacturing. The major constraint has been a shortage of manpower, the result of several factors: the indigenous populations are small – of the oil-rich countries only Libya and Saudi Arabia have over 2 million; the role of women in Islamic societies is such that female participation rates in the labour force are very low; there is a widespread scorn for manual work; and the

Table 9.4   Non-nationals in labour force of major labour-importing Arab countries, 1975–1976

	Total labour force ('000)	Non-nationals as % of labour force	% of all non-nationals in construction	Non-nationals as % of all construction workers
Bahrain	83	43·4	21·4	48·2
Kuwait	305	69·9	22·9	93·0
Libya	784	42·3	53·1	77·5
Oman	110	63·3	86·0	75·7
Qatar	66	80·0	18·8	97·3
Saudi Arabia	1,684	46·9	40·7	95·0
U.A. Emirates	298	85·4	37·4	82·4
All	3,294	51·9	41·2	85·6

Source: R.P. Shaw (1979), table 2

traditional paternal role of rulers often expresses itself in the creation of non-productive government posts for the indigenous population.

Importation of labour has been encouraged by the *laissez-faire* attitudes of most countries in the region to international labour movement. Spontaneity of movement has been facilitated by ethnic, linguistic and cultural affinites throughout the Arab world ('the circulation of Arab brethren'), and by the typically Third World conditions of population pressure and labour surplus in many non-oil countries of the region. In the late 1970s the major labour-exporting countries have been Egypt (20% of foreign workers in the Arab world), North Yemen (16%), Jordan (15%), Pakistan (10%), India (9%), Iran (6%), South Yemen (4%), Syria (4%), Lebanon (3%) and Tunisia (3%) (R. P. Shaw 1979). The flow patterns are strongly influenced by distance – hence the dominant flows into Libya from Egypt and Tunisia (although always subject to unstable political relations), into Saudi Arabia from the two Yemens, Jordan and Egypt, into Kuwait from Jordan, and into Oman and Bahrein from India and Pakistan. But there is also some occupational specialization by national origin. Thus, while the vast bulk of immigrants are required for unskilled labour, particularly in construction (Table 9.4), a significant proportion of Egyptians, Jordanians and Palestinians are employed throughout the Arab world as teachers, clerks and technicians – a reflection of higher educational standards at origin. In addition, highly qualified manpower is provided by expatriate communities of West Europeans and North Americans.

In the growing debate on the policy options open to labour-exporting and labour-receiving countries throughout the Middle East, those familiar with labour movements in other areas and other eras can hardly suppress a response of *déja vu*. In Kuwait, in particular, there is the familiar concern about the rapidly rising cost of infrastructure provision as dependants increasingly join the migrant workers; in Jordan, where a quarter of a million workers (one-third of the labour force) were working abroad in the late 1970s, labour shortages in some key sectors have led its government to view the rate of external migration as excessive; and in North Yemen, where over 80 percent of the GNP is provided by emigrant remittances, there has been a remittance-fuelled inflation rate of over 50 percent per annum.

Theoretical overviews

Classical theories of migration and of immigrant adaptation and assimilation are based on a functionalist perspective which views migration as an equilibriating response to spatial inequalities, as essentially voluntary in nature, as a rational attempt by migrants to maximize utility, and as a vehicle of upward social mobility. Although many international migrants enter a new society at the lowest economic and social strata, they are thought to have opportunities for improvement, certainly in subsequent generations, so that there is a progressive convergence of immigrant group characteristics towards those of the host community. Even when cultural pluralism persists, 'the functionalist approach tended to minimise the elements of conflict that pluralism created, emphasising the importance of the dominant value system in promoting consensual forms of pluralistic integration' (Richmond and Verma 1979, p.5).

A quite different interpretation of international migration is provided by the neo-Marxist conflict model, in which essentially coercive labour migration is a manifestation of an ongoing state of dependency which promotes underdevelopment in the periphery and overdevelopment at the core. Such analysis rejects the voluntary, rational and self-improving functionalist view of migration. Instead, the movement of labour from less developed peripheries to cores like northwestern Europe is seen as a further expression of exploitation of labour in a capitalist system. Such labour is simply part of Marx's 'reserve army of unemployed' at the beck and call of capitalist entrepreneurs, and suffering deprivations to sustain the living standards of the indigenous populations of advanced countries (Castles and Kosack 1973, Amin 1974, Nikolinakos 1975). Also integral to the conflict model is the view that migrant workers are prevented by discrimination from realizing the full range of labour market and housing market opportunities open to the indigenous population; they are trapped in occupational and residential ghettoes and become increasingly alienated from, and not assimilated into, the host societies. While in its purest form the functionalist view of migration is naive and excessively optimistic, the currently fashionable neo-Marxist interpretation suffers in turn from coarseness and rigidity.

1980 WORLD
POPULATION DATA

Reproduced from a sheet published by
the Population Reference Bureau, Inc.

Prepared by Carl Haub and Douglas W. Heisler,
Domographers, Population Reference Bureau.

Region or Country[1]	Population Estimate Mid-1980 (millions)[2]	Birth Rate[3]	Death Rate[3]	Rate of Natural Increase (annual, %)[4]	Number of Years to Double Population[5]	Population Projected for 2000 (millions)[6]	Infant Mortality Rate[7]	Total Fertility Rate[8]	Population under Age 15 (%)	Population over Age 64 (%)	Life Expectancy at Birth (years)[9]	Urban Population (%)[10]	Projected Ultimate Population Size (millions)[11]	Per Capita Gross National Product (US$)[12]
WORLD	4,414	28	11	1.7	41	6,156	97	3.8	35	6	61	39	9,832	2,040
MORE DEVELOPED[1]	1,131	16	9	0.6	111	1,272	20	2.0	24	11	72	69	1,372	6,260
LESS DEVELOPED[1]	3,283	32	12	2.0	34	4,884	110	4.4	39	4	57	29	8,460	560
AFRICA	472	46	17	2.9	24	832	140	6.4	45	3	49	26	2,051	530
NORTHERN AFRICA	110	42	13	3.0	23	186	121	6.2	44	3	54	42	370	790
Algeria	19.0	48	13	3.4	20	36.9	142	7.3	47	4	56	55	93.6	1,260
Egypt	42.1	38	10	2.7	26	64.9	90	5.3	40	4	55	44	90.0	400
Libya	3.0	47	13	3.5	20	5.7	130	7.4	49	4	55	60	11.7	6,910
Morocco	21.0	43	14	3.0	23	37.3	133	6.9	46	2	55	42	70.9	670
Sudan	18.7	48	18	3.1	22	31.8	141	6.6	44	3	46	20	88.8	320
Tunisia	6.5	33	8	2.5	28	9.7	125	5.7	44	4	57	50	14.4	950
WESTERN AFRICA	141	49	19	3.0	23	262	159	6.8	46	3	46	21	711	460
Benin	3.6	49	19	3.0	23	6.6	149	6.7	46	4	46	14	15.0	230
Cape Verde	0.3	28	9	1.8	38	0.4	105	3.0	36	4	60	20	0.6	160
Gambia	0.6	48	23	2.4	28	1.0	217	6.4	41	2	41	16	2.4	230
Ghana	11.7	48	17	3.1	22	21.2	115	6.7	47	3	48	36	56.6	390
Guinea	5.0	46	21	2.5	27	8.2	175	6.2	44	3	44	23	22.6	210
Guinea-Bissau	0.6	41	23	1.8	39	0.9	208	5.5	39	4	41	26	1.7	200
Ivory Coast	8.0	48	18	2.9	24	14.0	154	6.7	45	2	46	32	36.1	840
Liberia	1.9	50	17	3.2	21	3.5	148	6.7	48	2	48	29	8.6	460
Mali	6.6	49	22	2.7	26	11.6	190	6.7	48	1	39	17	27.9	120
Mauritania	1.6	50	22	2.8	25	2.9	187	6.9	42	6	42	23	7.2	270
Niger	5.5	51	22	2.9	24	10.0	200	7.1	47	3	42	11	23.7	220
Nigeria	77.1	50	18	3.2	22	148.9	157	6.9	47	2	48	20	434.7	560
Senegal	5.7	48	22	2.6	27	9.7	160	6.5	44	3	42	32	23.5	340
Sierra Leone	3.5	46	19	2.6	26	6.0	136	6.4	41	5	46	16	13.6	210
Togo	2.5	49	19	3.0	23	4.7	163	6.7	46	3	46	15	11.9	320
Upper Volta	6.9	48	22	2.6	27	11.8	182	6.5	44	3	42	5	24.2	160
EASTERN AFRICA	135	48	19	3.0	23	244	132	6.6	46	3	47	13	629	240
Burundi	4.5	47	20	2.7	25	7.8	140	6.3	44	2	42	5	19.9	140
Comoros	0.3	40	18	2.2	31	0.4	148	5.2	43	3	46	11	1.4	180
Djibouti	0.4	48	24	2.5	28	0.6	—	—	—	—	—	70	—	450
Ethiopia	32.6	50	25	2.5	28	55.3	162	6.7	45	3	39	13	136.5	120
Kenya	15.9	53	14	3.9	18	32.3	83	8.1	50	2	56	10	93.8	320
Madagascar	8.7	45	19	2.6	27	15.1	102	6.1	43	3	46	16	39.1	250
Malawi	6.1	51	19	3.2	22	11.5	142	7.0	44	4	46	9	31.3	180
Mauritius	0.9	27	7	2.0	34	1.3	35	3.1	37	4	67	44	1.8	830
Mozambique	10.3	45	19	2.6	27	17.9	148	6.1	45	2	46	8	44.0	140
Reunion	0.5	26	6	1.9	36	0.7	41	2.8	38	4	65	56	1.2	3,060
Rwanda	5.1	50	19	3.0	23·	9.6	127	6.9	47	3	46	4	24.7	180
Seychelles	0.1	26	8	1.8	38	0.1	43	4.5	42	6	65	37	—	1,060
Somalia	3.6	48	20	2.8	25	6.3	177	6.1	44	2	43	31	17.0	130
S. Rhodesia (Zimbabwe)	7.4	47	14	3.4	21	14.0	129	6.6	47	3	54	20	37.2	480
Tanzania	18.6	47	16	3.1	22	35.0	125	6.5	46	3	50	13	93.9	230
Uganda	13.7	45	14	3.0	23	25.5	120	6.1	45	3	52	7	57.9	—
Zambia	5.8	49	17	3.2	22	10.7	144	6.9	46	3	48	39	28.6	480
MIDDLE AFRICA	54	45	20	2.6	27	87	167	6.0	43	3	45	29	218	300
Angola	6.7	48	23	2.4	28	11.2	203	6.4	44	3	41	22	29.2	300
Cameroon	8.5	42	19	2.3	30	13.1	157	5.7	41	4	44	29	31.5	460
Central African Rep.	2.2	42	19	2.2	31	3.6	190	5.5	41	4	42	42	8.3	250

Pop. 1980   Birth Rate   Death Rate   Nat. Inc.   Doub. Time   Pop. 2000   Inf. Mort.   TFR   Pop. <15   Pop. >64   Life Expec.   Urb. Pop.   Ult. Pop.   GNP p.c.

Region or Country[1]	Population Estimate Mid-1980 (millions)[2]	Birth Rate[3]	Death Rate[3]	Rate of Natural Increase (annual, %)[4]	Number of Years to Double Population[5]	Population Projected for 2000 (millions)[6]	Infant Mortality Rate[7]	Total Fertility Rate[8]	Population under Age 15 (%)	Population over Age 64 (%)	Life Expectancy at Birth (years)[9]	Urban Population (%)[10]	Projected Ultimate Population Size (millions)[11]	Per Capita Gross National Product (US$)[12]
Chad	4.5	44	21	2.3	30	7.4	165	5.9	42	4	44	18	17.4	140
Congo	1.6	45	19	2.6	27	2.5	180	6.0	43	3	46	39	6.9	540
Equatorial Guinea	0.4	42	19	2.3	30	0.6	165	5.7	42	4	46	51	1.2	
Gabon	0.6	33	22	1.1	62	0.8	178	4.3	33	6	44	32	1.3	3,580
Sao Tome and Principe	0.1	45	11	3.4	21	0.1	64	—	—	—	—	24	—	490
Zaire	29.3	46	19	2.8	25	48.1	160	6.1	45	3	46	30	121.9	210
SOUTHERN AFRICA	**32**	**39**	**11**	**2.8**	**25**	**52**	**101**	**5.2**	**42**	**4**	**59**	**44**	**124**	**1,380**
Botswana	0.8	51	17	3.4	21	1.4	97	6.5	50	3	56	12	4.5	620
Lesotho	1.3	40	16	2.4	29	2.1	111	5.4	40	4	50	4	5.1	280
Namibia	1.0	44	15	2.9	24	1.7	142	5.9	44	3	51	32	4.5	1,080
South Africa	28.4	38	10	2.8	25	46.3	97	5.1	42	4	60	48	107.5	1,480
Swaziland	0.6	47	19	2.8	25	0.9	168	6.4	48	3	46	8	2.7	590
ASIA	**2,563**	**28**	**11**	**1.8**	**39**	**3,578**	**103**	**3.9**	**37**	**4**	**58**	**27**	**5,573**	**760**
SOUTHWEST ASIA	**98**	**40**	**12**	**2.7**	**25**	**164**	**117**	**5.8**	**43**	**4**	**56**	**46**	**281**	**2,280**
Bahrain	0.4	44	9	3.6	20	0.7	78	7.4	44	3	63	78	1.1	4,100
Cyprus	0.6	19	8	1.1	64	0.7	17	2.1	25	10	73	53	1.0	2,110
Gaza	0.4	53	18	3.5	20	0.7	137	—	48	5	52	87	—	—
Iraq	13.2	47	13	3.4	20	24.5	104	7.0	48	4	55	66	49.1	1,860
Israel	3.9	25	7	1.8	38	5.5	15	3.5	33	8	73	87	7.5	4,120
Jordan	3.2	46	13	3.3	21	5.9	97	7.0	48	3	56	42	11.8	1,050
Kuwait	1.3	42	5	3.7	19	3.1	39	7.0	44	2	69	56	5.3	14,890
Lebanon	3.2	34	10	2.5	28	4.9	65	4.7	43	5	65	60	7.6	—
Oman	0.9	49	19	3.0	23	1.7	142	7.2	45	3	47	5	3.2	2,570
Qatar	0.2	44	14	3.0	23	0.4	138	7.2	45	3	48	69	0.8	12,740
Saudi Arabia	8.2	49	18	3.0	23	15.5	150	7.2	45	3	48	24	30.8	8,040
Syria	8.6	45	13	3.2	21	16.2	114	7.4	49	4	57	49	32.7	930
Turkey	45.5	35	10	2.5	28	69.6	119	5.0	40	4	58	45	97.8	1,210
United Arab Emirates	0.8	44	14	3.0	23	1.6	138	7.2	34	3	48	65	2.5	14,230
Yemen, North	5.6	48	25	2.3	30	9.5	160	6.8	47	4	45	11	20.4	580
Yemen, South	1.9	48	21	2.7	26	3.4	155	7.0	49	4	45	33	6.9	420
MIDDLE SOUTH ASIA	**938**	**37**	**16**	**2.2**	**32**	**1,422**	**137**	**5.5**	**42**	**3**	**51**	**21**	**2,566**	**180**
Afghanistan	15.9	48	21	2.7	26	26.4	226	6.9	45	3	37	11	65.8	240
Bangladesh	90.6	46	20	2.6	27	156.7	153	6.3	44	3	46	9	334.5	90
Bhutan	1.3	43	21	2.2	31	2.0	147	6.2	42	3	43	4	4.0	100
India	676.2	34	15	1.9	36	976.2	134	5.3	41	3	52	21	1,642.8	180
Iran	38.5	44	14	3.0	23	66.1	112	6.3	44	4	58	47	101.0	—
Maldives	0.1	50	23	2.7	26	0.2	119	—	44	2	—	11	—	150
Nepal	14.0	44	20	2.4	29	22.0	133	6.4	40	3	43	4	51.4	120
Pakistan	86.5	44	16	2.8	25	152.0	142	6.3	46	3	52	26	334.6	230
Sri Lanka	14.8	28	7	2.2	32	20.0	42	3.4	39	4	63	22	30.3	190
SOUTHEAST ASIA	**354**	**36**	**13**	**2.2**	**31**	**539**	**96**	**4.7**	**42**	**3**	**53**	**21**	**915**	**400**
Brunei	0.2	28	4	2.4	29	0.3	20	5.1	43	3	66	64	—	10,640
Burma	34.4	39	14	2.4	29	53.7	140	5.5	40	4	52	24	92.3	150
Dem. Kampuchea	6.0	33	15	1.8	39	9.1	150	4.7	42	3	44	12	36.5	—
East Timor	0.8	44	21	2.3	30	1.1	175	6.1	42	3	42	12	—	—
Indonesia	144.3	35	15	2.0	34	210.6	91	4.1	42	2	50	18	356.8	360
Laos	3.7	44	20	2.4	29	5.7	175	6.2	42	3	39	15	11.1	90
Malaysia	14.0	31	6	2.5	28	20.7	44	4.4	41	3	61	27	29.5	1,090
Philippines	47.7	34	10	2.4	28	78.1	80	5.0	43	3	61	32	127.9	510
Singapore	2.4	17	5	1.2	59	3.0	12	1.9	31	4	71	100	3.7	3,260
Thailand	47.3	32	9	2.3	30	75.5	68	4.5	43	3	60	13	104.7	490
Vietnam	53.3	41	18	2.3	30	80.9	115	5.8	41	4	48	19	149.4	170

Pop. 1980   Birth Rate   Death Rate   Nat. Inc.   Doub. Time   Pop. 2000   Inf. Mort.   TFR   Pop. <15   Pop. >64   Life Expec.   Urb. Pop.   Ult. Pop.   GNP p.c.

Region or Country[1]	Population Estimate Mid-1980 (millions)[2]	Birth Rate[3]	Death Rate[3]	Rate of Natural Increase (annual, %)[4]	Number of Years to Double Population[5]	Population Projected for 2000 (millions)[6]	Infant Mortality Rate[7]	Total Fertility Rate[8]	Population under Age 15 (%)	Population over Age 64 (%)	Life Expectancy at Birth (years)[9]	Urban Population (%)[10]	Projected Ultimate Population Size (millions)[11]	Per Capita Gross National Product (US$)[12]
EAST ASIA	1,173	18	6	1.2	57	1,453	51	2.3	31	6	65	32	1,812	1,200
China[13]	975	18	6	1.2	58	1,212.3	56	2.3	32	6	64	26	1,530.0	460
Hong Kong	4.8	18	5	1.2	56	6.2	12	2.6	29	6	72	92	7.3	3,040
Japan	116.8	15	6	0.9	79	129.4	8	1.8	24	8	75	76	133.4	7,330
Korea, North	17.9	33	8	2.4	28	27.4	70	4.5	40	4	62	33	42.9	730
Korea, South	38.2	23	7	1.6	44	51.1	38	3.2	38	4	62	48	64.1	1,160
Macao	0.3	30	8	2.2	32	0.3	78	–	38	5	–	97	–	1,460
Mongolia	1.7	37	8	2.9	24	2.7	70	5.3	43	3	62	47	3.9	940
Taiwan	17.8	25	5	2.0	35	23.8	25	3.1	35	4	71	77	29.6	1,400
NORTH AMERICA	247	16	8	0.7	98	289	13	1.8	23	11	73	74	296	9,650
Canada	24.0	15	7	0.8	88	29.0	12	1.9	26	8	73	76	30.3	9,170
United States	222.5	16	9	0.7	99	260.4	13	1.8	22	11	73	74	265.5	9,700
LATIN AMERICA	360	34	8	2.6	26	595	85	4.5	42	4	64	61	955	1,380
MIDDLE AMERICA	91	38	7	3.1	22	168	72	5.3	46	3	64	59	274	1,180
Costa Rica	2.2	31	4	2.7	26	3.4	28	3.8	44	4	70	41	4.7	1,540
El Salvador	4.8	40	7	3.3	21	8.6	51	6.0	46	3	62	39	13.7	600
Guatemala	7.0	43	12	3.1	23	12.3	76	5.7	45	3	58	36	23.2	910
Honduras	3.8	47	12	3.5	20	7.1	103	7.1	48	3	57	31	15.3	480
Mexico	68.2	37	6	3.1	22	128.9	70	5.2	46	3	65	65	203.5	1,290
Nicaragua	2.6	47	12	3.4	20	4.8	122	6.6	48	3	55	49	9.3	840
Panama	1.9	28	6	2.2	31	2.9	47	4.1	44	4	70	51	4.5	1,290
CARIBBEAN	30	28	8	1.9	36	42	72	3.8	40	5	65	50	66	1,160
Bahamas	0.2	25	5	2.0	34	0.3	25	3.5	44	4	69	58	0.4	2,620
Barbados	0.3	16	8	0.9	80	0.3	27	2.2	32	10	70	44	0.4	1,940
Cuba	10.0	18	6	1.2	59	12.7	25	2.5	37	6	72	64	16.5	810
Dominica	0.1	21	5	1.6	43	0.1	20	–	–	–	58	27	–	440
Dominican Republic	5.4	37	9	2.8	25	8.5	96	5.4	48	3	60	49	15.1	910
Grenada	0.1	27	6	2.2	32	0.1	24	–	–	–	63	15	0.2	530
Guadeloupe	0.3	17	6	1.1	65	0.4	35	3.2	32	6	69	48	–	2,850
Haiti	5.8	42	16	2.6	26	9.9	130	5.9	41	4	51	24	16.3	260
Jamaica	2.2	29	7	2.2	31	2.8	15	3.7	46	6	70	41	5.3	1,110
Martinique	0.3	16	7	0.9	80	0.4	32	3.0	32	6	69	50	–	3,950
Netherland Antilles	0.3	28	7	2.2	32	0.4	25	3.1	38	6	62	48	–	3,150
Puerto Rico	3.5	23	6	1.7	42	4.5	20	2.4	36	6	73	62	–	2,720
St. Lucia	0.1	35	7	2.8	25	0.1	36	–	50	5	67	17	–	630
Trinidad and Tobago	1.2	25	6	1.9	37	1.4	29	2.6	38	4	67	49	2.2	2,910
TROPICAL SOUTH AMERICA	198	36	9	2.7	26	333	98	4.6	42	3	62	60	551	1,430
Bolivia	5.3	44	19	2.5	28	8.9	168	6.8	42	4	47	34	19.4	510
Brazil	122.0	36	8	2.8	25	205.1	109	4.4	41	3	64	61	341.0	1,570
Colombia	26.7	29	8	2.1	33	42.2	77	3.9	45	3	62	60	55.2	870
Ecuador	8.0	42	10	3.1	22	14.6	70	6.3	44	4	60	43	25.7	910
Guyana	0.9	28	7	2.1	33	1.2	50	3.9	40	4	69	40	2.0	550
Paraguay	3.3	39	8	3.1	22	5.6	64	5.8	45	3	64	40	9.2	850
Peru	17.6	40	12	2.8	25	29.2	92	5.3	44	3	56	62	54.6	740
Suriname	0.4	30	7	2.3	30	0.7	30	–	46	4	67	66	1.8	2,110
Venezuela	13.9	36	6	3.0	23	25.7	45	4.9	43	3	66	75	40.1	2,910
TEMPERATE SOUTH AMERICA	41	24	9	1.5	45	51	44	2.9	30	7	68	80	64	1,750
Argentina	27.1	26	9	1.6	43	32.9	45	2.9	28	8	69	80	41.0	1,910
Chile	11.3	21	7	1.4	48	15.2	40	3.0	35	5	66	80	18.6	1,410
Uruguay	2.9	21	10	1.1	65	3.5	46	2.7	27	10	69	83	4.5	1,610

Pop. 1980   Birth Rate   Death Rate   Nat. Inc.   Doub. Time   Pop. 2000   Inf. Mort.   TFR   Pop. < 15   Pop. > 64   Life Expec.   Urb. Pop.   Ult. Pop.   GNP p.c.

Region or Country[1]	Population Estimate Mid-1980 (millions)[2]	Birth Rate[3]	Death Rate[3]	Rate of Natural Increase (annual, %)[4]	Number of Years to Double Population[5]	Population Projected for 2000 (millions)[6]	Infant Mortality Rate[7]	Total Fertility Rate[8]	Population under Age 15 (%)	Population over Age 64 (%)	Life Expectancy at Birth (years)[9]	Urban Population (%)[10]	Projected Ultimate Population Size (millions)[11]	Per Capita Gross National Product (US$)[12]
EUROPE	**484**	**14**	**10**	**0.4**	**176**	**521**	**19**	**2.0**	**24**	**12**	**72**	**69**	**560**	**5,650**
NORTHERN EUROPE	**82**	**13**	**11**	**0.1**	**476**	**84**	**13**	**1.8**	**23**	**14**	**72**	**74**	**90**	**6,140**
Denmark	5.1	12	10	0.2	385	5.3	9	1.7	22	14	74	67	5.4	9,920
Finland	4.8	14	9	0.4	161	5.1	9	1.7	22	11	72	59	5.2	6,820
Iceland	0.2	19	6	1.2	57	0.3	11	2.3	30	9	76	87	0.3	8,320
Ireland	3.3	22	10	1.1	61	4.0	16	3.4	31	11	71	52	5.5	3,470
Norway	4.1	13	10	0.3	248	4.4	9	1.8	24	14	75	44	4.5	9,510
Sweden	8.3	11	11	0.0	1,386	8.6	8	1.7	21	15	75	83	8.2	10,210
United Kingdom	55.8	12	12	0.1	1,155	56.5	14	1.7	23	14	72	78	60.1	5,030
WESTERN EUROPE	**153**	**12**	**11**	**0.1**	**918**	**158**	**12**	**1.6**	**22**	**14**	**72**	**82**	**163**	**8,970**
Austria	7.5	11	12	-0.1	—	7.6	15	1.6	23	15	72	52	7.8	7,030
Belgium	9.9	12	12	0.1	990	10.7	12	1.7	22	14	71	95	10.4	9,070
France	53.6	14	10	0.3	198	57.5	11	1.9	24	14	73	73	60.7	8,270
Germany, West	61.1	9	12	-0.2	—	59.8	15	1.4	21	15	72	92	60.8	9,600
Luxembourg	0.4	11	12	-0.0	—	0.4	11	1.5	20	13	70	68	0.4	10,410
Netherlands	14.1	13	8	0.4	158	15.5	10	1.6	25	11	75	88	15.8	8,390
Switzerland	6.3	11	9	0.2	301	6.4	10	1.5	22	13	73	55	6.8	12,100
EASTERN EUROPE	**110**	**18**	**11**	**0.7**	**102**	**121**	**23**	**2.3**	**23**	**11**	**71**	**59**	**135**	**3,670**
Bulgaria	8.9	16	10	0.5	139	9.5	22	2.3	22	11	71	60	10.4	3,200
Czechoslovakia	15.4	18	12	0.7	100	17.2	19	2.4	23	12	70	67	19.0	4,720
Germany, East	16.7	14	14	0.0	—	16.6	13	1.8	21	16	72	76	17.7	5,660
Hungary	10.8	16	13	0.3	267	11.2	24	2.2	21	13	70	52	11.8	3,450
Poland	35.5	19	9	1.0	71	40.9	22	2.3	24	10	71	57	46.8	3,660
Romania	22.3	20	10	1.0	69	25.7	31	2.6	25	10	70	48	29.7	1,750
SOUTHERN EUROPE	**140**	**15**	**9**	**0.7**	**105**	**157**	**24**	**2.3**	**26**	**11**	**71**	**60**	**172**	**3,290**
Albania	2.7	30	8	2.2	32	3.8	87	4.2	37	5	69	34	5.7	740
Greece	9.6	16	9	0.7	98	10.6	19	2.3	24	12	73	65	13.2	3,270
Italy	57.2	12	9	0.3	224	61.3	18	1.9	24	12	72	67	62.6	3,840
Malta	0.3	17	10	0.8	92	0.4	16	2.0	25	9	71	94	0.4	2,160
Portugal	9.9	17	10	0.7	99	11.6	39	2.5	28	10	69	29	13.6	2,020
Spain	37.8	17	8	0.9	75	43.9	16	2.6	28	10	72	70	50.0	3,520
Yugoslavia	22.4	17	9	0.9	80	25.7	34	2.2	26	9	68	39	28.6	2,390
USSR	**266**	**18**	**10**	**0.8**	**82**	**311**	**31**	**2.4**	**24**	**10**	**70**	**62**	**360**	**3,700**
OCEANIA	**23**	**20**	**9**	**1.1**	**61**	**30**	**42**	**2.8**	**31**	**8**	**69**	**71**	**37**	**6,020**
Australia	14.6	16	8	0.8	86	17.9	12	2.1	27	9	73	86	18.5	7,920
Fiji	0.6	27	4	2.3	30	0.8	41	4.0	41	2	71	37	1.2	1,440
New Zealand	3.2	16	8	0.8	83	3.9	14	2.2	29	9	72	83	4.6	4,790
Papua-New Guinea	3.2	41	16	2.5	27	5.1	106	6.0	44	4	50	13	9.3	560
Samoa, Western	0.2	37	7	3.0	23	0.2	40	5.8	50	3	63	21	0.5	—
Solomon Islands	0.2	41	10	3.1	22	0.4	78	6.2	44	3	57	9	—	430

Pop. 1980   Birth Rate   Death Rate   Nat. Inc.   Doub. Time   Pop. 2000   Inf. Mort.   TFR   Pop. < 15   Pop. > 64   Life Expec.   Urb. Pop.   Ult. Pop.   GNP p.c.

General Notes

World Population Data Sheets of various years should not be used as a time series. Because every attempt is made to use the most recent and most accurate information, data sources vary and changes in numbers and rates from year to year may reflect improved source material, revised data, or a later base year for computation, rather then yearly changes.

Sources of data: Aside from population estimates and projections (see footnotes 2 and 6), number of years to double population (footnote 5), and per capita Gross National Product (footnote 12), most of the data in this *Data Sheet* were reported in the following United Nations (UN) publications: *Demog-*

raphic Yearbook, 1977 and *1978; Population and Vital Statistics Report, Data Available as of 1 January 1980,* Statistical Papers, Series A, Vol. XXXII, No. 1; and *World Population Trends and Prospects by Country, 1950—2000: Summary Report of the 1978 Assessment,* ST/ESA/SER.R/33 1979. Other sources were: U.S. Bureau of the Census, *World Population: 1977, 1978,* and *World Population: 1979* (forthcoming); unpublished reports of the Census Bureau's Foreign Demographic Analysis Division; World Bank, *Population Projections 1975–2000 and Long-term (Stationary Populations),* prepared by K. C. Zachariah and My Thi Vu of the Bank's Population and Human Resources Division, July 1979; Country Reports of the World Fertility Survey; official country publications; and special studies.

Figures for the regions and the world: Population totals (columns 1 and 6) take into account small areas not listed on the *Data Sheet.* These totals may also not equal the sums of their parts because of independent rounding. All other regional and world figures are weighted averages for countries for which data are available.

Footnotes

[1] The *Data Sheet* lists all geopolitical entities with a population larger than 200,000 and all members of the United Nations (UN) regardless of population size. Classification of "more developed" and "less developed" regions follows the latest (1979) practice of the UN. The "more developed" regions comprise all of Europe, North America (Canada and the United States), Australia, New Zealand, Japan, and the USSR. Cyprus, Israel, and Turkey, formerly included in the "more developed" region of Southern Europe, are now included by the UN with their region of location, Southwest Asia, and are thereby considered "less developed."

[2] Based on a population total from a very recent census or on the most recent official country or UN estimate; for almost all countries the estimate was for mid-1978. Each estimate was updated by the Population Reference Bureau to mid-1980 by applying the same rate of growth as indicated by population change during part or all of the period since 1970.

[3] Annual number of births or deaths per 1,000 population. For the more developed countries with complete or nearly complete registration of births and deaths, nearly all the rates shown pertain to 1977 or 1978. For most less developed countries with incomplete registration the rates refer to the 1975–80 period. These rates were used in the medium variant estimates and projections as assessed by the UN in 1978 (UN, *World Population Trends and Prospects . . .*). These figures should be considered as rough approximations only. Some estimates were obtained from published reports of the U.S. Bureau of the Census, the World Bank, the World Fertility Survey, government statistical offices, and special studies.

[4] Birth rate minus the death rate. Since the rates were based on unrounded birth and death rates, some rates do not exactly equal the difference between the birth and death rates shown because of rounding.

[5] Based on the current *unrounded* rate of natural increase and assuming no change in the rate.

[6] For most countries, projected by the Population Reference Bureau by applying the 1980–2000 growth rate implied by the UN medium variant projections to the country's estimated mid-1980 population total. For the United States, the projection shown is from the most recent Series II projection published by the U.S. Bureau of the Census. This projection assumes that birth rates in the U.S. will rise somewhat during the balance of this century until a total fertility rate (see footnote 8) of 2.1 is reached.

[7] Annual number of deaths to infants under one year of age per 1,000 live births. For countries with complete or nearly complete registration of births and deaths, nearly all the rates pertain to 1977 or 1978. For many less developed countries with incomplete registration, rates are the latest available estimates generally obtained from the sources noted above.

[8] The total fertility rate (TFR) indicates the average number of children that would be born to each woman in a population if each were to live through her childbearing lifetime (usually considered ages 15–49) bearing children at the same rates as women of those ages actually did in a given year. A TFR of 2.1 to 2.5, depending upon mortality conditions, indicates "replacement level" fertility – the level at which a country's population would eventually stop growing (or declining), leaving migration out of account. Most TFRs shown here refer to the 1975–80 period and are from UN, *World Population Trends and Prospects . . .*

[9] Average number of years a newborn child could be expected to live if current mortality conditions were to continue throughout his or her life-time. For the more developed countries with reliable mortality data, nearly all estimates shown pertain to part or all of the 1970–77 period. For most of

the less developed countries with unreliable mortality data, estimates refer to some part of the period since 1970 and were prepared by one of the following organizations: the UN Population Division; the Population Division of the U.S. Bureau of the Census; or the World Bank's Population and Human Resources Division. Estimates of life expectancy for most less developed countries should be considered as rough approximations only.

[10] Percentage of total population living in areas termed urban by that country.

[11] This column has been included in this year's edition of the *Data Sheet* in order to illustrate each country's potential population growth and the ultimate size that could eventually be achieved. These projections were prepared by K. C. Zachariah and My Thi Vu of the World Bank *(Population Projections, 1975–2000...)* and are not forecasts of what will necessarily happen, but could happen as a result of "long run implications of recent trends under a series of highly stylized assumptions." Specifically, the projections assume that fertility in all countries will someday arrive at replacement level (a TFR then of about 2.1) and remain there. For less developed countries, this is assumed to occur in the middle of the 21st century in Africa and somewhat earlier in Asia and Latin America. For more developed countries the arrival at replacement level fertility is placed about the year 2000. This assumes that the TFR will increase to 2.1 by that time in the many developed countries where fertiltiy is now below replacement level. The projections also assume that immigration will have no appreciable impact on the population growth of a particular country; this assumption tends to lower the "ultimate population" of the United States and a few other countries which can be expected to receive immigrants in the future. Several regional totals were adjusted by the Population Reference Bureau in order to agree with the geographical classifications used on the *Data Sheet.*

[12] Data refer to 1978 and are provisional. All data for individual countries are from the World Bank, *World Bank Atlas: Population, Per Capita Product, and Growth Rates, 1979.*

[13] Opinions vary widely on demographic measures for China. Those shown here come from official sources quoted in the *Guangming Daily* and *People's Daily* and UN sources noted above. Their accuracy is unknown. The projected population for 2000 shown here could be high in light of China's recently announced policy to encourage the one-child family and reduce population growth to zero by 2000.

REFERENCES

Abel-Smith, B., with Leiserson, A. (1978), *Poverty, Development and Health Policy*, Public Health Papers No. 69, W.H.O., Geneva

Abler, R., Adams, J. and Gould, P. (1971), *Spatial Organisation: The Geographer's View of the World*, Prentice-Hall, Englewood Cliffs, N. J.

Abu-Lughod, J. (1964), Urban-rural differences as a function of the demographic transition, *American Journal of Sociology* 69, 476–490

Abu-Lughod, J., Foley, M. and Winnick, L. (1960), *Housing Choice and Housing Constraints*, McGraw-Hill, New York

Adelman, I. (1963), An econometric analysis of population growth, *American Economic Review* 53, 314–339

Adelman, I. and Morris, C. (1967), *Society, Politics and Economic Development*, Johns Hopkins Press, Baltimore

Adegbola, O. (1977), New estimates of fertility and child mortality in Africa south of the Sahara, *Population Studies* 31, 467–486

Akhtar, R. and Learmonth, A. (1977), The resurgence of malaria in India 1965–76, *GeoJournal* 1.5, 69–79

Albuquerque, K.De, Mader, P. and Stinner, W. (1976), Modernization, delayed marriage and fertility in Puerto Rico 1950 to 1970, *Social and Economic Studies* 25, 55–65

Allen-Price, E.D. (1960), Uneven distribution of cancer in West Devon, *Lancet* 1, 1235–1238

Alonso, W. (1973), *National Interregional Demographic Accounts*, University of California, Berkeley

Amin, S. (ed.) (1974), *Modern Migrations in Western Africa*, Oxford University Press, London

Anderson, J., Cheng, M. and Fook-Kee, W. (1977), A component analysis of recent fertility decline in Singapore, *Studies in Family Planning* 8, 282–287

Anderson, T. (1955), Intermetropolitan migration: a comparison of the hypotheses of Zipf and Stouffer, *American Sociological Review* 20, 287–291

Andorka, R. (1978), *Determinants of Fertility in Advanced Societies*, Methuen, London

Anell, L. and Nygren, B. (1980), *The Developing Countries and the World Economic Order*, Pinter, London

Antonovsky, A. (1967), Social class, life expectancy and overall mortality, *Milbank Memorial Fund Quarterly* 45, 31–73

Armstrong, R. (1972), Computers and mapping in medical geography, in McGlashan (ed.), 69–85

Arriaga, E. (1970), The nature and effects of Latin America's non-Western trend in fertility, *Demography* 7, 483–501

Arriaga, E. and Davis, K. (1969), The pattern of mortality change in Latin America, *Demography* 6, 223–242

Askham, J. (1975), *Fertility and Deprivation: a Study of Differential Fertility amongst Working-class Families in Aberdeen*, Cambridge University Press, Cambridge

Baines, D. (1972), The use of published census data in migration studies, in Wrigley (ed.), 311–335

Bairoch, P. (1973), *Urban Unemployment in Developing Countries*, International Labour Office, Geneva

Baldwin, W. and Ford, T. (1976), Modernism and contraceptive use in Colombia, *Studies in Family Planning* 7, 75–79

Banks, J.A. (1954), *Prosperity and Parenthood*, Routledge & Kegan Paul, London

Barakat, H (1973), The Palestinian refugees: an uprooted community seeking repatriation, *International Migration Review* 7, 147–161

Barclay, G. (1958), *Techniques of Population Analysis*, Wiley, New York

Barrett, F. (1974), *Residential Search Behaviour: A Study of Intra-Urban Relocation in Toronto*, York University, Toronto

Baucic, I. (1973), Yugoslavia as a country of emigration, *Options Méditerranéennes* 22, 56–66

Beaujeu-Garnier, J. (1966), *Geography of Population*, Longman, London

Beaujot, R. (1978), Canada's population: growth and dualism, *Population Bulletin* 33 (2)

Beaumont, P. (1976), Assisted labour mobility policy in Scotland 1973–4, *Urban Studies* 13, 75–79

Beaumont, P. (1977), The assisted spatial mobility of unemployed labour in Britain, *Area* 9, 9–12

Beaver, M. W. (1973), Population, infant mortality and milk, *Population Studies* 27, 243–254

Beaver, S. E. (1975), *Demographic Transition Theory Reinterpreted: An Application to Recent Natality Trends in Latin America*, Lexington Books, Lexington

Becker, G. (1960), An economic analysis of fertility, in National Bureau Committee for Economic Research, *Demographic and Economic Change in Developed Countries*, Princeton University Press, Princeton, 209–231

Beckerman, W. (1974), *In Defence of Economic Growth*, Cape, London

Beier, G. J. (1976), Can Third World Cities Cope?, *Population Bulletin* 31 (4)

Bell, M. (1980), Past mobility and spatial preferences for migration in East Africa, in White and Woods (eds.), 84–107

Benjamin, B. (1965), *Social and Economic Factors Affecting Mortality*, Mouton, Paris

Berelson, B. (ed.) (1974), *Population Policy in Developed Countries*, McGraw-Hill, New York

Berelson, B. (1979), Romania's 1966 anti-abortion decree: the demographic experience of the first decade, *Population Studies* 33, 209–222

Berg, A. (1974), Nutrition, development and population growth, *Population Bulletin* 29 (1)

Berkner, L. and Mendels, F. (1978), Inheritance systems, family structure and demographic patterns in Western Europe 1700–1900, in Tilly (ed.), 209–224

Berry, B. J. (1980), Inner cities futures: an American dilemma revisited, *Transactions of Institute of British Geographers* 5, 1–28

Berry, B. M. and Schofield, R. (1971), Age at baptism in pre-industrial England, *Population Studies* 25, 453–463

Bhattacharyya, A. (1975), Income inequality and fertility, *Population Studies* 29, 5–19

Biggar, J. (1979), The sunning of America: migration to the Sunbelt, *Population Bulletin* 34 (1)

Birdsall, N. (1977), Analytical approaches to the relationship of population growth and development, *Population and Development Review* 3, 63–102

Birks, J. S. and Sinclair, C. (1977–1978), *International Migration Project Working Papers*, University of Durham

Birks, J. S. and Sinclair, C. (1979), The International Migration Project: an enquiry into the Middle East labor market, *International Migration Review* 13, 122–135

Blaikie, P. (1975), *Family Planning in India: Diffusion and Policy*, Arnold, London

Blake, J. (1961), *Family Structure in Jamaica*, Free Press, Glencoe, Ill.

Blake, J. (1968), Are babies consumer durables?, *Population Studies* 22, 5–25

Boddy, M. (1976), The structure of mortgage finance: building societies and the British social formation, *Transactions of Institute of British Geographers* 1, 58–71

Bogue, D. (1959), Internal migration, in Hauser and Duncan (eds.), 486–509

Bogue, D. (1969), *Principles of Demography*, Wiley, New York

Bogue, D. and Palmore, J. (1964), Some empirical and analytic relations among demographic fertility measures, with regression models for fertility estimation, *Demography* 1, 316–338

Böhning, W. R. (1977), *Compensating Countries of Origin for the Out-migration of their People*, Migration for Employment Working Paper 18F, International Labour Office, Geneva

Böhning, W. R. (1979), International Migration in Western Europe: reflections on the past five years, *International Labour Review* 118, 401–414

Boserup, E. (1965), *The Conditions of Agricultural Growth: The Economics of Agrarian Change under Population Pressure*, Allen & Unwin, London

Boserup, E. (1975), The impact of population growth on agricultural output, *Quarterly Journal of Agricultural Economics* 89, 257–270

Bourgeois-Pichat, J. (1974), France, in Berelson (ed.), 545–591

Bouvier, L. (1977), International migration: yesterday, today and tomorrow, *Population Bulletin* 32 (4)

Bouvier, L. (1980), America's baby boom generation: the fateful bulge, *Population Bulletin* 35 (1)

Brackett, J., Ravenholt, R. and Chao, J. (1978), The role of family planning in recent rapid fertility declines in developing countries, *Studies in Family Planning* 9, 314–323

Bradford, D. and Kelejian, H. (1973), An econometric model of the flight to the suburbs, *Journal of Political Economy* 81, 560–589

Brass, W. et al. (1968), *The Demography of Tropical Africa*, Princeton University Press, Princeton

Braun, R. (1978), Early industrialization and demographic change in the Canton of Zurich, in Tilly (ed.), 289–334

Bravard, Y. (1957) Sondages a propos de l'émigration dans les Alpes du Nord, *Revue de Géographie alpine* 45, 91–112

Breckenfeld, G. (1977), Business loves the sun belt and vice versa, *Fortune*, June, 132–146

Bright, M. and Thomas, D. (1941), Interstate migration and intervening opportunities, *American Sociological Review* 6, 773–783

Brookfield, H. (1957–1958), Mauritius: demographic upsurge and prospect, *Population Studies* 11, 102–122

Brookfield, H. (1973), On one geography and a Third World, *Transactions of Institute of British Geographers* 58, 1–20

Brookfield, H. (1975), *Interdependent Development,* Methuen, London

Brookfield, H. (1978), Third world development, *Progress in Human Geography* 2, 121–132

Brown, L. and Moore, E. (1970), The intra-urban migration process: a perspective, *Geografiska Annaler* 52B, 1–13

Brownlea, A. (1972), Modelling the geographic epidemiology of infectious hepatitis, in McGlashan (ed.), 279–300

Bruce-Chwatt, L. (1974a), Air transport and disease, *Journal of Biosocial Science* 6, 241–258

Bruce-Chwatt, L. (1974b), Resurgence of malaria and its control, *Journal of Tropical Medicine and Hygiene* 77 (4), 62–66

Bryant, C., Stephens, B. and McIver, S. (1978), Rural to urban migration: some data from Botswana, *African Studies Review* 21, 85–99

Buchanan, K. (1973), The white North and the population explosion, *Antipode* 5 (3), 7–15

Buksmann, P. (1980), Migration and land as aspects of underdevelopment: an approach to agricultural migration in Bolivia, in White and Woods (eds.), 108–128

Byrne, J. (1972), *Levels of Fertility in Commonwealth Caribbean 1921–65,* Institute for Social and Economic Research, University of West Indies, Jamaica

Caldwell, J. and Caldwell, P. (1977), The role of marital sexual abstinence in determining fertility: a study of the Yoruba in Nigeria, *Population Studies* 31, 193–217

Caldwell, J. and Okonjo, C. (eds.) (1968), *The Population of Tropical Africa,* Longman, London

Calot, G. and Hecht, J. (1978), The control of fertility trends, in Council of Europe (1978), 178–196

Campbell, A. (1974), Beyond the demographic transition, *Demography* 11, 549–561

Cannon, H. and Hopps, H. (1972), *Geochemical Environment in Relation to*

Health and Disease, Geological Society of America, Special Paper 140, Boulder, Colorado

Carlsson, G. (1966–1967), The decline of fertility: innovation or adjustment process, *Population Studies* 20, 149–174

Carrothers, G. (1956), An historical review of the gravity and potential concepts of human interaction, *Journal of American Institute of Planners* 22, 94–102

Castles, S. and Kosack, G. (1973), *Immigrant Workers and Class Structure in Western Europe*, Oxford University Press, London

Cavanaugh, J. (1979), Is fertility declining in less developed countries? *Population Studies* 33, 283–293

Cerase, F. (1974), Migration and social change: expectations and reality, *International Migration Review* 8, 245–262

Chambers, J. D. (1965), Three essays on the population and economy of the Midlands, in Glass and Eversley (eds.), 308–353

Chambers, J. D. (1972), *Population, Economy and Society in Pre-Industrial Britain*, Oxford University Press, London

Champion, A. (1976), Evolving patterns of population distribution in England and Wales 1951–71, *Transactions of Institute of British Geographers* 1, 401–420

Chapman, M. (1978), The cross-cultural study of circulation, *International Migration Review* 12, 559–569

Chen, P. (1975), Lessons from the Chinese experience: China's planned birth program and its transferability, *Studies in Family Planning* 6, 354–366

Cherry, S. (1980), The hospitals and population growth, *Population Studies* 34, 59–75

Childe, V.G. (1936), *Man Makes Himself*, Watts, London

Chilvers, C. (1978), Regional mortality 1969–73, *Population Trends* 11, 16–20

Chilvers, C. and Adelstein, A. (1978), Cancer mortality: the regional pattern, *Population Trends* 12, 4–9

Chisholm, A. (1972), *Philosophers of the Earth*, Sidgwick and Jackson, London

Chisholm, M. (1975), *Human Geography: Evolution or Revolution?*, Penguin, Harmondsworth

Chorley, R. and Haggett, P. (1965), Trend-surface mapping in geographical research, *Transactions and Papers of Institute of British Geographers* 37, 47–67

Cipolla, C. (1965), Four centuries of Italian demographic development, in Glass and Eversley (eds.), 570–587

Clark, C. (1967), *Population Growth and Land Use*, Macmillan, London

Clark, W. and Moore, E. (eds.) (1978), *Population Mobility and Residential Change*, Studies in Geography 25, Northwestern University, Evanston

Clarke, J. I. (1965), *Population Geography*, Pergamon, Oxford

Clarke, J. I. (1966), *Sierra Leone in Maps*, University of London Press, London

Clarke, J. I. (1973), Population in movement, in M. Chisholm and B. Rodgers (eds.), *Studies in Human Geography*, Heinemann, London, 85–124

Clarke, J. I. (1976), Population and scale: some general considerations, in Kosiński and Webb (eds.), 21–29

Clarke, J. I. (1977), Population geography, *Progress in Human Geography* 1, 136–141

Clarke, J. I. (1978), Population geography, *Progress in Human Geography* 2, 163–169

Clarke, J. I. (1979), Population geography, *Progress in Human Geography* 3, 261–266

Cliff, A. and Ord, J. (1973), *Spatial Auto-correlation*, Pion, London

Coale, A.J. (1969), The decline of fertility in Europe from the French Revolution to World War II, in Behrman, S. et al. (eds.), *Fertility and Family Planning: A World View*, University of Michigan Press, Ann Arbor, 3–24

Coale, A. J. (1974), The history of the human population, *Scientific American* 231 (3), 41–51

Coale, A. J. and Hoover, E. (1958), *Population Growth and Economic Development in Low-Income Countries*, Princeton University Press, Princeton

Coale, A.J. and Zelnick, M. (1963), *New Estimates of Fertility and Population in the United States*, Princeton University Press, Princeton

Cohen, M. (1974), *Urban Policy and Political Conflict in Africa: A study of the Ivory Coast*, University of Chicago Press, Chicago

Cohen, M. (1977), *The Food Crisis in Prehistory: Overpopulation and the Origins of Agriculture*, Yale University Press, New Haven

Cole, H., Freeman, C., Jahoda, M. and Pavitt, K. (1973), *Thinking about the Future: A Critique of The Limits to Growth*, Chatto and Windus, London

Collver, O. (1965), *Birth Rates in Latin America: New Estimates of Historical Trends and Fluctuations*, Institute of International Studies, Berkeley

Commission on Population Growth and the American Future (1972), *Final Report on Population and the American Future*, Signet, New York

Compton, P. (1969), Internal migration and population change in Hungary between 1959 and 1965, *Transactions of Institute of British Geographers* 47, 111–130

Compton, P. (1976), Religious affiliation and demographic variability in Northern Ireland, *Transactions of Institute of British Geographers* 1, 433–452

Compton, P. (1978a), *Northern Ireland: A Census Atlas*, Gill and Macmillan, Dublin

Compton, P. (1978b), Fertility differentials and their impact on population distribution and composition in Northern Ireland, *Environment and Planning* 10A, 1397–1411

Condran, G. and Crimmins-Gardner, E. (1978), Public health measures and mortality in U.S. cities in the late nineteenth century, *Human Ecology* 6, 27–54

Connell, K. (1950), *The Population of Ireland 1750—1845*, Clarendon Press, Oxford

Coombs, L. (1979), Underlying family-size preferences and reproductive behaviour, *Studies in Family Planning* 10, 25–36

Corsini, C. (1977), Self-regulating mechanisms of traditional populations before the demographic revolution, in International Union for the Scientific Study of Population, *International Population Conference Mexico 1977*, Vol. 3, Liege

Council of Europe (1978), *Population Decline in Europe: Implications of a Declining or Stationary Population*, Arnold, London

Cousens, S. (1960), The regional pattern of emigration during the Great Irish Famine 1846–51, *Transactions of Institute of British Geographers* 28, 119–134

Cowan, H. (1961), *British Emigration to British North America*, University of Toronto Press, Toronto

Coward, J. (1978), Changes in the pattern of fertility in the Republic of Ireland, *Tijdschrift v. E. S. G.* 69, 353–361

Cowgill, U. and Hutchinson, G. (1963), Sex-ratio in childhood and the depopulation of the Peten, Guatemala, *Human Biology* 35, 90–103

Cox, K. (1972), *Man, Location and Behaviour: An Introduction to Human Geography*, Wiley, New York

Crafts, N. (1978), Average age at first marriage for women in mid-nineteenth century England and Wales: a cross-section study, *Population Studies* 32, 21–25

Crawford, M. D. et al. (1961), Hardness of local water supplies and mortality from cardiovascular diseases in the county boroughs of England and Wales, *Lancet* 1, 860–862

Crawford, M. D. et al. (1968), Mortality and hardness of local water supplies, *Lancet* 1, 827–833

Crawford, M. D. et al. (1971), Changes in water hardness and local death rates, *Lancet* 2, 327

Croze, M. (1956), Un instrument d'étude des migrations interieures: les migrations d'électeurs, *Population* 11 (2)

Cunliffe, B. (1978), *Rome and her Empire*, Bodley Head, London

Curtin, P. (1969), *The Atlantic Slave Trade: A Census*, University of Wisconsin Press, Madison

Dando, W. (1980), *The Geography of Famine*, Arnold, London

Das Gupta, M. (1977), From a closed to an open system: fertility behaviour in a changing Indian village, in Epstein and Jackson (eds.), 97–121

Davis, K. (1967), Will current programs succeed?, *Science* 158, 730–739

Davis, K. (1974), The migrations of human populations, *Scientific American* 231 (3), 93–105

Davis, K. (1975), Asia's cities: problems and options, *Population and Development Review* 1, 71–86

Davis, Karen and Marshall, R. (1979), New developments in the market for rural health care, *Research in Health Economics* 1, 57–110

Day, L. (1968), Natality and ethnocentrism: some relationships suggested by an analysis of Catholic-Protestant differentials, *Population Studies* 22, 27–50

Day, L. (1978), What will a ZPG society be like?, *Population Bulletin* 33(3)

De Castro, J. (1952), *The Geography of Hunger*, Little Brown, Boston

Deevey, E. (1950), The probability of death, *Scientific American* 182, No. 4, April, 58–60

Demeny, P. (1972), Early fertility decline in Austria-Hungary: a lesson in demographic transition, in Glass and Revelle (eds.), 153–172

Demeny, P. (1974), The populations of the underdeveloped countries, *Scientific American* 231 (3), 149–159

Demko, G., Rose, H. and Schnell, G. (eds.) (1970), *Population Geography: A Reader*, McGraw-Hill, New York

Dennis, R. (1977), Intercensal mobility in a Victorian city, *Transactions of Institute of British Geographers* 2, 349–363

Department of Employment and Immigration, Canada (1979), *Annual Report to Parliament on Immigration Levels*, Ottawa

DeVise, P. et al. (1969), *Slum Medicine: Chicago's Apartheid Health System*, Community and Family Study Center, University of Chicago, Chicago

Drake, M. (1969), *Population and Society in Norway 1735—1865*, Cambridge University Press, Cambridge

Drewnowski, J. and Scott, W. (1968), The level of living index, *Ekistics* 25, 266–275

Dumond, D. (1975), The limitation of human population: a natural history, *Science* 187, 713–721

Dumont, R. (1974), Population and cannibalism, *U.N. Development Forum*, Sept–Oct

Duncan, O. (1959), Human ecology and population studies, in Hauser and Duncan (eds.), 678–716

Duncan, O. (1964), Residential areas and differential fertility, *Eugenics Quarterly* 11, 82–89

Duncan O., Cuzzort, R. and Duncan, B. (1961) *Statistical Geography*, Free Press of Glencoe, Glencoe, Ill.

Durand, J. (1960), Mortality estimates from Roman tombstone inscriptions, *American Journal of Sociology* 65, 365–373

Duza, M. and Baldwin, C. (1977), *Nuptiality and Population Policy*, Population Council, New York

Dwyer, D. (1975), *People and Housing in Third World Cities*, Longman, London

Earickson, R. (1970), *Spatial Behaviour of Hospital Patients*, University of Chicago Geography Research Paper 124, Chicago

Easterlin, R. (1968), *Population, Labour Force, and Long Swings in Economic Growth: The American Experience*, National Bureau of Economic Research, New York

Easterlin, R. (1976a), Population change and farm settlement in the northern United States, *Journal of Economic History* 36, 45–75

Easterlin, R. (1976b), The conflict between aspirations and resources, *Population and Development Review* 2, 417–425

Easterlin, R. (1978), The economics and sociology of fertility: a synthesis, in Tilly (ed.), 57–134

Easterlin, R. and Condran, G. (1976), A note on the recent fertility swing in Australia, Canada, England and Wales, and the United States, in Richards, H. (ed.), *Population, Factor Movements and Economic Development*, University of Wales Press, Cardiff, 140–151

Ebanks, G.E., George P. and Nobbe, C. (1974), Fertility and number of partnerships in Barbados, *Population Studies* 28, 449–461

Ebanks, G.E., George, P. and Nobbe, C. (1975), Emigration and fertility decline: the case of Barbados, *Demography* 12, 431–455

Economic Commission for Europe (1976), *Fertility and Family Planning in Europe around 1970*, U.N., New York

Ehrlich, P.R. (1971), *The Population Bomb*, Pan, London

Ehrlich, P.R. and Ehrlich, A. (1972), *Population, Resources, Environment*, Freeman, San Francisco

El Badry, M. (1969), Higher female than male mortality in some countries of South Asia: a digest, *Journal of the American Statistical Association* 64, 1234–1244

Elizaga, J. (1972), Internal migration: an overview, *International Migration Review* 6, 121–146

Enke, S. (1966), The economic aspects of slowing population growth, *Economic Journal* 76, 44–56

Enke, S. (1967), *Raising Per Capita Income Through Fewer Births*, General Electric-TEMPO, Santa Barbara

Enterline, P. (1961), Causes of death responsible for recent increases in sex mortality differentials in the United States, *Milbank Memorial Fund Quarterly* 39, 312–320

Epstein, T.S. and Jackson, D. (eds.) (1977), *The Feasibility of Fertility Planning: Micro Perspectives*, Pergamon, Oxford

Eversley, D. (1972), Rising costs and static incomes: some economic consequences of regional planning in London, *Urban Studies* 9, 347–368

Eversley, D. (1980), Social policy and the birth rate, *New Society* 52, No. 913, 9–11

Faulkingham, R. and Thorbahn, P. (1975), Population dynamics and drought: a village in Niger, *Population Studies* 29, 463–477

Federici, N. (1968), The influence of women's employment on fertility, in E. Szabady (ed.) (1968), *World Views of Population Problems*, Akadémiai Kaidó, Budapest, 77–82

Federici, N. et al. (1976), Urban/rural differences in mortality 1950–70, *W.H.O. Statistics Report* 29, 249–378

Fielding, A. (1971), *Internal migration in England and Wales*, Centre for Environmental Studies UWP 14, London

Findlay, A. and Findlay, A. (1980), *Migration Studies in Tunisia and Morocco*, Geography Occasional Paper 3, University of Glasgow, Glasgow

Flegg, A. (1979), The role of inequality of income in the determination of birth rates, *Population Studies* 33, 457–477

Fleury, M. and Henry, L. (1956), *Des Registres Paroissiaux à l'Histoire de la Population*, Institut National d'Etudes Démographiques, Paris

Flinn, M. (ed.) (1977), *Scottish Population History from the 17th Century to the 1930s*, Cambridge University Press, Cambridge

Flowerdew, R. and Salt, J. (1979), Migration between labour market areas in Great Britain 1970–71, *Regional Studies* 13, 211–231

Forbes, J., Lamont, D. and Robertson, I. (1979), *Intraurban Migration in Greater Glasgow*, Scottish Development Department, Edinburgh

Foreit, K., Koh, K. and Suh, M. (1980), Impact of the national family planning program on fertility in rural Korea: a multivariate areal analysis, *Studies in Family Planning* 11, 79–90

Forrester, J. (1971), *World Dynamics*, Wright-Allen, Cambridge, Mass.

Forster, C. and Tucker, G. (1972), *Economic Opportunity and White American Fertility Ratios 1800—60*, Yale University Press, New Haven

Forster, F. (1966), Use of a demographic base map for the presentation of areal data in epidemiology, *British Journal of Preventive and Social Medicine* 20, 156–171

Fox, C. (1947), *The Personality of Britain*, National Museum of Wales, Cardiff

Fox, J. (1977), Occupational mortality 1970–72, *Population Trends* 9, 8–15

Frank, A.G. (1969), *Capitalism and Underdevelopment in Latin America*, Monthly Review Press, New York

Frankel, F. (1971), *India's Green Revolution: Economic Gains and Political Costs*, Princeton University Press, Princeton

Frederikson, H. (1960), Malaria control and population pressure in Ceylon, *Public Health Reports* 75, 865–868

Frederikson, H. (1961), Determinants and consequences of mortality and fertility trends in Ceylon, *Public Health Reports* 76, 659–663

Freedman, D. (1963), The relation of economic status to fertility, *American Economic Review* 53, 414–426

Freedman, R., Whelpton, P. and Smit, J. (1961), Socio-economic factors in religious differentials in fertility, *American Sociological Review* 26, 608–614

Freeman, C. and Jahoda, M. (eds.) (1978), *World Futures: The Great Debate*, Martin Robertson, London

Frey, W. (1980), Status selective white flight and central city population change, *Journal of Regional Science* 20, 71–89

Friedlander, D. (1973–74), Demographic patterns and socio-economic characteristics of the coal-mining population in England and Wales in the nineteenth century, *Economic Development and Cultural Change* 22, 39–51

Friedlander, D. and Roshier, R. (1966), A study of internal migration in England

and Wales, *Population Studies* 19, 239–279 (Part I) and 20, 45–60 (Part II)

Frisch, R. (1975), Demographic implications of the biological determinants of female fecundity, *Social Biology* 22, 17–22

Fuller, G. (1974), On the spatial diffusion of fertility decline: the distance-to-clinic variable in a Chilean community, *Economic Geography* 50, 324–332

Galbraith, V. and Thomas, D.S. (1941), Birth rates and the interwar business cycles, *Journal of the American Statistical Association* 36, 465–476

Galle, O. and Taueber, K. (1966), Metropolitan migration and intervening opportunities, *American Sociological Review* 31, 5–13

Gardner, M. and Donnan, S. (1977), Life expectancy: variations among regional health authorities, *Population Trends* 10, 10–15

Gaunt, D. (1976), Familj, hushall och arbetsintensitet, *Scandia* 42, 32–59

Gendell, M. (1979), A 'population crisis' in Sweden again?, *Intercom* 7 (3), 7–9

George, P. (1951), *Introduction a l'Etude Géographique de la Population du Monde*, Institut National d'Etudes Démographiques, Paris

George, P. (1959), *Questions de Géographie de la Population*, Presses Universitaires de France, Paris

George, S. (1976), *How the Other Half Dies: The Real Reasons for World Hunger*, Penguin, Harmondsworth

Germani, G. (1965), Migration and acculturation, in Hauser, P. (ed.), *Handbook for Social Research in Urban Areas*, UNESCO, 159–178

Gilbert, A. and Sollis, P. (1979), Migration to small Latin American cities, *Tijdschrift v.E.S.G.* 70, 110–113

Gille, H. (1949–1950), The demographic history of the northern European countries in the eighteenth century, *Population Studies* 3, 3–65

Ginsberg, R. (1978), Probability models of residence histories, in Clark and Moore (eds.), 233–265

Glaser, W. (1978), *The Brain Drain: Emigration and Return*, Pergamon, Oxford

Glass, D. (1963–1964), Some indicators of differences between urban and rural mortality in England and Wales and Scotland, *Population Studies* 17, 263–267

Glass, D. (1967), *Population Policies and Movements in Europe*, Cass, London

Glass, D. and Eversley, D. (eds.) (1965), *Population History*, Arnold, London

Glass, D. and Revelle, R. (eds.) (1972), *Population and Social Change*, Arnold, London

Gober-Meyers, P. (1978), Interstate migration and economic growth: a simultaneous equations approach, *Environment and Planning* A 10, 1241–1252

Godlund, S. (1961), *Population, Regional Hospitals, Transport Facilities and Regions in Sweden*, Lund Studies B, No. 21

Goeller, H. and Weinberg, A. (1976), The age of substitutability, *Science*, Feb. 20, 683–689

Goldscheider, C. (1971), *Population Modernization and Social Structure*, Little Brown, Boston

Goldscheider, C. and Uhlenberg, P. (1969), Minority group status and fertility,

American Journal of Sociology 74, 361–372

Goldstein, S., Pitaktepsombati, P. and Goldstein, A. (1976), Migration and urban growth in Thailand, in Richmond and Kubat (eds.), 116–147

Goodman, L. (1959), Some alternatives to ecological correlation, *American Journal of Sociology* 64, 610–625

Gould, W.T. (1973), *Planning the Location of Schools: Ankole, Uganda*, UNESCO, Paris

Gould, W.T. (1974), International migration in tropical Africa: a bibliographical review, *International Migration* 8, 347–365

Gould, W. T. and Prothero, R. M. (1975), Space and time in African population mobility, in Kosiński and Prothero (eds.), 39–49

Gray, R. (1974), The decline of mortality in Ceylon and demographic effects of malaria control, *Population Studies* 28, 205–229

Greaves, T. (1972), The Andean rural proletarians, *Anthropological Quarterly* 45, 65–83

Green, A. (1976), *Immigration and the Post-War Canadian Economy*, Macmillan of Canada

Greenwood, M. (1970), Lagged response in the decision to migrate, *Journal of Regional Science* 10, 375–384

Greenwood, M. (1975), Research on internal migration in the United States: a survey, *Journal of Economic Literature* 13, 397–433

Griffin, K. (1969), *Underdevelopment in Latin America*, Allen & Unwin, London

Griffin, K. (1974), *The Political Economy of Agrarian Change: An Essay on the Green Revolution*, Macmillan, London

Griffith, G. T. (1926), *Population Problems of the Age of Malthus*, Cass, London

Griffiths, M. (1971), A geographical study of mortality in an urban area, *Urban Studies* 8, 111–120

Grigg, D. (1976), Population pressure and agricultural change, *Progress in Geography* 8, 133–176

Grigg, D. (1979), Ester Boserup's theory of agrarian change: a critical review, *Progress in Human Geography* 3(1), 64–84

Grigg, D. (1980), Migration and overpopulation, in White and Woods (eds.), 60–83

Gugler, J. (1969), On the theory of rural-urban migration: the case of subSaharan Africa, in Jackson (ed.), 134–155

Gugler, J. (1976), Migrating to urban centres of unemployment in tropical Africa, in Richmond and Kubat (eds.), 184–204

Guillet, E. (1963), *The Great Migration*, University of Toronto Press, Toronto

Guralnick, L. (1963), *Mortality by Industry and Cause of Death*, Vital Statistics Special Reports 53, U.S. Department of Health, Education and Welfare

Gutkind, P. (1975), The view from below: political consciousness of the urban poor in Ibadan, *Cahiers d'études africaines* 15, 5–35

Habbakuk, H.J. (1971), *Population Growth and Economic Development since*

1750, Leicester University Press, Leicester

Hagerstrand, T. (1957), Migration and area: survey of a sample of Swedish migration fields and hypothetical considerations on their genesis, *Lund Studies in Geography* 13B, 27–158

Hagerstrand, T. (1967), *Innovation Diffusion as a Spatial Process*, University of Chicago, Chicago

Haggett, P. (1972), *Geography: A Modern Synthesis*, Harper & Row, New York

Haggett, P. (1976), Hybridizing alternative models of an epidemic diffusion process, *Economic Geography* 52, 136–146

Haines, M. (1977), Fertility, nuptiality and occupation: a study of coalmining populations and regions in England and Wales in the mid-nineteenth century, *Journal of Interdisciplinary History* 8, 245–280

Hajnal, J. (1965), European marriage patterns in perspective, in Glass and Eversley (eds.), 101–143

Hanley, S. (1977), The influence of economic and social variables on marriage and fertility in eighteenth and nineteenth century Japanese villages, in Lee (ed.), 165–199

Hansen, J.C. and Kosiński, L. (1973), *Population Geography 1973*, IGU Commission on Population Geography, Bergen

Harris, A. and Clausen, R. (1966), *Labour Mobility in Great Britain 1953–63*, Government Social Survey, London

Harris, J. and Todaro, M. (1970), Migration, unemployment and development, *American Economic Review* 60, 126–142

Hart, J. (1971), The inverse care law, *Lancet* 1, 405–412

Hartshorne, R. (1939), *The Nature of Geography*, Association of American Geographers, Lancaster, Pa.

Harvey, D. (1974), Population, resources and the idology of science, *Economic Geography* 50, 256–277

Hauser, P. (1967), Family planning and population programs: a book review article, *Demography* 4, 397–414

Hauser, P. and Duncan, O. (eds.) (1959), *The Study of Population: An Inventory and Appraisal*, University of Chicago Press, Chicago

Hawley, A. (1944), Ecology and human ecology, *Social Forces* 22, 398–405

Hawthorn, G. (1976–1977), A review of: Family Planning in India (P. Blaikie), *Journal of Development Studies* 13, 442–443

Hawthorn, G. (ed.) (1978), *Population and Development, High and Low Fertility in Poorer Countries*, Cass, London

Heenan, L. (1967), Rural-urban distribution of fertility in South Island, New Zealand, *Annals of Association of American Geographers* 57, 713–735

Heer, D. (1966), Economic development and fertility, *Demography* 3, 423–444

Heer, D. (1979), What is the annual net flow of undocumented Mexican immigrants to the United States?, *Demography* 16, 417–423

Heijke, J. and Klaassen, L. (1977), *Human Reactions to Spatial Diversity: Mobility in Regional Labour Markets*, Netherlands Economic Institute, Rotterdam

Helleiner, K. (1957), The vital revolution reconsidered, *Canadian Journal of Economics and Political Science* 23, 1–9

Henripin, J. and Peron, Y. (1972), The demographic transition of the province of Quebec, in Glass and Revelle (eds.), 213–231

Henry, L. (1956), *Ancien Familles Genevoises*, Institut National d'Etudes Démographiques, Paris

Henry, L. (1957), La mortalité d'après les incriptions funéraires, *Population* 12, 149–152

Henry, L. (1967), *Manuel de Démographie Historique*, Librarie Droz, Geneva

Henry, L. (1972), Historical demography, in Glass and Revelle (eds.), 43–54

Henry, L. and Lévy, C. (1960), Ducs et pairs sous l'ancien régime, *Population* 15, 807–830

Herbert, D. (1973), The residential mobility process: some empirical observations, *Area* 5, 44–48

Hermalin, A. (1972), Taiwan: appraising the effect of a family planning program through an areal analysis, *Population Papers of the Institute of Economics, Academia Sinica*, No. 2

Hermalin, A. (1975), Regression analysis of areal data, in C. Chandrasekharan and A. Hermalin (eds.), *Measuring the Effect of Family Planning Programs on Fertility*, International Union for the Scientific Study of Population, Dolhain, Belguim, 245–299

Hermalin, A. and Van de Walle, E. (1977), The Civil Code and nuptiality: empirical investigation of a hyhothesis, in Lee (ed.), 71–111

Hiemenz, U. and Schatz, K. (1977), *Transfer of Employment Opportunities as an Alternative to the International Migration of Workers*, Migration for Employment Project Working Paper 9, International Labour Office, Geneva

Hilton, T. (1960), *Ghana Population Atlas*, Nelson, Edinburgh

Hirschman, A. (1958), *The Strategy of Economic Development*, Yale University Press, New Haven

Hirst, M. (1977), Recent villagization in Tanzania, *Geography* 63, 122–125

Hofstee, E. (1968), Population increase in the Netherlands, *Acta Historiae Nederlandica* 3, 43–125

Hofsten, E. (1966), Population registers and computers, *Review of the International Statistical Institute* 34, 186–193

Hogan, D. and Berlinck, M. (1976), Conditions of migration, access to information and first jobs: a study of migrant adaptation in Sao Paulo, in Richmond and Kubat (eds.), 225–238

Hoggart, K. (1979), Resettlement in Newfoundland, *Geography* 64, 215–218

Hollingsworth, T. (1970), *Migration: A Study Based on Scottish Experience Between 1939 and 1954*, Oliver and Boyd, Edinburgh

Hollingsworth, T. (1972), The importance of the quality of the data in historical demography, in Glass and Revelle (eds.), 71–86

House, J. (1973), Geographers, decision takers and policy makers, in M. Chisholm and B. Rodgers (eds.), *Studies in Human Geography*, Heinemann, London, 272–305

House, J. et al. (1968), *Mobility of the Northern Business Manager*, Papers on Migration and Mobility, Department of Geography, University of Newcastle-upon-Tyne

Howe, G.M. (1970a), *National Atlas of Disease Mortality in the United Kingdom*, Nelson, London

Howe, G. M. (1970b), Some recent developments in disease mapping, *Royal Society of Health Journal* 90, 16–20

Howe, G. M. (1972), *Man, Environment and Disease in Britain*, David and Charles, Newton Abbot

Howe, G. M. (1979), Mortality from selected malignant neoplasms in the British Isles: the spatial perspective, *Geographical Journal* 145, 401–415

Howe, G. M. and Lorraine, J. (1973), *Environmental Medicine*, Heinemann, London

Howell, N. (1979), *Demography of the Dobe !Kung*, Academic Press, London

Hull, T., Hull, V. and Singarimbun, M. (1977), Indonesia's family planning story, *Population Bulletin* 32 (6)

Hunter, J. (1967), Seasonal hunger in a part of the West African Savanna, *Transactions of Institute of British Geographers* 41, 167–185

Hurst, M. E. (1973), Establishment geography: or how to be irrelevant in three easy lessons, *Antipode* 5(2), 40–59

International Geographical Union (1978a), *Policies of Population Redistribution: A Symposium*, Commission on Population Geography, University of Alberta, Edmonton

International Geographical Union (1978b), *Population Redistribution in Africa*, Commission of Population Geography, University of Alberta, Edmonton

Isbell, E. (1944), Internal migration in Sweden and intervening opportunities, *American Sociological Review* 9, 627–639

Jack, A. (1971), Interregional migration in Great Britain: some cross-sectional evidence, *Scottish Journal of Political Economy* 18, 147–160

Jackson, J. (ed.) (1969), *Migration*, Cambridge University Press, Cambridge

James, P. (1954a), The geographic study of population, in P. James and C. Jones (eds.), *American Geography: Inventory and Prospect*, Syracuse University Press, Syracuse, 106–122

James, P., (1954b), The field of geography, in P. James and C. Jones (eds.), *American Geography: Inventory and Prospect*, Syracuse University Press, Syracuse, 2–18

Janowitz, B. (1971), An empirical study of the effects of socio-economic development on fertility rates, *Demography* 8, 319–330

Janowitz, B. (1973), An econometric analysis of trends in fertility rates, *Journal of Development Studies* 9, 413–425

Jansen, C. and King, R. (1968), Migrations et 'occasions intervenantes' en Belgique, *Recherches Economiques de Louvain* 4, 519–526

Jerome, H. (1926), *Migration and Business Cycles*, National Bureau of Economic Research, New York

Johnson, B. L. (1969), *South Asia*, Heinemann, London

Johnson, G. (1963–1964), Health conditions in rural and urban areas of developing countries, *Population Studies* 17, 293–309

Johnson, J. H., Salt, J. and Wood, P. (1974), *Housing and the Migration of Labour in England and Wales*, Saxon House, Farnborough

Johnson, J. H. and Salt, J. (1978), Labour migration policies in Great Britain, Paper presented at I.B.G. Population Geography Study Group Conference on Population Policies at University of Durham

Johnston, R. J. (1978), *Multivariate Statistical Analysis in Geography*, Longman, London

Johnston, R. J. (1979), *Geography and Geographers: Anglo-American Human Geography since 1945*, Arnold, London

Jones, D. W. (1975), *Migration and Urban Unemployment in Dualistic Economic Development*, University of Chicago Geography Research Paper 165, Chicago

Jones, E. F. (1971), Fertility decline in Australia and New Zealand 1861–1936, *Population Index* 37, 301–338

Jones, E. F. and Westoff, C. (1979), The end of 'Catholic' fertility, *Demography* 16, 209–217

Jones, H.R. (1970), Migration to and from Scotland since 1960, *Transactions of Institute of British Geographers* 49, 145–159

Jones, H. R. (1974), *Newtown: A Case Study of Migration to a Growth Point in Mid-Wales*, Occasional Geographical Papers 2, University of Dundee, Dundee

Jones, H. R. (1975), A spatial analysis of human fertility in Scotland, *Scottish Geographical Magazine* 91, 102–113

Jones, H. R. (1976), The structure of the migration process: findings from a growth point in Mid-Wales, *Transactions of Institute of British Geographers* 1, 421–432

Jones, H. R. (1977), Metropolitan dominance and family planning in Barbados, *Social and Economic Studies* 26, 327–338

Jones, H. R. (1978), Canada reviews immigration policy, *Geography* 64, 217–219

Jones, H. R. (1979), Modern emigration from Scotland to Canada, *Scottish Geographical Magazine* 95, 4–12

Jones, R. E. (1976), Infant mortality in rural North Shropshire 1561–1810, *Population Studies* 30, 305–317

Joseph, G. (1975), A Markov analysis of age/sex differences in inter-regional migration in Great Britain, *Regional Studies* 9, 69–78

Kahn, H. et al. (1976), *The Next 200 Years: A Scenario for America and the World*, Morrow, New York

Kane, P. (1977), Population planning in China, in Epstein and Jackson (eds.), 207–217

Katz, M. (1976), *The People of Hamilton, Canada West: Family and Class in a Mid-Nineteenth Century City*, Harvard University Press, Cambridge, Mass.

Keeble, D. (1977), Spatial policy in Britain: regional or urban?, *Area* 9, 3–8

Kemper, R. (1971), Rural-urban migration in Latin America, *International Migration Review* 5, 36–47

Kennedy, R. (1973), Minority group status and fertility: the Irish, *American Sociological Review* 38, 85–96

Kennett, S. (1980), Migration within and between the Metropolitan Economic Labour Areas of Britain 1966–71, in J. Hobcraft and P. Rees (eds.), *Regional Demographic Development*, Croom Helm, London, 165–187

King, R. (1973), Geographical perspectives on the Green Revolution, *Tijdschrift v. E.S.G.* 64, 237–244

King, R. (1976) The evolution of international labour migration movements concerning the EEC, *Tijdschrift v.E.S.G.* 67, 66–82

King, R. (1978), Return migration: a neglected aspect of population geography, *Area* 10, 175–182

Kirk, D. (1942), The relationship of employment levels to births in Germany, *Milbank Memorial Fund Quarterly* 28, 126–138

Kirk, D. (1966), Factors affecting Moslem natality, in Berelson, B. et al. (eds.), *Family Planning and Population Programs*, University of Chicago Press, Chicago, 561–579

Kirk, D. (1971), A new demographic transition?, in *Rapid Population Growth: Consequences and Policy Implications*, Johns Hopkins Press, Baltimore, 123–147

Kiser, C. and Whelpton, P. (1953), Résumé of the Indianapolis study of social and psychological factors affecting fertility, *Population Studies* 7, 95–110

Kitagawa, E. and Hauser, P. (1973), *Differential Mortality in the United States: A Study in Socioeconomic Epidemiology*, Harvard University Press, Cambridge, Mass.

Klaassen, L. and Drewe, P. (1973), *Migration Policy in Europe*, Saxon House, Farnborough

Kloos, H. and Thompson, K. (1979), Schistosomiasis in Africa: an ecological perspective, *Journal of Tropical Geography* 48, 31–46

Knights, P. (1971), *The Plain People of Boston 1830–60*, Oxford University Press, New York

Knodel, J. (1966–1967), Law, marriage and illegitimacy in nineteenth-century Germany, *Population Studies* 20, 279–294

Knox, P. (1978), The intraurban ecology of primary medical care, *Environment and Planning* A10, 415–435

Kocher, J. (1973), *Rural Development, Income Distribution and Fertility Decline*, Population Council, New York

Koller, S. (1963), The development of the excess male mortality, in International Union for the Scientific Study of Population, *International Population Conference New York 1961*, Vol. 1, 675–684

Kono, S. (1971), Evaluation of the Japanese population register data on internal migration, in International Union for the Scientific Study of Population, *International Population Conference London 1969*, Vol. 4, Liège, 2766–2775

Kormoss, I. and Kosiński, L. (1973), *Population Mapping 1973*, IGU Commission on Population Geography, Bruges

Kosiński, L. (1970), *The Population of Europe*, Longman, London

Kosiński, L. (1978), Federal programs directly affecting migration in Canada, in International Geographical Union (1978a), 21

Kosiński, L. and Prothero, R. M. (eds.) (1975), *People on the Move: Studies on Internal Migration*, Methuen, London

Kosiński, L. and Webb, J. (eds.) (1976), *Population at Microscale*, IGU Commission on Population Geography and New Zealand Geographical Society, Christchurch

Krause, J. (1958), Changes in English fertility and mortality 1781–1850, *Economic History Review* 11, 52–70

Krause, J. (1965), The changing adequacy of English registration 1690–1837, in Glass and Eversley (eds.), 379–393

Kuhn, W. (1978), Guest workers as an automatic stabilizer of cyclical unemployment in Switzerland and Germany, *International Migration Review* 12, 210–224

Kulischer, E. (1948), *Europe on the Move: War and Population Changes 1917–47*, Columbia University Press, New York

Kulldorff, G. (1955), *Migration Probabilities*, Lund Studies in Geography B No.14, Gleerup, Lund

Kwofie, K. (1976), A spatio-temporal analysis of cholera diffusion in western Africa, *Economic Geography* 52, 127–135

Ladinsky, J. (1967), The geographical mobility of professional and technical manpower, *Journal of Human Resources* 2, 475–494

Land, K. (1969), Duration of residence and prospective migration, *Demography* 6, 133–140

Langer, W. (1963), Europe's initial population explosion, *American Historical Review* 69, 1–17

Langer, W. (1974), Infanticide: a historical survey, *History of Childhood Quarterly* 1

Langer, W. (1975), American foods and Europe's population growth 1750–1850, *Journal of Social History* 5, 51–66

Lapham, R. and Mauldin, W.P. (1972), National family planning programs: review and evaluation, *Studies in Family Planning* 3 (3), 31–34

Law, C. and Warnes, A. (1976), The changing geography of the elderly in England and Wales, *Transactions of Institute of British Geographers* 1, 453–471

Lawton, R. (1968), Population changes in England and Wales in the later nineteenth century, *Transactions of Institute of British Geographers* 44, 55–74

Lawton, R. (ed.) (1978), *The Census and Social Structure: An Interpretative Guide to Nineteenth Century Censuses for England and Wales*, Cass, London

Lawton, R. and Pooley, C. (1976), *The Social Geography of Merseyside in the Nineteenth Century*, Report to Social Science Research Council

Leach, G. (1976), *Energy and Food Production*, IPC Science and Technology Press, London

Learmonth, A. (1972), Atlases in medical geography, in McGlashan (ed.), 133–152

Learmonth, A. (1977), Malaria, in G. M. Howe (ed.), *A World Geography of Human Diseases*, Academic Press, London, 61–108

Learmonth, A. (1978), *Patterns of Disease and Hunger*, David and Charles, Newton Abbot

Lee, E. (1966), A theory of migration, *Demography* 3, 47–57

Lee, R. D. (ed.) (1977), *Population Patterns in the Past*, Academic Press, New York

Lee, R. B. and DeVore, I. (eds.) (1976), *Kalahari Hunter Gatherers*, Harvard University Press, Cambridge, Mass.

Leete, R. and Fox J. (1977), Registrar General's social classes: origins and uses, *Population Trends* 8, 1–7

Lenski, G. (1961), *The Religious Factor: A Sociological Study of Religion's Impact on Politics, Economics and Family Life*, Doubleday, New York

Levine, D. (1974), The Demographic Implications of Industrialization: A Study of Two Leicestershire Villages 1600–1851, Unpublished Ph.D dissertation, University of Cambridge

Levy, R. (1972), *Use of a Geographic Base File in a Health Information System*, Computerized Geographic Coding Series GE 60 (3), U.S. Bureau of the Census, Washington D.C.

Lewis, O. (1959), *Five Families: A Mexican Case Study in the Culture of Poverty*, Basic Books, New York

Leys, C. (1975), *Underdevelopment in Kenya: The Political Economy of Neo-colonialism 1964–71*, Heinemann, London

Lightfoot, P. (1979), Planning issues in the urbanization of Thailand, Paper given at Conference on Population and Development, Developing Areas and Population Geography Study Groups of Institute of British Geographers, University of Cambridge

Lipton, M. (1977), *Why Poor People Stay Poor: a Study of Urban Bias in World Development*, Temple Smith, London

Livi-Bacci, M. (1972), Fertility and population growth in Spain in the eighteenth and nineteenth centuries, in Glass and Revelle (eds.), 173–184

Livi-Bacci, M. and Hagmann, H. (eds.) (1971), *Report on the Demographic and Social Pattern of Migrants to Europe*, Council of Europe 2nd European Population Conference, Strasbourg

Lloyd, P. (1979), *Slums of Hope*, Penguin, Harmondsworth

Logan, W. (1976), Cancers of the alimentary tract, *W.H.O. Chronicle* 30, 413–419

Long, L. (1970), Fertility patterns among religious groups in Canada, *Demography* 7, 135–149

Long, L. and Hansen, K. (1979), *Reasons for Interstate Migration*, U.S. Bureau of the Census, Washington

Lopes, J. (1978), Capitalist development and agrarian structure in Brazil, *International Journal of Urban and Regional Research* 2, 1–11

Lowry, I. (1966), *Migration and Metropolitan Growth: Two Analytical Models*, University of California Press, Los Angeles

Mabogunje, A. (1970), Systems approach to a theory of rural-urban migration, *Geographical Analysis* 2, 1–18

McCrone, G. (1969), *Regional Policy in Britain*, Allen & Unwin, London

MacDonald, E. (1976), Demographic variation in cancer in relation to industrial and environmental influence, *Environmental Health Perspectives* 17, 153–166

MacDonald, J. and MacDonald, L. (1964), Chain migration, ethnic neighbourhood formation and social networks, *Milbank Memorial Fund Quarterly* 42, 82–97

McFalls, J. (1979), *Psychopathology and Subfecundity*, Academic Press, New York

McGinnis, R. (1968), A stochastic model of social mobility, *American Sociological Review* 33, 712–722

McGinnis, R. (1974), Review of: The Limits to Growth, *Demography* 10, 295–299

McGlashan, N. (1967), Geographical evidence on medical hypotheses, *Tropical and Geographical Medicine* 19, 333–343

McGlashan, N. (ed.) (1972), *Medical Geography, Techniques and Analysis*, Methuen, London

McGlashan, N. (1972), Food contaminants and oesophageal cancer, in McGlashan (ed.), 247–257

McGovern, G. (1964), *War Against Want*, Walker, New York

McGranahan, D. et al. (1972), *Contents and Measurement of Socioeconomic Development*, Praeger, New York

McInnis, R. M. (1977), Childbearing and land availability, in Lee (ed.), 201–227

Mackay, D. (1969), *Geographical Mobility and the Brain Drain: A Case Study of Aberdeen University Graduates 1860—1960*, Allen & Unwin, London

McKay, J. and Whitelaw, J. (1977), The role of large private and government organizations in generating flows of inter-regional migrants: the case of Australia, *Economic Geography* 53, 28–44

McKeown, T. (1976), *The Modern Rise of Population*, Arnold, London

McKeown, T. and Brown R. (1955), Medical evidence related to English population changes in the eighteenth century, *Population Studies* 9, 119–141

McKeown, T., Brown R. and Record, R. (1972), An interpretation of the modern rise of population in Europe, *Population Studies* 26, 345–382

McNabb, R. (1979), A socio-economic model of migration, *Regional Studies* 13, 297–304

McNamara, R. (1977), Possible interventions to reduce fertility, *Population and Development Review* 3, 163–176

McNicoll, G. (1978), Population and development: outlines for a structuralist approach, in Hawthorn (ed.), 79–99

Madigan, F. (1957), Are sex mortality differentials biologically caused?, *Milbank Memorial Fund Quarterly* 35, 202–223

Malawi Population Change Survey 1970–72 (1973), National Statistical Office, Zomba, Malawi

Mamdani, M. (1972), *The Myth of Population Control: Family, Caste and Class in an Indian Village*, Monthly Review Press, New York

Mandelbaum, D. (1974), *Human Fertility in India: Social Components and Policy Perspectives*, Oxford University Press, Delhi

Mandle, J. (1970), The decline in mortality in British Guiana 1911–60, *Demography* 7, 301–315

Mann, M. (1973), *Workers on the Move: The Sociology of Relocation*, Cambridge University Press, Cambridge

Margolis, J. (1977), Internal migration: measurement and models, in A. Brown and E. Neuberger, *Internal Migration: A Comparative Perspective*, Academic Press, New York

Martine, G. (1972), Migration, natural increase and city growth: the case of Rio de Janeiro, *International Migration Review* 6, 200–215

Mason, T. et al. (1975), *Atlas of Cancer Mortality for U.S. Counties 1950–1969*, Government Printing Office, Washington D.C.

Masser, I. (1970), *A Test of Some Models for Predicting Intermetropolitan Movement of Population in England and Wales*, Centre for Environmental Studies UWP 9, London

Matras, J. (1965), The social strategy of family formation: some variations in time and space, *Demography* 2, 349–362

Matthiessen, P. (1972), Replacement for generations of Danish females 1840/44–1920/24, in Glass and Revelle (eds.), 199–212

Mauldin, W. P. (1978), Patterns of fertility decline in developing countries 1950–75, *Studies in Family Planning* 9, 75–84

Mauldin, W. P. and Berelson, B. (1978), Conditions of fertility decline in developing countries 1965–75, *Studies in Family Planning* 9, 89–147

May, J. (1950), Medical geography: its methods and objectives, *Geographical Review* 40, 9–41

May, J. (1958) *The Ecology of Human Disease*, M D Publications, New York

May, J. (1961), *Studies in Disease Ecology*, Hafner, New York

Meade, M. (1977), Medical geography as human ecology, *Geographical Review* 67, 377–393

Meadows, D. H. et al. (1972), *The Limits to Growth, a Report for the Club of*

Rome's Project on the Predicament of Mankind, Universe Books, New York

Meegama, S. (1967), Malaria eradication and its effect on mortality levels, *Population Studies* 21, 207–237

Mesarovic, M. and Pestel, E. (1974), *Mankind at the Turning Point*, Hutchinson, London

Mitchell, J. C. (1959), Labour migration in Africa south of the Sahara, *Bulletin of the Inter-African Labour Institute* 6, 12–47

Mitchell, J. C. (1969), Structural plurality, urbanization and labour circulation in Southern Rhodesia, in Jackson (ed.), 156–180

Moreira, M. de M., Da Silva, L. and McLaughlin, R. (1978), *Brazil*, Population Council, New York

Moriyama, I. et al. (1958), Observations on possible factors responsible for the sex and race trends in cardiovascular-renal mortality in the United States, *Journal of Chronic Diseases* 7, 401–412

Moriyama, I. and Guralnick, L. (1956), Occupational and social class differences in mortality, in *Trends and Differentials in Mortality*, Milbank Memorial Fund, New York

Morrill, R. (1965), The Negro ghetto: problems and alternatives, *Geographical Review* 55, 339–361

Morrill, R. et al. (1970), Factors influencing distances travelled to hospitals, *Economic Geography* 46, 161–171

Morris, L. et al. (1978), Contraceptive prevalence in Paraguay, *Studies in Family Planning* 9, 272–279

Morris, L. et al. (1979), Contraceptive use and demographic trends in El Salvador, *Studies in Family Planning* 10, 43–52

Morrison, P. (1967), Duration of residence and prospective migration, *Demography* 4, 553–561

Morrison, P. (1973), Theoretical issues in the design of population mobility models, *Environment and Planning* 5, 125–134

Moseley, M. (1979), *Accessibility: The Rural Challenge*, Methuen, London

Mourant, A. et al. (1978), *Blood Groups and Diseases*, Oxford University Press, Oxford

Murray, M. (1967), The geography of death in the United States and the United Kingdom, *Annals of Association of American Geographers* 57, 301–314

Muss, D. (1962), Relationship between water quality and deaths from cardiovascular disease, *Journal of American Water Works Association* 54, 1371

Muth, R. (1971), Migration: chicken or egg?, *Southern Economic Journal* 37, 295–306

Mwansasu, B. and Pratt, C. (eds.) (1979), *Towards Socialism in Tanzania*, Tanzania Publishing House, Dar es Salaam

Myrdal, A. (1945), *Nation and Family: The Swedish Experiment in Democratic Family and Population Policy*, Routledge & Kegan Paul, London

Myrdal, G. (1940), *Population: A Problem for Democracy*, Harvard University Press, Cambridge Mass.

Myrdal, G. (1957), *Economic Theory and Under-developed Regions*, Duckworth, London

Myrdal, G. (1974), The transfer of technology to underdeveloped countries, *Scientific American* 231 (3), 173–182

Myrdal, A. and Myrdal, G. (1934), *Kris i Befolkingsfragan*, Albert Bonniers Forlag, Stockholm

Nag, M. (1971), The pattern of mating behaviour, emigration and contraceptives as factors affecting human fertility in Barbados, *Social and Economic Studies* 20, 111–133

Nalson, J. (1968), *Mobility of Farm Families*, Manchester University Press, Manchester

Nam, C. (1979), The progress of demography as a scientific discipline, *Demography* 16, 485–492

Nam, C. and Gustavus, S. (1976), *Population: The Dynamics of Demographic Change*, Houghton Mifflin, Boston

Nelson, P. (1959), Migration, real income and information, *Journal of Regional Science* 1, 43–73

Newman, P. (1965), *Malaria Eradication and Population Growth with Special Reference to Ceylon and British Guiana*, School of Public Health, University of Michigan, Ann Arbor

Newman, P. (1970), Malaria control and population growth, *Journal of Development Studies* 6, 133–158

Newsholme, A. (1929), *The Story of Modern Preventive Medicine*, Williams and Wilkins, Baltimore

Newton, M. and Jefferey, J. (1951), *Internal Migration: Some Aspects of Population Movements within England and Wales*, H.M.S.O., London

Ng, R. (1975), Internal migration in Southeast Asian countries, in Kosiński and Prothero (eds.), 181–192

Nicholas, D. et al. (1976), Attitudes and practices of traditional birth attendants in rural Ghana, *W.H.O. Bulletin 54*

Nikolinakos, M. (1975), Notes towards a general theory of migration in late capitalism, *Race and Class* 7, 5–16

Noin, D. (1979), *Géographie de la Population*, Masson, Paris

Nortman, D. (1977), Changing contraceptive patterns: a global perspective, *Population Bulletin* 32 (3)

Oechsli, F. and Kirk, D. (1974–1975), Modernization and the demographic transition in Latin America and the Caribbean, *Economic Development and Cultural Change* 23, 391–419

Office of Population Censuses and Surveys (1978a), *Trends in Mortality 1951–1975*, Series DHI no. 3, H.M.S.O., London

Office of Population Censuses and Surveys (1978b), *Occupational Mortality*, Series DS no.1, H.M.S.O., London

Office of Population Censuses and Surveys (1978c), *Birth Statistics 1976*, H.M.S.O., London

Office of Population Censuses and Surveys (1981), *People in Britain: A Census Atlas*, H.M.S.O., London

Ogden, P. (1980), Migration, marriage and the collapse of traditional peasant society in France, in White and Woods (eds.), 152–179

Ogilvy, A. (1980), *Inter-regional Migration since 1971*, Occasional Paper 16, Office of Population Censuses and Surveys, H.M.S.O., London.

Ohlin, P. (1961), Mortality, marriage and growth in pre-industrial populations, *Population Studies* 14, 190–197

Oliver, F. (1964), Interregional migration and unemployment 1951–61, *Journal of Royal Statistical Society* A 127, 42–75

Olsson, G. (1966), Distance and human interaction: a migration study, *Geografiska Annaler* 47B, 3–43

Omran, A. (1977), Epidemiologic transition in the U.S., *Population Bulletin* 32 (2)

Omvedt, G. (1975), The political economy of starvation, *Race and Class* 17, 111–130

Orubuloye, I. and Caldwell, J. (1975), The impact of public health services on mortality differentials in a rural area of Nigeria, *Population Studies* 29, 259–272

Osborne, R. (1958), The movements of people in Scotland 1851–1951, *Scottish Studies* 2, 1–46

Paine, S. (1979), Replacement of the West European migrant labour system by investment in the European periphery, in Seers et al. (eds.), 65–95

Park, R. (1936), Human ecology, *American Journal of Sociology* 42, 1–15

Peach, C. (1965), West Indian migration to Britain: the economic factors, *Race* 7, 31–46

Peach, C. (1966), Factors affecting the distribution of West Indians in Great Britain, *Transactions of Institute of British Geographers* 38, 151–163

Peach, C. (1975), Immigrants in the inner city, *Geographical Journal* 141, 372–379

Pearce, D. and Britton, M. (1977), The decline in births: some socio-economic aspects, *Population Trends* 7, 9–14

Pebley, A., Delgado, H. and Brinemann, E. (1979), Fertility desires and child mortality experience among Guatemalan women, *Studies in Family Planning* 10, 129–136

Petersen, W. (1969), *Population*, Macmillan, New York

Poleman, T. (1975), World food: a perspective, *Science* 188, 510–518

Pooley, C. (1977), The residential segregation of migrant communities in mid-Victorian Liverpool, *Transactions of Institute of British Geographers* 2, 364–382

Pooley, C. (1979), Residential mobility in the Victorian city, *Transactions of Institute of British Geographers* 4, 258–277

Power, J. (1976), *Western Europe's Migrant Workers*, Minority Rights Group Report No. 28, London

Preston, S. (1976), *Mortality Patterns in National Populations*, Academic Press, New York

Preston, S. (ed.) (1978), *The Effects of Infant and Child Mortality on Fertility*, Academic Press, New York

Preston, S. (1980), Causes and consequences of mortality declines in less developed countries during the twentieth century, in R. Easterlin (ed.), *Population and Economic Change in Developing Countries*, University of Chicago Press, Chicago, 289–360

Preston, S. and Nelson, V. (1974), Structure and change in causes of death: an international summary, *Population Studies* 28, 19–51

Preston, S. and Van de Walle, E. (1978), Urban French mortality in the nineteenth century, *Population Studies* 32, 275–297

Pritchard, R. (1976), *Housing and the Spatial Structure of the City*, Cambridge University Press, Cambridge

Prothero, R. M. (1965), *Migrants and Malaria*, Longman, London

Prothero, R. M. (1972), *Reports on Commission on the Geography and Cartography of World Population 1964–72*, IGU Commission on Population Geography, Edmonton

Prothero, R. M. (1974), Foreign migrant labour for South Africa, *International Migration* 8, 383–394

Pryor, R. (1971), *Internal Migration and Urbanization*, University of N. Queensland, Townsville

Pryor, R. (1975), Migration and the process of modernization, in Kosiński and Prothero (eds.), 23–38

Pyle, G. (1971), *Heart Disease, Cancer and Stroke in Chicago*, Geography Research Paper 134, University of Chicago, Chicago

Pyle, G. (1979), *Applied Medical Geography*, Wiley, New York

Pyle, G. and Rees, P. (1971), Modeling patterns of death and disease in Chicago, *Economic Geography* 47, 475–488

Quigley, J. and Weinberg, D. (1977), Intra-urban residential mobility: a review and synthesis, *International Regional Science Review* 2, 41–66

Ravenstein, E. (1885), The laws of migration, *Journal of the Royal Statistical Society* 48, 167–227

Razzell, P. (1965), Population change in eighteenth century Britain: a re-appraisal, *Economic History Review* 18, 312–332

Razzell, P. (1974), An interpretation of the modern rise of population in Europe – a critique, *Population Studies* 28, 5–17

Razzell, P. (1977), *The Conquest of Smallpox: The Impact of Inoculation on Smallpox Mortality in Eighteenth Century Britain*, Caliban Books, Firle, Sussex

Reddaway, W. (1939), *The Economics of Declining Population*, Macmillan, London

Redford, A. (1926), *Labour Migration in England 1800–50*, University of Manchester, Manchester

Rée, G. (1977), Schistosomiasis, in G. M. Howe (ed.), *A World Geography of Human Diseases*, Academic Press, London, 17–31

Rees, G. and Rees, T. (1977), Alternatives to the census: the example of sources of internal migration data, *Town Planning Review* 48, 123–140

Rees, P. (1977), The measurement of migration from census data and other sources, *Environment and Planning* A, 247–272

Rees, P. and Wilson, A. (1977), *Spatial Population Analysis*, Arnold, London

Reichert, J. and Massey, D. (1979), Migration from a rural Mexican town, *Intercom* 7 (6), 6–7

Reid, D. (1973), Arteriosclerotic disease in relation to the environment, in Howe and Lorraine (eds.), 145–153

Repetto, R. (1978), The interaction of fertility and the size distribution of income, in Hawthorn (ed.), 22–39

Repetto, R. (1979), *Economic Equality and Fertility in Developing Countries*, Johns Hopkins University Press, Baltimore

Revelle, R. (1974), Food and population, *Scientific American* 231(3), 161–170

Rich, W. (1973), *Smaller Families through Social and Economic Progress*, Overseas Development Council, Washington D.C.

Richmond, A. and Kubat, D. (eds.) (1976), *Internal Migration: The New World and the Third World*, Sage Publications, London

Richmond, A. and Verma, R. (1978), The economic adaptation of immigrants: a new theoretical perspective, *International Migration Review* 12, 3–39

Riddell, J.B. (1978), The migration to the cities of West Africa: some policy considerations, *Journal of Modern African Studies* 16, 241–260

Rindfuss, R. and Sweet, J. (1977), *Postwar Fertility Trends and Differentials in the United States*, Academic Press, New York

Roberts, B. (1978), *Cities of Peasants: The Political Economy of Urbanization in the Third World*, Arnold, London

Roberts, G. (1955), Some aspects of fertility and mating in the West Indies, *Population Studies* 8, 199–227

Roberts, R. and Lee, E. (1974), Minority group status and fertility reviewed, *American Journal of Sociology* 80, 503–523

Robertson, I. M. (1972), Population distribution and location problems, *Regional Studies* 6, 237–245

Robertson, I. M. (1974), Scottish population distribution: implications for locational decisions, *Transactions of Institute of British Geographers* 63, 111–124

Robinson, A. H. (1956), The necessity of weighting values in correlation analysis of areal data, *Annals of Association of American Geographers* 46, 233–236

Robinson, W. C. (1961), Urban-rural differences in Indian fertility, *Population Studies* 14, 218–234

Robinson, W. C. (1974), Review of: The Limits to Growth, *Demography* 10, 289–295

Robinson, W. S. (1950), Ecological correlations and the behaviour of individuals, *American Sociological Review* 15, 351–357

Rogers, A. (1966), A markovian policy model of interregional migration, *Papers of Regional Science Association* 17, 205–224

Rogers, A. (1967), A regression analysis of interregional migration in California, *Review of Economics and Statistics* 49, 262–267

Rogers, A. (1968), *Matrix Analysis of Interregional Population Growth and Distribution*, University of California, Los Angeles

Romaniuk, A. (1968), Infertility in Tropical Africa, in J. C. Caldwell and C. Okonjo (eds.), *The Population of Tropical Africa*, Longmans, London, 216–224

Romaniuk, A. (1980), Increase in natural fertility during the early stages of modernization: evidence from an African case study, Zaire, *Population Studies* 34, 293–310

Rose, H. (1971), *The Black Ghetto: A Spatial Behavioural Perspective*, McGraw-Hill, New York

Rosing, K. and Wood, P. (1971), *Character of a Conurbation: A Computer Atlas of Birmingham and the Black Country*, University of London Press, London

Rossi, P. (1955), *Why Families Move: A Study in the Social Psychology of Urban Residential Mobility*, Free Press, Glencoe, Ill.

Rostow, W. (1960), *The Stages of Economic Growth*, Cambridge University Press, Cambridge

Rowntree, J. (1957), *Internal Migration: A Study of the Frequency of Movement of Migrants*, H.M.S.O., London

Ryder, N. and Westoff, C., (1971), *Reproduction in the United States 1965*, Princeton University Press, Princeton

Sandbach, F. (1978), Ecology and the 'Limits to Growth' debate, *Antipode* 10 (2), 22–32

Sauer, R. (1978), Infanticide and abortion in nineteenth century Britain, *Population Studies* 32, 81–93

Sauvy, A. (1975), *Zero Growth*, Blackwell, Oxford

Schroeder, H. (1960), Relation between mortality from cardiovascular disease and treated water supplies, *Journal of American Medical Association* 172, 1902–1908

Schultz, T. P. (1980), An economic interpretation of the decline in fertility in a rapidly developing country, in R. Easterlin (ed.), *Population and Economic Change in Developing Countries*, University of Chicago Press, Chicago, 209–265

Scottish Economic Planning Board (1970), *Migration to and from Scotland*, Edinburgh

Scrimshaw, S. (1978), Infant mortality and behaviour in the regulation of family size, *Population and Development Review* 4, 383–403

Seers, D., Schaffer, B. and Kiljunen, M. (eds.) (1979), *Underdeveloped Europe: Studies in Core-Periphery Relations*, Harvester Press, Hassocks

Shannon, G. and Dever, G. (1974), *Health Care Delivery: Spatial Perspectives*, McGraw-Hill, New York

Shaw, J. M. (ed.) (1979), *Rural Deprivation and Planning*, Geo Abstracts Ltd., Norwich

Shaw, R.P. (1975), *Migration Theory and Fact*, Regional Science Research Institute, Pennsylvania

Shaw, R.P. (1979), Migration and employment in the Arab world: construction as a key policy variable, *International Labour Review* 118, 589–605

Shin, E. (1976–1977), Socioeconomic development, infant mortality and fertility, *Journal of Development Studies* 13, 398–412

Short, J. (1978), Residential mobility, *Progress in Human Geography* 2, 419–447

Shorter, E., Knodel, J. and Van de Walle, E. (1971), The decline of non-marital fertility in Europe 1880–1940, *Population Studies* 25, 375–393

Shrewsbury, J. (1970), *A History of Bubonic Plague in the British Isles*, Cambridge University Press, Cambridge

Shryock, H. and Siegel, J. (1976), *The Methods and Materials of Demography* (Condensed edn. by E. Stockwell), Academic Press, New York

Sigerist, H. (1943), *Civilization and Disease*, Cornell University Press, Ithaca, New York

Silk, J. (1971), *Search Behaviour*, University of Reading Geography Paper 7, Reading

Silver, M. (1965), Births, marriages and business cycle in the U.S., *Journal of Political Economy* 74, 237–255

Sinha, R. (1976), *Food and Poverty*, Croom Helm, London

Smith, D. M. (1975), *Patterns in Human Geography*, David and Charles, Newton Abbot

Smith, D. M. (1977), *Human Geography: A Welfare Approach*, Arnold, London

Smith, D. S. (1977), A homeostatic demographic regime: patterns in West European family reconstitution studies, in Lee (ed.), 19–51

Smith, T.L. (1976), *The Race between Population and Food Supply in Latin America*, University of New Mexico Press, Albuquerque

Snyder, R. (1976), *The Biology of Population Growth*, Croom Helm, London

Solomon, M. (1969), *Population Dynamics*, Arnold, London

Speare, A. and Goldstein, S. (1978), Summary of comparative studies of migrant adjustment in Asian cities, *International Migration Review* 12, 114–116

Spengler, J. (1938), *France Faces Depopulation*, Duke University Press, Durham

Spengler, J. (1975), *Population and America's Future*, Freeman, San Francisco

Srinivasan, K., Reddy, P. and Raju, K. (1978), From one generation to the next: changes in fertility, family size preferences, and family planning in an Indian State between 1951 and 1975, *Studies in Family Planning* 9, 258–271

Stamp, L.D. (1964), *The Geography of Life and Death*, Collins, London

Staveley, M. (1978), Resettlement and centralisation in Newfoundland, in International Geographical Union (1978a), 30

Stewart, C. (1960), Migration as a function of population and distance, *American Sociological Review* 25, 347–356

Stewart, J.Q. (1947), Empirical mathematical rules concerning the distribution and equilibrium of population, *Geographical Review* 37, 461–485

Stocks, P. (1947), *Regional and Local Differences in Cancer Death Rates*, H.M.S.O., London

Stone, P. (1978), The implications for the conurbations of population changes, *Regional Studies* 12, 95–123

Stouffer, S. (1940), Intevening opportunities: a theory relating mobility and distance, *American Sociological Review* 5, 845–867

Stouffer, S. (1960), Intervening opportunities and competing migrants, *Journal of Regional Science* 2, 1–26

Strachan, A. (1980), Government sponsored return migration to Guyana, *Area* 12, 165–169

Strodbeck, F. (1949), Equal opportunity intervals: a contribution to the method of intervening opportunity analysis, *American Sociological Review* 14, 490–497

Stycos, J.M. (1968), *Human Fertility in Latin America*, Cornell University Press, Ithaca

Stycos, J. M. (1971a), Family planning and American goals, in D. Chaplin (ed.), *Population Policies and Growth in Latin America*, Heath, Lexington, 111–131

Stycos, J. M. (1971b), *Ideology, Faith and Family Planning in Latin America*, McGraw-Hill, New York

Stycos, J. M. (1977), Population policy and development, *Population and Development Review* 3, 103–112

Stycos, J. M. (1978), Recent trends in Latin American fertility, *Population Studies* 32, 407–425

Stys, W. (1957), The influence of economic conditions on fertility of peasant women, *Population Studies* 11, 136–148

Sublett, M. (1975), *Farmers on the Road*, University of Chicago Geography Research Paper 168, Chicago

Sun, T.-H., Lin, H.-S. and Freedman, R. (1978), Trends in fertility, family size preferences, and family planning practice: Taiwan, 1961–76, *Studies in Family Planning* 9, 54–70

Sundquist, J. (1975), *Dispersing Population: What Americans can Learn from Europe*, Brookings Institute, Washington, D.C.

Svart, L. (1976), Environmental preference migration: a review, *Geographical Review* 66, 314–330

Sween, J. and Clignet, R. (1969), Urban unemployment as a determinant of political unrest, *Canadian Journal of African Studies* 3, 463–487

Swindell, K. (1979), Labour migration in underdeveloped countries, *Progress in Human Geography* 3, 239–259

Taeuber, I. (1958), *The Population of Japan*, Princeton University Press, Princeton

Taeuber, I. (1965), Policies, programs and the decline of birth rates: China and the Chinese populations of East Asia, in M. Muramatsu and P. Harper (eds.), *Population Dynamics*, Johns Hopkins Press, Baltimore, 99–104

Taeuber, K., Chiazze, L. and Haenszel, W. (1968), *Migration in the United States: An Analysis of Residence Histories*, U.S. Dept. of Health, Education and Welfare, Washington, D.C.

Tapinos, G. (1966), Migrations et particularismes régionaux en Espagne, *Population* 21, 1135–1164

Tarrant, J. (1980), The geography of food aid, *Transactions of Institute of British Geographers* 5, 125–140

Taylor, C. E. (1979), Estimating Canada's emigration, *Intercom* 7 (5), 7–9

Taylor, C., Newman, J. and Narindar, K. (1976), The child survival hypothesis, *Population Studies* 30, 263–278

Taylor, P. J. (1979), 'Difficult-to-let', 'difficult-to-live-in', and sometimes 'difficult-to-get-out-of': an essay on the provision of council housing, *Environment and Planning* 11A, 1305–1320

Taylor, P. J. (1980), A pedagogic application of multiple regression analysis, *Geography* 65, 203–212

Taylor, R. C. (1969), Migration and motivation, in Jackson (ed.), 99–133

Taylor, R. C. (1979), Migration and the residual community, *Sociological Review* 27, 475–489

Teitelbaum,, M. (1972), Fertility effects of the abolition of legal abortion in Rumania, *Population Studies* 26, 405–417

Terry, G. (1973), The interrelationship between female employment and fertility, Ph.D dissertation, Florida State University

Thirlwall, A. (1966), Migration and regional unemployment, *Westminster Bank Review*, Nov., 31–44

Thomas, B. (1954), *Migration and Economic Growth: A Study of Great Britain and the Atlantic Economy*, Cambridge University Press, Cambridge

Thomas, B. (1972), *Migration and Urban Development; A Re-appraisal of British and American Long Cycles*, Methuen, London

Thomas, D. S. (1938), *Research Memorandum on Migration Differentials*, Social Science Research Council, New York

Thomas, D. S. (1941), *Social and Economic Aspects of Swedish Population Movements 1750–1933*, Macmillan, New York

Thomas, E. and Anderson, D. (1965), Additional comments on weighting values in correlation analysis of areal data, *Annals of Association of American Geographers* 55, 492–505

Thomas, I.D. (1968), Geographical aspects of the Tanzania Population Census 1967, *East African Geographical Review* 6, 1–12

Thomas, I. D. (1972), Infant mortality in Tanzania, *East African Geographical Review* 10, 5–26

Thomlinson, R. (1965), *Population Dynamics*, Random House, New York

Tilakaratne, W. (1978), Economic change, social differentiation and fertility: Aluthgama, in Hawthorn (ed.), 186–197

Tilly, C. (1978), The historical study of vital processes, in Tilly (ed.), 3–56

Tilly, C. (ed.) (1978), *Historical Studies of Changing Fertility*, Princeton University Press, Princeton

Tirasawat, P. (1978), Economic and housing adjustment of migrants in Greater Bangkok, *International Migration Review* 12, 93–103

Titmuss, R. and Abel-Smith, B. (1961), *Social Policies and Population Growth in Mauritius*, Methuen, London

Toney, M. (1976), Length of residence, social ties, and economic opportunities, *Demography* 13, 297–309

Trewartha, G. (1953), A case for population geography, *Annals of Association of American Geographers* 43, 71–97

Trewartha, G. (1969), *A Geography of Population*, Wiley, New York

Tromp, S. (1973), The relationship of weather and climate to health and disease, in Howe and Lorraine (eds.), 72–99

Tsui, A. and Bogue, D. (1978), Declining world fertility: trends, causes, implications, *Population Bulletin* 33(4)

Tuyns, A. (1970), Cancer of the oesophagus: further evidence of the relation to drinking habits in France, *International Journal of Cancer* 5, 152–156

Udo, R. (1976), *Applied Population Geography: A Survey*, IGU Commission on Population Geography, Edmonton

U.N. Dept. of Economic and Social Affairs (1970), *Methods of Measuring Internal Migration*, Population Studies 47, New York

U.N. Research Institute for Social Development (1974), *The Social and Economic Implications of Large-Scale Introduction of New Varieties of Foodgrain*, Geneva

U.S. Agency for International Development (1973), *Population Program Assistance: Annual Report 1973*, Washington D.C.

U.S. Bureau of Census (1960), *Historical Statistics of the United States*, Washington D.C.

Valentine, C. and Revson, J. (1979), Cultural traditions, social change and fertility in sub-Saharan Africa, *Journal of Modern African Studies* 17, 453–472

Van Amersfoort, J. (1978), Migrant workers, circular migration and development, *Tijdschrift v.E.S.G.* 69, 17–26

Van de Kaa, D. (1978), Towards a population policy for western Europe, in Council of Europe (1978), 215–230

Van de Walle, E. (1972), Marriage and marital fertility, in Glass and Revelle (eds.), 137–151

Van de Walle, E. (1978), Alone in Europe: the French fertility decline until 1850, in Tilly (ed.), 257–288

Van de Walle, E. and Knodel, J. (1967), Demographic transition and fertility decline: the European case, in International Union for the Scientific Study of Population, *Contributed Papers to 1967 Sydney Conference*, 47–55

Van de Walle, E. and Knodel, J. (1980), Europe's fertility transition: new evidence and lessons for today's developing world, *Population Bulletin* 34 (6)

Van Heek, F. (1956–1957), Roman Catholicism and fertility in the Netherlands, *Population Studies* 10, 125–138

Vanhove, N. and Klaassen, L. (1980), *Regional Policy: A European Approach*, Saxon House, Farnborough

Vedder, R. and Gallaway, L. (1970), Settlement patterns of Canadian emigrants to the United States 1850–1960, *Canadian Journal of Economics* 3, 476–486

Vining, D. and Kontuly, T. (1978), Population dispersal from major metropolitan regions: an international comparison, *International Regional Science Review* 3, 49–73

Wade, R. (1979), Fast growth and slow development in southern Italy, in Seers et al. (eds.), 197–221

Warren, H. et al. (1967), Possible correlations between geology and some disease patterns, *Annals of New York Academy of Science* 136, 657–710

Warren, H. (1973), Some trace element concentrations in various environments, in Howe and Lorraine (eds.), 9–24

Watson, W. (1964), Social mobility and social class in industrial communities, in M. Gluckman (ed.), *Closed Systems and Open Minds*, Oliver and Boyd, Edinburgh, 129–157

Weeden, R. (1973), *Interregional Migration Models and their Application to Great Britain*, Cambridge University Press, Cambridge

Weintraub, R. (1962), The birth rate and economic development: an empirical study, *Econometrica* 15, 182–217

Welch, R. (1970), *Migration Research and Migration in Britain: A Selected Bibliography*, Centre for Urban and Regional Studies, University of Birmingham, Birmingham

Welch, R. (1971), *Migration in Britain: Data Sources and Estimation Techniques*, Centre for Urban and Regional Studies, University of Birmingham, Birmingham

Weller, R. H. (1979), The differential attainment of family goals by race, *Population Studies* 33, 157–164

Wentholt, R. (1961), Characteristics of Dutch emigrants, in G. Beijer (ed.), *Characteristics of Overseas Migrants*, The Hague, 145–278

Westoff, C. (1975), The yield of the imperfect: the 1970 national fertility study, *Demography* 12, 573–580

Westoff, C. and Bumpass, L. (1973), The revolution in birth control practices of U.S. Roman Catholics, *Science* 179, 41–44

Westoff, C. and Ryder, N. (1977), The predictive validity of reproductive intentions, *Demography* 14, 431–453

White, P. (1980), Migration loss and the residual community: a study in rural France 1962–75, in White and Woods (eds.), 198–222

White, P. and Woods, R. (eds.) (1980), *The Geographical Impact of Migration*, Longman, London

Wilkinson, T. (1967), Japan's population problem, in S. Chandrasekhar (ed.), *Asia's Population Problems*, Allen, London, 100–118

William-Olsson, W. (1963), *Report of the IGU Commission on a World Population Map*, prepared for 1964 International Geographical Congress, London. Reprint of 9 papers from *Geografiska Annaler* 45, 243–291

Williams, L. (1979), Changes in Asian breastfeeding patterns, *Intercom* 7 (4), 7–9

Williams, P. (1978), Building societies and the inner city, *Transactions of Institute of British Geographers* 3, 23–34

Willis, K. (1972), The influence of spatial structure and socio-economic factors on migration rates, *Regional Studies* 6, 69–82

Willis, K. (1974), *Problems in Migration Analysis*, Saxon House, Farnborough

Wilson, C. (1954), *The History of Unilever*, Vol. 1, Cassell, London

Wilson, F. (1972), *Labour in the South African Gold Mines 1911–69*, Cambridge University Press, Cambridge

Wilson, F. (1976), International migration in southern Africa, *International Migration Review* 10, 451–488

Wilson, M. G. (1968), *Population Geography*, Nelson, London

Wilson, M. G. (1971a), Alternate measures of human reproduction – some geographical implications, *New Zealand Geographer* 27, 185–196

Wilson, M. G. (1971b), The spatial dimension of human reproduction in Victoria, *Proceedings, Sixth New Zealand Geography Conference*, N.Z. Geographical Society, 258–264

Wilson, M. G. (1978a), A spatial analysis of human fertility in Scotland: reappraisal and extension, *Scottish Geographical Magazine* 94, 130–143

Wilson, M. G. (1978b), The pattern of fertility in a medium-sized industrial city, *Tijdschrift v.E.S.G.* 69, 225–232

Wolpert, J. (1965), Behavioural aspects of the decision to migrate, *Papers of the Regional Science Association* 15, 159–169

Wolpert, J. (1966), Migration as an adjustment to environmental stress, *Journal of Social Issues* 22, 92–102

Wolter, F. (1975), Relocation of production in developing countries, *Intereconomics* 12, 366–368

Woods, R. (1979), *Population Analysis in Geography*, Longman, London

Wooldridge, S. W. and East, W. G. (1951), *The Spirit and Purpose of Geography*, Hutchinson, London

World Health Organization (1976), Health care in rural areas, *WHO Chronicle* 30, 11–17

World Health Organization (1978), *The Promotion and Development of Traditional Medicine*, Technical Report Series No. 622, Geneva

Wrigley, E. A. (1961), *Industrial Growth and Population Change*, Cambridge University Press, Cambridge

Wrigley, E. A. (ed.) (1966a), *An Introduction to English Historical Demography*, Weidenfeld and Nicolson, London

Wrigley, E. A. (1966b), Family limitation in pre-industrial England, *Economic History Review* 19, 82–109

Wrigley, E. A. (1967), Demographic models and geography, in R. Chorley and P. Haggett (eds), *Socio-economic Models in Geography*, Methuen, London, 189–215

Wrigley, E. A. (ed.) (1972), *Nineteenth Century Society: Essays in the Use of Quantitative Methods for the Study of Social Data*, Cambridge University Press, Cambridge

Wrigley, E. A. (ed.) (1973), *Identifying People in the Past*, Arnold, London

Wynne-Edwards, V. (1962), *Animal Dispersion in Relation to Social Behaviour*, Hafner, New York

Wynne-Edwards, V. (1965), Self-regulating systems in populations of animals, *Science* 147, 1543–1548

Yasuba, Y. (1961), *Birth Rates of the White Population in the United States 1800–1860*, Johns Hopkins Press, Baltimore

Yeates, M. and Garner, B. (1971), *The North American City*, Harper & Row, New York

Young, J. (1972), *Some Aspects of the Medical Geography of County Durham*, Ph.D. thesis, University of Durham

Zarate, A. (1967), Fertility in urban areas of Mexico, *Demography* 4, 363–373

Zelinski, W. (1966), *A Prologue to Population Geography*, Prentice-Hall, Englewood Cliffs, N.J.

Zelinsky, W. (1971), The hypothesis of the mobility transition, *Geographical Review* 61, 219–249

Zelinsky, W. (1978), Is nonmetropolitan America being repopulated?, *Demography* 15, 13–39

Zimmer, B. (1955), Participation of migrants in urban structures, *American Sociological Review* 20, 218–224

Zipf, G. (1946), The P_1P_2/D hypothesis: on the intercity movement of persons, *American Sociological Review* 11, 677–686

Zipf, G. (1949), *Human Behaviour and the Principle of Least Effort*, Hafner, New York

SUBJECT INDEX

AUTHOR INDEX